Bouquet of Shale

Jeff Scott

Methanol Press

In memory of
Ian Thomas (1942–2011)
Joyce Blythe (1947–2011)
Eileen Shepherd (1931–2010)

th blu nyt
th stRs u cant c
th hum that nevr gOs awy

Jennifer Egan

First published in Great Britain by
Methanol Press
2 Tidy Street
Brighton
East Sussex BN1 4EL

For a complete catalogue of current and forthcoming publications
please write to the address above, or visit our website at
www.methanolpress.com

ISBN 978-0-9568618-0-1
A catalogue for this book is available from the British Library

Editor in absentia: Michael Payne
Word Wrangler: Graham Russel
Stenographer: Vy Shepherd
Book Design: Vicky Holtham
Cover Design: Rachael Adams
Cover Photograph: *Northern Echo*/David Wood

Printed in the UK by Imprint Academic

INTRODUCTION

The book you have in your hand continues my examination of the question 'what is speedway?' I started my quest to find of answer this question in 2005 when I travelled to every track in the country and have continued to try to do so every year since then. This odyssey has, so far, resulted in the publication of the books *Showered in Shale, Shifting Shale, Concrete for Breakfast, Quantum of Shale* and *Shale Trek*. This latest book is really more of the same but also something different. It's also not a club history nor the (auto) biography of a rider but a snapshot and my personal journey round every stadium that staged the sport in Britain – this time during 2010. Again, it was a pleasure to be able to have a reason to visit pretty well every track in the country (except those where I was no longer welcome). Though I could only write about what I encountered, I have again tried to capture some of the characters that make up some parts of the speedway world as well as vaguely attempt to delve beneath the surface of what I've seen. All of life was there at speedway in our nation and many people went out of their way to be kind, tell me their thoughts on speedway or comment on my books. What notionally started out as a philosophical quest has continued to take a somewhat anthropological turn but, hey, that's how things happen.

Choosing a snappy title – preferably involving the word Shale – gets trickier each year. This book is dedicated to three people who've all sadly left us. Ian Thomas always took a keen interest in my writing – well, my sales and the crowd sizes I saw on my travels – and gave prompt, honest feedback. I always enjoyed any meeting with Ian and he's greatly missed on the speedway scene. Also greatly missed is the lovely Joyce Blythe whose mix of kindness and plain speaking clearly signalled her love of people and conversation. Joyce also took immense pride in her work at the Coventry trackshop (for both speedway and stock cars). Trips to the Isle of Wight, still don't seem right without Eileen Shepherd sat by the pits perimeter fence overlooking the fourth bend. Along with "the best cup of coffee on the Island", to go along with her curiosity about people, Eileen also had an inexhaustible supply of various chocolate biscuits and welcome snacks she insisted you ate in large quantities. Ian, Joyce and Eileen all immeasurably brightened my experience of the speedway world. It's easy to imagine what a greater loss to their loss to their families and loved ones they are.

When writing this book I have tried to adhere to the lessons I was given previously by my editor, mentor, advisor and writing coach Michael Payne as well as encouragement from the late Michael Donaghy who suggested I write about what I know or love.

Sadly, anyone familiar with my blog or my previous books will know that I'm not adverse to some pointless navel-gazing, pretentiousness and facetiousness. Nonetheless, I hope that you can forgive these faults and mostly enjoy the chance to travel to the tracks again in my company as much as I relished the visits.

Lastly, without the riders prepared to risk their lives on high-powered bikes without brakes on various different tracks – for our entertainment and to make their living – there would be no sport to watch in this country. In our everyday lives, we often take our own mortality for granted and, equally, we make light of speedway injuries as part and parcel of the sport. The 2010 season was another poor one for serious injuries in the UK and, clothed in their racing gear, unlike their loved ones, we often forget that every rider is someone's brother, son, partner, husband or father. Hopefully we can all remember this every time a critical comment nearly passes our lips without need of further injury to remind us of the real situation.

There you have it. I hope that you enjoy your journey.

Brighton

8 April 2011

CONTENTS

5

CHAPTER 1

Lakeside

"We're clearly not the rubbish team that the experts claimed we were!"

14th May

Even after only a few weeks of the 2010 Elite League season, it's already clear that – barring significant injury – the Poole Pirates will run away with things at the top of the Elite League qualifying table. With the modern day play-off system, their strength in depth or number of victories makes very little difference since the Elite League table topper then has to compete with the three teams below them in order to determine who will be crowned champions. The rejuvenated Lakeside of the Stuart Douglas and Jon Cook era – during the close season, the club will win the BBC London Outstanding Contribution to London Sport Award 2010 – are widely considered to be another club likely to qualify from the remaining eight teams that comprise the 2010 version of the top tier of British speedway. Prior to Lakeside's Elite League 'A' fixture at Wimborne Road, co-promoter and team manager Jon Cook stressed the psychological and tactical need for any visiting team to put on a good performance in Dorset in order to (hopefully) encourage Poole to initially decide to avoid you in the all-important play-off semi-finals. "You want to be sure that if you join Poole in the play-offs, then you want to be the team they want to avoid, and the way to do that is to put on an impressive show both home and away against them. It means that you will then probably meet them in the final and anything can happen at that stage with all the pressures etc that cup finals provide." Despite Poole's home strength, prior to the meeting Jon still felt confident of a creditable performance from the Hammers. "We do have a couple of riders who are familiar with the Poole track, Krzysztof Kasprzak and Daniel Davidsson, so I can't see any reason why we shouldn't be looking to go down there and give a very good account of ourselves and maybe persuade Poole that they would rather not face us in the play-off semi-finals, assuming that we earn our place in the play-offs when they come along." The best laid plans go awry and so it proves when Hammers No. 1 Krzysztof Kasprzak fails to ride in the meeting and, thereby, scuppers Lakeside's chances of a close contest. His absence undoubtedly hastens his departure from Thurrock, but also ensures their use of the rider-replacement facility is a poor substitute for the points his familiarity with the Wimborne race circuit would usually ensure. Nonetheless, any 70-24 defeat captures the eye (even if there were mitigating circumstances).

Just over two weeks later, for the return fixture the Hammers draft back in their 2009 No. 1, Lee Richardson, in place of their recalcitrant stay-away Pole. In his programme notes, "the guvnor" Stuart "Stan" Douglas comments, "Dropping Krzysztof was not an easy decision. As I have stated openly, I am very fond of the lad, but there are conditions surrounding his service with us that were becoming untenable. …With slightly different circumstances, I will always be open to including KK in our plans, but I'm not sure how readily those circumstances will change." Before his departure from the team, Krzysztof did reappear in the Hammers' race tabard – posting points tallies of 6 and 7 points – against Ipswich and Wolverhampton, but didn't really advance his case for continued inclusion. Commenting upon the "straight replacement" that Lee Richardson's arrival represents in his programme column, Jon Cook notes, "We hold no animosity towards Krys. It's just fair to say that things have not worked out for either party this time around. His reasons for absence a fortnight ago for our visit to Poole and the resultant humiliating defeat were weak at best. His progression in the GP qualification makes us fear for future short-term illnesses. His form and presence as a No. 1 has been lacking. … It's important for the club's finances that we recoup a large chunk of the investment we have made in Krys, so it's highly likely he will return to the Elite League fairly quickly elsewhere." A sign of maturity is an ability to admit error and correct previous decisions. Jon Cook continues, "In truth the year hasn't felt right to me or Stuart ever since Press and Practice day when Lee quietly packed his stuff away as the photos were being taken having practised earlier. When you make a mistake it's best to put it right as soon as you can and without going into great detail we all would have handled that November situation a bit differently with the benefit of hindsight."

Dave Robinson in Refs Box

With Lee Richardson restored to the pits, many fans also feel confident that a whole new spirit and culture now energises the club. Four hours before the scheduled start time, inside the First Place Diner (located adjacent to the first bend under the raceway tavern) opinions vary as to whether the Pirates will drive back onto the M25 as victors or the vanquished. Nick Newton briefly interrupts his late afternoon full English breakfast to ask, "Have you seen the start gate? They ripped it up on Wednesday, put new clay down and now it's perfection! Robbo has a new engine, JD is in the points and DD shoots away from the start line like he's been fired off an aircraft carrier!" How wonderfully

Concentration in the Pits

appropriate for a speedway team sponsored by the Royal Navy. Nick takes delight in Daniel's rich vein of recent form, "As soon as he sees the magnets move, he's off and got his foot down in the first corner." Friendly blonde manageress of the First Place Diner, Tracy Manning, isn't so confident of the outcome tonight. "You know what the result is going to be!"
[Jeff] "I dunno, I think you're going to win."
[Nick] "I think we are too! I can't wait for the meeting to start."
If the Hammers might shock the Pirates, then someone else who's in for a surprise when he walks into the café is Terry, whose 70th birthday results in an impromptu celebration-cum-commemoration of the big day in the form of a wall display of photos, balloons and assorted memorabilia. Echoing changes by Jon Cook to the Lakeside team line-up, Tracy also refreshes the quality of the product offerings from the First Place Diner to ensure ongoing customer

Lakeside: *"We're clearly not the rubbish team that the experts claimed we were!"*

satisfaction. "This year we're doing traditional puddings. Last week it was rice puddings and, this week, it's apple and blackcurrant crumble. They're very popular!"

Outside the Lakeside Speedway Office Adam Shields sports the casual attire of British-based Australian speedway riders everywhere – shorts, black T-shirt, stubble and, as a concession to the British climate, an open zipped tracksuit top. In his case a rather stylish version emblazoned with the Lakeside logo that's just right for our summer. Adam is about to set off to the pits having been unable to get to the bottom of some mystery, "They said, 'It was someone from the speedway.' I said, 'That narrows it down – but not by very much!'" There's a proper nautical theme around the club tonight with the visit of the Pirates and, of course, the sponsorship of the Royal Navy. Programme Editor Alan Sargent amended the Royal Navy advert on page 2 of tonight's programme accordingly, "I changed the copy for the Navy advert to be more topical." [1]

The door of the speedway office opens and tonight's SCB official Dave Robinson exits clutching a briefcase and match programme. "I suppose I better get off and look as though I know what I'm doing!"
[Alan Sargent] "You must prefer the smaller tracks."
[Dave] "Why?"
[Alan] "Cos the track walk is much shorter."

Hardworking speedway reporter Paul Burbidge whose responsibilities now require that he roves internationally parks up on the rough-hewn Lakeside car park adjacent to the clubhouse. "Phil Chard's not feeling well so I've come over for him. The first GP [Leszno] was excellent and I'm not just saying that because I do the website for them! The second one had a final that you couldn't take your eyes off because you never quite knew what would happen."
[Jeff] "The wet spoilt it!"
[Paul] "What are you going to do when there's 10,000 people in the stadium and most of the riders have to race in Poland the next evening? It was great to see Kenneth Bjerre do so well!"
[Jeff] "What about Nicki?"
[Paul] "It takes a while to get settled in with new people at anyone's work and Nicki has a whole new pit crew this season!"

In the referee's box perched above the start/finish line of the Thurrock raceway, music man Steve Gobey gets ready for the night ahead accompanied by his son John (Dave Robinson tells me, "also known as Oliver"). From this vantage point, the view is excellent but conditions are cosy – particularly since referee Dave Robinson is already in situ after a (short) track walk and safety furniture inspection. Out talk almost inevitably turns to the rich tapestry of characters working behind the scenes within British Speedway. It's a sport where passions run high in private but also in public. Though some promoters claim black is white and deny that they jump up and down on the centre green like a cartoon character, others have made quite a name for themselves with their distinctive centre-green antics and celebrations. Dave Robinson asks, "Have you seen Malcolm Vasey jump around the centre green – they call him the epileptic scarecrow!"

When the turnstiles open, a tanned Jon Cook is there to meet and greet the early arrivals. The Lakeside fans are in happy mood after the previous night's away victory at 'local' rivals Ipswich.

---

[1] The advert features the Royal Navy logo along with a red-helmeted Lee Richardson in the foreground next to a smartly dressed flat-capped Navy officer attired in an epauletted shirt with tie. Staring on in the background is a blurry headphone wearing Steve Brandon whose presence indicates that this must be a photograph from a televised Sky Sports meeting. In bold letters the header of the advert copy shouts "Why We Need a Navy". Perhaps cost cutters from the Coalition could take note of the answer to this rhetorical question! "Britain relies on the sea, over 90% of our trade travels by sea in containers or tankers. The Royal Navy protects the sea-lanes ensuring our trade is safe, HMS Kent is currently operating around the UK in support of this. Last year HMS Kent was deployed to the Middle East countering pirates and so know all about tonight's opponents and therefore good luck Hammers against tonight's opponents Poole Pirates."

"Great win last night!" a man in a stylish Hammers anorak that's almost smart enough to wear away from speedway tells a smiling Jon ("It was!") Another fan butts into their congratulatory conversation, "They rode as a team, that's why!" On the raffle stall Phillipa ("two ll's and one p") Thomas from Standford-Le-Hope tries to interest passers-by to chance their luck. She's enjoyed the recent resurgence in Hammers fortunes. "I suppose it must be eight years or so now we've been coming. We did come before but stopped coming. Actually it must be more than eight years. I don't know how we'll do tonight. I've been coming to speedway for too long to make any predictions!" Phil Morris's dad stops to rehearse an old joke, "I'll do a strip for £1 – you wouldn't want me to mind!" His son Phil's career took in many British speedway clubs including Reading and, most recently, Lakeside. Understandably his dad's proud of his son's on-track exploits but also, away from the shale, his burgeoning television career. It's proved quite lucrative, "£93,000 allowed him to set up a business. He's got a quarter of a million turnover, which is good from sandwiches! He didn't drink and didn't smoke and looked after himself and wasn't short of money, but it really did set him up. Quarter of a million really isn't bad from sandwiches." Though I really can't believe it's not butter given his success in the world of catering, Phil Morris knows what side his bread is buttered. The lady with Phil's dad stresses that Phil works hard at his television career. "He did about eight or nine shows. More than people know! Not all of them for money but for the appearances and they paid his expenses and that."

It's over two decades since Allen Rob junior visited the stadium, "It's the first time I've been here since 1989 [studies the nearby gate] that wasn't here last time I was here!" Raffle lady Phillipa hopes that success on the track away at Foxhall Heath will translate into more fans through the turnstiles. "If people see we've won last night they should come. It should give the team some confidence!" Her partner Ivor has his doubts, "We won here last week against them [Ipswich] – by 6 points – but it was a boring meeting."
[Phillipa] "Whereas last night was a really good meeting."
[Ivor] "This is probably the biggest meeting of the season, so far."
[Phillipa] "There's loads of them [Poole fans] coming cos they think they're going to win."

Since my last visit to Lakeside, Alf Weedon's retired from the last bastion of his trackshop empire – the outlet in the parade of shops at the bottom of the clubhouse building overlooking bends 1 and 2. Though the sign above the shop ("Speedway and Bangers Souvenir Shop") remains unchanged, the internal fixtures and fittings are transformed under the new management of friendly trackshop lady Justine Potter. The range of clothing emblazoned with the distinctive Hammers logo has increased exponentially and, as befits an outlet that also serves the stockcars, the range of model cars should be breathtaking for all avid collectors. Justine's isn't the only outlet in this parade to enjoy a makeover since – between her shop and the refreshingly totally unaltered sweetshop concession, notably for its reluctant customer service – there's now a seafood stall that sells (in true East End, almost by the Thames fashion) various fish snacks. Sittingbourne's Graham Arnold avoids the fish but is, as usual, at Lakeside on race night. He worries about Sittingbourne's future at the Iwade track, despite the fact that they no longer compete in the costly National League. "It's getting harder because the BSPA have put the bond up to £2,000 and told us we have to pay by the 20th!" Ex-sports editor of the *Romford Recorder*, Peter Butcher, now works as the communications administrator for the Isthmian Football League and remains a keen Lakeside fan. "The team is all about juggling personalities and getting the team together. If you have a 4-point away win and then you've got a home meeting against the League leaders you can't ask for more than that!"

Race nights at Thurrock over recent seasons have been notable for the buzzy atmosphere and growing crowd (including the 260 fans who bought season tickets for the 2010 season). Obviously,

Lakeside: *"We're clearly not the rubbish team that the experts claimed we were!"*

though this is closely related to the quality and performance of the team on the track, but it's also down to the ebullient spirit of the staff engendered by the confident management of Stuart Douglas and Jon Cook. The work of announcer Bob Miller and his race-night co-worker presenter, Geoff Cox, also contributes to the sparky atmosphere. Just prior to the first race, over the loudspeakers the crowd get a reminder of their possible contribution to proceedings, "It's going to be an absolute cracker! You are our eighth man so to speak – let's get behind the Hammers!" Another factor in the Hammers favour tonight will be the absence of Darcy Ward from the Poole Pirates team though, that said, they cover his unavailability through rider replacement. Even more significantly, the Pirates wonder reserve Artur Mroczka – already ninth in the Elite League averages on 8.60 – is also absent tonight. Poole team manager Neil Middleditch (or Meil as he's called in the programme) sends out Redcar Captain and ex-World Champion Gary Havelock (who is the Pirates official declared No. 8) for the first of Darcy's rides. It's a competitive race won by newly minted GP star Chris Holder to immediately puncture the Lee Richardson triumphant return to Thurrock balloon. With Gary Havelock third ahead of Stuart Robson, the visitors open with a heat advantage. However, it's not a sign of things to come and, despite the instant opportunity to size up the track, Gary Havelock again finishes third in heat 2 trailed off behind the fast starting Hammers pair of Daniel Davidsson and Paul Hurry. Nonetheless, Poole have strength in depth throughout their line-up as illustrated by a win for Bjarne Pederson in the drawn Heat 3. When Daniel Davidsson wins heat 4 followed home by his race partner Adam Shields, this second 5-1 of the night for the Hammers extends their early meeting lead to 6 points (despite the attentions of Messrs Watt and Havelock). Sat in the grandstand bar overlooking the Thurrock raceway, raceday meteorologist and telephonist, Bryn Williams worries about maltreatment of the older members of the speedway fraternity, "I reckon Middlo should be reported to Age Concern – Havvy was out in heats 1, 2 and 4!" Having temporarily broken off from his concentrated texting, Bryn's attention soon returns to his mobile phone, "I got lumbered with the flippin' updates tonight."

Another welcome development of the Douglas/Cook era is the arrival of temporary crowd control barriers on the back-straight stockcar track. These provide a close-to-the-action vantage point. Until tonight's heat 5, I'd not sampled the Lakeside experience from this particular location. It's a tremendously exciting viewing position that provides an excellent view of the start/finish line while any battle for dominance on bends 1 and 2 takes place right there in front of you. This proximity to the shale action emphasises and exaggerates the speed at which the riders loom up and zoom past. It's completely thrilling and really fires the imagination – exactly what speedway spectating should be about everywhere! Though Jason Doyle wins heat 5, the eye is caught by Jonas Davidsson's battle for third place with Chris Holder. Jonas bests his rival at the flag by the proverbial tyre knobble! Symptomatic of the economic malaise of 2010 that affects speedway clubs throughout all three British leagues is the lack of sponsorship for heat 6 ("Please telephone 01708 863443 to sponsor this heat"). Heats 9 and 15 are similarly unsponsored. If a go-ahead club like the Lakeside Hammers – who, arguably, outline the sport's most eloquent and persuasive sponsorship proposition in their glossy deluxe brochure – struggle to sell all their heat sponsorships then those clubs with inferior presentational skills (or offerings) really do have a thankless task in the present economic environment. Though without sponsorship, the show must go on – Lee Richardson emerges triumphant with his first home race win since his re-engagement back onto the staff at Lakeside.

Adam Shields and Paul Hurry combine in the seventh to bang in the third Hammers maximum heat advantage of the night. With the scores less than poised at 27-15, Middlo explores all his tactical options to bring Davey Watt in for Darcy Ward's rider-replacement ride wearing the black-and-white helmet colour. This looks an inspired move when Watt initially leads the race. Sadly he's almost immediately outfoxed by Daniel Davidsson and, in a close clash as they rip in and rip out, both run to ruin the double runs the Hammer in that surface. With more than three points to land in his rival, Watt's rush of blood rightly earns him a disqualification and, as an additional bonus, constructive feedback from the Hammers faithful as he takes a lengthy walk back to the pits. In the rerun, Gary Havelock fails to provide any effective resistance to Davidsson (D.) and Paul Hurry racking up yet another Lakeside 5-1. A hangover from last season's averages manipulation allegations continues to linger when, with the scores at an unexpected 32-16, some home fans speculate, "It makes you wonder what Poole are up to?" While we wait for the start of heat 9, returned prodigal son, Lee Richardson publicly professes delight but also emphasises that his joy at racing regularly again at Thurrock is an acquired taste. "I used to hate the place when I came back here last year but I'm delighted to be back." While the tractor circles grading the track, raffle ticket sellers 'Scary' Sheila La-Sage and Cameron Saveall wander throughout the stadium to drum up interest in tonight's cash (£86) prize. Throughout, Scary also kindly up-sells my recently published *Track Directory* as tonight's must-have accessory for Hammers fans bookshelves. Sheila is always an engaging and friendly saleswoman.

Though they don't probably appreciate their good fortune, Hammers fans are fortunate to enjoy their speedway at a circuit where you can watch the action without restriction from almost any vantage point within the stadium. Though it's an unscientific survey, it looks to me that there are probably more garden chairs at Lakeside than at any other British speedway track! There is, of course, a lack of hard concrete standing surfaces here. Heat 9 takes considerable time to run to completion. First time out the race stops at the start and erroneous rumours claim disqualification for Davey Watt for having no dirt deflector. Helpfully, after some further faff and delay, we get a complicated explanation of the referee's interpretation of the situation and the rules that apply, "Davey would be allowed back into the rerun of the race from off 15 metres but, after he's excluded, for failing to get to the tapes under the two-minute time allowance, he's replaced by Gary Havelock who is able to compete from the start line." After a ragged restart, referee Dave Robinson again illuminates the red stoplights. It's a decision only vaguely supported by the ineffectual half-hearted waving of the red flag by the centre-green staff member on the first bend. Leon Madsen then leads the re-rerun right until the moment Jonas Davidsson overtakes on the second bend of the last lap. The message that he's been vanquished doesn't compute with Leon who, then, snatches back his victory on the finish line.

For the neutral, tonight's meeting serves up an entertaining mix of competitive races and eye-catching overtaking manoeuvres. It's an experience somewhat at odds with traditional historic perceptions of the level of speedway entertainment allegedly served up in Thurrock. Heat 10 also starts dramatically when Jason Doyle – who's fourth into the first bend – throws himself theatrically off his bike to fall dramatically onto the shale. It's a manoeuvre that actually impresses referee Dave Robinson enough to order a rerun with all four back – possibly in admiration of his artistry and flamboyant execution. It proves a worthwhile swallow-dive-cum-gamble since, in the rerun, Doyle grabs third place ahead of Stuart Robson (though the heat itself is drawn after another race win for Lee Richardson). Heat 11 finds Chris Holder in the black-and-white helmet colour, headgear he wears with great success. With Leon Madsen third, the ungainly Pirates 2-7 narrows the score to 41-28. Despite this success, in the First Place Diner Tracy Manning holds her hand up, "I was so wrong wasn't I?!" Madsen's out again in heat 12 where he combines with race winner Bjarne Pedersen to ram home successive heat advantages for the visitors to reduces their deficit to a mere 9 points.

Poole captain Davey Watt's disappointing night continues into the first corner of the next race when Adam Shields rides hard underneath him in as they battle for third place. Referee Dave

Robinson ignores this fall – possibly since it lacks the prerequisite theatricality – and the Aussie takes no further part in another race yet again won by Lee Richardson. Watt's performance has been so poor that you could half suspect that he's forgotten he no longer wears the 2009 Eastbourne Eagles kevlars. Yet more drama arrives in the penultimate race of the night. On the back straight of the second lap Jason Doyle passes Paul Hurry but, when the Lakeside reserve tries to cut back up inside on the fourth bend to repay the favour, he inadvertently catches Doyle's back wheel to send them both cart-wheeling down the section of the home straight directly in front of the referee's box. Though Doyle led his erstwhile rival and was clearly clipped from behind by Paul Hurry, weirdly referee Dave Robinson decides to disqualify the Australian. Though the two leading riders were on their third lap because the two fallers had yet to complete two laps, the race is rerun. Fast-gating Leon Madsen leads the restart until on the back straight of the last lap where Jonas Davidsson overtakes to win (while his brother David finishes third). With the result beyond doubt, the last race of the night is completely academic, but nonetheless keenly contested. Chris Holder lowers Lee Richardson's colours for the second time this evening in their own mini series of three races.

Interviewed over the loudspeaker system immediately after Lakeside's surprisingly comfortable 53-40 victory, Jon Cook strikes an ebullient tone. "We've taken 7 points in two days! We're clearly in second place – 6 points ahead of our nearest rivals. We're clearly not the rubbish team that the experts claimed we were!" Reluctant to get too over-confident about the future, nonetheless Jon celebrates the "good team spirit" of the past two meetings and highlights the contrast with earlier attitudes he believes this indicates. "Something didn't feel right all season but we were getting the results – but we've put our finger on that now." The 2010 Elite League season will suffer disruption from the Football World Cup. "We've had a good crowd on an almost warm night. The summer will probably come for two weeks when the World Cup is on. We've had a fantastic atmosphere and shown, once again, that Lakeside is the team for the people of Essex and Kent and all around!" Jon also publicly savours the return of Lee Richardson, it's a signing that should enable the club to 'kick on' throughout the remainder of their EL campaign. "We've never lost contact with Lee. He came to the Press Day. I first spoke to him after the draw at Eastbourne and we were looking to go in another direction. After Krzysztof Kasprzak decided to go missing I approached Lee, but he said it wasn't to be. Overnight he thought about it – texted and that was delightful!"

14th May Lakeside v. Poole (Elite League) 53-40

CHAPTER 2

Eastbourne
"He had such a talent and never knew it"

15th May

With the 2010 speedway season quarter of the way through, there's already a possibly poignant double End-of-Era mid-May meeting at Arlington Stadium in East Sussex. The Eagles decision to switch their regular race night from their 'traditional' Saturday to Thursday fittingly enough finds the "last ever" Saturday night meeting combined with (what the front of the commemorative programme bills as) "David Norris presents Floppy's Farewell in the Last King of Arlington". Given David Norris's importance to the club over recent years along with his idiosyncratic approach to life – never mind his dry wit – it promises to be much more than your usual Benefit meeting. With an attractive field of 16 riders, further interest is provided by a variety of off-track events. These include a raffle for the chance to press the start button for the Grand Final (and present the trophies) as well as an auction of the riders' race jackets in the clubhouse plus a disco afterwards until midnight.

Wheelie

The commemorative programme is both informative and fun as well as a fitting memento. Most of all – in the self-deprecating fashion of notionally repressed Englishmen everywhere – it's affecting, almost moving. Along with the raft of photographs, adverts, heartfelt messages and the meeting scorecard, space is found for David to pen unique profiles on every rider participating in the event. Columns from Mike Bellerby/Trevor Geer, Dean Barker, Jon Cook and, of course, David Norris, supplement all this. Bringing the curtain down on a speedway career that "has been my life for 29 years" could prove to be difficult but, in this instance, is handled with some aplomb. Making a list of people to thank inevitably ensures that you miss someone off. After paying tribute to the fans, David proceeds to thank Alan Crompton, Lesley Watkins, Dean Barker, the Dugard family, Roy and Darren Prodger, his mum, dad and sister, as well as his wife Ellie and their sons Ashley and Jack. Everyone has quirks and flaws to balance their notable qualities. Indeed, both Dean Barker's and Jon Cook's columns are further distinguished by the way they mix wit, honesty and affection. Dean notes, "Flop has been like a

Roving reporter

brother to me, he is my best friend who has made me laugh every single day for the last 25 years… except the four years when we didn't speak!" Nonchalance and self-deprecation can be a convenient mask to hide behind, let alone disguise soul-searching self-analysis. Dean emphasises the successful on-track aspects of their enduring relationship, "We went on to race many times for England and to race in the World Team Cup. Flop also rode in the GP which was great for him, he had such a talent and never knew it. I think Flop's turning point in speedway was when he didn't have me around to distract him!"

Widely acknowledged for the quality and honesty of his public pronouncements (whether verbal or written), Jon Cook proceeds to exceed his own high standards with a two-page information-packed retrospective. He recalls the winter of 1992-1993 that saw Len Silver's arrival at Eastbourne to try to revitalise the club. "Len was keen, as were Charlie and Bob Dugard, to bring back the young fresh look of British youth to the team and I was charged with finding out if David would like to come home from Ipswich, 'tapping up' in real terms." The usual rose-tinted spectacles you'd expect to go hand-in-hand with such recollections are notable by their absence. "David was a constant in my time here, on his day he could be both brilliant and frustrating in equal measure. Some of his rides and defeats of opponents will stick with me forever but so too will his ability to fall off when wide in the first turn or his mid-season loss of form which would be replaced by an end-of-season burst being enough to guarantee a contract for the following year." Jon is keen to highlight David's "absolute blistering season of 2003" during which he reached a 10-point average and also rode in the Cardiff GP as well as in the World Team Cup. "That season and its high points are a legacy that David can never be denied and it marks him down as a rider who should be greatly respected by all. That respect is sometimes lost because of his stupid 'Floppy' nickname and perhaps now is the time to come clean and say that I never liked that moniker. The result of a comment by his engine tuner at the time, Neil Evitts, it stuck with David at a time when he was known here as 'The Wild Thing' cueing the Troggs tune blaring from the PA every time he won a race. Floppy sounds too cuddly and friendly. Ask David's opponents; 'Wild Thing' was always more fitting." After a career on the shale, what the future clearly holds for any rider is rarely certain. "His place in Eagles history is assured and hopefully in time he will play a role off the track in the sport. He has much to offer and Sky's coverage is certainly a sadder place without his dry wit and tell it as it is, rather than the more mainstream BBC-like safety of Kelvin Tatum *et al*."

Synchronistically enough the issue of the *Speedway Star* on sale at the trackshop features an interview by Peter Oakes that ranges widely and captures the David Norris worldview. Floppy dismisses the idea that he took to speedway naturally and goes out of his way to thank "Terry Rowlands, who was Alan Johns's partner and mechanic who helped run the track, took me onto the car park and just drew me this tiny little circuit." Gareth Rogers gave David his debut ride in the National League (the old second division) in a meeting on August 21st 1988 v. Stoke. When I caught up with Gareth at Newport Speedway he recalls, "I put Dave Norris into his first ever meeting aged 16 years and one day. He scored 8 plus 2. He had two heat wins and equalled the track record on his debut! The next night – at Exeter where he'd never ridden before – he beat Alan Rivett who was their Australian No. 1. Every single away meeting, he won a heat that season. At every away track during August to October, he won a race. When we went to Newcastle, Barry Wallace was taking the mick over the tannoy, 'There's this wonder kid from Eastbourne. This David Norris has won a lot of heats, let's see how he gets on here heh, heh!' And then David won heat 3!"

David famously grew up in East Sussex close to the track with his parents and sister in Upper Dicker (nowadays he still lives locally in Hailsham). Though often a cliché, nonetheless David worked hard to fulfil his ambition to become a speedway rider, "When I was a schoolboy, I'd pick all the

14

litter up at Arlington after the speedway and stockcars. I would think I was 13 when I started doing it. That's a massive job really, I had to pick it up, bag it and bin the rubbish. I got 24 quid a week… did two paper rounds in the morning – Upper Dicker is a sparse village, so I'd probably be doing three or four miles on the paper round, go to school and then go to work at the stadium on a Monday, Tuesday, Thursday and Friday. … it was really hard after stockcar meetings, they'd get 4,000 fans there and I remember one meeting when they were giving out free newspapers. They tore them up and left the pieces all over the place. I think that sort of background gives you an edge." David used to chant Colin Richardson's (Lee Richardson's father) name and identifies him as his first hero. However, "My first real idol was Kelly Moran. I still remember when I went up to him for an autograph, he asked my name and I thought I was in trouble for something. Then he signed my autograph book, 'To David, Best Wishes, Kelly Moran'. …What he did has always stuck with me and if I have got the time, I'll ask the name of someone asking for an autograph and if it's a little girl, I will put a little kiss underneath. Then you'll become their favourite rider, little things like that mean a lot."

Aged nine, David nearly died in hospital, "My appendix was upside down and rubbing on my bowel and I was proper, proper ill". Kelly Moran rang him a couple of times and, prompted by Margaret Dugard, Ron Preston, Lars Hammarberg, Gordon Kennett and Dave Kennett all visited. Though he has his memories David also has his mementoes, "Programmes – no, race-jackets – I was a massive hoarder of them. I had every one in the loft until we stopped having them when team kevlars came in." David rates Dean 'Deano' Barker as the best rider he rode with, "I think we were great at team riding – and I mean proper team riding, not what some people sometimes call team riding." David ranks Bobby Ott ("He was absolutely crazy on the bike. Off it as well") and Peter Karlsson ("He would be fearless and still is") as the best riders he raced against. Like Frank Sinatra, Norris also has the odd regret – injuries, basically. However, he stresses, "There are no decisions I would have done different. People say that year I gave up drinking and smoking and got fit was something I could have done ten years before. No, I couldn't. I have lived my life how I wanted to live it."

The chance to pay respects to David Norris as well as contribute to his well-earned tax-free testimonial monies attracts a large crowd of regular fans but also lapsed and occasional visitors including ex- Eastbourne promoter Bob Brimson. Bob's company, Propeller Media have an airfence banner on the first corner and an advert in the programme (where Bob sports the rather impressive moniker of "Consultant Director of Creative Services Universal Music UK"). Bob nowadays lives in North London so, ignoring the regular demands of his work, he finds it harder to get to Eastbourne. As if to underline the importance of this event, Bob's brought along Katie ("lifelong friend, government aparatchik, biker, Ramones fan and like me, professional chain-smoker") to her first ever speedway meeting. She's no stranger to two wheels since she's the holder of an advanced motorbike licence. Her knowledge, understanding and advanced qualification is a source of pride for Bob: "It's the same as a police one or something like that." Bob isn't a complete stranger to Arlington over recent years, "I came twice last season. One meeting against Coventry was brilliant and the other was absolutely dire!" Bob waves his arm expansively in the general direction of the track and nods towards the stadium infrastructure as he tells Katie, "It's a very working class sport!" Famously attracted into speedway promotion by the gateway path of rider sponsorship – in his case, Bob further appreciated the matter-of-fact heroism of the competitors after he saw David Norris make a roll-up between races. Bob now has enough time and distance from his promotional reign to put it into some sort of perspective. "If Nicki hadn't been world champ that year and we'd had him a bit more, I think we would have got into the play-offs. When everyone was happy it went well. But, I think I signed a few too many old 'uns and then kept faith too long – thinking, hoping – they would come back! I look back on those years with a lot of

15

affection". He explains those times to Katie, "I work in a tough business but speedway's tougher! It's like going into a darkened room and being held upside down until all the money has been shook out of your pockets! At times it was a nightmare but I only have positive memories, good memories now. I set myself an amount of money I wouldn't go over but I did! Another problem was that the club wasn't worth anything if you sold it, so that is something!" Bob asks whether I still go round the tracks every season.

[Jeff] "I enjoyed Lakeside last night."

[Bob] "I don't want to talk about them as I'm sure you understand! How did they do?"

[Jeff] "They beat Poole."

[Bob] "That's not what I want to hear!"

The meeting line-up is pretty well as per programme except for the withdrawal of the star attraction Leigh Adams who's replaced by Richard Sweetman. Presenter Kevin Coombes informs us over the loudspeaker system, "Leigh Adams has been recalled by his Polish club". This prompts groans from the crowd but a quick defence from trackshop man Nick Barber, "Leigh Adams isn't one of those who always pulls out – unlike some other riders – he always rides!" The parade truck does a slow celebratory circuit of the stockcar track so that David Norris, wife Ellie, children Ashley and Jack along with fan club secretary, Lesley Watkins, can wave to the crowd. As a noticeable surge of Arlington adulation swamps the parade truck, Kevin Coombes intones, "He's made us laugh, he's made us cry" but fails to mention anything about making us angry and, instead, defaults to a revelationless observation, "We've got the weather." Lap of honour over, Floppy joins the parade of riders stood in front of the back-straight grandstand just prior to their introductions. From his vantage point adjacent to the start line, John Hazelden spots the already perma-tanned Jon Cook sat next to Bob Dugard on the centre green, "Cookie's here!" Kevin articulates the emotions of the moment, "The man who's going to be shaking hands with the friends who raced against him on the track for these past 21 years." Never lost for words, witticism or eccentric comment, David launches headlong into his farewell meeting. "It's been mad getting here. It's a nightmare. I've 16 geezers who mean more to me than anything [voice cracks with a thin wire of emotion]. I'm gonna cry! Thanks for coming and let's look for the next Floppy!"

Though Kevin Coombes introduces each rider capably, Floppy's own programme pen portraits arguably capture them much better. Edward Kennett ("Makes me feel real old. I have seen Ed grow ever since he was a wee one. ... has the added advantage of John Davis as a future father-in-law."), Jason Doyle ("I don't know too much of Jason, other than he is here for me at the drop of a hat. ...he unfortunately tore his rotator cuff in his shoulder which ended his 09 season. Time out can make you go one of two ways, and mate he's going all the way.") Hans Andersen ("We used to meet up a few times after racing in Sweden at the airport. Always made each other laugh and had more of my sense of humour than me!"), Danny King ("To be a great rider he has it all except our backing") Joe Screen ("Makes me proud that he and others alike were the benchmark for my generation of speedway. I think because of the era Joe started in he was probably slightly unappreciated. If there was a Joe Screen today the world would speak of little more. Emil-esque.), Cameron Woodward ("What a nice guy, raised by his parents in a firm and proper manner, polite and bashful...he is his own biggest critic which is fine as long as he takes praise when given. I've got all the time in the world for him – except evenings and weekends!"), Lewis Bridger ("I'm disappointed that still no one has taken the reins for him in the form of a manager"), Lukáš Dryml ("I'm not saying that he falls off a lot but he is my king of crash. If he has one it's normally proper only to be followed by the most passionate and perfectly detailed step by step account of said crash. Brilliant"), Adam Shields ("Life's fun with Adam around. He too loves it deep and wide, it's amazing what a guy will tell you in a hot tub! One of my favourite memories is when Adam's love for snow lasted two minutes in Sweden one year. Stick to the beach buddy!") and Ben Barker ("I met Uncle Ben at the British Under-21s at Eastbourne two years ago. He was a breath of fresh air, reminded me of the good old days, me and Deano spoke to him about gearing but he was off but said, 'Ah don't worry I shall just ride it flat out anyway'. He had never seen Eastbourne before and I think he made Top 4. I said if this guy ever got a good bike under him watch out. Well guys I guess you better watch out.") For this meeting, Ben wears the No. 16 race tabard and Kevin excitedly tells us he's also "wearing a pair of Floppy's leathers; that brings back memories, last-minute entry Ben Barker!"

The parade photo (including David Norris) nearly goes awry until Kevin issues instructions in the patient tone of someone speaking to recalcitrant children, "Helmets off – sorry Lewis – that looks better!" Photograph over, the riders take a few practice laps, while we're encouraged to wish the meeting away and look forward to the Grand Final, "That's when we find out who is the unofficial King of Arlington!" Kevin bigs up the official on the buttons, "The world's best referee – Tony Steele is here! No pressure then. He hasn't ref'd at Eastbourne for about five years. Is it the tea or what? He rang Floppy and asked, 'Would you like me to do it?'" Almost forgotten in the excitement, Kevin also reminds us *en passant*, "It's our last Saturday night for 2010 – what a way to bow out with Floppy's big one!"

Contemporary life is full of needless safety and/or public information announcements that we heedlessly ignore as background chatter. At our peril we discount Kevin's warning that during tonight's meeting David will also have a microphone in his hand – albeit of the roving variety. "Floppy will be grabbing one or two of his heroes every fourth race – just a reminder, he's had a pint of cider already, so anythink could happen!" One of those genuinely keen to tilt at and land the unofficial King of Arlington crown is Edward Kennett. However, just as the riders come under orders for the first race, he pulls back suddenly. Edward's mechanic Chris Geer promptly races out onto the centre green but, just as he arrives alongside the defective bike, it fires back into life. Resuming his place off gate 3, Edward finds his main rival Scott Nicholls off the inside gate – separated by Richard Sweetman in the No. 2 Leigh Adams race tabard. Scott and Ed proceed to race neck and neck alongside each other until the exit from bend four, where Scott nudges-cum-brushes underneath his rival to establish the dominance he requires to win the race. Daniel King wins heat 2 ahead of Hans Andersen while, at the rear of the race, an out-of-sorts David Mason retires when already a considerable distance adrift. Out on the centre green, Bob Dugard and Jon Cook chat animatedly throughout the initial racing, apparently oblivious to the track action.

From the referee's box alongside Tony Steele, Kevin Coombes provides us with another public service announcement. "I have been asked by Bob Dugard to point out that stockcar racing starts here next Saturday. Run by Speedworth International – it's a big gamble for them moving from Wednesdays." Keen that we should support this venture, Kevin concludes, "It's an absolutely amazing spectacle!" Probably aware of the irony, although he doesn't acknowledge it, Kevin fails to mention that it's a similarly 'brave' (possibly more dramatic) move for the Eastbourne Eagles promotion to decide to voluntarily switch from their long time Saturday race night to their new 'regular' Thursday night slot. While I'm sure stockcar races get the juices flowing, I'm not convinced that it beats the absolutely amazing spectacle of a top-notch competitive speedway race. Understandably, the Eastbourne managerial team publicly put a brave face on this change of race night away from the weekend. They acknowledge the fears of the fans but proceed to point to the harsh commercial reality that competition with the Speedway Grand Prix series on too many Saturdays throughout the summer speedway months is a thanklessly uneconomical proposition on a long-term basis. Simon Stead comfortably wins heat 3 while behind him three riders regularly trade position. Nicolai Klindt rears out of the gate to relegate himself to last position. On the second bend of lap 2, Joe Screen zooms past Cameron Woodward apparently oblivious to the mogul run of bumps on that particular bend. Next time round, this insouciance proves fatal when a badly discombobulated Joe gets so badly out of position that Nicolai and then Cameron easily pass. John Hazelden glances appreciatively round the stadium, "I tell you what – it's a bigger crowd than I expected! I was here for Floppy and Deano's testimonials and there's definitely more here."

Testimonials, invitations and rider benefits often attract a high calibre field but inevitably (but also sensibly), the riders tend to err on the side of caution. Though this might be standard practice, it's a message that clearly hasn't got through to either Ben Barker or Lewis Bridger since they race throughout heat 4 like it will decide the eventual whereabouts of the world championship crown. Ben Barker looks likely to shade it until the third lap where, as the riders transition from the first to the second bend, Lewis dives dramatically under Ben before drifting wide to occupy his racing line. It's effectively race over as Lewis then proceeds to power towards the chequered flag sat astride his bike in his usual distinctively comfortable riding the sofa style.

Already a fluent performer from his televised work for Sky Sports, David Norris with the roving mic in his hand at his own farewell meeting enjoys *carte blanche* so gives full reign to his natural broadcasting ability. "We're with the crowd on the second bend. It's as raw as it gets! It's as random as it gets! Let's ask the man in the purple-and-yellow top what he's doing here." The man in question is an Oxford fan, "Sadly, I have to watch Swindon now but they've started to lose!" David spots some people he knows, "These are the Carpenter brothers. Kevin Carpenter, he's a professional golfer, freestyle. I met them two years ago coming back from Bydgoszcz." Floppy's microphone enables the brothers to fulfil their dream to sing in public for a large audience. Either that or they've been at the falling down juice. The Arlington version of the Carpenters enthusiastically launch into their marvellously atonal rendition of "I'm forever blowing bubbles". From the safety of the referee's box Kevin Coombes quick-wittedly quips, "You can get their CD as you leave the stadium tonight!"

Heat 5 starts with the unusual sight of Lewis Bridger leading from the tapes but, unfortunately, when he rears on the back straight Scott Nicholls slips past for an easy win. Kevin's appreciative of what he's just seen, "Second win of the night. A little bit of a purple patch for Scott Nicholls and that's exactly where he needs to be." Last-minute Leigh Adams replacement (and tabard wearer) Richard Sweetman channels the spirit of the great man to win heat 6. It's a sight to savour for John Hazelden, "He's a good little rider." Collectively we – the crowd – learn that there's no meeting reserve when Adam Shields fails to appear for the seventh race because of "serious bike trouble". John Hazelden voices his suspicions, "I 'spect he only brought one bike!" From the way the riders ride the second bend, it's clear that the mogul run of bumps there continue to cause problems. Edward Kennett soon finds himself a long way behind Hans Andersen but proceeds to apply his extensive experience of the Arlington track to ride a very wide line in pursuit. His exciting full-throttle style quickly makes up the initial gap but can't quite overcome it.

This season some of the Australian riders have come over all Teasy-Weasy and (it appears) also had a bet amongst themselves to not cut their hair. Whether or not dyeing it is part of the equation is impossible to establish exactly. Poole's Davey Watt is definitely one of those involved – 'how age inappropriate' is the general consensus but, then, if you (allegedly) have the smallest ears in speedway this sort of thing is bound to happen. Cameron Woodward is also involved. While he gardens by the tapes prior to the start of heat 8, dark brown dyed coloured hair shows beneath the back of his helmet. Only those in the know appreciate the full intricacies of this wager. These luxuriant hairstyles wouldn't look out of place if Cameron or Davey became members of a heavy metal band (although, perhaps, Pre-Raphaelite curls would be more authentic). That said, given the artificial lustre of the hair dye colour they look to have chosen together in Superdrug, there's a strong element of Fisher Price toy about their present tonsorial style. Hidden beneath his helmet, Ben Barker's hair is completely unremarkable. However, when interviewed at the live meetings shown on Sky Sports, it's always hard to throw off the impression that the pitch of Ben's voice is some form of tribute to the late Alan Ball. Required to ride not speak, Ben wins comfortably.

David Norris continues to throw himself into the roving aspect of his microphone duties with due seriousness, "I've secretly come down to beneath your box!" Gremlins creep into the system to interrupt the flow of his interviews with selected friends and fans. David shrieks, "Save it! Save it! You'll ruin it! We can't quite hear what they're saying." These technical issues disappear as quickly as they arrive to allow Wild Thing back to full flow. "This is speedway – don't be scared! I was drunk last night thinking what I was going to do to make this different? Where is Karen Walker? We're gonna beat these Dryml people." Regular Lukáš Dryml chants are nowadays fashionably *de rigueur* amongst a select but noisy section of fans usually located in the home-straight grandstand. Wild Thing is keen to resurrect the defunct Arlington tradition of E.A.G.L.E.S. chants. David appeals to the Eastbourne fans in the back-straight grandstand to indulge him with a spontaneous toasting contest. "You lot over there, open your mouths – give me an 'E.'" The Eagles versus Dryml's chant-off doesn't approach hip-hop standards of aggression or word play and also doesn't meet Wild Thing's satisfaction. In possible sympathy, heat 9 ends dissatisfactorily and is awarded after the enthusiasm of the third-bend gate operative temporarily overwhelms his ability to count to four. His sudden loss of numeracy nearly ends in disaster. On lap three with Ben Barker flying up front and Scott Nicholls in close pursuit – the Ipswich favourite and ex-Eagle suddenly shows lightning reactions to pull up dramatically when the gate-cum-fence panel unexpectedly swings outwards onto the track to impede his high-speed chase round the outside. As quick as the gate swings open, it swings shut again to prompt much mystification amongst the less eagle-eyed members of the Eastbourne congregation. Kevin Coombes explains, "Heat 9 being awarded because the gate opened slightly earlier – one lap earlier than it needed to be." Opposite the third-bend gate is the tractor turnaround point. Already retired from the race and safe from harm at the time of the incident – ready to exit the raceway – a nonplussed David Mason looks on. As a last-minute replacement for Paul Hurry, John Hazelden doesn't expect he'll trouble the scorer, "The only way David Mason will get a point is if someone falls off."

David and Kevin do the raffle draw during the interval. It features some unique prizes. Kevin's focuses upon the raffle prize that most appeals to him, "pressing the button for the last heat. You can touch Tony Steele but only on the shoulders, present trophies and also win some signed hoodies and Danny King's goggles from last season's Under-21s!" David draws the winning ticket but the lucky holder isn't so easily found. "Where are you? It took me ages to think of this prize! The prize of a lifetime! Come on or I'm gonna claim it myself! Some of the guys who couldn't make it – donated someint personal, things money can't buy. If I was a fan, I'd be wanting this stuff. Tony Steele has done it for free. He should have said, 'Dave you come up and start the last race'. We've got an auction in the bar – in the clubhouse – after the meeting and, then, a disco. You can bid for the riders' race jackets. There's only 18 in the world! It's signed by all the riders which slightly devalues it!" Second prize in the raffle is an Eastbourne race jacket. David wonders, "Signed is it? I want to describe this – it's a peachy-flesh colour – just how I like it."
[Kevin] "It's a salmon colour, that's what we say in the business."
[David] "It's a caviar colour."
[Kevin] "I know you're the fisherman. You're showing off now!"

Talk of fishing and David's love of fish is borne out in the commemorative souvenir programme with a full-length photograph of a quizzically proud Floppy holding a large fish in all its glory. The look on his face confirms suspicions that Wild Thing caught it all by himself. Nowadays no self-

19

respecting sport or hobby is without its complete range of accoutrements and paraphernalia. Indeed, in the background of this photograph, there's an impressive sized tent and comfy chair positioned by a large lake that (disappointingly as I'd like to think David's catch took more skill, guile and cunning) I suspect is packed with fish. The brute reality of said photograph is that it's really an advert placed by Hawkhurst Fish Farm. It's slightly less hunter-gatherer than tradition dictates but, nonetheless, the sense of achievement in landing this whopper is still there for all to see on David's slightly bearded face. Back out on a centre green devoid of fish, David's in full effect, "PK was meant to do my meeting and he abandoned me, he's got family commitments which, as an old guy, I understand. I've got his gloves and goggles from two or three weeks ago when he spanked our bots!" Yellow ticket number 450 wins this particular PK memorabilia prize while, "white – colour of a cloud – 343" wins "Danny King's World Cup goggles from 2009 when he became a bit of a hero in some quarters!" David regales us, almost without drawing breath, "Lee Richardson couldn't be here tonight, unfortunately he's in Las Vegas."

[Kevin] "What do you think of it so far?"

[David] "They're all brilliant! I love Ben Barker – he's so old school! He's so on it! I had a late night last night but didn't get drunk. Ben's come here last minute and he's flat out!"

[Kevin] "Give us an 'E!'"

[David] "I used to sit in the blue section as a child – now the grey section – unless you give it your all, you can't come back next week!"

[Kevin] "We're not here next week – in a fortnight."

Quixotic as ever, David demands a delay in the chant-off until cheerleader-in-chief, Karen Walker can be found to lead the chorus. Away from the madding crowd, on the other side of the perimeter fence adjacent to the St John Ambulance hut (during this extended interval prior to heat 11) Adam Shields's van reverses and leaves.

When the race action resumes, Edward Kennett initially leads heat 11 until passed by a superfast Danny King on the back straight. Lewis Bridger makes it two wins in three races when he overtakes Jason Doyle at the start of the second lap of heat 12. To celebrate his race win, Lewis showcases a trademark wheelie for a complete lap! The promise (warning?) that every four laps the microphone will be under David's control goes awry after the exertions of the interval draw. David's slightly lost sense of time, "Sorry, I was talking to me mum! Go away mum." While he gathers himself, Kevin again reminds us, "Don't forget stockcars start next Saturday at 6.45." John Hazelden knows his stockcars, "It can be wonderful but it can be dreadful! But then so can speedway." With Karen Walker found, prior to the chant-off David riffs, "Lukáš Dryml is Eastbourne end of story. I love him to bits. Not being funny, you're honoured to have him here. In time old-fashioned style, I give you Karen the original cheer girl!" Enthusiastically Karen leads the back-straight grandstand fans in the traditional Arlington war cry, "Give us an 'E', give us an 'A', give us a 'G', give us a 'L', give us an 'E', give us a 'S'. What have you got? EAGLES!" The Lukáš Dryml fan club chant back noticeably less loudly. Up for the challenge, Karen resumes with yet another war cry, "Give me a 'D', give me a 'D', give me a 'D', give me an 'A' give me a 'V', give me an 'I', give me a 'D', What have you got? D-D-DAVID!"

Despite a poor start to his season at Peterborough – where he's fallen short of the expectations of the Panthers management, fans and, of course, himself – Lewis looks an altogether different rider in this particular part of East Sussex. Indeed, he wins heat 14 so easily that he wheelies over the finish line during laps two, three and four! Between races Kevin Coombes reviews last night's results including the Lakeside score, "53-40! Poole showing they're human. Lee Richardson taking over from Krzysztof Kasprzak – things weren't quite right there – were they?" Though the odd race has a going through the motions element, the way Coventry Bees team mates Ben Barker and Edward Kennett line-up closely to each other on gates 1 and 2 before heat 15 shows they take their personal duels very seriously. Edward easily wins their race to the first bend while the diminutive Barker suffers mechanicals. When his bike finally splutters back into life Ben's so far behind he pulls a few perfunctory wheelies before he retires. John Hazelden's earlier confident prediction that David Mason won't score proves misguided when the lack of meeting reserve in heat 16 (to replace the absent Adam Shields) requires that he only needs to finish to score. "Mason's gonna get a bloody point!"

The prize for the winner of the Grand Final is ostentatiously brought onto the centre green and deposited close to the start gate for later presentation. From the image on the side of the box, said prize is a large sized television (or, possibly, a small sized television in a large box). Kevin exults, "There's a flat screen TV for the meeting winner!" Some fans wonder whether the box is empty while others question whether it sustained damage in its alleged fall off the back of a lorry. With most riders racing almost every night during the speedway season, often in different countries, the burning need for a television isn't completely clear? Irrespective of their domestic viewing arrangements, heat 17 features another three-rider race. It's won comfortably by Scott Nicholls after he's given Danny King a gratis gating lesson. Joe Screen supplements this impromptu education when he reels in and passes the promising young Ipswich rider. Kevin salutes the 12-point haul for Scott Nicholls that ensures his qualification for the Grand Final before he then drops his voice to inform us, "Joe Screen finishes with 6 points not really getting out of the gate, unfortunately."

With 9 points from four rides, Edward Kennett needs to win heat 19 to guarantee his shot at the flat screen telly via victory in the Grand Final. Though Edward leads Lewis from the gate – as they enter the second bend – Bridger drives into the dirt out by the airfence to accelerate in jet-propelled fashion into a lead he fails to relinquish. A win for Jason Doyle in heat 20 would see him equal Edward Kennett's 11-point tally and gain last-gasp qualification to the Grand Final by virtue of his greater number of race wins. In order to do so, Jason showcases a carbon copy of Lewis's manoeuvre from the previous race to find the 'same dirt' in the same place on the second bend of the first lap. It provides all the acceleration he needs to fire into the lead. Up above the action in the referee's box, Kevin Coombes snatches a few words with referee Tony Steele about Mr Norris. "David is, I think, a bit special. You can talk to him about everything! He knows not just about himself but all the teams and the riders."

[Kevin] "He always stepped up to the plate in the Team GB kevlars."

[Tony] "He did! He's very much going to be missed at Eastbourne – at all the tracks and amongst the officials. David was always very fair and very honest and is a hard act to follow!"

Raffle prizewinner and Canterbury fan, Debbie is also alongside Tony Steele with her forefinger positively itching to press the start button. Kevin investigates her speedway pedigree, "We've been coming here since Canterbury closed. We pick and choose our meetings and we're here today following David." Whether through inexperience or nerves, Debbie holds the Grand Final tapes far too long. This (along with the thought of a new flat screen telly) lures Hans Andersen into breaking the tapes. If this were anything other than Floppy's Farewell, then Hans would lose the opportunity to become "the Last King of Arlington" or take home a new flat screen TV. His disqualification would go against the spirit of the meeting and the fun of the day so it's hardly a surprise when Kevin tells us, "We'll try again with all four riders and Alan [Rolfe] going to get another set of tapes." Said rerun of the Grand Final is worth the proverbial admission money alone since it serves up a determined, passionate contest that makes you realise how rarely we get to see them nowadays! Though Hans Andersen and Jason Doyle also compete, after the second lap it's effectively a two-rider match race over two laps between Scott Nicholls and Lewis Bridger.

Both Scott and Lewis rear massively at full power as they vie for the front. On the back straight of the third lap Scott grabs back the lead with a superpowered rearing manoeuvre that looks like it will be enough to get additional value from his television licence fee right until the moment Lewis returns the superpower compliment with a cut back underneath him on the third bend of the last lap to gain victory and stir the crowd. After these two last laps of total commitment, Lewis celebrates his inauguration as the Last King of Arlington exuberantly. Wholehearted and keenly contested, this race is a fitting finale to East Sussex based David Norris's Eastbourne career.

15th May Last King of Arlington Winner: Lewis Bridger

Eastbourne: *"He had such a talent and never knew it"*

CHAPTER 3

Newport

"I'm not telling anyone what to do! I just advise if they want it! Some of them do need it"

30th May

The Queensway Meadows Industrial Estate in Newport is bathed in Bank Holiday weekend sunshine when I pull up outside Hayley Stadium, home to the Newport 'Darlows' Wasps. Staff on the gate of the club's rough-hewn car park currently outnumber parked cars with 90 minutes to go before the scheduled start time of 2.30 p.m. Over by the pits gate entrance Workington Comets team manager, Ian Thomas pulls up in a well-polished rather spiffy-looking German car. Last night his team suffered a surprise home defeat at Derwent Park against Sheffield in the Premier League. Ian's deep in a mobile conversation so I don't get the chance to ask him if he heard Jon Ronson discussing the (ultimately abortive) US smell warfare programme plans to drop two different chemicals onto Iraq to create enough confusion – by turning their soldiers gay and give them halitosis – to enable them to invade successfully and take control. Though it's a long drive down from the North West (or Yorkshire in Ian's case) Comets riders won't have time to dwell upon this reverse and, indeed, probably arrive full of confidence at their prospects this afternoon against Newport. Though the Wasps have only lost three home meetings this season to date (out of a possible nine), by all accounts last weekend's defeat was ignominious enough to prompt joint team manager Kevin Brown to issue a public apology. Given the strength of the Birmingham Brummies this season and their record of success on the road, this sounds a somewhat drastic reaction. That said the 39-52 scoreline only gives us the broad numerical facts rather than any true insight into the calibre or effectiveness of the Wasps performance.

At this time of year by early afternoon the Newport pits are a suntrap bathed in almost Mediterranean brightness. Club photographer Hywel Lloyd and Wasps incident recorder Gavin Morrison are deep in conversation. They pause their chat long enough for Hywel to gnomically observe, "You

Paperwork

Rider parade

23

got here for our last meeting then!" I'm en route to the Hay Festival and, given its comparative proximity to Newport, the opportunity to take in a speedway meeting in South Wales is impossible to resist. It's hard to tell whether Hywel is joking or serious. This week's *Speedway Star* does carry news that Newport's Nick Mallett's promoter's licence has been withdrawn by the Speedway Control Bureau for the rest of the 2010 season, "after he made derogatory comments about Weymouth on the social networking site Facebook." He won't be the first, let alone the last to make critical public statements about Mr Philip Wayne Bartlett. That said, ownership of a promoter's licence carries responsibility and involves obligations including respectful behaviour towards fellow colleagues. Nonetheless, if the youngest promoter in British speedway struggles to understand the dynamics and visibility of such newfangled technology what hope is there for the rest of us? [1]

When I question Hywel about his earlier observation of doom he comes over all reluctant, "I'm not saying anything! Things aren't looking good. Have you seen the programme? Then I suggest that you go and get one!" What exactly promoter Steve Mallett has written in his "Waspland whisperings" column does – if you listen to Hywel – sound earth-shatteringly apocalyptic. However, when I finally get to see a copy – given last season's frequent similar rumblings – it's actually (in film terms) much more *Groundhog Day* than *2012*. [2]

Stood on the periphery of the bustle of activity that is the visitors' side of the pits, Wasps Programme Editor and Public Relations Officer Gareth Rogers's cheerful mood matches the brightness of the sunshine. We reminisce about the 16-year old David Norris early impact in the sport (prompted by talk of his Benefit meeting at Arlington) until a casually dressed Benji Compton interrupts us to express his surprise that he hasn't heard anything from Redcar. Gareth solicitously listens to Benji's concern before he promises, "I'll mention you asked to Brian [Havelock]. They did make some changes to the team but things got worse then. Like they did when we made changes here last season, we went to the bottom!" Away from Newport, Gareth has restarted his presentational duties on race night at Redcar Speedway. "Redcar haven't won since I went back. They won here and have had a draw at home but, apart from that, they've lost everything! The crowd has held up well though. When, at the end of the meeting I'm changing my shoes, one of the old fans – and I mean one of the old blokes – said to me, 'We had ten years without speedway so we're going to keep coming. It'll pick up eventually!' Brian rang me after

[1] The SCB statement on the matter noted, "The Speedway Control Bureau, at its recent meeting, reviewed the position of Mr Nicholas Mallett holding a promoter's licence for Newport speedway. The outcome is that Mr Mallett's SCB licence has been withdrawn for the duration of the 2010 season. Mr Mallett has been advised of the Speedway Control Bureau's decision." Though the posting on the Facebook site has been deleted 23-year old Nicky allegedly criticised Weymouth officials on the running of the Dorset club. Fortunately many members of the British Speedway Forum do not hold promoters' licences otherwise they too would find themselves in exile with Nicky Mallett. Fellow Newport co-promoter and Nicky's father, Steve commented, "Nick has had his licence suspended and he is entitled to reapply for it at the end of the season. His comments formed part of a private conversation he had with someone on Facebook. He left his profile open and that's how the comments were discovered. I don't believe he ever wanted them to be made public." If this is the only reason for the suspension of Nicky's promoter's licence, then it seems that the SCB wish to send a general message that they disapprove of the use of new social networking communication channels (a.k.a. Facebook) by speedway officials. Punishment served, Nick regains his licence prior to the 2011 season

[2] On page 3 of the programme Steve's "Waspland whisperings" outline the hardy perennial of his ongoing concern at crowd levels – or the lack of them – and the implications the resulting lack of finances might possibly have for the continuation of the club. "Meanwhile our concern over attendances continues. Last Sunday we had some extra bodies here courtesy of the travelling support for the Brummies but there were still nothing like the number of home supporters that we need. It was not only the Somerton Park days of yore that saw Newport as one of the best attended tracks in the sport but here at Queensway Meadows from 1997 when the sport was revived after a 20-year absence. When my family re-opened the doors in 2009 we invested heavily both on track with respect to the circuit and an airfence coupled with radically improving changing and medical facilities behind the scenes....Trouble is that we cannot afford to carry on as we are unless together we can convince the former fans to get down here and show there is still a demand for us in the city. The family will be monitoring the gate today and tomorrow when the successful Newport Hornets face the Dudley Heathens and we face a difficult decision about our own continuity. As I say – we need your help to get the turnstiles ticking again otherwise speedway will be just a memory."

Newport: *"I'm not telling anyone what to do! I just advise if they want it! Some of them do need it"*

they lost at Sheffield [3] and asked, 'What did I think?' which is a start." Our conversation is interrupted again, this time by the shouts of a man on the other side of the pits. His loudness draws attention but so too does the headscarf tied round his head in the manner of a pirate or heavy metal roadie. Gareth harrumphs, "They're shouting every week at Newport!"

Stood close by to us, apparently serenely oblivious to the shouting, is 79-year-old speedway legend and Wasps joint team manager Neil Street. Though he's lived in England for a significant number of years, despite the warmth of the late May sunshine, Neil wears his trademark jumper. Though you can take the man out of Australia, you can't take Australia out of the man. Modest, friendly, hugely knowledgeable with time for absolutely everyone, Neil exudes contentment and fascination in equal measure. Huge numbers of grateful pupils have passed through Neil's capable hands. His quietly spoken advice is endlessly relevant to anyone's speedway education but, equally importantly, his attitude to life and towards people is even more instructive. The hierarchy and power relationships implied by the concept of management, doesn't sit easily with Neil's style of guidance. "I'm not managing anybody! I'm just here to advise the youngsters. They're here to learn or, at least, they should be! They're apprentices learning their trade. If they learn it properly, they'll have a good career! But, if they just think they can pick it up as they go along, then they won't."

[Jeff] "They're lucky they've got you to listen to."
[Neil] "I'm not telling anyone what to do! I just advise if they want it! Some of them do need it. [smiles] It keeps me going."

Though it isn't long until the scheduled start time, there's hardly a flood of fans inside the stadium. However, there's quite a queue at the burger van including an energetic Ian "I'm 68, I look 78 but feel 58" Thomas, the Workington Comets' ebullient team manager. While they wait, he chats with Workington programme seller Liz, "Briggo sold 12 in the Directors' box!" "That's good, it's been out a while. [Turns to me] We put on a show for Briggo. We had a massive poster with Briggo's Ride written on it at Workington. It covered two-thirds of the track and Briggo rode through it."
[Jeff] "I hope you got a photo."
[Ian] "What do you think?! We got photos before, during and after!"
[Jeff] "Just teaching you to suck eggs."
[Ian] "They say there are 300 here! What do you think?"
[Jeff] "It's not a large crowd."
[Ian] "That's an understatement. I'd commit suicide if we had this!"
[Jeff] "Are you going to introduce the riders to the crowd?"
[Ian] "No, the crowd to the riders!"
[Jeff] "I don't have your wit."
[Ian] "What have the crowds been like where else you've been?"
[Jeff] "The Isle of Wight wasn't big but it's not the summer yet when they get most of theirs. Eastbourne had a good crowd for the Norris meeting but the switch to Thursday will be a test. Lakeside was impressive against Poole but they promote it aggressively to the people in their area who can get there easily – along the A13 and the A12 – rather than those who have to travel any distance round the M25. It seems like lots of them can get there easily and do! Some say Poole is down and others say it's massively up."
[Ian] "That's not entertaining winning by so much! Crowds are down at Birmingham because of that!"
[Jeff] "Have you seen the programme?"

[3] Redcar lost 67-25 in the Premier Trophy on 27th May

[Ian] "Why does it slag me off then?"

[Jeff] "No. There's doubt about their future here."

[Ian] "Oh. People can slag me off, I don't care!"

A fan comes up to quiz Ian about whether or not the bridge in Workington is open.

[Ian to Liz] "It's been open about six weeks now."

[Fan] "I knew the footbridge was open."

[Ian] "It's not a footbridge – it's for cars only."

[Fan] "Oh. I'm coming to Northside when they have the Under-15s there."

[Ian] "They haven't hardly had anything there this year."

[Fan] "What time do they start?"

[Ian] "I dunno."

[Fan] "What date is it?"

[Ian] "I dunno."

[Jeff] "July 17th"

[Fan] "Do you do second half still?"

[Ian] "If riders want to ride, we do."

[Fan] "So, no programmed second halves!"

[Ian, studiously but politely] "If riders are ready to ride and want to, they can!"

[Fan] "What are you going to do next season?"

[Ian] "Why?"

[Fan] "Your lease expires."

[Ian] "Does it?"

[Fan] "They say so in the press! Do you want to say anything?"

[Ian] "If I did, I would say it in the press not on the terraces at Newport."

[Fan] "I'm sorry if I offended you by asking. Sometimes people can say things unofficially."

Ian cuts short the conversation for more pressingly important matters, namely he's at the front of the queue so needs to place his order for a burger and a can of full-fat Coco-Cola. The fan – who only joined the queue to quiz Ian – wanders off. Ian's order arrives quickly and, as Ian walks back towards the pits, he bites hungrily into his burger, "This is awful! I'm a diabetic, I shouldn't be eating this!"

The Newport track surface receives far more criticism than other similarly allegedly 'difficult' tracks. Whatever the reason for this attention, there's absolutely no doubt that before the racing gets underway promoter Steve Mallett works away at it industriously. Doubtless, he drives his tractor to prepare the shale in the manner that he deems most likely to ensure a smooth surface, good racing and a Wasps victory. The results of his handiwork are there for all to see at the start line since this area enjoys his particular attention. Steve moves clods and lumps of shale in all directions to create a rough, surprisingly contoured surface. On the centre green, this afternoon's SCB official Dale Entwistle, looks on disconsolately with an expression on his face that brings to mind a phrase from one of A. A. Gill's recent restaurant reviews, "It was like a wine gum filled with pus but tasted less nice."

Before the racing starts the announcer informs the assembled crowd, "I dunno if you heard, we had a break-in at the stadium last week!" Thieves can't have stolen the Newport 'Darlows' Wasps mojo, since last weekend's result against Birmingham showed they'd already lost it. What exactly has gone missing isn't made clear, nonetheless, we're told, "We'll be having a collection at the interval. Todd Kurtz was one of those that suffered." Todd rides at reserve for the Wasps with an assessed average of 3. Attaining and maintaining competitive equipment is increasingly hard for

26

any rider but probably more so for one who's thousands of miles from home (albeit with an opportunity to learn under the expert tutelage of Neil Street). The meeting gets underway with a particularly ragged start as some riders belie the name of the sport to depart the start line exceptionally slowly. Referee Dale Entwistle immediately stops the race and the announcer informs us, "Well, dunno what happened there! Referee Dale Entwistle says it's his fault. Nice of him when it's easier to blame an electrical fault! He had a problem with the button." Given the opportunity to showcase his lightning-fast reflexes for a second time, André Compton forgets his experience and fails to live up to the billing implied by his No. 1 race tabard to finish comprehensively last. It's a race won by the resurgent Newport captain Leigh Lanham escorted home by the similarly experienced Craig Watson. Fortunately for Newport, the programme scorecard shows Leigh and Craig will ride together three times this afternoon. Many wouldn't have predicted an opening Wasps 5-1. Heat 2 sees white-helmeted Comets reserve Richard Lawson fire from the tapes into the lead but, unfortunately, he can't quite cope with his own velocity so nearly strikes the safety fence as he exits the second bend. Somehow Lawson retains control but drops to second and then falls off his bike on the next bend when Todd Kurtz drives underneath him. Rusty Harrison's race win ensures the heat is drawn. Craig Cook and Chris Schramm then combine in the third race for a Comets 5-1 that levels the cumulative score. Tim Webster finishes last and it's impossible to avoid the thought that rider replacement for Kyle Legault would be more favourable for Newport.

The strength of the sunshine prompts a brief delay to allow a few circuits for the bowser to dampen down dust levels. Heat 4 pits two highly regarded No. 5s against each other. Workington's stylish Dane Peter Kildemand zooms from the start line and, though at the end of the first lap he comes under brief pressure from the Wasps Kim Nilsson, he responds by going faster. Kildemand looks extremely quick to the naked eye. It's an effect exaggerated by his rather stylish but idiosyncratic manner on his bike that sees him raise his right leg to horizontal as he broadsides into each corner. He definitely looks quite an acquisition for the Comets. Over the remaining three laps, Kildemand further catches the eye each time he exits the fourth bend since – as he arrows towards the safety fence – he rears as if the sheer power of the bike nearly runs away with him. Recommended to the Comets promoters by that shrewd judge of speedway flesh – Denmark team manager Jan Stæchmann – Kildemand is another graduate from the Danish junior rider development programme. He's progressed from racing 80cc machines to the 500cc beasts that are nowadays his living at Workington and Fjelsted. With Rusty Harrison third, the visitors gain a heat advantage and immediately follow it up with another after André Compton wins heat 5 comfortably. Tim Webster again fails to trouble the scorer but battles determinedly throughout the race making light of a solo mid-race fall to swiftly remount. The nice cooling breeze is ideal for the fans on a sunny day but suboptimal for track curation since no sooner has the bowser dampened the shale than it quickly gets dry and dusty again.

Heat 6 gets no further than the second bend where a slow-motion Richard Lawson falls back first into the airfence. Ignoring the virtuosity of his dismount, referee Dale Entwistle disqualifies him from the rerun (even while Lawson is still prone on the track surface). Once back on his feet, Richard stomps back to the pits to the warm applause of the crowd in the home-straight grandstand. When Lawson draws level with the referee's box, he angrily points to his own eyes twice. It's gesture unseen on *Vision On* but does prompt some good-natured jeers from the Newport faithful in the grandstand. Lolling against the pits gate, Newport promoter Steve Mallett – defiantly dressed in jeans and black T-shirt rather than the collar and tie that regulations dictate should be worn along with his BSPA jacket – greets Richard with a toothy but not altogether affectionate grin along with a meaningful stare usually practised just prior to bar-room discussions breaking down into physical confrontation. Like photographers throughout British speedway,

27

Hywel Lloyd's work allows him the privilege of watching from the centre green. He's dismissive about Richard Lawson's protestations to the referee, "There was nothing wrong! He was miles behind when he fell."

[Jeff] "And on his own."

[Hywel] "He was."

The rerun of heat 6 is a dramatic affair. Blue-helmeted Craig Watson flies from gate 3 with Peter Kildemand in close pursuit until Leigh Lanham nips around him on the fourth bend through the proverbial nonexistent gap. It's a manoeuvre that spurs Kildemand to chase even more enthusiastically. On the back straight of the second lap – as they transition from bends 2 to 3 – Kildemand almost draws alongside outside Lanham and close to the safety fence. Holding his throttle open, the young Dane draws level but then appears to suddenly realise he has too much speed going into the corner. Backing off fractionally too late ensures the inevitable consequence of Peter hammering into the airfence. Kildemand then jumps to his feet angrily and gestures wildly to imaginary persons unknown. Referee Dale Entwistle ignores his tai-chi-meets-kung-fu-fighting style appeal for leniency in favour of disqualification. Dale also awards the race though two laps have not been completed. This 5-0 heat advantage gives Newport a narrow lead at 18-17. Kildemand stomps unhappily back to the pits where, once again, Steve Mallett greets the return of another irked and dust speckled Comets rider with his silent trademark broad smile. From his endlessly changing vantage points, Hywel captured the money shot of the Kildemand outside attempted overtake as Lanham and the Dane rode neck and neck into the third bend. Contrary to the implication of the Comet heat leader's protestations and body language, Hywel's photo shows a clear gap between the two riders a fraction of a second before the fall. "'That's the one you want!' I said to Leigh Lanham. 'Lucky you're not a fat bastard like me otherwise he wouldn't have been able to try to get round!'"

Some delay follows for airfence repairs. The bowser circles in soporific fashion while the camera operatives inside the ReRun Productions film tower located on the first bend take a well-earned but brief break. To my untutored eyes, this is the only new item of furniture inside Hayley Stadium since my last visit. After the inflatable equipment repairs and much diligent curatorial work, referee Dale Entwistle rules the initial attempt to run heat 7 as an unsatisfactory start. The rerun features a dramatic coming together on the first bend after birthday boy Chris Schramm tootles from the tapes, wobbles and falls only to find himself clipped by his equally tardy race partner Craig Cook who, as a result, straightens and fires into the second-bend airfence. With both Newport riders ahead at the time of the stoppage, there appears ample ground for disgruntlement amongst either the Wasps management or fans when the referee, slightly strangely, rules this also to be an unsatisfactory start. Without even a second glance, let alone animosity, Steve Mallett and Ian Thomas chat absorbedly together at the foot of the stepped viewing platform on the Workington side of the pits during the latest break in proceedings. The re-rerun of heat 7 sees Newport's reserve on an assessed 5-point average, Alex Davies, look good, comfortable and fast in third position until the second bend where he smashes into the airfence to earn a disqualification. The announcer tells us understatedly, "He was drawn into the airbags there!" The re-re-rerun of heat 7 features a delightful shimmy from Kim Nilsson past Craig Cook on the first bend. It gives him a lead he doesn't relinquish and afterwards celebrates with some virtuoso wheelies.

Always likely to do well in heat 8 given his experience, Craig Watson wins comfortably and in the process gains his 2,000th point for Newport. With the scores evenly poised at 24-23, the Comets Peter Kildemand and Richard Lawson both bounce back from tumbles and disqualifications in their previous rides to win heat 9 imperiously. They accomplish this in conditions that closely resemble a dust storm that natural selection dictates camels have temporarily sealable nostrils to overcome. With ongoing understatement, the announcer hails their untroubled heat maximum as "quite decisive". Any race that pits Leigh Lanham and Craig Watson against Chris Schramm and Craig Cook is always likely to be one to savour. So heat 10 proves as Watson and Cook exit the second bend almost neck and neck. Leigh Lanham would have been alongside but – with experience, discretion and three and a half laps still on his side – he backs off slightly so that, by the third bend, Chris Schramm catches him. To my untutored eye, Lanham appears marginally out of control and under pressure. It's not a complete surprise when he smashes into the airfence with gusto. After some delay, Leigh's back gingerly onto his feet holding his left elbow sporting the pained expression of a man who's just dropped his ice cream. Laurence Rogers escorts him back towards the pits area and, when he reaches the pits gate, theatrically stares up at the red disqualification light, shakes his head and makes a two-armed gesture to the referee that probably isn't officially in the Signing Dictionary. Though no Marcel Marceau, his gesture nevertheless clearly implies Laurence's displeasure and belief that Chris Schramm's move-over knocked off Leigh Lanham. If Hywel's camera contains photographic evidence that confirms (or denies) this narrative, he doesn't share it with me. The first bend of the rerun more closely resembles skittles than speedway. Craig Cook takes Craig Watson's back wheel away – those who like the Workington rider would describe it as determinedly aggressive while those don't could see the same manoeuvre as wilfully reckless. The conflagration suddenly appearing in front of him prompts the quick-thinking Chris Schramm to take evasive action, albeit at the expense of ramming the second-bend airfence so brutally that it punctures. Despite the lack of fans here this afternoon, there's still impressively loud – almost pantomime – cries of disbelief from the home-straight grandstand and its environs when Dale Entwistle rules that this is an "unsatisfactory start". Back on the Workington side of the pits, an animated discussion ensues between Watson and Cook, both of whom continue to courteously wear their helmets. Their colleagues, teammates, rubber-neckers and well-wishers quickly surround them. Their discussions go no further than a frank exchange of opinions until both groups part in the manner of repelling magnets. Laurence Rogers tries to bridge the physical gap to go back over to the Workington side of the pits for further discussions but is stopped by a protective Ian Thomas shouting, "Go back!" Double-underlining his request, Ian waves his arms as if landing a plane on an aircraft carrier while again loudly insisting, "Go back!"

During the wait for yet another restart, Laurence goes on a walkabout to cool his heels in the shade of the home-straight grandstand and, possibly, make accidental but meaningful eye contact with Dale Entwistle. "I've seen some bad refs like Watters and the like but this bloke is something else! Cook took Watto's wheel away! I've got the thing [memory stick] for the match report but I don't know where to stick it!" In the re-rerun of a protracted heat 10, Craig Watson tacitly acknowledges the combatively strong opponent he faces on the track. Indeed, with discretion being the better part of valour, Craig conspicuously doesn't race into the first bend. However, by the fourth bend of the second lap he's got the time, speed and confidence to attempt an outside pass only for Cook to skilfully force him wide. It's a manoeuvre that wastes his rival's forward momentum as they enter the first bend of the third lap vying for second place. Ahead of them, the ease of Chris Schramm's victory further confirms the health protective qualities of airfence safety furniture at speedway and, with his partner Cook second, provides Workington with successive 5-1s to balloon the Comets advantage to 7 points at 26-33. On the warm-down lap Craig Watson conspicuously ignores the consolation wave of Craig Cook's hand. The interval is taken one heat early so that both the crowd and the track can enjoy a well-earned drink.

Co-author of the still indispensable *Homes of British Speedway* reference book, John Jarvis sits in the shade of the section of the home-straight grandstand that overlooks the first bend. John points to an old age pensioner and asks, "Do you know who that is?" I don't. Apparently, it's ex-Newport

Newport: *"I'm not telling anyone what to do! I just advise if they want it! Some of them do need it"*

and Wolverhampton rider Cyril Francis. "They let him in free each week." John then asks rhetorically, "You've come to see the end?" Like many who care about this South Wales speedway club, John has concerns at the size of the crowd. "There can only be 350 here when he [Steve Mallett] needs 800 to break even. You need 300 to make the National League pay. Tomorrow he'll get 200 maybe 250 if Dudley bring some down. Birmingham brought some last week. They say Tony Mole is looking at it in case Birmingham doesn't run next year.

[Jeff] "He's here today."

[John] "In his Workington top this week, he was in his Birmingham top last! I haven't been anywhere else this season – not Swindon or Somerset – just here! I haven't missed a single meeting Premier League or National League. I like to support Steve Mallett because he's a nice man. His mum is nice too."

[Jeff] "She's the one walking the dog."

[John] "She works in the burger bar at National League meetings. He must be losing money every week. It's a question of when he stops! They're all nice, only the son is a prat! It's amazing how things change. You ask Glyn Shailes – in '98 or '99 when Swindon did the fixture list they'd say 'Put in Newport first meeting, they'll bring 600!' It's a natural cycle for clubs. They come back and attendances are high and then it falls off. Look at Birmingham!"

After the interval, Kim Nilsson races to his second win in three rides (to take his points tally to 8) but it's only enough to ensure a drawn heat. After a last place, a disqualification and heat 9 race win, Richard Lawson banishes unpredictability with another win in heat 12 closely followed home by Chris Schramm. With the scores to a mathematically still retrievable 30-41, predictably enough Kim Nilsson appears in the black-and-white helmet colour for heat 13. From gate 2 Leigh Lanham fires from the tapes but then further showcases his team riding credentials by dawdling for an apparently becalmed Kim Nilsson. While Leigh waits for an acceleration that fails to materialise, Compton recovers from yet another slow start to zoom past into the lead. Leigh Lanham immediately abandons his forlorn escort duties to fruitlessly chase Compton. Behind him on the fourth bend of the first lap, Kildemand cuts off Nilsson's nose to simultaneously relegate him to fourth place and also nullify any potential tactical points advantage. The Comets 4-2 heat win guarantees what, ultimately, is an extremely comfortable away win. Rusty Harrison wins the penultimate race of the afternoon to become the fifth Comet to taste victory in South Wales this afternoon. Confirming that Newport are down to their loyal hardcore of support, complaints and discontent remain on mute. The harshest criticism I overhear remains mild, "The track is pants and the team is pants!" Sat on the steps of the brightly coloured trackshop, Anita Lewis soaks up some late afternoon sunshine. "At least I get a tan while I wait for the customers to arrive! What was the score?"

[Jeff] [As the riders flash past having just finished heat 15] "If that was a 3-all then you lost by 15."

[Anita] "Oh!"

[Jeff] "It was a good meeting. You were close till about half way through then you fell away. Lanham and Watson are quite a pairing. I don't suppose 15-point defeats have people flooding in to buy merchandise."

[Anita] "It doesn't!"

In his report on the meeting afterwards in the *Speedway Star* Terry Daley remarks, "Last week it was Birmingham who slaughtered the home team, a performance and result which prompted team manager Kevin Brown to issue a public apology. I didn't get an opportunity to speak with

Newport: *"I'm not telling anyone what to do! I just advise if they want it! Some of them do need it"*

him this time around, although he could well have spoken the exact same words after this defeat, the Wasps sixth in their opening seven league fixtures." [4]

30th May Newport v. Workington (Premier League) 37-52

4 A few weeks later promoter Steve Mallet announces that Newport Speedway are saved and that the club's management have already started to plan for their 2011 Premier and National League campaigns. Wasps shareholder Peter Mole – a Midlands-based dentist – stepped forward with financial aid to ensure the club's future. Putting two and two together often finds the wrong conclusions but, though not mentioned in the press or by the club, it wouldn't be a surprise if the new Mole (P.) investor is related to the famous speedway investor and "Kidderminster-based businessman" Mole (T.). Either way, Newport Press Officer Gareth Rogers welcomes developments to stare cheerily into the future, "It's very much secure after a lot of speculation and, I have to say, some negativity, which in one sense is understandable with the sort of statements we are sometimes capable of putting out. I was partially responsible for introducing Peter Mole into the club through my sporting contacts in the Midlands and he's been a factor here since the end of last season. The speculation is now over and the club will definitely see the season out and is already talking about 2011."

Newport: *"I'm not telling anyone what to do! I just advise if they want it! Some of them do need it"*

CHAPTER 4

Sheffield
"When the flag drops the bullshit stops"

3rd June

Though the speedway season is less than three months old, the highly fancied Birmingham Brummies are back in Sheffield for the third time. They've already won at Owlerton in the Premier Trophy and Knock-out Cup so, given comparative team strengths let alone recent form, they'll arrive for this Premier League meeting confident of completing a hat trick of victories. In a sun-kissed Owlerton car park I bump into ex-Sheffield Tigers co-promoter, Malcolm Wright. Though there's over three hours till the scheduled start time a couple of Birmingham Brummies fans are also already here, "I see the Brummies fans have arrived."
[Malcolm] "Where?"
[Jeff] "There's two of them over there."
[Malcolm] "They're here then!"
[Jeff] "Let's open up and start now."
[Malcolm] "They'll bring a few tonight. They've won twice here already this season and will want to see them win in the League!"

Inside the warm confines of the ('Thank you for smoking') Sheffield Speedway Office smokers – Neil Machin and Mitch Shirra – outnumber the non-smoker, Julie Reading. New Zealander Mitch still looks extremely youthful as well as wiry and athletic with only a vague hint of a paunch (when seated). He sports the casual clothes uniform of antipodeans everywhere: T-shirts, shorts, black peaked cap with Aussie cricketer style sunglasses jauntily perched on top. Mitch clutches a packet of fags and a flat-screen mobile in one hand as he gestures with the other. It seems a lifetime ago since Mitch made his British speedway debut in 1974. When it turned out he was only 15, Mitch was banned until 1975 when he rode for Coventry and Coatbridge. His baby-faced looks exaggerated his youthful precociousness. Sheffield co-promoter Neil Machin and Mitch need no second invitation to take a trip down memory lane. Though it's the theft of Mitch's red-and-black double-sized enviromat the last time he visited Owlerton ("there were only the sidecar boys left") that immediately concerns them. Neil and Mitch agree that its distinctive size and colour should make it easy to spot if they ever set eyes on it again. Their consensus is that its double-sized appeal prompted its theft while Mitch loaded his van, "They lifted off me toolbox and took it!"
[Malcolm] "Right, at least they didn't steal the toolbox."
[Neil] "The sidecar boys are here next week. We'll be on the lookout – it's just the right size for them!"

There's no speedway at Owlerton next week – instead they'll stage the final of the British sidecars. Tonight's programme advises would-be patrons that it'll be "a terrific spectacle over 20 heats". Sheffield season tickets will be valid, let alone there's the added attraction of the "normal restaurant carvery" in the expensively revamped Panorama Room. Also, to treble underline the possible appeal to any waiverers, Tigers reserve Paul Cooper "will passenger for former British Champion Rob Bradley." Neil asks Malcolm, "Are you coming next week?"
[Malcolm] "No, if it's sunny I'll go to Brighton."
[Neil] "What chance have we got if we can't get you to come? Mitch Shirra is coming."

[Malcolm] "You like bikes!"

Mitch has been there, done that and got the T-shirt when it comes to speedway. Obviously this means he's got a rich fund of stories and recollections.

[Mitch] "I signed for Coventry at 15 in 1975 and they immediately loaned me to Coatbridge. Charles Ochiltree used to make sure he collected his £80 a meeting!"

[Neil] "Charles Chocolatetree."

[Mitch] "£80! That's why I got £1.25 a start and £1.25 a point."

[Neil] "We want that back."

[Mitch] "Ha ha."

[Neil] "Still it was £1,000 for a bike."

[Mitch] "I could get a Weslake engine for 350 quid. I sold my 2-valve Jawa for £140."

Speedway office

[Neil] "When I'd rooted my engine it was better to buy one off Arnie Haley for 170 quid than repair it!"

The arrival of Birmingham's Gary Patchett interrupts their talk.

[Mitch] "I must introduce myself."

[Gary] "The name [points to pocket] gives it away."

[Neil] "What BRC Roofing?"

While they exchange pleasantries and gossip, Tigers trackshop franchisee Jeff Dooley hovers in the speedway office doorway.

[Gary] "I know what I meant to ask – how's Ricky's hand?"

[Neil] "It's getting better. When the flag drops the bullshit stops."

[Jeff] "He'll be ok as long as he holds on."

[Neil] "He couldn't hold on the other day."

[Mitch] "We need to put the magic spray on it."

[Neil] "Ah, the magic spray – put it on and they can ride with a broken leg!"

Panoramic view

Gary departs but the crisscross of memories flow thick and fast.

[Neil] "When Kelly [Moran] went to his first World Final at Gothenburg…"

[Mitch] "His first was Poland 1979."

[Neil] "His second, anyway, he didn't even know he'd been there."

[Mitch] "When we were at Pocking it was the Pairs."

[Neil] "Was that when they had six riders in a race?"

[Mitch] "Nah, it must have been the Four Team; New Zealand, England, Czechoslovakia and the US. Kelly and Shawn used to wear those full-face helmets with the chin guard and Kelly got it knocked [makes skewed gesture] so he rode three and a half laps only able to see out of one eye, at best! He was effectively blind but you wouldn't

33

know if you watched him."

[Neil] "Did you know that Roman Matousek rode in five world finals? He used to go the Eastern European qualification route."

Such talk prompts Mitch to recount a convoluted ice speedway story. Though everyone else appears to know who they're talking about, I slightly lose the plot. The focus of a story is a rider whose bike was sabotaged one year in Russia, got food poisoning another year and yet, on another occasion in the manner of all good folk tales, eventually emerges victorious. In the year said 'mystery rider' won in Finland, "He locked his bike up so no one could touch it. They used to run them over two days then. It took until the 39th race for him to win it! When we went out that night, he showed us the bike! All the paint had gone cos of the spikes, his leathers were in shreds, even the casing had gone cos he got that close to them!

[Neil] "They used to have mobile operating theatres at every [ice speedway] meeting. When those spikes went down your leg they used to have to sew you up quick; it wasn't just a scratch on your arse! His dad died in Amsterdam at the Olympic Stadium in the summer – ice racing! Volvo were going to sponsor speedway but pulled out after that!"

[Jeff Dooley] "I was looking at the Sheffield versus USSR [F.I.M. Inter-club match] programme from 1976 it was 51-26 or something."

[Neil] "Didn't the track record go about five times that night?"

[Jeff] "The Russians won only one race when Carl Glover lent them a bike. The crowd went mad at the idea he'd do something like that."

[Neil] "They used to just ride the factory equivalent – as it was, without modifications."

[Mitch] "They just got on them and rode."

[Neil] "Trouble was, if they were on tour and later – after they'd lost at Exeter and other places by massive scores – you just couldn't sell it!"

Julie Reading doesn't join in the conversation, "I'm not saying anything to you. My mouth is zipped."

[Jeff] "It was accurate, wasn't it?"

[Julie] "Yes, but what if Chris Mills sees it?"

[Neil] "He won't read it."

[Julie] "But what if he does?

[Neil] "Dave [Hoggart] reads quicker than us so he gets to see the proof. [To Julie] Let me check the programme for mistakes we haven't seen till now!"

A short distance away from the speedway office, Sheffield Tigers sound and music maestro Shaun Leigh arrives in his speedway rider-esque big white van. He parks up in strategic fashion by the stairs that lead up to the bar area adjacent to the Panorama Room. He's happy to chat as he unloads his sound equipment.

[Shaun] "Speedway's getting so expensive nowadays."

[Jeff] "It's nearly £20 for an adult at some speedway meetings if you include the programme."

[Shaun] "Yeh – for 15 minutes of entertainment – that's why so many people come along! It's a scandal when you think how many come along and what they pay to watch crap football."

[Jeff] "You do [announce] Sheffield Wednesday don't you?"

[Shaun] Yeh!"

[Jeff] "So you've seen Michael Gray."

[Shaun] "He's retired now. Nice bloke. Modest. When you think how old he is, he's amazingly fit – gives lots of the youngsters the run-around! He could go all day!"

Shortly afterwards, the man with many hats at GRT Media, Bob Tasker, arrives to take his altogether much lighter equipment up the same staircase. "If you wait a minute, I'll show you a view of Owlerton you won't have seen before!" In the upstairs bar, Bob retrieves the key for a door to

34

behind the scenes at Owlerton. Things look much different where only staff have any access. "Ten million pound refurbishment and you can see where it ended!" Bob bustles along a narrow passageway and up yet more stairs until we find ourselves perched on a gantry that overlooks bend one. From this vantage point we've an excellent view of the stadium, its terraces as well as the beauty of the surrounding area. "Even if I say so myself, the DVDs don't do it justice! It's 140 miles each way to get here but it's worth it for later when Richard Hall will be dashing round there [points to bend four] – as he will be!"

It's the first night *Shale Trek* goes on sale. Just inside the turnstiles, I set myself up with a small table borrowed from the bar just inside the turnstiles. Though in prime position, many fans walk purposefully by with their eyes studiously fixed on a point in the near distance as if they'd just seen a long lost friend they're dead keen to speak to or, alternatively, need to determinedly concentrate so they don't forget something crucial. Another man in a Birmingham BRC Roofing collared shirt strides into the stadium. It's Mick Bratley who, until the end of last season, was one of the head honchos at the East of England showground. He asks playfully, "You're not banned from here yet?"
[Jeff] "No, I'm the acceptable face of speedway writing here."
[Mick] "Right, I'll go and have a word with Neil and get you banned!"
Shortly afterwards Neil strides up to the table and asks, "Don't you have a poster to tell them who you are?"
[Jeff] "No, I did well to carry all this stuff up on the train."
[Neil] "I was joking."

Before Neil can take up position to linger by the turnstiles to meet and greet early arrivals or make last-minute checks on housekeeping arrangements, Shaun Leigh bounds up and asks one of the great philosophical questions, "How old is Nicky Mallett?"
[Jeff] "Maybe 22 or 23? I went last Sunday, the racing was good but Monday was the day to go."
[Shaun] "Why?"
[Neil] "He threw a punch on the track."
[Jeff] "He had his arm in a sling."
[Neil] "Okay – he threw a punch over the fence at someone, allegedly."
[Jeff] "A fan?"

Neil clutches a guest list in his hand in a manner that suggests it might be a sacred artefact. It'll be useful for the gate operatives when they get to see it. Neil's notorious for his close attention to detail. He calls out to a passing rider in a pair of shockingly bright box-fresh trainers, "What do you call those birds – Louise and Gemma?"
[Rider] "Gemma and Nicola."
[Neil] "Oh flippin' heck, I've got the wrong names!"

After he's passed on the amended list and chatted to all and sundry, Neil briefly returns to absent-mindedly finger a copy of my new book. He has little inclination to glance inside until I tell him that it includes his favourite speedway poem (written by Nigel Boocock), *Gresham's Lament*. Neil concentratedly reads the poem lost in thought, "What a great poem!"
[Jeff] "*Green Light and Go* is in there too."
[Neil] "I didn't quite get on with that one."
[Fan] "I didn't know he could read!"
[Neil, with the book inches from his face] "It's me eyes – this type is very small."

Where would speedway be as a spectacle without shale? Amazingly, some clubs economise with this vital ingredient. According to trackshop man Jeff Dooley, Sheffield isn't one of them. "The last two weeks the racing has been superb. The meeting versus Berwick was absolutely top drawer! It's nice when a team will come and really race you. The weather has been consistent so the track has been perfectly prepared which you can't do when there might be rain. Josh Auty is so exciting, fantastic; you'll love him tonight! He can't gate but he's so exciting. He went to Oz [last winter] as a boy and has come back a man!" Another Tigers fan looks on approvingly towards the track, "Wet and lots of dirt! Those Birmingham Aussies will love it! Not too much dirt though. We really need the Halifax Dukes to ride the dirt when it's deep. Leicester is coming back next year, I hope. I've told them at work I'll be booking the date. I'll get down there early – have a sleep in the car and get in because there'll be loads of people going." Shaun Leigh's extensive speedway duties also take him every week to Scunthorpe, "Last week there was no dirt and it was slick. There was no passing at all! Once they went and were set, it didn't change. No overtaking and this was Scunny! The home of overtaking! The times weren't that slow."

Stadium Assistant Safety Officer Ron Clayton patrols the grounds but is also curious enough to stop to briefly look at my books. From the way he talks about his work I imagine that Ron's worked here forever but that isn't the case, "I started on Tuesday working for Matt Hamilton". A few minutes later, a man asks, "Did you get the job then?" and learns, "I'm on probation for six months – I've been on probation all my life." Like his father, Ron's a diehard Sheffield Wednesday fan. "My dad's season ticket for the 1953-54 season cost five guineas whereas mine is the best part of £300. He sat in a different part of the ground – the South Stand – where the Sheffield Wednesday establishment sit. I'm in the North Stand where the most vociferous supporters stand (when they can afford to graduate from the Spion Kop). It's named after the Second Boer War battle, the one that Winston Churchill described as 'an acre of massacre.'" Having retired early to go on probation at Owlerton, despite his uniform, it transpires Ron's an historian who specialises in the history of Sheffield. He's published three books: *Hillsborough: Then and Now*, *Ron Clayton's Hillsborough and Beyond* and, along with Martin Rodgers, he's co-written *River Loxley from Source to Confluence*. Inevitably, he's fount of local information. "Did you know there's a cemetery behind the stadium – World's End. Nobody knows if its name was to do with the final judgement or because the place is so isolated! The cemetery is the most neglected cemetery in Sheffield. Lieutenant George Lambert – Sheffield's most forgotten VC winner – is buried there. His VC was won in 1857 in the Indian Mutiny. He was in the 84th Foot Regiment, part of the Yorkshire and Lancashire Regiment (until they were disbanded in 1968). Have you heard of Loxley? It's supposedly the birthplace of Robin of Loxley, reputedly Robin Hood. I'm hoping to get a statue – of him as a small boy – of this Yorkshire hero put up here! They've a statue of him at Doncaster airport – Sean Bean and Brian Blessed opened it. I've actually played Friar Tuck in *In Search of Robin of Loxley*. We're trying to get the legend that he was born in Loxley widely known. I've now recruited my third and fourth Maid Marion!" Ron's extremely proud of Sheffield's rich history. It's a source of endless fascination. There are so many tales to tell and important historical facts to recall, including "uncovering the remains of Sheffield Castle – under Castle Market – and, of course, we got the Manor Lodge in Sheffield where Mary Queen of Scots was held captive for the best part of 14 years." Ron updates me on Owlerton Farm until a couple of Sheffield Tigers fans interrupt our conversation. One of them is also an historian, "Malcolm Nunn is the local expert on the Sheffield Flood of 1869". Close attention to dates and detail are essential to rigorous historical study so, understandably, Malcolm immediately corrects Ron, "You got it wrong, it's 1864". Malcolm's also written a number of books. "I've done various ones, *Loxley Valley* from Amberley Press down in Gloucestershire and two Bradfield books by Tempus Publishing. My great-great-grandfather's brother – William Horsfield – was the one who found the crack in the Sheffield dam!" As an ignorant Southerner I hesitate to admit that news of the Sheffield Flood has passed me by.

Birmingham speedway fan and modest inventor of his own virtual speedway competition – The Platinum Helmet – Mike Butler wanders through the Owlerton turnstiles, "I've come along to stand with the people I stand with at Birmingham." Nonetheless, his thoughts are partly elsewhere at Arlington stadium where they'll stage the first ever Thursday night Elite League meeting in East Sussex, "Will there be a big crowd at Eastbourne tonight?" The crowd through the turnstiles here at Owlerton tonight arrive at the rate of a steady trickle until about 20 minutes before tapes up when things turn frenetic with people keen to see if Birmingham can defeat Sheffield for the fifth time already this season. At 7.35 p.m. the impressive Owlerton loudspeaker system crackles into life to treat us to a pre-recorded announcement that sounds as if it were 'laid down' (as we say in the music business) roughly around the time that Michael Jackson recorded *Thriller*. In the type of portentous slightly other-worldly voice they usually reserve for horror films (or health and safety advice) we're told, "Ladies and Gentlemen – from the darkest depths of your imagination… this is Owlerton Stadium – home of the Sheffield Tigers!" Out on the centre green, it's club co-promoter Dave Hoggart's job – in his capacity as meeting presenter – to guide us on another Thursday night journey into the darkness of our souls. As usual it sounds effortless. By the start line, Dave provides the various introductions for both teams during the rider parade but prefaces these observations with the news, "And, in case you didn't know, that's the Tigers that won twice on the road this week!"

So far this season, the Birmingham BRC Roofing Brummies have pretty well swept all opposition before them – both home and away, albeit mostly in the Premier Trophy. Always in need of a real, imagined or ludicrously sanitised story, early doors the speedway trade press seized upon the composition of the Brummies as a talking point since their original team line-up comprised six Aussies and an American. However, with their sole non-antipodean rider (Chris Kerr) injured, tonight Australian Rusty Harrison replaces him. This would mean that the Birmingham septet only feature riders from Down Under but for the stubborn fact that Bath-born Kyle Newman now rides at reserve in the No. 7 race tabard. Hoggy's introduction of the Sheffield Window Centre Tigers captain, subtlety promotes next week's meeting, "At No. 6 – he'll be riding sidecars next week – Paul Cooper!" Apart from team motivation, another essential duty of team captaincy is the fabled coin toss. Providing little in the way of breathless anticipation, Paul Cooper and Jason Lyons quickly do the honours to decide that the Tigers will take gates 1 and 3 in the first race.

Though very few speedway teams are renowned for the volume of their fans who travel to away meetings, most clubs have a loyal hardcore of supporters who always take to the road. Numbers vary between the various teams from the noticeable to the pitiful. Dave Hoggart is keen to acknowledge the dedication of the Tigers faithful, "Thank you for following us on the road. It's greatly appreciated as you could see from the celebrations at Workington – thank you for suffering with us!" Sheffield appear set for an opening race 5-1 until their promising Australian No. 2 with the speedway appropriate surname, Hugh Skidmore, reveals the limits of nominative determinism on the second lap when he grinds to a halt with an engine failure on the back straight when ahead of his guest teammate Peter Kildemand (on his first ever visit to Sheffield). Visibly dissatisfied to the point of extreme frustration, Hugh rides his bike onto the centre green to theatrically dump it down opposite the bend-four pits gate. Hugh lashes his equipment to the ground so suddenly you could be forgiven for thinking that it's caught fire. In fact, it has! What would have been a Tigers 5-1 transmogrifies into a drawn heat that, rather surprisingly, sees Jason Lyons finish third. Dave Hoggart offers his "Commiserations to Hugh, I'm not quite sure what happened there!" Some fans in the crowd offer coarse suggestions about Dave's eyesight and, afterwards, Sheffield co-promoter Neil Machin reveals that we'd all witnessed "one of the biggest engine blow-ups for years". The instantaneous destruction of the engine scatters debris across the track to create immediate pressure on High Skidmore's bank account and intense heat to his nether regions. Neil Machin marvels at events and draws some technical conclusions. "No one had seen a blow-up like that one for a long time. The thing was split in half with valve stems shooting out, which could have been pretty nasty had one caught Hugh. Then it all caught fire – all very dramatic, but all Hugh could do was throw it in a skip afterwards, it was such a write-off. It's just another part of the story that engines are revving too highly these days and unless we curb it, riders are going to keep on facing big repair or replacement bills."

One drawn heat often follows another and so it proves with the reserves race (heat 2) and also heat 3 where the bend-four outside line dramatics from Richard Hall completely fail to materialise as he runs a last. A significant factor in Sheffield's recent success on the road is the improved form and confidence of their young heat leader Josh Auty. After a winter in Australia, Josh nowadays scores the points that are the responsibility of any heat leader who wears a No. 5 race tabard. Though he's yet to master the art of swift gating, Josh's dander is completely up so no matter who leads him, he rides with the speed and confidence of a man convinced that four laps provide more than enough opportunity to rectify things. Brummies experienced Aussie, Steve 'Johno' Johnston leads heat 4 until on the third lap Josh swoops round the outside (of bends 3 and 4) to gain a lead that he fails to relinquish. With the exotically named Australian Arlo Bugeja in third, the Tigers gain a race advantage to give them a narrow 2-point lead.

One of speedway's glamour couples and certainly one of the happiest, Scunthorpe Scorpions Mark 'Buzz' Burrows and Weymouth-based photographer Julie Martin stop by at my display table for a discussion of life and speedway. Dressed smartly in his casual clothes, Buzz cuts a slim line wiry figure – much more so than you'd expect if you only saw him suited and booted on any speedway work night. It must be the bulkiness of the safety equipment worn or else the unflattering cut of his kevlars. A quietly spoken man, Buzz tells me, "I'm gonna ride the season for Scunthorpe and see how it goes from there."
[Jeff] "And ride another season?"
[Buzz] "Hum."
[Julie] "No!" [1]

Julie and Buzz have a two-city relationship (what the Dutch call 'living apart together') with Julie in Weymouth and Buzz in Sheffield. Before the meeting starts, they linger in the pits where, for the first time, Julie bumped into Birmingham Brummies co-promoter and team manager Graham Drury. "I just met Graham Drury. I was leaning over the fence chatting to Kyle Newman and he said to Buzz, 'Is she your daughter?' I like him!" Though you can take the girl out of Dorset – and

[1] Off the track a week later, Buzz would celebrate his 46th birthday (June 10th) while on the track he would make a slow start to his 2010 campaign for the Scunthorpe Saints. Sheffield-born Burrows made his speedway debut in North Lincolnshire for Scunthorpe in 1984, aged 19. With considerable speedway experience, Buzz easily identifies the underlying issues behind his results this season. "It's been silly mechanical gremlins which have been the major problem so far. That, and the fact that I'm nowhere near match fit, which doesn't help." Addressing the issue of fitness Buzz continues, "There's no trouble from last year's crash but I really need about three weeks of constant racing to get match fit." Unfortunately his fitness is going to elude Buzz for a little while longer since he's off on a 10-day break to the South of France, "It was booked in February because I didn't think I was going to be riding so there's not a lot I can do about it now." Investment could potentially cure his mechanical ills but, in the traditional chicken-and-egg situation, Buzz needs to score points in order to get the capital to finance equipment expenditure. "Who knows what's going to happen? I take it day by day now. When things are going right, I'm alright, but I've only got the one bike now because I had one pinched during the winter and I blew my GM up big time when I started practising. I'm doing it while the bike lasts and when it goes, that's it, I'm done. That will be the end of it. It just doesn't pay to go out and buy a new bike. You're looking at over three grand for a new engine these days and two grand for a rolling chassis, just a basic one, so you're looking at about six grand for a brand new bike. My engines are at least 2005 and the rolling chassis is 2008. The damage to the one I blew up is well over a grand, a piston's £300, a rod's £300, a barrel's £300, so you're looking at £1,000 for starters and that's just not cost effective to repair. Will it be my last season? I don't know. Who knows? You never know what is going to happen but if anything happens to the one bike between now and the end of the season, then I'm probably not going to make it to the end of the season. It's got to last me."

ban her from Radipole Lane (despite many years' service as track photographer and press officer) – Julie still very much has her finger on the pulse of the soap opera that is life in the National League for the Weymouth Wildcats. Despite promoter Phil Bartlett's over-lavish praise of his partner Sam Knight's business acumen ("I know she's my partner but, from a business point of view, having her on the team is the best thing that has ever happened to the Wildcats since I've been involved with the place"), her appointment as Weymouth Wildcats commercial director has failed to deliver the commercial results envisaged. During the 2009 close season, trade press reports said Weymouth's average crowd fell from 380 in 2008 to 320 in 2009. Unfortunately, 2010 saw further shortfalls in paying customers prepared to come through the turnstiles.[2] Inevitably, this ongoing lack of punters creates cash-flow problems and, allied to rumours of disgruntled staff, fans and riders (let alone talk of bouncing cheques and unpaid invoices), the future doesn't look bright in speedway terms without some dramatic change in a town fabled for its sunshine. Julie tells me, "The best crowd they've had is 340 for Newport. Ten of the track staff didn't turn up so they had to advertise for eight more. They were looking for a new team manager but haven't found one. The burger van has blown up. Last week, they say the landlord's blokes came down and asked for the rent and Phil went up to the ref's box to see Sam but she told him to give them a cheque. They refused and wanted cash. The landlord's blokes apparently said if they didn't get paid they'd lock the gates." Even if you discount the element of exaggeration or inaccuracy that Bartlett's own will to unpopularity sometimes attracts, it's definitely suboptimal for any business to have real or perceived payment problems with their suppliers. That said things can't be as bad as people make out since – contrary to the prophets of doom – the club continue to fulfil their fixtures home and away. Later this week in Dorset, they face the rejuvenated Buxton. However, not everyone will have to pay to get in according to Julie, "Last weekend they were giving out 'buy-one-get-one-free' leaflets on the seafront so I grabbed a handful and gave them to my brother. When he went in with one, Sam went mad with Phil saying she hadn't seen them, 'They're undated – they'll be coming in all season with these!' She wasn't happy at all!" While we natter about Weymouth, Buzz chats amiably with a steady stream of well wishers and fans keen to learn about developments in his career or establish his opinions. With a break in both sets of conversations, Buzz directs his girlfriend to the bar, "She got in free – she can buy the drinks!"

The fifth race of the night provides the Tigers with their second successive heat advantage in a race won by Ricky Ashworth. Jason Lyons shows comparative improvement with a second place but still falls short of his own exalted standards. Richard Hall gets his first point of the night after a tussle with the Brummies Aaron Summers. At this point, the racing is temporarily interrupted by news from the pits, "All four riders have come in from the last race and, to put it politely, have complained about the sunshine! This is the fastest racetrack in Britain and it is dangerous!" Announcement over, music man Shaun Leigh wryly slaps on Steve Harley and Cockney Rebel who blast out their famous chorus of "Here Comes the Sun". Sunshine can be big news in South Yorkshire so it's little surprise that Dave Hoggart frequently updates us on the progress of the setting sun, "I can tell you ladies and gentlemen that things are progressing nicely – the sun is going down, as it would!" While we admire the end of another day over the steel city "Ain't No Sunshine When She's Gone" blares out. Trackshop man Jeff Dooley's wife Ann can't quite believe it, "Who'd have thought it would be the sun that delays things!" Prior to my visit to Sheffield Bryn Williams warned me, "Remember if you're up North it's cold, wet and grippy – even if it's sunny!" Around 8.30 p.m. (after the sun falls below the height of the stadium roof), we get underway again but Hugh Skidmore's poor evening continues with another last in a heat 6 won by Johno to tie the score at 18-18. Often excoriated on the Internet forums for their alleged inability to even

[2] They would fall by around another 23% to the region of circa 245 per meeting

39

be able co-ordinate visits to drinking establishments, during the close season the BSPA set in motion a country-wide initiative to promote the sport. Not by setting in place a much-needed programme of British young rider development initiative but by commissioning some uniquely distinctive pens with a pull-out poster and banner. Trackshop man Jeff Dooley had firsthand involvement in the central purchasing of said pens. To be fair, just when you thought there could be no surprises on the pen front, these particular pens really do have to be seen to be believed! I keep my suspicions that demand levels have been low to myself. This isn't to doubt the complexity of their manufacture, sourcing or design but rather the fundamental need for a pen with a pull-out poster! Jeff comments, "The pens were purchased from me by Neil on behalf of the BSPA, with the intention of each club having 400: 200 to give away and 200 to sell. The cash from the sale of the 200 was to cover the cost of the 200 given away. Glasgow and Edinburgh said 'bring it on!' and 'let's purchase more things centrally so we can get rock bottom prices!' Poole didn't want their 400 cos Doodsons [specialist insurance company] have their logo on it and their sponsor is Castle Cover. They wanted 2,000 so they put a map on theirs there instead."

Heat 7 initially sees Justin Sedgmen and Richard Sweetman threaten another 5-1 until a super quick Josh Auty blasts round both on the fourth bend. Out on the centre green a gaggle of sponsors enjoy the luxury of a unique vantage point to savour this race. Dave Hoggart advises us upon their sponsorship and services, "Our driving school guests from AA Driving School – the only national driving school with fully qualified instructors – are here enjoying themselves and I hope you are too! If you need to learn to drive just say you heard about them at Sheffield speedway to get a great discount!" Call me old-fashioned but I rather imagined most driving schools had fully qualified instructors? Heat 8 sees Hugh Skidmore finally put his gremlins behind him with a super-fast start. Sadly his renaissance only lasts until the second bend where Aaron Summers overtakes him. Hugh and Aaron proceed to entertain with a lusty battle for supremacy throughout the remainder of the race. Though they look mighty quick, somehow this is the slowest time of the night so far, 62.5 seconds. An engine failure for Rusty Harrison along with third place for Arlo Bugeja ensures another drawn heat – the fifth in eight races.

Johno leads heat 9 comfortably until bends 3 and 4 of the second lap where Richard Hall winds it on to pass him in the exact spot that Mystic Bob (Tasker) prophesied hours earlier! Confirming the race result, Dave Hoggart prefers to praise third-placed Ricky Ashworth, "A good race from Ricky too – he's had some knocks but never mind!" Only declared fit to ride just prior to the meeting, these would be the only points Ricky drops all night. Dave Hoggart treats us to a joke that I lose the thread of that involves, I gather, an overweight woman ("she was packing for the weekend, it took her three hours just to fold her undies").

The speedway gods don't bless Hugh Skidmore tonight. With just over a lap of heat 10 to go, Hugh attempts another blast round the outside in his duel for second place with Richard Sweetman. With great spacial awareness the Brummies No. 4 sharply blocks Skidmore's line – this prompts Hugh to lock, pirouette and fall. Following closely behind, Peter Kildemand takes prompt evasive action but still thumps his bike into the fence at the apex of the bend. Good value entertainment because of his youthful enthusiasm, Skidmore rises from the shale to push his bike the considerable distance home to the finish line only to then find himself disqualified by referee Michael Breckon. The referee awards the race as a Brummies 5-1 (giving them a 29-31 lead) and also publicly commends Sheffield's guest from Workington, "Thank you to Peter Kildemand for getting off so quickly and avoiding a nasty accident!" Heat 11 starts well from a neutral's point of view since Josh Auty completely fails to gate. While Aaron Summers and Jason Lyons zoom away, on the first lap Auty initially looks so out of sorts that Paul Cooper appears the Sheffield rider most likely to mount any challenge. However, Cooper's *joie de vivre* and speed dissipates after

40

Auty locks-up in front of him on bend two of the second lap. Correcting his posture and angle of approach, Auty zooms down the back straight and, on the fourth bend, goes outside Jason Lyons prior to a scythe up the inside of race leader Aaron Summers (who, sensibly, backs off). The sheer aggression and velocity of this manoeuvre nearly causes Auty to lock and fall. Somehow he hangs on and, to noisy adulation from the more voluble Sheffield faithful who cluster under the home-straight grandstand, accelerates away to win.

With the Brummies still 2 points to the good, their team manager Graham Drury nonetheless thinks ahead so rings the changes prior to heat 12. Though nominated to ride, Graham discards Rusty Harrison in favour of the pointless Kyle Newman to complete his regulation three rides and, thereby, enable the more competitive Harrison to race in Kyle's place in heat 14. However, if Kyle Newman's only included to be a make-weight, someone's clearly forgot to clue him up on this expectation since he repels Arlo Bugeja on the first lap. Occupying a possibly vital third place, Newman races doggedly to remain ahead of Bugeja who, though he rides as if trying to generate sufficient speed to pass, you somehow just know that this is really only an empty gesture since the Australian is never likely to actually attempt an outside pass. Equally, perhaps, Bugeja creates this impression of intense pressure in the hope that inexperience prompts an error from Newman. Concentratedly determined, Newman does slightly lock-up on the back straight of the last lap. It briefly allows Bugeja up his inside before he shuts the door to gain his only point of the night. Given the delicately poised closeness of the meeting, Newman's third place point could be significant.

Each and every race that features Josh Auty fascinates! The back straight of the second lap of heat 13 sees Josh go outside Jason Lyons and then cuts hard inside Steve 'Johno' Johnston for the lead by they reach the apex of the next bend. Once again his determination and virtuosity make Josh worth the admission money alone. In the trackshop, Jeff Dooley looks on with admiration. "He's better round here than some of the senior riders. It is his track! He's rode here since he was 13 so he's done a lot of laps. You just know if he's within a couple of bike lengths going into the last lap that he'll pass two of them!" Despite the Auty heroics, with Kildemand fourth the heat is drawn so, with two races to go, the Brummies retain their 2-point advantage.

Sheffield take their quest for victory seriously enough to send Paul Cooper out on Ricky Ashworth's bike for the penultimate race. It's a sensible decision since he finishes third ahead of Rusty Harrison. Up front the two Richards – Hall and Sweetman – duel for position. On the first lap round bends 3 and 4, Hall passes Sweetman riding fast, brave and close to the safety fence. At the start of lap three, Sweetman returns the favour with a blast up the inside only to then see Hall make his Owlerton experience count with another blast round the outside on the next bend to ensure a Tigers heat advantage that levels the scores at 42-42. Little excuse is ever needed to blare 'Tiger Feet' out over the loudspeaker system. The £10 million refit of the Panorama Room provides – for all patrons lucky enough to watch this (or any) meeting from there – an excellent view of proceedings. It's a facility that runs to its own particular schedule if we heed David Hoggart's advice, "At 9 o'clock the buffet turns into sandwiches. I don't know what the time is [pause] 9.16 – there's sandwiches!"

Though he rode more impressively than his points tally of 5 indicates, Peter Kildemand fails to make the cut for the vital nominated heat 15. Nonetheless, David Hoggart sings his praises, "We want to thank Peter Kildemand – it's the first time he's seen Sheffield." The Tigers last-heat power partnership of Ashworth and Auty will want to translate their alphabetical priority over Johnson and Lyons into points. Prior to tapes up, Jeff Dooley points out that all the non-riding members of the Tigers team sit on the Pukka Pies centre green advertising hoarding to watch, "This is new too, this season – Cooper gets them all out on t'middle for the last race!" Heat 15 is a truly fitting finale to this close fought contest but also showcases the verve, power, dynamism and excitement that are the hallmarks of all great speedway races. From the tapes Jason Lyons finally finds his gating gloves to lead with Johno second. They hold the advantage until Ricky Ashworth passes both on the transition between bends 3 and 4 of the first lap. With the daredevil Auty close behind, the Brummies Aussie pair can't afford any complacency. Jason Lyons signals the collective desire of the early-season 2010 version of the Brummies to repass Ashworth for the lead on the back straight of the second lap. Josh Auty sizes up and, eventually, reels in Johno on the fourth bend of the third lap. With all four riders racing close enough together to fit under the proverbial blanket, Johno nearly but doesn't quite return the favour on the second bend of the last lap. Fortunately for Sheffield, Johno's dash for fresh air ends with a sudden engine failure for race leader Jason Lyons that immediately prompts Johno to back off. It's a dramatic, high action corner that leaves the Tigers in command on a 5-1 until Auty gets out of shape on the last bend – allowing Johno back past into second place – to end his hopes of an all-action paid maximum. Nonetheless the 4-2 heat advantage seals the win for the Tigers. On the terraces, Buzz is full of admiration for the action we all just witnessed. "I think that's one of the best races I've seen in a while! I think Lyons and Johno had it sorted until he broke down. But for that, I think it would have been a 4-2 to the Brummies or, at least, a 3-all!" With her natural love of and bias toward the National League and its riders, Jules prefers to appreciate Kyle Newman's earlier efforts for third place in heat 12. "Kyle did well. My heart was in my mouth! Did I tell you I did the update for Bournemouth versus the Isle of Wight? I was stood with Ray and Robin – there was about ten of us. They helped me. I can't tell who is who after the second bend. I try to get in as many clichés as possible. I don't think they'll ask me again!"

Most speedway nights in Sheffield, there's usually a second half. In this instance, there are four races won respectively by Ashley Morris (twice), Tyson Nelson and James Sarjeant. It's my first chance to watch Mitch Shirra's prodigy Tyson Nelson. He features in three races – a win and two engine failures. Jeff Dooley studies Tyson with curiosity, "I think Mitch Shirra's over for a few months looking after him." After the second half, the crowd ebb away to the car park or adjourn upstairs to throng the bar adjacent to the Panorama Room. Neil Machin quizzes me about my evening, "How did you do?"
[Jeff] "I sold as many as there were Josh Auty passes."
[Neil "What, loads?"
[Jeff] "Three."
[Neil] "I tell you what mate, that is what speedway's all about! Every time there's someone in front of him, you think he's going to pass. He's got 58 points in four meetings and three of them were away!"

Since I'm due at a Latin Dance Night held every Thursday at the Polish Hearth Club on Eccleshall Road, Neil volunteers to find Simon Parker to give me a lift. He's the Tigers understudy track photographer, sponsor of heat 1 (West Riding Toyota and Lexus) and the father of affable helpful trackshop stall worker Dan. Neil surveys the bar ("I can't recognise him without his camera round his neck"). While he goes off to search, Neil proudly and proprietarily insists that I "get a look at the Panorama Room – it's plush, it overlooks the fourth bend and the pits and, I know I'm biased after the £10 million refit, but is there a better view from a restaurant in speedway?" As we glide over to the other side of the town in his sleekly impressive Lexus, Simon exalts in the victory, the inspiration passing of Josh Auty but, most of all, the privilege of working with Sheffield Tigers track photographer Chris Spires. "He's away this week – I'm his assistant and I'm very respectful of that! It's a privilege and an honour to do a job like this. I work in the motor trade really – we

42

sponsor heat 1. We used to sponsor heat 14 but that doesn't always get run whereas heat 1 always does!"

3rd June Sheffield v. Birmingham (Premier League) 46-44

43

Sheffield: *"When the flag drops the bullshit stops"*

CHAPTER 5

Rye House

"No one breathes Rye House more than Chris Neath. Cut him in half and he'd be coloured blue and yellow!"

5th June

Three hours before the PL Knock-Out Cup Second Leg encounter between Rye House and Edinburgh there's a sultry microclimate at Len Silver's stadium in Hoddesdon. Ignoring threatening dark clouds in the distance, one of the raffle ladies confidently advises not to worry, "We always get a nice breeze here because of the river [Lea] being so close!" Shortly afterwards they study an iPad, the first I've seen up close and personal. Whatever its functionality, they're only interested in the photographs of baby Zak who weighed in at 8lb 10 oz on Tuesday. Doubtless Zak's parents Darren and Becky are as extremely proud as iPad owners everywhere are with their wildly hyped gizmo. Though Zak's only five days old, he's already the talk of the terraces. Hardworking Lisa takes a brief break from her many race-night duties to update the raffle ladies, "Most babies come out looking old and wrinkled but not Zak!"

George and Linda Barclay also arrive early. Linda's another who takes extreme pride in youth. "Three of our lads were in the recent Southern Riders [championship] and they finished first, second and third! Len [Silver] has given them their first ever second half as a reward tonight. Jack Nottingham was about 13 when he started at Sittingbourne, Joe Exley might have ridden at Lydd starting around 18 months ago while Jake Hallett has only been here probably since the beginning of last year. They're all 15 and they're all really keen!"
[George] "They're all J's!"
[Jeff] "All the best people are."
[George] "They've all been coming virtually every week since we started."
[Linda] "It's so popular, Len's letting us put on an extra day."
[George] "It's nearly always over-subscribed. Tonight their names are in the programme! Wow! You can imagine the thrill! They always used to put me in as A.N. Other."
[Linda] "It's really some incentive for the lads. The hardest thing is to get them in their age groups so you can put them out together. I dunno if it's right but, I'm told, there's hardly any 14-year olds. We're running an extra session tomorrow. Shame it said on the website Saturday 6th June. People have been ringing to find out if it's the day or the date that's right. They had to ring anyway to book. Most weeks we get 18; 20 is the maximum. They're split into three groups and taught by Len, Alan Mogridge and George. It's the tuition and individual attention that makes the difference!"

A similarly delighted Debs Nottingham arrives – she used to work at the Speedway Museum and, nowadays, is often found at Sittingbourne – and struggles to contain her excitement. "I've something to tell you! You know my little Jack who's bimbled around, well he's riding! In the Southern Track Riders he was third cos he was an absolute idiot. He'd won all of his races except his last one when he spun the bike round. Mark Morley, who was mechanicing for him, told him

44

to calm down and he did okay in the rerun – given he had to start off 15 metres. Jack started on a 100cc at Sittingbourne in 2007 and he started at the training schools here last year. He's also been to Paul Hurry's Training Schools. Paul's brilliant! He watches them and then he picks off their bits and pieces. Sitting position, handlebars, everything. He's fantastic with all the riders – a brilliant bloke! Before he starts the coaching session, he makes sure everyone is happy with their starting positions and that. I can't wait for the second half!"

One of the biggest fans of my speedway writing, Gaz, takes a brief break from multi-tasking at his refreshment kiosk duties to collect two red-and-white aprons from Andy Griggs at the trackshop. "They're fantastic! How much do I owe you?" Who would have thought that Gaz would like to dress up in a pinny? He's so chuffed it's a shame no one asks him to put them on and give us an Anthea Redfern style twirl. Apparently unfeminised by his love of aprons, Gaz calls over, "I'm not speaking to you – you're dangerous! Have you sold many? You can put down 'it's all bollocks!'"

Twenty minutes after the turnstiles open so do the heavens for around three-quarters of an hour. Weather forecasters would probably call it a "sharp shower". Everyone retreats under shelter while the track shale takes on a dark deeper hue. One of those ducked out of the rain is Michael Addison who spent 20 years working at the BSPA during the most recent glory years of speedway. He spent many of those years finding sponsorship for the sport. Mike established sponsorship links with household names such as Gulf Oil, Strongbow, WD&HO Wills and Skol. Mike's British Speedway heyday was a promotional era full of strong personalities and, often, similarly sized egos. Despite his experience with the movers and shakers of speedway, Michael expresses delight that he's on page 42 ("That's the year I was born") of my latest book *Shale Trek*. His general enthusiasm for life, love of speedway and interest in people comes across in conversation. Nowadays Michael gets his speedway kicks at Rye House and Wolverhampton. He used to regularly patronise Poole but recently abandoned Wimborne Road in favour of Monmore Green because they no longer serve meals on race night on the South Coast. His visits to Hertfordshire invariably take Michael down memory lane. "I remember when I first came here in 1955 and there was just a wooden rickety fence. Now look what Len has done to it! He's always investing in the stadium. It looks funny with the seats in here, doesn't it? I can't get used to it. It looks immaculate. There used to be long grass in the middle. The first promoter here used to

Raffle

Medical attention

Rye House: *"No one breathes Rye House more than Chris Neath. Cut him in half and he'd be coloured blue and yellow!"*

be George Kaye – a very nice man. He started my programme collection when he gave me 500 at Harringay. The announcer was the late Peter Arnold – he was killed in a car crash. I can even tell you what that first meeting was! It was the Roosters – at the front of the race jacket was a big RH – versus California from near Wokingham. It was in the Southern Area League. There were five tracks in that. Rye House, California, Brafield and Eastbourne, that's five – no – that's four, I can't remember the other one." Michael's eyesight is similarly as impressive as his memory, "Look at that swarm over there by the pylon!" Away on the near distance horizon – against the dark sky and rain – it's just about possible to make out the cloud around the pylon. Maybe it's an invasion of flying killer ants? Instead I ask, "What are they, bees?" Though a city dweller nowadays, Michael knows country ways, "It's too light for bats to be out!"

Always smartly dressed, knowledgeable and extremely well prepared Rye House presenter Craig 'Mr Potassium' Saul arrives with his son but without his trademark banana. Ducking out of the heavy rain he says, "Look at that swarm by the pylon!"
[Jeff] "What is it?"
[Craig] "I dunno! I worry this won't be on!"
[Jeff] "It should help you pull back your 12-points deficit."
[Craig] "Why's that? Edinburgh are the form team. They're very impressive! No one can take them for granted."

Never knowingly under-researched, Craig's already read much of *Shale Trek* but, as he flourishes his notepad, he double-checks, "How many Edinburgh chapters are there then?"

Close by Michael Addison falls into conversation with Len Silver who, as usual, looks immaculate. Len's BSPA jacket buttons are well polished. So much so they shine in the comparative gloom of the late afternoon. Len also wears a harassed expression but, when he spots a copy of his autobiography in Michael's hand, remarks instructionally, "Read it from cover to cover – you'll enjoy it more than most!"

[Michael] "Because I can remember it!"
[Len] "We can."
[Michael] "Those were the days!"

Notoriously a capable meeter and greeter, Len invariably needs no second invitation to work any speedway audience. Today he stares distractedly and morosely off into the middle distance. Even Len can't control the weather, "I can't do anything about it! I don't know what to do!" Michael asks "Can you remember what Johnny [Hoskins] used to do?" If Len can, he doesn't let on as he walks away to disappear inside the Speedway Office. Given the strength of the rain, if it subsides the meeting should go ahead. Dependent, of course, on how thoroughly they watered the track earlier this afternoon. I quiz Michael about what Johnny Hoskins used to do. "If the weather looked doubtful, he used to come out in his sombrero thing and put a finger in his mouth, hold it up like that and say in a loud voice, 'it's okay, the meeting will go on!'"

Rye House pits marshal, Steve Webb [a.k.a. Webby] lingers by my bookstall. If his distinctive multi-patterned safari style suit (set off by pink plimsolls) is anything to go by, Webby is off duty! It's rained so heavily that he won't have need for his usual constitutional (accidental) swim in the nearby River Lea (recently reported by the *Speedway Star*). Webby spots the sun-dappled early autumn afternoon panoramic shot of the Rye House stadium home-straight grandstand that's the cover image of *Shale Trek*, "Len will be so pleased with that – it's lovely!"

With the rain over, a trickle of fans come through the turnstiles. A couple of early arrivals (Rye House fans) wonder, "Where's the Edinburgh fans then? There's usually load of them!" Shortly afterwards, sight of a BSPA Edinburgh press pass arouses scepticism in the turnstile operative, "He

46

Rye House: *"No one breathes Rye House more than Chris Neath. Cut him in half and he'd be coloured blue and yellow!"*

still has to pay, don't he?" Honorary Edinburgh Monarchs fan and Sittingbourne pits marshal Dick Jarvis arrives barely able to contain his glee at the havoc he expects the wet track will wreak amongst the home riders. "This should be interesting! Last weekend the home team just couldn't ride it against Buxton. They just didn't want to know! Jamie Smith got 2 and he was lucky to get those."

[Jeff] "This is the Premier League so they'll ride it better."

[Dick] "I hope not, obviously! You got another new book out?"

[Jeff] "Your photo is in it."

[Dick] "That'll stop people wanting it."

[Jeff] "No they'll be flooding to get a copy. Here it is – it's a distant shot."

[Dick] "That's okay then!"

Norrie Tait arrives and immediately starts to regale Dick with tales of alleged shenanigans at last night's Armadale Premier League derby meeting between the Edinburgh Monarchs and Glasgow Tigers. It was a night that featured a catalogue of engine failures, retirements and falls before it finished 64-26 in favour of the Monarchs (a significant contrast to earlier in the season when the Tigers were surprise victors at the Scotwaste Arena). The way Norrie recounts it, last night many Glasgow riders were reluctant to actually race. It's quite a tale of woe. Travis McGowan endured an engine failure at the start of heat 1, James Grieves trailed way off at the back in heat 3 but still gained a point (mainly because the Tigers Australian Michael Penfold also featured in the race). Josh Grajczonek stopped in the fourth race while Travis McGowan and Lee Dicken rode so slowly at the back of the race in heat 5 that they bumped into each other and Travis fell off. Jamie Courtney retired in heats 8 and 12 while Josh Grajczonek again retired in heat 9. Apparently, if any Tigers rider found themselves in the lead (or second) they then often operated on an 'after you Claude' basis. If events prior to heat 15 raised eyebrows, then the final race of the night took them above the metaphorical hairline. To Edinburgh fans with a suspicious cast of mind, heat 15 conclusively 'proved' that some form of averages manipulation – widely viewed as necessary in order to make rumoured team changes – definitely applied to this meeting. The final race saw first-lap retirements for Matthew Wethers (Edinburgh) and James Grieves (Glasgow). This was then compounded by the fall of race leader Kalle Katajisto (Edinburgh). Inadvertently, Travis McGowan became the only Glasgow Tigers race winner of the night after referee Graham Flint awarded him victory. Norrie delights at this turn of events, "Actually they might have screwed it because they got a 3-0 in heat 15!" Norrie relates these shenanigans with equanimity in contrast to his disgruntlement at the perceived mistreatment of the Tigers joint top scorer James Grieves (widely rumoured to be the rider that the Glasgow management would drop in order to make team changes), "The fans knew before Grievesy did!" Dick isn't so sure, "It wouldn't have made any difference!" The newly slim line Reading Racers official historian Arnie Gibbons arrives and, as ever, remains frighteningly well informed about numerous aspects of national (and international) speedway. "Apparently the Tigers are 0.06 shy of getting down to what they wanted to get down to! If McGowan had managed to fall off before Katajisto did, they could have brought in Screen for two of the tail-enders and now they have to do something more drastic! They'll definitely get rid of Penfold – the useless Australian – that's not fair of me, he's overmatched. One thing no one seems to be saying is maybe the reason Edinburgh won 64-26 last night is because they're so strong! It's also funny how both Edinburgh riders – who were on maximums – managed not to finish in heat 15!"

Due to his involvement with the Liberal Democrats, this season Arnie hasn't seen as much speedway as he'd like but did get to Norway to see the Eurovision Song Contest! "Apparently Norwegian TV aren't showing the World Cup because they spent all their budget on staging the Eurovision Song Contest! They say Germany won because they're the only country who can afford to stage it! My husband was there to watch the Eurovision (held at the Tele Nord Arena in Oslo), I also went to watch two speedway meetings! Both in the Norwegian League – Saturday in Oslo and Sunday at Drammen. Norway was so expensive, it made Sweden appear cheap!" The UK government coalition is founded upon the unlikely bedfellows of the Conservative Party and the Liberal Democrats. In speedway party political terms, there are now closer links between Nick Barber (Conservative councillor in Felixstowe) and Arnie. I had expected a greater degree of scepticism from politically experienced Arnie about the benefits of the new coalition but, with the levers of power so close at hand, (at least with me) Arnie enthusiastically advocates the expected Party line on the benefits the Coalition can and will deliver. That said, Arnie does adopt a slightly querulous tone on some matters. "It's the first time I can get up in the morning and know that Liberal Democrat policies have actually got passed into law! Labour did pass some of our policies into law but pretended they were their own. Both of them [Cameron and Clegg] can use the Coalition to discard any policy they don't like! On Europe, Cameron can renege on his European policies saying 'it's to keep the Lib Dems happy' and Clegg can say 'I can't talk about it in case it upsets the Tory right'! It's the first time I can say I know five cabinet ministers! All that about politicians travelling second-class on the train doesn't mention that their red boxes travel by car for security! This is my local track, my most-visited track and this is my third time here." Our talk of politics ends when the dulcet tone of Len Silver booms out over the stadium loudspeaker system. "We're not doing a parade tonight because of the threat of showers. I'm afraid the track is less than perfect after that three-quarters of an hour shower that passed through. Edinburgh will be difficult to beat with their 12-point advantage. The riders have agreed to go ahead and we thank them for that!"

Invariably diplomatic, Arnie's got strong opinions on governance of British Speedway and the recent controversies provoked by allegations of average manipulation. "I think you'll find the failure of the BSPA was to be sufficiently robust on Poole because it's so hard to prove! Any club can basically do what they want and take the piss with impunity! If you recall, Joe Screen rode in Sweden in five races and didn't fall off the night before the disputed meeting in Poole. People posted on the BSF saying he fell off and aggravated an injury forgetting that Swedes post on there too and they said he didn't. Joe then flew back to Manchester and yet a doctor in Poole – who clearly hadn't seen him – signed him off causing him to miss the meeting at Swindon and all that resulted from that. Now, if McGowan had managed to fall off in the recent Edinburgh v. Glasgow match then they could have brought in Screen." Suddenly it all falls into place – kindly Joe Screen is the common link and, perhaps, he's the real Mr Big pulling the puppet strings of British speedway! Probably fearful of the consequences if news of his disloyalty gets through to Mr Big, Arnie laughs off my suggestion of Joe's political ruthlessness. Heat 1 gets underway but stops after an engine failure for Jordan Frampton on the second bend, "See – whenever this happens – people can always say 'they're fixing their averages!'" The rerun sees the Monarchs partnership of Ryan Fisher and, their recently recruited German rider, Tobias Busch, race to a comfortable 5-1 ahead of Luke '747' Bowen. Arnie likes what he's seen, "They said last night Tobias Busch didn't have any opposition but he didn't look too bad there!" The rider whose name sounds like an obscure martial art, Kalle Katajisto, wins heat 2. With yet another Monarchs German rider amongst the points (Max Dilger in third) Edinburgh gain a 4-2 heat advantage helped in some small part by Kyle Hughes' retirement. Arnie's already got his card marked, "Hughes blows hot and cold – if he doesn't fancy it, he doesn't turn up!" The next race sees Edinburgh track yet another (impressive) German rider, in this case Kevin Wolbert who wins accompanied by partner Matthew Wethers to record the Monarchs second maximum heat advantage in three races. Rye House Rockets team captain, Chris Neath retires from this race but, worse still, smashes up his "number one engine" so much that he has to resort to his second bike for the rest of the meeting. With the

Rye House: *"No one breathes Rye House more than Chris Neath. Cut him in half and he'd be coloured blue and yellow!"*

Monarchs already 10 points to the good, Arnie ponders the situation, "Rye House has a strong team and a nice home advantage – maybe the track is upsetting them more than the away riders?" Less politely, 22 points ahead on aggregate some Edinburgh fans playfully wonder, "Are you Glasgow in disguise?"

Heat 4 sees Andrew Tully and Linus Sundström race neck and neck until the third bend of the first lap before the Scotsman then pulls away. After we collectively mark up our programmes appropriately (a Monarchs 4-2 heat advantage taking the score onto 6-18), there's an inordinate delay to confirm the result. Eventually Craig Saul says, "The referee has been in consultation with the pits and has confirmed that the rider in white [Tully] was not in possession of a dirt deflector at the start of the race and has been disqualified." With our scorecards a mess, the reversed result (from 2-4 to 4-2) amends the cumulative scoreline to a comparatively more benign 8-16. However, this Rockets 'reprieve' is only short-lived since the Monarchs race to another heat advantage via a win from Ryan Fisher. This heat showcases another fall for the luckless Rockets captain, Chris Neath. Three consecutive drawn heats follow providing race wins for Andrew Tully, Linus Sundström and Kalle Katajisto. Heat 8 includes a fall for Tobias Busch to become the first visiting rider (and the first German rider) to really appear to struggle to master tonight's slippery conditions at Hoddesdon. That said, the speeds generated by the Edinburgh riders indicate that the circuit is eminently raceable and, with the scoreline at 19-29 after eight races, it appears that the spirit they require for a fight-back long since deserted the Rockets riders.

Between races I catch up with obsessive collector Roger Adams. "Since I've seen you last I've got into water towers in a big way! The woman who used to live next door to me knew I took photos of water towers and she knows a bloke – who I meet in the coffee place in the Tesco at Braintree – who fits aerials for mobiles and I go round with him. I've got just over 100 different water tower photos. I've branched out into Suffolk. You wouldn't believe there's so many different designs and that. Unbelievable! I do buses and lorries – Eddie Stobart's ladies names and fleet numbers on the front of cabs – it's terrible. I've been carrying a photo of Mick Bates round with me for ages and ages and, because he's the referee here tonight, I finally got it signed!" Roger chooses his hobbies discriminatingly, "I nearly got into pylons myself but didn't." Gaz stops by as Roger departs so I ask him, "Guess what he collects?" Gaz pulls a strange expression, "Does he look up women's skirts?" When I explain Roger's love of water towers, sacks and lorries, Gaz pulls a quizzical face before he dismissively exclaims, "He's a flippin' saddo! Speedway is full of weirdos." Though he's at the speedway every week, Gaz clearly exempts himself from such judgements.

Another passionate speedway man is Peter Butcher. He's nattily dressed this evening in a cream linen suit. Earlier he'd a surprise at the turnstiles, "I'm in a state of shock. I don't know quite what to say!" When I ask, "Why?" Peter sheepishly holds up an "Admit One OAP" ticket. While we chat, the on-track spectacle comes to an abrupt halt after the usually super reliable Chris Neath suffers further traction and/or balance problems with tonight's gloopy version of the Hoddesdon track. Chris is trapped under the third-bend safety fence, surrounded by track staff members, fellow riders and the medical team. One fan isn't sympathetic about his predicament, "Why has he fallen off?" Peter has his own questions, "Do you know a rain dance? I expect they said 'Stay down, Chris, there's rain forecast!'" With concern in his voice, over the stadium speakers Craig Saul reminds us, "No one breathes Rye House more than Chris Neath. Cut him in half and he'd be coloured blue and yellow!" It's an image to conjure with. It sounds much more *Star Trek* than speedway. After about five minutes down, Chris rises to a polite almost cricket-esque smattering of applause. Without the obstruction of a fallen rider and medical team, we enjoy the treat of a 15-minute virtuoso exhibition of track grading. The curatorial work goes on so long I even question Gaz, "The dirt has gone out a bit wide and they're pulling it back." Peter Butcher is

Rye House: *"No one breathes Rye House more than Chris Neath. Cut him in half and he'd be coloured blue and yellow!"*

suspicious, "I expect Edinburgh are chuffed with how long that track grade went on. If it gets stopped, say, after ten [heats] will Edinburgh still be the winners?" Better minds than mine need to answer this question, "I dunno – this is speedway!"[1]

Chris Neath's travails symbolise the Rye House Rockets evening. If there is such a thing as gating gloves, then Edinburgh are definitely the only team in super-strength versions this evening. They look confident on the track, so much so that you could half believe that they were at home. It's men against boys stuff. That said, Linus Sundström of the Rockets threatens each time he takes to the track as, to a lesser extent, do both Stefan Ekberg and Luke Bowen. The fight also temporarily returns to the hugely experienced Jordan Frampton, to the extent that he initially leads heat 10. However, the significant action is all behind him where Rye House No. 2, Luke Bowen, attempts to assert himself with an aggressive second-lap charge (from fourth) round the third and fourth bends. Like so many of his teammates previously, (compared to normal) the damp conditions hamper his battle for better position. Predictably, Luke soon loses traction (on bend four) to somehow manage to wedge himself under the kickboards – fractionally ahead of his bike before it joins him. Understandably, since he's the cause of the stoppage, Mick Bates disqualifies '747' and though Jordan Frampton led first time out, in the rerun he's a conclusive third. Heat 11 features a superb wide overtake on the first lap by Tobias Busch past Linus Sundström as they transition from bends 1 to 3. Unfortunately Busch loses power on the back straight next time round to enable Sundström to power underneath him for a comfortable victory. With three Germans in the side, towel-draped start tapes remain a possibility. Heat 12 produces Kevin Wolbert's third win in four races, while Craig Saul looks on approvingly, "The 24-year-old German's first ever visit to Rye House has been successful – he's only dropped 1 point!"

Super7evens start girls organiser Shelly-Ann Willetts stops by my display table for a few words. Along with her colleagues, Shelly-Ann adds some much-needed glamour to the cover of my book *Concrete for Breakfast* and gets a few mentions in *Shale Trek*. She carefully inspects my merchandise and it's not long before she offers a few matter-of-fact corrections, "I'm not a speedway fan and I'm not from Stourbridge!"
[Jeff] "There's a photo of you at Swindon."
[Shelly-Ann] "You know, I can't even remember that one!"
[Jeff] "You were holding a Scott Nicholls window sticker with Hans Andersen and Ben Barker."
[Shelly-Ann] [laughs] "Oh, yeh, I remember!"

Book in hand, Shelly-Ann calls loudly to her boyfriend, "Oi Adam – come here!" Adam Roynon approach extremely silently – despite his crutches – and, stepping back, I tread very heavily on his healthy foot. Adam laughs off my apologies, "That's alright." With eyes fixed on the action until the race ends, he can confirm the exact result of the heat (13) I miss, "It was a 4-2 to Edinburgh's Fisher, Sundström and Tully." This result takes the Monarchs past the magical 45-point mark. At least it usually would be magical, except for the 29-49 scoreline from the first leg that put the contest beyond doubt quite a few races back. Kalle Katajisto's third win of the night in heat 14 allows Saul to showcase his pronunciation abilities, "Kally Kat-y-yisto." Shelly-Ann shows Adam Roynon the *Concrete for Breakfast* cover.
[Adam] Which one are you?"
[Shelly-Ann] "The one in the middle."
[Adam] "When did you have blonde hair?"

---

[1] Len Silver explains his track grading philosophy in a close season letter to the *Speedway Star*. "Since all tracks deteriorate as each race goes by, it is a necessary evil to try to keep the surface consistent and smooth as far as that is possible… At Rye House, the tractor usually does two laps of the circuit between races far from the seven minutes Mr Thompson suggests is the norm at Swindon. This increases to four laps about twice in a meeting and when a rider has two races on the trot."

Rye House: *"No one breathes Rye House more than Chris Neath. Cut him in half and he'd be coloured blue and yellow!"*

Though sharp eyed when it comes to the race action on the track, Adam fails to clock the fair highlights in Shelly-Ann's hair. Andy Griggs can't quite believe my clumsiness, "Well, you stood on the only foot he has! You wouldn't believe that in a novel. And, to think, he only came out of hospital today!"

Though he's notionally only a reserve, Edinburgh team manager John Campbell rewards Kalle Katajisto's Hertfordshire exploits with a nomination in heat 15. As they transition from the start line to bend, Linus Sundström makes a point to deliberately clip Kalle's elbow as they fly into the corner. It only fractionally discombobulates Katajisto but his momentary correction is enough to allow Linus to escape and, with Stefan Ekberg third, their 4-2 heat advantage – the only other prompted by Andrew Tully's lack of a dirt deflector after he'd won the race – massages the final scoreline to a fractionally more acceptable 35-55.[2] It's a result that tells Arnie something, "That explains why you only need three drops of rain at 11 a.m. for a Rye House meeting to be called off!" One notable feature of the Premier League Knock-Out Cup competition is the absence of double-point tactical rides. Invariably a fount of information, Arnie provides further insight. "Even tacticals wouldn't have saved Rye House tonight! The history of the introduction of the tactical is interesting. Initially it was solely in the [Premier League] Knock-Out Cup – it was proposed by Len Silver, no less – who now says how horrible they are but he was the one who introduced them!" News that I'd stomped on Adam Roynon's good foot prompts Arnie to speculate, "I can't quite make my mind up about Adam Roynon. Either he's extraordinarily unlucky or, if not, there's something else going on!"

The first race of a "second-half race (to be run if riders are available)" between Tom Stokes and Shane Hazelden only lasts until bend three of the second lap. Shane somehow manages to strangely extend his leg, slip and execute a 270-degree twirl before trapping himself underneath his bike. It's quite a manoeuvre! With some understatement, Arnie observes, "Hum, ungainly fall." The next race features the 'Three Js' a.k.a. up-and-coming riders of the future: Joe Exley, Jake Hallett and Jack Nottingham. Delighting his mum Debs (and any other family member present), Jack wins their race in a time of 76.7 seconds.

The third race of tonight's second half appears to only feature one rider. Concerned that my eyesight has deteriorated further I check with Arnie, "How many people are in this race?" [Arnie] "One! This is the full second half we were promised. I think Tom Stokes might win." This must be what the programme means by "if riders are available"! Shane Hazelden's first race fall either damaged the rider or his equipment. Without any other riders on the track, Tom Stokes looks fast but also quite stylish. Craig Saul greets his display with enthusiasm, "Four solo laps there for 16-year-old prospect Tom Stokes."

The 'Three Js' race again. Joe Exley wins with Jack Nottingham second while Jake Hallett retires. The fifth second half heat sees Tom Stokes improve his solo race time to 60.9 seconds. The final race of the night again showcases the talents of riders who came through the Rye House Training School system. As he exits the fourth bend on his second lap Jake Hallett pulls up. Again I turn to Arnie for guidance, "You can't tell if it's crisis of confidence or an engine failure?" At the moment Arnie swivels round and notes, "He had an engine failure in the last one," Jake's bike suddenly

---

[2] Edinburgh Monarchs co-promoter and away fixtures team manager John Campbell noted afterwards, "We were about 10 miles out on the M25 motorway and I said to my travelling companions, 'Why are the cars coming the other way with their headlights on?' It didn't take long to find out as we were soon into heavy rain. It rained the rest of the way but then, when we got to the stadium, the rain had cleared. On entering the stadium Rye House team manager, John Sampford, was standing in the middle of the pits car park and I shouted over to him, 'Is it on?' 'Of course it is!' was his reply and I knew then that we would win. I hadn't even looked at the track but I knew it would be much more like an Armadale surface than the normal Rye House track. And so it turned out to be." Len Silver would later say this meeting took place on a "filthy wet night."

Rye House: *"No one breathes Rye House more than Chris Neath. Cut him in half and he'd be coloured blue and yellow!"*

splutters back into life. He resumes some distance back in third. Jack Nottingham triumphs in a time of 71.9 seconds to score 8 (out of a possible 9 points).

Speedway enthusiast Mike Hunter wears many different metaphorical hats on behalf of the Edinburgh Monarchs. Tonight, he speaks as a genuine burstingly proud fan. Though by inclination not prone to over-exuberance or hyperbole, the manner and nature of tonight's victory prompts – in Mike's terms – the equivalent of a prolonged scream of celebration. "That was amazing! We were fantastic! I know the conditions didn't suit the home team but we were exceptional! Busch has made all the difference. We were a good team before but, now, possibly a great team! Everyone liked Tabaka but Busch is exceptional!" Hemel Hempstead based Scots ex-rider (and provider of illuminating insight into the Speedway Grand Prix via his reports in the *Speedway Star*) Bert Harkins stands with an excited gaggle of Edinburgh fans. Mike kindly praises my speedway books. "Jeff is very dedicated. He works hard writing them and then he works hard making sure they're available." In a similar style to the Queen – who notoriously likes to put people at their ease with the question, "How was your journey here today?" – Bert trots out his own conversational relaxer: "Do you go to many tracks?" Perma-smiling Dick Jarvis tries to savour the Monarchs triumph in silence but fails, "I don't have to make any comment [pause] but Neath – what a tart! I think Rye House have a complex about wet tracks! Edinburgh just attacked the track and, to be honest, it was nowhere near as wet as last week."

5th June Rye House v. Edinburgh (Knock-Out Cup Second Leg) 35-55

Rye House: *"No one breathes Rye House more than Chris Neath. Cut him in half and he'd be coloured blue and yellow!"*

Mildenhall

"There are excellent sight lines. Every track should be like this!"

6th June

The venue for the 2010 National League Four Team Championship Finals is West Row Stadium, home of the Mildenhall Tigers. This particular BSPA shared event features eight teams, so it'll be cosy in the compact Mildenhall pits with 32 riders, their mechanics and equipment. The teams selected to compete will race over a possible 25 heats to determine the eventual winner. However, since the National League comprises 11 teams, this meeting will go ahead without the participation of Newport, Plymouth and Scunthorpe! In his column in the programme, Mildenhall Chairman Ray Mascall expresses both delight and pride that the Fen Tigers club will stage "this prestigious event – well-known as producing a great family day out with very exciting racing". The meeting (along with the Mildenhall Fen Tigers) is sponsored by Angela and Neil Watson via their company Art and Stitch. In the car park beforehand, smartly dressed in his BSPA jacket, Ray diffidently supervises the myriad of last-minute tasks any speedway meeting requires. Today it's also imperative the club puts its best foot forward on behalf of the National League tier of racing and, of course, the sport of speedway in general.

Crowded pits

Without the enthusiasm or the £21,000 investment of Ray and Jean Mascall, it's unlikely that Mildenhall Speedway would still exist to entertain the Suffolk speedway public. It's widely rumoured the Mascalls put their life savings into the club to ensure the sound of speedway engines continue to echo round the West Row Stadium on many summer Sunday afternoons. Sadly Ray's wife Jean passed away three weeks ago and, understandably enough, though publicly he bears up, this loss has irrevocably changed his outlook on life and his attitude towards speedway. "We were together 30 years. We met at speedway and now she's gone. It's just not the same anymore! If the right offer came along, I'd let someone else take it off my hands and have all the hassle. If they wanted, I'd be happy to come and do

Head plant

53

whatever needed doing, watch the speedway and enjoy it, and then go home! At the moment, I don't get a minute. When I get home, I have to think about doing up the riders' wages, planning for the next meeting, doing the paperwork – the BSPA always wants something! Speedway clubs don't run themselves; it's amazing how much there is to do. It's not the same, anymore. Jean had been ill for a while and, eventually, I said to her I can't do any more for you – you're going to have to go to the hospital, which she didn't want to do. I rang on the phone and my son from my first marriage – who's a paramedic – rushed over but by the time I'd put the phone down and walked back, she'd gone! It was so sudden! The way I look at it is she's not in any pain but there was no time to say goodbye!" Ray's eyes betray his matter-of-fact tone and demeanour. [1]

On the A11 en route to the Four Team, I pass the light metallic green Ford that Isle of Wight co-team manager Kevin Shepherd drives. His family recently lost his charming mother, Eileen. "Mum went in on Valentine's Day with DVT and she went in again exactly two months later. On the Tuesday, my dad went home that night and they called him the next morning and, by that night, she was gone!" Though probably unknown to each other, Jean Mascall and Eileen Shepherd shared a love of speedway. They both touched the lives of many people outside their immediate family because of this deeply held enthusiasm. Both remain sadly missed.

Over at the area of the home-straight grandstand that traditionally houses the trackshop tables, Mildenhall regular Michael Slattery is comparatively pleased to see me. "I didn't know you were coming! Johnny [Barber] didn't tell me. He probably didn't want to spoil the surprise! [Points to smoke on the horizon] There's a fire over there – did you start it? Maybe we could burn your new book?" Moments later Phil Hilton – speedway photographer and Johnny Barber's chauffeur-cum-Boy-Friday arrives with Johnny in tow. Phil nods towards the tractor that circuits the track, "Look at that! I think it's the nicest I've ever seen it. It looks smart and tidy, there's a lot of shale on it too!" Elsewhere in the stadium, Craig Saul helps test the loudspeaker system.
[Disembodied voice] "Testing, testing, how's that?"
[Craig] "We're at unequal levels – as they say."
[Disembodied voice] "Testing, testing, how's that?"
[Craig] "Just a little too loud."
[Disembodied voice] "Testing, testing, testing, how's that."
[Craig] "I think we'll be okay once we've got the riders and the crowd making some noise!"

Sound check over, Craig wanders over to find out about new merchandise and special offers available at the trackshop. Still shell-shocked from Rye House's surprise home defeat to Edinburgh, Craig tells Johnny, "I'm recovering after last night."
[Jeff] "The Edinburgh fans were very happy."
[Johnny] "It wasn't just the Edinburgh fans!"
Michael interrupts the conversation, "I won't buy it [Shale Trek] if I'm not in it!"
Suddenly it's clear there are a good number of fans inside the stadium grounds keen to find prime

[1] Three weeks after the NL 4TT the *Speedway Star* reports, "Mildenhall Speedway is up for sale and searching for its seventh owner in ten years following club owner Ray Mascall's decision to quit....The local couple who were married for 30 years, achieved a life-time ambition when they saved the West Row club from closure following the King's Lynn decision to buy and sell at the end of the 2008 season." Taking stock of the situation after Jean's funeral service, attended by more than 50 people Ray commented, "After the events of the last couple of months, my future in the sport is coming to an end. Jean said to me before she died that if anyone makes an offer, let them run it. Speedway meant a lot to us both, it is where we met but has all become too much. There was Jean's passing, then a run of home meetings, which took a lot of organising, as well as arranging the funeral and a few other matters. It all came at once and took its toll. It is the culmination of everything happening and I don't want it to be to the detriment of my health, which has already happened with stress. My friends and family mean a lot more to me than being involved in speedway in this way." The prospective sale didn't go smoothly. Not only were stadium owner Dave Coventry and Ray unable to reach agreement but, according to Ray, the BSPA didn't cover themselves in glory, "I'm afraid the way the BSPA has treated me has left me very disillusioned. At the moment, I don't even want to watch another speedway meeting, and I've been a lifelong supporter."

Mildenhall: *"There are excellent sight lines. Every track should be like this!"*

locations for their garden furniture. "Have they opened the gates early?"

[Johnny] "I think they're expecting a bumper crowd and I'm expecting a bumper late night home."

[Jeff] "What time will it finish? Seven?"

[Johnny] "Hum."

[Jeff] "Eight?"

[Johnny] "You keep dreaming!"

There could be further delay if there's any crashes. Stadium soundman Trevor voices his anxiety, "We just hope the owner doesn't come along to the stadium. Last week he came just before the parade and turned the volume right down! Blayne [Scroggins] tried to make the announcements but no one could hear him. People booed. We said 'no one can hear him!'"

[Jeff] "Pardon?"

[Trevor] "I use that joke. The track looks nice. Usually the stadium won't let them onto it until, at least, one. Today it looks ripped! He mustn't have been around."

[Michael Slattery] "We haven't had Michael Jackson yet."

[Trevor] "We haven't forgotten. We wouldn't forget. *Billy Jean* will be on in a moment. You should do a book on him."

[Jeff] "Maybe next year!"

[Trevor] "He's much sharper than he pretends."

Another early arrival is Graham Rouse. Unusually, he's at a speedway meeting without his wife. "Hilary can't come today. She's working at the shop I can't tell you the name off. Jason Crump was in again the other day." Graham refuses to be drawn on what exactly Jason shops for on his visits to this mystery shop Hilary works in. My suggestions – Monster Energy drink, Australian honey, Paris Hilton sex videos – fall on good natured but deaf ears. I rib Graham about the stuttering start to the season his beloved Peterborough Panthers have enjoyed so far – particularly on the rider changes front. He bats away my joshing out Karol Zabik and Lewis Bridger, "Ipswich and Eastbourne are dustbin teams. They look at what's left after everyone else has had their pick!" Before I can defend the team selection honour of the Witches and the Eagles, an old age pensioner with an American accent interrupts to ask, "I've come over from the airbase. I live in New York State. We have four tracks there. I just want to see some good racing – where would be the best place to sit that's not on concrete? It's hot here. I'll have to take my jacket off."

[Jeff] "I must apologize that there's no bowler hats and there's no fog."

[US airbase man] "Actually, there was fog when we arrived in Prestwich."

[Jeff] "Prestwick."

[US airbase man] "Yes, they landed us there and we spent a day and a half in Ayr."

[Jeff] "Not much happens in Ayr."

[US airbase man] "It's a nice village and would be good to visit for an hour. I came years ago with a buddy and we rode round the country on a motorbike with a sidecar. I'd never been in a sidecar before or on that side of the road. We went round a few circles the wrong way but, luckily, there wasn't any traffic. We rode to Norway too." Mildenhall Speedway occupies a stadium where there is a wealth of interesting vantage points for any keen photographer, even those unprepared to stand or sit on concrete.

With 32 riders along with their mechanics, helpers or family members to accommodate in the pits, even the overflow areas have overflow areas. There's bustle and hubbub everywhere. Weymouth team manager Jem Dicken's in deep conversation with his riders in the small area that serves as the Wildcats section of the Mildenhall pits area. When I suggest that people claim that current uncertainty about the future of the Wildcats (as well as rumour of a rider with a bouncing cheque) might be an unwelcome distraction, Jem point blank dismisses such naysayers. "Looking

Mildenhall: *"There are excellent sight lines. Every track should be like this!"*

around, we've got a side as good as anyone so I think we've got a good chance!" When I enquire if lovebirds Phil Bartlett and Sam Knight are here yet, Jem glances theatrically round the pits, studies the nearby grandstand and says sarcastically, "Don't let them see me talking to you!" "It's a shame Sam's not here because on the Wimbledon Yahoo forum [Johnny Barber would later ask, "Have Wimbledon still got a forum?"] she said my book is rubbish – well she used another less polite word."

[Jem] "Don't take any notice of her, no one else does."

[Jeff] "I admire the way she's bravely gone public about her incontinence problems!"

[Jem] "Her what?"

[Jeff] "She signs off her posts with pmsl. When I checked on the online Urban Dictionary they said it was the "most banally stupid acronym of the text message era." With important team management issues to manage, Jem doesn't have time to discuss any real or feigned bladder control issues.

Johnny Barber delights at the sight of speedway historian Arnie Gibbons, "The important question – what did you think of Eurovision?" Arnie smiles, "I loved the Belgium entry, *Me and My Guitar*. It was fantastic!" Johnny and Arnie chatter animatedly about Eurovision! Mr Barber concludes their conversation with the immortal words, "As long as the speedway nations keep winning that's the main thing!" Photographer Phil Hilton stares anxiously at the already extremely crowded Mildenhall pits area, "I dunno how they're gonna fit them all into the pits." Surveying the stadium I tell Johnny, "It isn't the biggest crowd I've ever seen – there's probably more of a crowd in the pits." This is no surprise to Johnny, "That's always the way at Mildenhall!"

Johnny leafs through a hot-off-the-press copy of *Shale Trek*. Invariably he quickly finds mistakes. So far he hasn't done so. "Look at that! I turn straight to the Mike Moseley photo! Having read what I said about Mike Bennett and Kevin [Moore], I dunno if they're going to be plugging the trackshop this year!" Phil Hilton's got a clear idea of what's wrong with British speedway, "He tried to sell me a bag for 14 quid, that's why speedway is dying! Put that in your next book." Ipswich fan Adie arrives inside the stadium at the same time as the first hint of drizzle. "I went to Poland with Milesy [Steve Miles] – £50 on the plane booked six weeks before – to see Torun versus Zielona Gora. It was great to see a meeting with heat leaders like Gollob, Pedersen, and Zagar versus Andersen, Miedzinski, Holder and Ward. There was only 8,000 there but they jump up and down like a football crowd. The prices were amazing! We had an hour train journey from Torun to Bydgoszcz that cost £2 and a meal for four that cost 28 quid. Do you see they brought in Ales Dryml for Vissing at Ipswich? He didn't do well at Peterborough for us but there's a few that could go. I said to John Louis, 'What's this about them wanting £14,000 for Sundström?' And he said, 'We ride him as often as we can!' When we all know they don't want him to have an average. There was a letter in the paper asking why Chris Louis wouldn't speak to the fans. Sometimes we have a meeting and he's away working with Sky! When he is there, he says nothing."

The light drizzle that affects the first race (won by Dudley's Lee Smart) increases in intensity. Though this spells disaster for the likely quality of the racing, Adie still marvels at the spectacle, "Look at that rain!" The first race of the second semi-final only reaches the second bend of the second lap before Byron Bekker falls. Referee Margaret Vardy apparently anticipates his demise since he'd barely hit the floor before she flicks on the red lights. While we wait for confirmation of Byron's inevitable disqualification, Adie clearly hasn't browsed the Internet or listened to the speedway bush telegraph. "What happened at Rye House last night?"

[Jeff] "They lost 35-55."

[Adie] "You're kidding me! I was gonna go! But I'd been working on the roof all day and it was hot yesterday in Suffolk and, after I'd had one beer, you're not going to go are you?"

Mildenhall: *"There are excellent sight lines. Every track should be like this!"*

The rerun of the initial heat of semi-final 2 proceeds uneventfully in the rain until Mark Baseby rears as he exits the fourth bend (on lap 2). Unluckily, he somehow manages to hit the home-straight safety fence at the only point of its length where there's a gap! Mark smashes dramatically into this edge of the fence with his head. It throws him – like the proverbial ragdoll – from his bike. The impact and velocity of his contact smashes the fence to bits, almost as if it's stage scenery rather than genuine safety equipment. An impressive sized crowd of paramedics quickly circle Mark Baseby after his "face plant" as he lies prostrate on the shale. Arnie Gibbons strikes a concerned but sardonic note, "You'd think that Mark Baseby of all people would know his way round Mildenhall!" It certainly looks a horrible incident, particularly when the ambulance rushes onto the track. Mark eventually gets to his feet to wipe the collective grimace from the faces of the crowd. The crowd greet his recovery with warm applause as Craig Saul observes, "They build them tough". [2]

The vastly experienced Dean Felton wins the second race of semi-final group one while the also well travelled but much younger Chris Mills emerges victorious from the second heat of the second group semi-final. Jem Dicken's prediction of a challenge from the Weymouth Wildcats looks a trifle over-optimistic, particularly since – after two races – they're the only team (in either semi-final) to fail to trouble the scorer. This afternoon the run into the finish line appears to represent greater difficulty than the weather conditions, if judged by the way diminutive Jon Armstrong rears and nearly falls from his bike in the fifth race of the afternoon. Meteorological observations obsess the crowd almost as much as the on-track action. Like a land-bound sea-dog, Johnny Barber sniffs the air and nods towards a weather system massing impressively in the near distance (in the rough vicinity of the third bend), "If that black cloud over there hits we're in trouble!" Weymouth finally gain their first point in their fourth race but only after Daniel Halsey falls and, thereby, gifts it to Tom Brown who – at that precise moment – is trailed off badly at the rear. Johnny Barber's got such an uncanny ability to interpret cloud types – from cumulus to nimbus via cirrus or cirrocumulus – that Michael Fish should update his résumé. The rain is now constant and verges on the point of heavy. Johnny's resigns himself to an abandonment and an early night back home, "This looks like it could be in for the night!" Adie's equally downcast, "It's peeing down." Heat 6 of semi-final group 2 illustrates the deleterious effect of the rain upon the racing. In a slithery race, Tom Brown leads until an aggressive Karl Mason overtake on the third bend of the first lap. By the second bend of the third lap, Matt Wright loses traction but, somehow, manages to stay upright but, sensibly, decides to only idle round the circuit contentedly (but injury free) at the rear. To call it a race would over-egg the pudding. Nonetheless, Tom Brown's second place transforms the Weymouth Wildcats aggregate points tally by tripling it to 3 whole points!

Despite the ferocity of the downpour, with only two races left in each semi-final to complete this initial qualification stage of the competition, perhaps there's a case for waiting for the rain to clear. There are grumbles that the referee hasn't run the meeting as speedily as the weather forecast dictates. Given the strength of the rain, it could now take quite some time to clear. Arnie Gibbons isn't optimistic, "I can't see this going unless it stops raining soon and the sun comes out and dries the track. It's not as if they're only three or four races from the end or there's a shortage of rain-off dates, like there would at the end of the season." Arnie channels the spirit of Donald Rumsfeld to come up with his own multiple-choice scenario to cover an impressive range of known knowns,

[2] Interviewed afterwards, Mark describes the incident evocatively. "I had Luke Priest in front of me. But he was going so slow I went for the cutback to try and pass up the inside of him and got a bit of extra drive, my bike lifted I thought I could correct it in time, but just caught the fence. I had a face plant straight into the fence, but I'm okay, I just had a sore neck. It could have been a lot worse for me injury-wise. The main thing is I'm alright. I've a bent bike, but that can be straightened." Face plant is a wonderful use of the English language but still doesn't do full justice to the dramatic spectacle of its execution.

unknown knowns, unknown unknowns and known unknowns. "What will happen? It's a big mystery? Will we (a) have a long delay and 12 more heats of racing or (b) the meeting will be called off!" Hardworking West Dorset based ("proper Dorset") speedway reporter Phil Chard came to Suffolk this afternoon to report on the activities of the Bournemouth Buccaneers for the *Bournemouth Echo*. "The *Bournemouth Echo* has a circulation of 40,000 plus there's the *Dorset Echo* coverage". When it arrives, the abandonment announcement isn't a shock, "Safety is paramount so there's no surprise there." In speedway coverage terms, the Buccaneers are the amuse-bouche to the appetiser, main, dessert, cheese and biscuit courses (with wine, port and digestifs) that is the acres of newsprint commanded by the Poole Pirates. Last season Poole were, unusually, one of the basement clubs of the Elite League. The 2010 season has seen a dramatic transformation in their fortunes. Though the one-sided score lines could lead you to think otherwise, Phil Chard praises the calibre of the racing on offer at Wimborne Road, "If any of the Pirates don't make the gate, they really still go for it – despite the large wins! The racing is ten times better than it was last season. Crowds are going up! The fans love the excitement! The atmosphere is great!"

[Jeff] "You are the Real Madrid of speedway."

[Phil] "They prefer to be called the Manchester United of speedway not Chelsea."

Inside West Row stadium this afternoon, there are more speedway reporters than you can easily shake a stick at. Intrepid *Express and Star* speedway reporter Tim Hamblin this season adds (National League) Dudley to his speedway coverage portfolio to go along with his responsibilities for Elite League Wolverhampton. It's Tim's first trip to West Row and, typically given his cup half-full outlook on life, he's positively evangelical about speedway in Suffolk at this particular location. "I think it's terrific! There are excellent sight lines. Every track should be like this! There's nice fish and chips; Craig Saul – who I think is excellent – presents; you can see what's going on in the pits – every county should have one like it! I think it's absolutely superb! There's even a bar, though I couldn't because I'm working." While everyone sensibly shelters from the torrential rain, out on the track a young kiddie can't resist a quick circuit of the track on his BMX. Tim looks on approvingly, "Taking the Rickardsson line and making quite good time!" The colours of the youngster's replica football top create some mystery about his allegiances, despite the name Ronaldinho emblazoned on the reverse. Ever the diligent investigative reporter, Tim breaks off to rush over to the far side of the pits to check its exact provenance with the owner and returns with news, "it's the Barca second strip!"

Whether the whole meeting will have to be rerun, or the meeting rerun from the stage it was abandoned or, indeed, if the four finalists can be chosen from the present points position remains definitively unclear. When news of the abandonment appears on the BSPA website (along with the scores), it advises "BSPA to rule on possible restaging". Privy to the discussions between the team managers and the National Development League co-ordinator Peter Morrish in the pits this afternoon immediately after the abandonment decision, Craig Saul reveals, "There were four team managers who thought the teams ahead when the meeting was abandoned should qualify and four who didn't!" A predictable response, given that Weymouth is the only team to have no chance of qualification. Craig continues, "It was a shame we couldn't tell the public the decision but, sensibly, Peter Morrish wasn't going to be rushed into a snap decision. It wasn't the time. He'll go away and think about it and let everyone know in due course. Given that neither semi-final reached a decisive point – plus seven teams remain in arithmetical contention to qualify – it's likely that the next NDL management committee meeting will rule that the whole event should

Mildenhall: *"There are excellent sight lines. Every track should be like this!"*

be rerun." [3]

While Tim and Craig kindly help to carry boxes of unsold stock back to my car, they chat amiably. "Hopefully we'll see you at Rye House soon?" News that Tim Hamlin used to visit to Hoddesdon between studies in the 1970s prompts some joyful naming of the riders from that era. It's a time Tim recalls with great affection, "I used to go on the train via Broxbourne when I was rich (as rich as you ever are as a student) and walked when I wasn't. I walked to a rain-off once, which was a bit of a blow. I was at Harlow Technical College doing a one-year National Council for the Training of Journalists course in journalism (natch). It was 1977-78 academic year, I believe. Sunday afternoon racing, obviously. I still have a few of the programmes. The era of Bob Garrard, Kelvin Mullarkey, Ashley Pullen, Hugh Saunders, etc. After that time, it was 30 years before I returned. I drove down to see the semi-final of the World Under-21 championship and it was as if nothing had changed (except they now have the excellent fish and chips). Rye House were a strong team at that time. My one abiding memory through the years is of a match against Ellesmere Port when John Jackson was in his pomp. The Gunners were up against it and the public address system failed. Len Silver marched a lap of the track carrying a piece of hardboard with 'John Jackson tactical substitute' plus the relevant helmet colour chalked on it. He got back to the pits gate where the riders were all seated, ready to come out, and then brandished the board under the noses of the two home riders as if to say 'Have you seen this?' knowing, of course, that Jackson was seated on his bike next to them. Happy days! I didn't pay much attention to the riders, to be honest, because I wasn't a Rye House fan. It was speedway for the sake of watching speedway. Actually, during that year I also hitchhiked after lessons at Harlow to Milton Keynes and back on a Tuesday night to see Workington who duly lost 40-38 in a last-heat decider. Arthur Price, if memory serves, scored a 15-point maximum. I was getting close to the track (it was the Groveway stadium) but running out of time when I saw a car carrying a Milton Keynes Knights sticker. I had a big metal programme board at the time – covered with stickers from various tracks – including a large one for Workington. Out shot the board and, bless the driver, in pulled the car. That's speedway fans for you!"

6th June National League Four Team Championship Finals: meeting abandoned

[3] The restaging of the 4TT was to prove a complicated affair not unconnected to but, equally, not wholly explained by the mid-season demise of Mildenhall peedway club. By mid-August the NL decision-making wheels of power had ground out a solution to questions surrounding the restaging line-up, venue and date. Headlined on the BSPA website as "NL Weekend at Rye", the official statement released by Peter Morrish revealed that Buxton, Bournemouth, Dudley and Rye House would compete for the silverware at Hoddesdon on Saturday October 2nd (with the NLRC staged at the same venue the next afternoon). Poor weather, logistical complexity prompted by the end-of-season NL play-offs alongside Rye House's ongoing involvement in the final stages of the Premier League consolation tournament (for the Young Shield) led to a need for flexibility. In a fast-changing and fluid situation, plans for a double-header staging at Hoddesdon of the NL 4TT and the NLRC on Saturday 16th October came to naught during the week beforehand. Derek Barclay reacted on the BSF with his usual *sang froid*, "This to me is the final nail in the coffin of the third tier which, this year, has plummeted from the highs of former Conference seasons to a totally marginalised league now." The Rye House website put things slightly differently, "The BSPA Management Committee has instructed Rye House that it must give precedence to the staging date of its Young Shield Semi-Final tie against Newport over the National League Fours and Riders Championship. The latter – scheduled to be held at Hoddesdon this Saturday – has therefore reluctantly been postponed, with the Silver Ski Rockets instead meeting the Newport Wasps at Rye House on Sunday, October 17th, with a 1 p.m. start (gates open at 11 a.m.). This earlier than usual start time is to allow Newport's Swedish riders to catch evening flights out of Stansted. The BSPA's decision is based upon the need to complete the Young Shield competition, allowing for any bad weather, before the season-ending deadline of October 31st and the option to find an alternative date for the National League event. Rye House apologises to any supporters inconvenienced by this late change, which is due to a directive beyond its control." Continuing as usual to tightly grasp his telescope the wrong way round, Derek's curiosity prompts him to (in trademark fashion) rage impotently, "I wonder exactly WHEN the decision to scrap the NLRC & Fours was made..?" It's a question that will forever remain unanswered. Shortly afterwards, Derek goes on to demand that Wolverhampton stage the meeting. In the end, the NLRC ran on the last weekend of the season while the abandoned 4TT completely disappeared from the schedules.

Mildenhall: *"There are excellent sight lines. Every track should be like this!"*

CHAPTER 7

Swindon

"I'd heard he was, then I heard he wasn't and Davey Watt was and then I heard he was again!"

8th July

The month-long Football World Cup in South Africa disrupted speedway scheduling across all three leagues and, it's widely reported, had a deleterious impact upon crowd levels. The experienced Swindon Speedway promotional team did plan ahead to minimise the impact upon the home fixtures at the club instead staging meetings against fellow Thursday night clubs, Eastbourne and Ipswich. Neither team is likely to provide significant opposition nor fire into rapture the collective imagination of the Wiltshire speedway public. Only a fortnight ago, the Robins hammered the Eagles 60-36 in the Elite League 'A' fixture. In his programme notes, Swindon co-owner Gary Patchett seeks to partially exonerate the visitors, "we were comfortable victors in the 'A' fixture not least because of the injuries sustained by Ricky Kling in heat 2 that forced him to withdraw from the meeting". Gary then highlights the potential threat posed by "former Robin Matej Žagar". The Slovenian thrilled the Blunsdon faithful during the 2009 season and, allegedly, prompted some soul searching amongst the Robins management team before the exigency of the points limit led them to (reluctantly) release Matej.

So far, the 2010 Eastbourne No. 1 hasn't set the world alight at Eastbourne, let alone taken to the heart of the majority of Eagles fans. Matej's early-season performances have been variable. He's looked disinterested in the pits and isn't ineffective in the early heats (particularly heat 1). His average fell, almost precipitously, from 9.15 to 7.18 while, in parallel, rumbles of discontent from the terraces (and even in the usually relentless positive local media coverage) increasingly gain momentum. Though notoriously robust, Matej's an unusual speedway rider frequently laid low by sudden illnesses with peculiar almost tactically variable impacts upon his health. As a case in point, last Thursday saw Matej miss Eastbourne's home meeting with Coventry, then ride twice in Poland over the weekend before missing the Eagles Sky televised Monday night fixture against Peterborough. Ever diplomatic, Eastbourne co-promoter and team manager Trevor Geer retains his equanimity, "Matej is suffering quite badly with hay fever and a few things at the moment and has been advised not to fly, which makes it awkward coming over here." Fortunately for the club and the rider, Eastbourne received a medical certificate by fax from the rider on Monday prior to the televised meeting. Nonetheless his absence through illness should, if the letter of the law of the speedway regulations are consistently adhered to, result in a 28-day ban for 'withholding his services'. But – as is the obsessively philosophical and 'make it up as you go along' wont of the sport's governing bodies – it transpires that though he intended to miss the Peterborough meeting through illness, Matej was, in fact, already serving a one-match suspension as punishment for his earlier absence! With sightings of a smiling Matej Žagar in the Eastbourne pits almost as rare as unicorns galloping on the seafront, it's a situation that nowadays even invites (faux) concern from others. Peterborough team manager Trevor Swales spotted that Žagar rode in a GP qualifier and a Polish league meeting over the weekend prior to the Panthers televised fixture, "Yet he is again too ill to come to England on Monday and that is not on. It is something the authorities have to look at. No one should think that I'm having a pop at Eastbourne because that is not the case. I feel sorry for them after being left in an awkward position by a rider who has been blatantly unfair to his club and fans over here." If Eastbourne wish to perform creditably at Abbey Stadium tonight or (even) mount a serious EL challenge this season, then strong performances from Matej Žagar are imperative. Obviously, Matej remains keen to remind the Robins management of his effectiveness round Blunsdon.

Curatorial team

The Abbey Stadium at 4 p.m. bathes in a scorching hot 26 degrees. Sat on his tractor, track curator and club co-promoter Ronnie Russell is stripped to the waist with the tan of a farm worker. He goes round and round the track with a green grunge speckled bowser that looks as if it's been freshly slimed on the set of *Ghostbusters*. The letter pages of recent editions of the *Speedway Star* frequently debate track conditions at Blunsdon. [1] Even without such encouragement Ronnie searches, nay quests, for Japanese production operations management levels of continuous improvement. Indeed, last week's meeting versus Ipswich saw a hot and windy day play havoc with the track surface (particularly on turns 1 and 2), so Ronnie intervened and, afterwards, told the *Speedway Star*, "After it was so inconsistent I decided to rip the track up and relay it."

Harold & Rob

After numerous further circuits of the massive 363-metre Blunsdon track, chocolate-tanned Ronnie Russell breaks off to confer with some of his curatorial colleagues including Blunsdon blogger Graham Cooke. Looking much more prosperous after his successful battle with cancer, Ronnie dismisses criticism of the track as ill-informed opinion. "We put 226 tons – not counting what we started off with as surplus (about 10-12 tons) on the track so far this season. We've completely reshaped the track and, if you talk to the riders, they'll tell you it's faster! This is a very big track and

[1] Scott Smedley from Bath shared his thoughts on the recent slump in attendances at Swindon. "Most of the blame for this lies in the track. I'm no expert on track grade preparation but a good track should allow for plenty of action and multiple racing lines. …what makes this even more disappointing is that Ronnie Russell said he could sort the track out and turn it into a proper 'racing' track, when it actually didn't need fixing! The track was one of the best for racing action during 2007, 2008 and 2009 when Russell was not responsible for track preparation! So if Swindon want to see attendances improve, the first thing to do is not replace riders but provide a track that could provide good racing." Derek Hayward from Basingstoke – track staff member at Smallmead for 15 years and on the fourth bend for the last year and a half at Swindon – responds the next week with a different perspective. "Scott says Ronnie ruined it in 2009, but what he failed to realise is that Ronnie took over track preparation in April 2009 when Gerald fell ill and was unable to carry on as track curator. I see the track from the inside and I know there's more shale on that track at the end of 15 than there was at the start of heat 1 at Reading. So I say to Ronnie, keep up the good work, we may have only been the third best track (across all three divisions of British speedway) as voted by the referees and officials in 2009 but carry on as we are and we will be number one this year." They were actually voted 2nd best track in 2010.

Swindon: *"I'd heard he was, then I heard he wasn't and Davey Watt was and then I heard he was again!"*

when you're creating those sort of speeds – like we are – that's why the surface gets so hard! People say they create dirt at Eastbourne but that's nothing like what we have to work with here. [Points to mini-track on the Abbey Stadium centre green] it could fit on there easily!" Never lost for words, Ronnie's in affable mood, "I'm the same colour as the track, I need a flashing light on my head so they don't run me over!" Given the width of a speedway tyre, its knobbles and the number of racing lines found on any speedway track, it's quite an achievement that bikes here manage to thoroughly cover so many millimetres of the track to pack it down so tightly. Later, another long-time fan takes a different view, "Terry tells Ronnie to pack down the track because that's how he likes it!"

Though battered in last week's crash with Robert Miśkowiak, Thomas H. Jonasson is keen to race for the Robins tonight. Thomas sustains concussion, yet he wants to race! Whereas Matej Žagar has a touch of hay fever but decides not to fulfil his contractual obligations. Ronnie admires Jonasson's determination but, though sympathetic, he's adamant that the Robins management team won't risk Thomas's health. "He's dizzy and sick but he said 'Let me come here at least!' And, when he got here, then we told him he couldn't ride!" The new Eastbourne reserve power partnership (Gustafsson and Dryml) have only ridden once together and won't again tonight since an illness for Simon Gustafsson keeps him away. It's not so long ago that the speedway authorities (and the promoters) gave chapter and verse explanations about the absence of almost any rider. Nowadays sudden and/or downright peculiar absences occur frequently but get greeted with a shrug of the shoulders and vague talk of the rider "being ill". This isn't, of course, to take Simon Gustafsson's name in vain – despite the usual information vacuum meaning no one is really able to throw any sensible light on the specifics of tonight's illness. Instead, Kyle Hughes rides. Though he's improved significantly (and will, ultimately, probably grace the top tier of British speedway) there's no doubt that the Hughes/Dryml partnership inspires much less fear for Swindon than the alternative. News that Kyle rides prompts ex-teacher Graham to chip in, "I taught him – not very much – but I did teach him. He's a Chippenham lad." Wayne Russell is a big fan of the absent young Swede, "Did you see the way Gustafsson's team rode Dryml on Monday night? Simon struggled a bit when he was second in Eastbourne's averages – he's only young and it's a lot of responsibility – but he is good enough! I really rate him. I thought with Gustafsson and Dryml at reserve it would be a really close meeting! What can you do about all these riders missing? [shrugs]" If Wayne does have answers about how British speedway solves unexpected rider absences then, sadly, I don't get to hear because we're interrupted by a fan asking querulously, "Is Žagar here?" In his trademark taciturn unflustered fashion Wayne replies, "I'd heard he was, then I heard he wasn't and Davey Watt was and then I heard he was again!"

In recent years the Robins have challenged hard to become Elite League champions but this season, by their own recent high standards, the Robins aren't quite of the same vintage. Nonetheless, they could still make the lucrative Play-off stage of the season and that, after all, is the real strategic financial aim of any Elite League club. Apparently forgetting that for many years Swindon rode in the Premier League, many fans nurse a grievance about this loss of potency so much so that many nowadays stay away or, alternatively, moan at length on the forums (or in person). Blunsdon blogger Graham Cooke is sick of these complaints, "There's a lot of negativity! I remember when earlier in the season people were saying this is the worst Swindon team they've ever seen! What about 1983 with Phil Crump and six assorted others who got thrashed at home and away! This is a nice little team – not a championship winning team – but a nice one!" Such negative chatter and diminishing crowd numbers saw Swindon co-owner Terry Russell warn Robins fans (after the recent Knock-Out Cup meeting with Peterborough) about future doomsday scenarios. Apparently reading phrases in green biro from the well-thumbed copy of the Mallett promotional playbook, Terry's irritation burst forth in the local media and pages of the *Speedway*

Swindon: *"I'd heard he was, then I heard he wasn't and Davey Watt was and then I heard he was again!"*

While Ronnie returns to his track curatorial work, I follow Graham through the pits towards number 96 – a.k.a. the track staff rest and recreation room. Opposite there's now a temporary building with an impressive array of tables and chairs outside. "It's our new catering area where we eat our food. Terry [Russell] buys us our chicken and chips – they're like emu pieces, they're enormous – fish and chips or pie and chips." Though there's much curatorial housekeeping work to be done still at Blunsdon before the tapes rise, Graham has half a mind on his annual sojourn behind the scenes at the Cardiff Grand Prix inside the Millennium Stadium. "My lad Dave is working with me at Cardiff this year." It's unlikely SGP lightning strikes twice since 2009 saw a pit gate fight – images of which flashed Graham's anxious expression worldwide. "There's no Sayfutdinov but there's still a few punchy little blighters!" Graham's *Blunsdon Blog* – speedway's equivalent of *The Archers*, albeit with added shale – continues to enthral online. There's almost insatiable demand for his charmingly detailed 'Life behind the scenes at Blunsdon' stars a rich array of genuine characters that make speedway what it is. Dedicated volunteer track staff are the centrepiece of the blog but, pretty well anyone you care to name within the speedway world, at some point gets a gently but incisively observed walk-on part. "We cracked our millionth visitor last weekend. I feel kinda sad!" To overcome his feelings of melancholy, Graham retreats to number 96 where he sets about refreshment duties for everyone there (Keith, Mark and myself). Ernie interrupts the comparative calm restfulness of few minutes away from track curatorial duties, "Did you find a battery charger here last week?

[Graham] "Nah!"

[Ernie] "Morten's lost one."

[Graham] "The rate things go here, that's gone! Nothing's safe! We've even lost the radio fascia from the tractor! The bolt cutters went missing! The small electric generator and Punch's petrol disc cutter also went."

When you're a vital part of the fabric of a club, inevitably you get to see and hear many things as well as form a pretty accurate picture of the personality and character of riders, officials, management and colleagues alike. Graham recalls the recent Swindon versus Belle Vue meeting, "The funniest heat we've seen this season was when Jordan Frampton beat Hans Andersen. You could almost see the fear in his eyes on turns 3 and 4. They were all gathering behind him and he was going faster and faster, just staying ahead of them. Hans Andersen pressured him throughout.

---

[2] "Quite simply we aren't prepared to pour money down the drain with heavy losses so if the fans are that fickle, I can only ask them if they want a speedway team at Blunsdon? If they aren't going to support us then there won't be a team, it is that simple. The crowd was very poor [versus Peterborough] and we held an emergency meeting afterwards to discuss whether there were any reasons why. In my six years at Swindon we have generally had good support, and in all of the last four seasons we have made the Play-Offs. We also promoted this meeting big time by taking out a full-page advert in the Wembley Soccer play-off promotion clash programme between Swindon and Millwall. The deal was to show your Wembley ticket stub and get £5 off. Some 37,000 Swindon people reportedly went and clearly that promotional effort did not work. After topping the league table last year it was spelled out to us in the harshest of terms that you merely need to get in the Play-Offs, especially this year with the abolition of a points advantage for the top two teams in the semi-finals. …I am not aware that there was any other major event on locally, and the World Cup football hadn't started. The match was not under threat from the weather and while there was plenty of cloud, all the weather forecasts indicated no rain for our area. Perhaps Peterborough's inclusion of two guests and rider replacement for Troy Batchelor put some people off, but in fact, I think we faced a more powerful team on the Blunsdon track than their regular seven. I don't think the fact that we've been running fortnightly affects us either, it should mean that speedway is less of a drain on fans' pockets – and I think it is the way for the Elite League speedway to go – and of course, mirrors football." Responding to criticism from a small section of fans about Mads Korneliussen and Morten Risager, Terry Russell went on, "I'm not the sort of person to sack two riders I think are putting in the effort because of largely Internet-led moaners. I'm sure the fans miss Matej Žagar, but we could realistically only have kept him if we had done the unthinkable and not used Leigh Adams. …the bottom line however is that the level of support for speedway at Swindon has to be much greater than it was last Thursday or there won't be a team. If fans are that fickle then the owners will not risk their overall livelihood." It's a theme that Swindon Robins co-owner Gary Patchett echoes, "We are scratching our heads for sure. 2009 was a year of great recession but our crowds held up. Sadly, I can only agree with everything Terry has said and if crowds don't improve dramatically, the future is bleak." After the 2010 season closed, Ronnie Russell reveals that the club made an operating loss of £154,000!

Swindon: *"I'd heard he was, then I heard he wasn't and Davey Watt was and then I heard he was again!"*

When he finished he jumped into the arms of his mechanic and celebrated like he'd become world champion! It was probably three seconds a race faster than he ever went before or went since!"

The red truck outside the track staff cubbyhole has – using the argot of senior management everywhere – been re-designated. In other words, given a new name to go with an additional function without anything really changing on the investment front. "Terry Russell last week mentioned we need a Rapid Response Unit so we can rush out onto the track to make repairs wherever they're needed. So the red truck has been promoted to a Rapid Response Unit. We are the RRT – the Rapid Response Team!" If injuries are a matter of life or death at speedway, mandatorily every track enjoys the services of medics and an ambulance. Away from the febrile atmosphere necessitated by the television schedule led Speedway Grand Prix Series and televised live Sky Sports meetings, most people might feel that there's minimal need for genuine urgency at any speedway meeting for instantaneous track furniture repairs. Graham begs to differ, "When people start dismantling airbags – i.e. Eastbourne in heat 2 when Kling rode into Gathercole and when Mads on the wind-down lap, for reasons best known to himself, plunged into the airbags and ripped it last week (we've had to reduce the airbags on turn 3) – you definitely need to get on with repairs quickly! We've got everything you need on board: airbags, four lots of air pipes to link to the airbags, a couple of rubber kickboards, toolkit, drill, glue, patches, cable ties, screwdriver, hammer, nails, everything you can think of! When Miśkowiak straightened up and T-boned Thomas Jonasson, they flew into the safety fence and destroyed the wooden kickboard – which we didn't have a spare of. And they punctured the airfence for which we didn't have a big enough cutter for in the van – not surprising when it's a big steel safety fence! The velocity was such that Jonasson's handlebars ripped a hole in it and, to add insult to injury, Thomas was excluded." Talk of recent speedway accidents inevitably brings Adam Skornicki's recent crash to mind. By all accounts, Adam's clutch lever knocked through his front teeth and went out again through his cheek after his crash during the Wolves meeting against Belle Vue. A few days later on the Sunday, Adam then rode in the Poland but only managed three races before commonsense dictated he took no further part in proceedings. Sensibly, Skornicki then had a week off to recover from his facial injuries.

Disgruntled terrace talk about the quality of the team and the product on show at Blunsdon continues to irk Graham. "If the crowds at Eastbourne are as fickle as they are here, you'll have problems. When we lost to Lakeside you'd have thought the world had ended! The things you hear. People always say things like 'I've been coming 45 years and I've never seen such a bad track, bad team, bad management' – you name it – they blame it!" A short distance away from the business end of the pits – where the riders and mechanics congregate – there's an impressive sized area Swindon use to store their shale. Graham proudly shows me a shale pile of approximately 20 tons, "You should have seen how far it came out when we just had a delivery!" Only seconds after I've admired the Team Holta sticker on the side window of Graham's car, Graham jubilantly receives news that Team Holta have just arrived within the Abbey Stadium grounds. I'm shocked that Rune would come all the way to Swindon the night before a Grand Prix practice! Graham quickly disabuses me of my misapprehension, "It's Krzystof Nyga and Michal Ciurzynski – Team Holta! Rune flies in tomorrow."

Over on the sloped tarmac terraces adjacent to the start line, Roy Hicks sports an impressive amount of safety equipment for his bicycle ride his home (for a well-earned bite to eat after a hard day's work at the track). Roy's fortunate to only live a quarter of a mile away as the crow flies, three-quarters of a mile away if you travel on the uniquely complex redesigned road network that nowadays surrounds Blunsdon. Though he's excited about the Robins versus Eagles clash,

Roy's mind is also already elsewhere – in Cardiff for the SGP round staged there in two days' time. "We've got a trailer home and, sounds silly to say and people don't believe you, but we stay 10 minutes away from the stadium as Cardiff has a caravan park by Sophia Gardens. We'll go on Friday – there's a real party atmosphere with the same people going each year (we'll book again) – and with the earlier start time we'll be back early and have a barbecue!" Later Robins Pit crew co-ordinator (and zealous advocate of its membership benefits), Darcia Gingell wants to know what direction I approached this remarkable road network from when I came to the stadium. "Did you come in the front or the back way?" The way I came meant I didn't experience the unique section of road where everyone heading south needs to be in the left-hand lane to turn right. I also completely fail to notice the nearby 'encroaching' housing developments that make Darcia anxious for the future. "Over there they're building loads of houses – there's rumours again about the stadium!" My supposition that such things must surely be on the back burner ("I thought there was a recession") fails to understand the innate magnetism of Swindon as a destination of choice (actually Swindon is something of a boom town with low unemployment figures), "Not round here. They need more and more houses." This is Darcia's seventh season at speedway. She remains fanatical about all things Swindon Robins, "I've only ever known Elite League – we started coming half way through the first season in 2004. This season there's been loads of good racing. Loads of people just moan and moan but don't seem to notice the quality of the racing!" Darcia doesn't take comfort in the ease of the Robins victory over the Eagles a fortnight ago. Indeed, pretty well every Swindon fan I meet echoes what sounds like a pre-agreed mantra to bemoan the (apparently) massively significant absence of Thomas Jonasson. Darcia is no exception, "We haven't got Jonasson!" Like pretty well every Robins fan, she's completely unfazed about the Eagles absentee, Simon Gustafsson. However, Darcia does have a soft spot for fellow reserve, Lukas Dryml. "He's lovely Lukas, isn't he? He can't half chat though! One night he chatted to us so much in the bar that his brother had to come and rescue us. If only all speedway riders where like him! But they're not…"

Tonight's crowd is swollen by touring Edinburgh Monarchs fans, "There's 21 of us on the trip – we're staying at the Blunsdon Hotel. It was Rye House on Saturday, Newport on Sunday, we watched the football on Tuesday and Wednesday, we're here tonight, going to the Pairs at Somerset tomorrow and Cardiff on Saturday before going back on Sunday. There's another bus coming down at midnight tonight to avoid the traffic." BBC Radio Wiltshire, top performer and Swindon speedway presenter Richard Crowley bigs up the programme edited by Chris Seaward to the crowd on account of its production quality, "Your all-colour speedway programme at Swindon this year!" At first glance the cover for tonight's League 'B' meeting appears to promote the joys of motorcycling for old age pensioners. A grey haired model named Barry stares out at us. Smartly dressed in a hi-vis fluorescent yellow motorcycle jacket, Barry's must be absent minded since he's without a helmet or motorcycling gloves. Mounted on his handlebars are some water bottles, a cuddly toy and a camera. What safety message the club or Barry wish to send out remains mysterious? [3] Over recent years, my book display at Blunsdon wouldn't be complete without the presence of ex-*Antiques Roadshow* worker, Harold Davies (90). As usual, he arrives with Anthony Roberts (a.k.a. Rob) shortly before the rider parade and introductions. Because my display table temporarily occupies their regular viewing position we – in the spirit of

[3] Swindon legend and four-times World Champion Barry Briggs is on a nationwide tour of speedway tracks to raise money for his "Briggo Sport Relief Ride" charity. It's a schedule that would tire a man half his age. Indefatigable, Barry has a fundraising target of £120,000 that will be used to help injured speedway riders. He's also got a book (*Wembley and Beyond*) to promote but this takes a back seat to his summer of charity work fundraising at speedway tracks throughout Britain (along with selected parts of Europe). At the end of his lengthy travels, 76-year-old Briggo raised a fantastic £68,463.58 in total. Many injured speedway riders benefitted including Garry Stead, Per Jonsson, Steve Weatherley, John Simmons, Krzysztof Cegielski, Graham Miles, Neil Hewitt, Paul Mitchell, Alan Wilkinson, Lawrence Hare, Joe Owen and Pip Lamb who were all either presented with (or sent) a cheque – some for £5,157.27 – by Briggo.

65

Swindon: *"I'd heard he was, then I heard he wasn't and Davey Watt was and then I heard he was again!"*

speedway fans everywhere – amicably rub along together. Harold rummages inside his jacket pocket for his wallet and, for half a moment, I think he's about to buy a book. Instead, as befits a proud Bristol Bulldogs fan, he takes out a clipping from the Letters page of the February 8th edition of the *Bristol Times*. "I've been keeping lots of clippings by my chair for you but you haven't been here! When will you next be here? We go to the New Forest on the 17th."

[Jeff] "Will you be horse riding?"

Last year Harold needed two sticks to walk but, this year, he's down to one. "Ho, ho! Not with my hip! It's been a year now. It's just getting a little bit better and now it's the other one. I have some ointment but I don't know if that will help? They've re-laid the track you know."

[Jeff] "Yes, I'd heard. Is it any better?"

[Harold] "I dunno! You should've seen the crash here last week. We went to Somerset and saw their captain [Jason Lyons] go straight up in the air and his bike followed him. We saw an England and Australia match once where one rider swallowed his tongue. He never rode from that day till this. I forget his name. What's this with Poole? It's a carve-up! I reckon that Žagar wanted to come back here. Poole had pulled the eyes over the Control Bureau and they wouldn't let us keep Žagar. It's all wrong! He wanted to stay – he don't want to ride there [Eastbourne]. They say he has what's it – hay fever – but I don't know. What's this with Poole at Belle Vue? 50-40! Bristol used to do that when they were getting 5-1s all the time. No one wants to see that. They'll make that up in no time [at Wimborne Road] and get a crowd to see it!"

Leigh Adams beats Žagar to win the first race. Eastbourne track their new Polish No. 2 Tomasz Jedrzejak but the real interest of the heat resides in the form of Australian Cory Gathercole who rides so wildly that it verges on the dangerous. Three times on the second bend, Cory cuts the corner and scythes across the track in an attempt to outwit Jedrzejak. Ignoring "s'lee Adams" fast time, Harold takes a generous view of Cory's calculated but dangerous riding manoeuvres, "You should see Cory at Somerset – he's great!" Guarding the hash-marked area at the bottom of the grandstand stairs that lead down from the toilets, the bar and the Legends Lounge, Blunsdon's security man Neil Scott looks wistfully out over the track. "Trouble is Mr Russell prepares it a bit heavy for the first three or two heats. It's grippy in parts and not in others till it settles! Cory looked like he didn't have the right setup for that race." Eastbourne's potential meeting-winning reserve, Lukas Dryml suffers no such problems with his setup so jets from the tapes to lead comfortably until he falls second time around on the apex of the first corner. Marooned back in fourth by some considerable distance, Simon Gustafsson's reserve replacement, Kyle Hughes, unfortunately doesn't spot his stricken Eagles colleague until the very last moment. Laying his bike down very late, Kyle glides into a surprised but still prone Dryml. The innocuous incidents are often the most devastating. Medical personnel in brightly coloured clothing gather for some time before they transport Lukas back to the pits with injuries unknown. Either referee Stuart Wilson possesses a wicked sense of humour or, perhaps, a desire to encourage young riders because before the rerun of the race (without the disqualified Dryml) we're told, "SCB official Stuart Wilson congratulates Kyle Hughes for trying to lay his bike down!"

During this slightly extended delay, I quiz speedway historian Robert Bamford who's something of an occasional Boy Thursday behind the tables of the trackshop at Blunsdon. Any conversation with Robert behind his trackshop table inevitably comes with the equivalent of a health and safety announcement about his choice of location. "As purely the place he stands so that good friends Lucy Aubrey and Lee Poole can keep an eye on him following health issues in recent months". Perhaps he could get a card printed with his mantra? Our talk about the opening line of Cliff Richard's autobiography ("To this day I can't be sure whether monkeys swim under water") prompts Robert to ruminate, "I have a good opening line – actually a question: Do people dream in colour? And can you see text or read signs in dreams? I think not! If I get my enthusiasm back,

---

Swindon: *"I'd heard he was, then I heard he wasn't and Davey Watt was and then I heard he was again!"*

I'm going to go round and write the real *Shale Trek* and quote you all the time!" If tonight's speedway ornithological battle already weighs in favour of the Robins, then a three-rider race that features Kyle Hughes as Eastbourne's sole representative doesn't bode well. This unpromising situation quickly worsens with his engine problems throughout the rerun. When race winner Justin Sedgmen (in place of Thomas H. Jonasson) crosses the finish line, Kyle remains over half a lap behind.

A season without obviously great promise, even for relentlessly optimistic Eastbourne fans, is soured for many by the lackadaisical attitude of the Eagles so-called No. 1 Matej Žagar. From a School of Thought that dictates the cup will often be broken or, only rarely half full, Martin Dadswell isn't a happy bunny stood guesting behind the tables of the Swindon trackshop, "If Dryml is injured we're really ******!" With Martin's 'hopes' already in a critical condition on life support, Richard Crowley's announcement ("We understand it will be three riders only for heat number 3") would prompt any responsible person to remove all sharp objects from Mr Dadswell's vicinity, "We've got no number 8 again too!" Eastbourne's sole representative Ricky Kling does arrive second into the first bend but – for reasons best known to himself – then drifts away towards the bend-2 airfence. Effectively lost from contention from that point on, by the start of lap three Kling appears nearly as demotivated as Martin Dadswell. Ricky signals his disillusion by riding into the corners with his bike upright! No longer bothering to even pretend to try to slide his equipment, Kling eventually completes the remainder race and prompts some quizzical Swindon fans to wonder "should he be disqualified for failing to race?" With three heats gone, Eastbourne trail 13-5. Though he claps the action in front of him, Harold's still preoccupied with the thought that speedway might return to Bristol, "They said the council would decide in May but it's gone quiet and we ain't heard anything since!"

Elsewhere in the stadium, Clive Fisher catches up Leigh Adams to confront the Australian with some hard-hitting questions about the first race, "That was a fast time!" Resisting the temptation to – as usual – talk about himself in the third person, Leigh replies modestly, "Well, you know, it was just a fast start!" Pressed for more insight Leigh confesses, "There was a bit of dirt round the inside." Resisting the follow-up question about Leigh's favourite helmet colour that is doubtless on the tip of his tongue, Clive Fisher instead provides some brief, broad brush analysis of the future, "It's the big one – Cardiff – on Saturday, are you missing it?" Still manfully avoiding the royal plural, Leigh remains stoically philosophical, "I can honestly say no! It's a pretty heavy schedule. In a few years' time maybe I'll miss it but, for now, I'm just enjoying my racing and my testimonial and my book – we've finally got that out!"

Any Eastbourne fans prone to pessimism have their anxiety levels stoked by another heat disadvantage in a race won by Simon Stead. Matej Žagar then restores some semblance of dignity with a race win in black-and-white to reduce the deficit to a much more acceptable margin of 5 points. Generate, the lemony flavoured drink that Robert Bamford raved about during the Blunsdon leg of last season's Elite League Play-Off final, has benefited from its initial regional trial in Gloucestershire and Wiltshire to go on nationwide distribution. Paul Oughton (from the Robins commercial team) introduces Kieron Lewis – the man behind the Generate relationship with Swindon speedway. "I live locally and I'm a Swindon fan." The pep-you-up drinks market is extremely competitive but dominated by major players like the increasingly visible Red Bull or its lesser rival, Monster. Working on the assumption we all know as much as he does about this particular drinks category, Kieron tells me that the metaphorical heat of the kitchen is too much for some of the lesser lights, "Relentless have got out of motor sports and now concentrate on water sports and festivals!" Unable to compete with the marketing and sponsorship spend of Red Bull or Monster, Generate need to live up to their brand name and seize greater market share

Swindon: *"I'd heard he was, then I heard he wasn't and Davey Watt was and then I heard he was again!"*

by garnering positive word of mouth. Kieron's two years in the job successfully oversaw market testing of the product in Gloucester and Wiltshire (including Abbey Stadium). Competition for market share is a literal and metaphorical pissing contest. "It's a natural drink not a diuretic and it also doesn't give you massive highs and lows like the other drinks. Athletes aren't allowed to drink Red Bull or Monster anyway! They sponsor everything so it's very competitive. If I was offered it [as a sportsman] I'd take it. We've sponsored Chris Harris at Cardiff, which is very exciting. Speedway fans are very loyal – it's glamorous but underrated. I'm mainly motocross this year. We've a couple of very exciting developments but I can't tell you about those." While we chat, out on the track Eastbourne stabilise their position with a drawn heat helped by a fall for Cory Gathercole. Paul Oughton shrugs philosophically, "He's trying too hard."

Ricky Kling continues his torpor in heat 7 and easily secures last place in heat 7. Luckily for Eagles fans, Tomasz Jedrzejak remains true to his Polish roots so adapts easily to the fast Blunsdon track for a win ahead of the Robins in-form heat leader Simon Stead. Kieron studies Stead intently as he fails to reel in Jedrzejak, "I'd expect him to do better." Stead cuts a distinctive figure on the track – partly because of his riding style but mostly because of his uniquely coloured crash helmet. It's almost fluorescent and heads more toward the colour orange than any other hue. Surely the rules prohibit notionally 'red' coloured helmets in non-traditional Pantone hues? Recovering in Lazarus-like fashion, Lukas Dryml shows no obvious visible ill effects after missing his scheduled heat 4 ride when he takes his place at the start line for heat 8. Yet again, each time round Cory Gathercole tries to cut the corner of the first bend. When he falls on the third lap, his disqualification sees the referee awards the race in favour of Jedrzejak (his second win in successive races) and Dryml to take the scoreline to an ungainly and slightly astonishing 26-25.

Heat 9 is worth the admission money alone. Mads Korneliussen passes Joonas Kylmakorpi on lap 2 to slot into second place behind his fast-starting Polish teammate, Grzegorz Zengota. With commitment to both the Eastbourne cause and his duty to entertain, Joonas returns the favour on the second bend of lap 3 and holds off Korneliussen's attentions despite a last-gasp dash from the bend to the finish line. The bare detail of the result (Robins heat advantage) fails to capture the full excitement of their contest. Eastbourne fan and dedicatedly well-travelled Manchester United season ticket holder Noel admires Joonas's commitment, "When Mads passed him I thought that was it but, fair play to him, JK fought back intelligently!" Heat 10 sees Eagles Kling and Dryml surprisingly out-gate the master of Blunsdon, Leigh Adams. Their glory is short-lived since Adams scythes through them both on the back straight of the first lap. Absorbed by the action, Harold also ventures down memory lane, "My wife died in 2006. We emigrated to the US in the 1950s but my wife didn't like it and we came back. Her sister was over there. New England. We only stayed a month so it was like a long holiday."
[Jeff] "When did you get married?"
[Harold] "It was the 12th June [eyes dance] 1947!"

With the scores still comparatively poised, Eastbourne desperately need Matej Žagar to win heat 11 but, instead, he rides like a novice into the first bend. Since the margin for error is slight at the upper levels of speedway, this advantage is sufficient enough for Simon Stead to capitalise upon his escape to win by the proverbial mile. Though he lives in Bristol, Harold won't go to the Cardiff Grand Prix. "I went the first year but it was too noisy. I didn't have any earplugs and I don't like the indoor. Speedway should be outside. I didn't like it so I didn't go again. When the girl was singing, ugh! It's better like this!" Harold waves proprietarily at the panoramic vista that is the Abbey Stadium home straight. Harold isn't happy with the volume levels at Blunsdon either. "The music is too loud here I told them. You can hardly hear or have a conversation. I'd prefer to listen to 'Red Sails in the Sunset', bet you don't know that?" I don't so Harold gives his West Country

Swindon: *"I'd heard he was, then I heard he wasn't and Davey Watt was and then I heard he was again!"*

accented rendition of the song.

[Jeff] "You should volunteer to sing on the centre green."

[Harold] "Ha ha ha."

[Jeff] "I'd come to see that."

[Harold] "Lots of the old songs would be good."

[Jeff] "It's right for the demographic."

Heat 12 sees Lukas Dryml and Justin Sedgmen exchange second position for a couple of laps before Lukas finishes second behind Zengota (with Kling last). The Robins lead by 5 points with three races to go. Žagar sets his inconsistency aside with a comfortable win in heat 13. Behind Matej there's a battle royal that sees Joonas Kylmakorpi hold off the attentions of Leigh Adams throughout laps two and three. His cause is helped by what appears to be a single racing line that offers no real way past, even for someone as experienced round Blunsdon as the Robins talismanic Australian. On the final lap, Simon Stead who powers alongside Kylmakorpi on the back straight then makes a poised but sharp cut back up the inside on the apex of the third and fourth bends to snatch second on the race to the line. It's a well-practised impressive high-speed manoeuvre that enraptures the Blunsdon faithful and claws back a potential Eagles 5-1 into a much more manageable 4-2. Heat 14 completely undermines impressions that Kyle Hughes' inclusion is as a makeweight last-minute replacement for Simon Gustafsson since he gamely pressures Justin Sedgmen for third place throughout the final lap. Afterwards the announcer passes on the admonishment of referee Stuart Wilson, "Warning to the rider in white – Kyle Hughes – to remain still at the tapes!" With one heat still to go, tractors take to the shale for last-minute curatorial repairs. With the scoreline at 46-41, the Eagles will only snatch a draw in the unlikely event that both Robins riders suffer mechanical difficulties (or fall). With the Blunsdon circuit suitably dressed, Clive Fisher celebrates the handiwork of the track staff, "The tractors have now departed from the circuit and the track is in tiptop condition." Clive Fisher then enthusiastically greets news of Matej Žagar's nomination for heat 15 as if he's discovered the fifth Beatle. He also uses what is to my ears a unique pronunciation, "Matej Jag-ar".

[Jeff] "What, Matej Jaggar?"

[Rob Bamford] "It is Yen-zay-ar to say it correctly. If you see Žagar written down correctly there's a diacritic over the Z."

[Jeff] "It's not Jaggar though, is it?"

[Rob] "No, but he was close."

[Jeff] "Sounds like he's struggling with his teeth."

Typifying his early-season form in an Eagles race tabard, Žagar finishes a comprehensive and disappointing last – possibly overwhelmed by Clive's various pronunciations ("It's Matej Zag-har"). Until the last bend Tomasz Jedrzejak looks likely to emerge victorious until, once again, Simon Stead executes another dramatic trademark high-speed cutback (where he feigns to go round the outside of his rival before he zooms down the inside to snatch victory). Like many other ecstatic Swindon fans in the crowd, Harold throws his arms in the air and, temporarily forgetting his hip problems, vaguely leaps upwards. Security man Neil Scott savours the spectacle, "Who says speedway is all about procession? Steady is superb this year – he should be in the England team. We have been getting some good racing here to be fair!" You can't gainsay that the Swindon promotion endeavour to provide an entertainment during a night of speedway at Blunsdon. The rider victory parade is a staple at pretty well every track (weather permitting) though, from that point on, the norm is for riders to leave the pits and stadium as though they wish to escape the scene of a hit-and-run accident because of a lack of insurance. They're so thorough in Wiltshire that Master of Ceremonies Clive Fisher interviews every rider (rather than just the odd one). Clive's got a unique line in closed questions that either presumes their answer or, in the case of

Swindon: *"I'd heard he was, then I heard he wasn't and Davey Watt was and then I heard he was again!"*

riders with poor English, really require no answer at all but still inform/entertain the crowd. Clive tells Leigh Adams, "What a great meeting!" Leigh's in full agreement, "Yeh, it was. … you know, towards the end, it just felt right to me … Steady did really well there. It was a great meeting – awesome crowd and great atmosphere!" Morten Risager gets a small walk on part in Clive's questioning master-class, "It was a classic to watch, was it a classic to ride in?" Apparently, it was! In response to the question, ("Cory, it just wasn't your night, was it?") the young Australian is bluntly honest "I was a bit tired. I got up but it was one of those meetings where you wished you hadn't bothered with it." During his interrogation, Mads Korneliussen is left nowhere to go so replies, "The track was superb." Employing his own version of positive psychology about what sounds like a momentously dangerous trip ahead, Clive looks ahead to the future on Mads's behalf, "Are you in a confident frame of mind to go to the Midlands on Monday?" Clive then "pays special tribute to Justin Sedgmen" who confirms the pleasurable experience of his 7-point haul at reserve from five rides ("I really enjoyed it"). Simon Stead deservedly receives the Man of the Meeting trophy award and soon has Clive's endorsement ringing in his ears, "It's what speedway is all about! It's what you live for!"

[Simon] "It is! I'm really, really, happy! The track staff all do a good job and it's great to race on."

On his way out to the emptying car park, youthful Robins press officer and programme editor Chris Seaward walks with Swindon incident reporter (as well as ex-Reading Racers and Oxford Cheetahs timekeeper) Roger Nettlefold. "As Roger says, 'Stead is carrying speed better than I've ever seen him.'"

[Roger] "He doesn't lock-up in every corner like he used to."

[Chris] "We had a slow start to the season but, now things have picked up, the belief has come into the side and I think we'll make the play-offs!"

Chris modestly bats off compliments about the quality of the Swindon programme and the depth of information he helps provide on the club website, "I chat to Ronnie Russell every week for the website and, in 15 minutes, you can have tons of material. He's great!" Wayne Russell also smiles about the quality of the racing served up tonight. "It looked dead early but turned into a great meeting and we got 3 points. They really livened up after the 7-2."

[Jeff] "Stead should be in the Great Britain team."

[Wayne] "I think he will be. He's riding really well here."

[Jeff] "He should be excluded for his incorrect Pantone coloured red helmet."

[{Wayne] "That's just pedantic that is!"

[Jeff] "It is!"

Some of the few remaining fans inside the stadium still have two unanswered questions: 'why didn't Eastbourne have two riders in heat 3?' and, more peculiarly, 'why did Žagar go on victory parade with the Robins?' [4]

8th July Swindon v. Eastbourne (Elite League) 50-43

[4] Due to injury, Eastbourne captain Cameron Woodward deputised as Matej Žagar's mechanic at Blunsdon. Afterwards he questions why some Eastbourne fans choose to jeer the Slovenian. "It was even more disappointing when the crowd came across to have a go at Matej. He was trying all night. We were chasing setups and he was really giving it everything. I don't know why the crowd are getting at him. I like Matej, I've only really known him this season but he is very professional. When he is disappointed he doesn't show it by throwing his helmet around or anything like that. Maybe fans think he doesn't care."

Swindon: *"I'd heard he was, then I heard he wasn't and Davey Watt was and then I heard he was again!"*

CHAPTER 8

Cardiff

"Michael Lee says on his DVD, 'The people who used to run the sport didn't want it to get too big!'"

10th July

Speedway publishing's equivalent of a solar eclipse takes place in an upstairs room at Cardiff Rugby Club clubhouse prior to the tenth staging of a Grand Prix in the Millennium Stadium. A perfect storm sees the (almost) simultaneous launch and publication of autobiographies by six-times World Champion Ivan Mauger (*The Will to Win*), one-time Speedway World Champion Michael Lee (*Back from the Brink*) and the soon-to-retire Leigh Adams – the most surprising rider of his generation not to become World Champion who's here with his evocatively titled *Leigh Adams: The Book*. All of these luminaries will release their personal stories into an unsuspecting world at the Cardiff Speedway Memorabilia Fayre annually organised by Nick Barber and his family. In view of the anticipated crowds that these book launches will provoke, Nick Barber places all their promotional stalls next to each other. Just prior to the official opening of the Fayre, the Ivan Mauger display table suddenly but mysteriously moves position to occupy significantly more space than originally allocated. Perhaps Nick chose the order of the tables based on world championship trophies? Whatever the criteria, Ivan is next to Michael Lee/*Backtrack* who are next to Leigh Adams who is by the stall that sells the Alan Wilkinson biography. Also on the window side of the room, albeit never having thrown their legs over a bike, there are also stalls for GRT Media stall – run by its owner, cameraman, film editor and marketer Bob Tasker (helped by his wife Suzi) – and hardy speedway fayre perennials ReRun Productions headed up by owner cameraman, film editor and marketer Steve Girdwood (ably assisted today by Jacqueline). My stall is opposite Ivan's and next to John Chaplin's who is here with his writing partner Norman Jacobs (who arrives late after a tyre blew out on the motorway to Cardiff) ably assisted by John's ex-rider son, Chris. They're here to promote the Tom

Ivan Mauger

71

Farndon book. Further along we're joined by Devon Shirts (replica tabards stall) and – all the way from Poland – Pawel Ruszkiewicz with a cornucopia of speedway memorabilia. There's also a comprehensive photographic display. Situated in pride of place at the head of the room – close to the entrance – are the various Barber stalls. At the opposite end of the room – though the space they'd booked and paid for is partly occupied by the Ivan Mauger team – are a friendly couple that sell a wide range of anoraks and other clothing conspicuous for not being Wulfsport.

Though apparently size isn't everything, like fishermen recalling the highlights of their career on the riverbank, talk inevitably soon turns to confidential commercial matters. I'm curious to learn how the exceptionally well-promoted Alan Wilkinson book has sold, especially since this is a charitable venture that sees its publisher remit all monies (after deductions for print/promotion costs) to the rider himself, Alan Wilkinson. "No it's not a rude question at all – 800 so far! We've given a substantial cheque over – I won't say how much – the book is stocked in Waterstones Manchester, Stockport and now, Bolton. There's lots of books out this year." Leigh Adams arrives with his son along with a display stand they together struggle to install. Alan's publisher Ian Corcoran nods over to the nearby Ivan Mauger stall where there's a pile of handsomely produced books (448 pages, 200 pictures with a 16-page colour section) sat ready for sale on a table covered with a trademark Ivan Mauger black-and-white chequered patterned tablecloth. "I counted 480 books there last night. He's used the same printer as us – I'd be interested to know what price he got. I reckon he'll do well! He's got another 600 in the van outside. Speedway fans are the sort of people who buy all the books so we should be fine!" Sadly this forecast would prove to be inaccurate since – in a time of economic recession – difficult choices have to be made by governments and speedway fans alike. Consequently those with sufficient budget to only purchase one copy were left with a difficult choice between Ivan, Michael and Leigh. Those sufficiently flush to purchase all three books would have little change from £60 so probably wouldn't have enough (discretionary) money left to lash out on DVDs, tabards, photographs, memorabilia or other books. GRT Media supremo Bob Tasker chats while he sets up his stall, "I've already interacted with Welsh people this morning and it's downhill from here!" There's an image of Lee Strudwick on screen as Bob cues up his demonstration DVD. My question, "Did I see a Lee Strudwick interview there?" gets an affirmative.

Twenty minutes prior to the official opening time the *Backtrack* display table collapses under the weight of unsold copies. Fellow stallholders rush to help, thankful that no one's crushed under their sheer weight. I thank my lucky stars that fastidiously professional Stoke promoter Dave Tattum isn't at the Fayre since I hate to think what his reaction would be to another publisher with defective display equipment. Also personing – as we say in modern politically correct parlance – the Ivan Mauger stall is his co-author Martin Rogers. He'll enthusiastically work the crowd around this stall all day with his energetic and outgoing wife Lin. Prior to the widely anticipated rush, Martin snatches a few words, "I'm choosing my words carefully – because you know how important that is – but I wish your breath of fresh air had arrived before when the sport was something different."
[Jeff] "You're working hard to make your book a success."
[Martin] "Thank you."
[Jeff] "I believe Ivan is going to 17 tracks pressing the flesh. What a joy for people!"
[Martin] "It should be fun and attract lots of attention."
[Jeff] "I go to every track every year."
[Martin] "He has a few more years on you!"

Ivan's appearance belies the fact that he's 70 years old. Given how much attention each Ivan track visit will inevitably and understandably create, his 17-gig book-signing tour is bound to be both exhilarating and tiring. The same can be said for the creation of the book itself – developed from an idea that had been in gestation for quite some time. Martin Rogers glosses over the considerable demands that the creation and production of any book involves ("it was an exciting journey"), let alone one so comprehensive or lavishly illustrated as Ivan's autobiography *Will to Win*. Obviously enough, you don't get to achieve excellence or become six-times World Champion without plenty of ability, effort, determination, exhaustive attention to detail (verging on the relentless) and general all-round professionalism. Best of breed isn't ever accidental. The traits that served Ivan so well on shale are nowadays applied with vigour elsewhere. Though still remarkably youthful himself, Martin lives Down Under but still fondly remembers his own full and varied speedway life as well as his British journalistic roots. "I started in sports journalism – in football and cricket – but it was only speedway that let me in. Everyone else keeps you on the periphery but, as you know, speedway is a special sport and community." That's so very true, "Yes, it's very welcoming. You can come as you are!"

Nick Barber interrupts all our conversations when he loudly advises "30 seconds!" I half expect him to shout, "Achtung! Achtung! Dive! Dive!" Instead without ceremony, downstairs the Fayre is officially declared open and, after some rumbles from the stairwell, the first eager arrivals burst through the Fayre doors at the far end of the room. Though he lacks the healing touch of Jesus, Ivan's presence provokes a "pick up thy bed and walk" mentality amongst the initial group of super keen old age pensioners keen to savour his unmediated presence. They rush, almost sprint, in order to claim their place in the quickly forming queue. Joyful cries of "Ivan! Ivan!" immediately ring out. With the comparative solitude of the room shattered, the Speedway Memorabilia Fayre is suddenly the mini equivalent of Bedlam. Substantial queues soon form at all three stalls that sell these newly released speedway rider autobiographies. So much so that it's not long before a long line stretches back down the room and, very effectively, blocks the GRT Media and ReRun Productions stalls from sight. Unfortunately for them, this, thereby, immediately severely restricts the likelihood of impulse purchases from those stalls. Thankfully my display isn't blocked but, if the room was an ocean and my table a boat, then my vessel remains completely becalmed. The only people who stop by my stall in the first hour either enquire if they can buy the Ivan Mauger book, or alternatively, stop for a chat. This is always welcome particularly when it's John Jarvis co-author (with Robert Bamford) of the justifiably acclaimed *Homes of British Speedway* reference work that's a must-have for any speedway fan's bookshelf. John has yet to miss a Newport meeting this season. Last night's encounter with the Weymouth Wildcats was no exception. "The meeting took a long time to run last night. Steve [Mallett] had put a ton of brick dust – not shale – down on the track and watered it so conditions were horrendous! It took an hour to run the first four races. Tim Webster went off to hospital with a suspected broken shoulder that's just deep bruising, apparently. He had a fall and exclusion. They had a big delay to scrape it all off again. It was this [gestures] thick [circa six inches]. Everyone's bike kept rearing. There was about 400 to 450 people there." Opposite us there's a three-deep gaggle of prospective book purchasers, "You're going to have a tough day against Ivan. Yours are the best-written books. I think [Brian] Burford ghosted the Leigh Adams book."

[Jeff] "Martin Rogers ghosted Ivan's and Tony McDonald's knocked Michael Lee's into shape though it had originally been written ages ago."

[John] "Tony McDonald used to edit the *Speedway Mail*. Do you think he'd like to buy some unsold copies? I have hundreds! [I suspect that Tony wouldn't like any more unsold inventory] They're putting new floodlights up at Newport."

[Jeff] "Do they have permission to run late?"

[John] "What, the lease you mean? It's owned by a London company – London and Scottish something. They wanted £85,000 per annum or something like that but Steve negotiated them

Cardiff: *"Michael Lee says on his DVD, 'The people who used to run the sport didn't want it to get too big!'"*

down to £60,000. They're running till the end of the year definitely! A dentist called Mole is backing them. I wonder if he's related [to Tony]?" John politely ignores my tried and tested dentist puns ("Well the Newport management and fans were down in the mouth but his support definitely fills a hole!"). "Perhaps everyone is called Mole who'd like an interest in Newport?"

Johnny Barber is happy to forecast likely book sales activity at the Fayre. "I reckon Ivan will sell 500, Leigh Adams should do well cos he's in the Fanzone and Michael Lee should also be very popular!" There's definitely a danger that Ivan will suffer repetitive strain injury from the sheer volume of signatures he'll be required to give in such a short space of time. However, like all success stories, these things don't happen by accident and require dedication as well as hard work. Martin Rogers and his wife Lin work tirelessly to attract possible purchasers or wavering ditherers by loudly letting people know that Ivan is here, the book is available and that he's happy to pose for photographs or dedicate copies to purchasers. Arguably of the right height to be a speedway rider himself, Martin holds a copy of the book aloft in the manner of a drama student perfecting their "I'm a teapot" mime. At Guantanamo Bay, the home of physical and psychological torture techniques, it's common practice to try and break the resolve of prisoners by making them stand with their arms outstretched for hours on end while they're bombarded with atonal, almost unlistenable to, music. Or, alternatively, they play tunes that offend the supposed religious sensibilities of the prisoners (thereby, ensuring Cliff Richard rarely gets on the playlist). Thankfully spared any awful music – later this will be inflicted upon luckless early arrivals inside the Millennium Stadium by SGP organisers BSI/IMG who this year spared at all costs by hiring Ruth Lorenzo and Miss Frank as their pre-meeting entertainment – Martin appears to have voluntarily co-opted himself to suffer some low-level torture by holding copies of the magnum opus he helped create at arm's length. Lin energetically works the line of prospective punters. She funnels them with production line efficiency towards the impressive pile of books adjacent to Ivan on the table repeatedly chanting in the manner of a Buddhist mantra, "Ivan Mauger book anyone?" When Lin occasionally tires of that phrase, she has an extensive repertoire of additional interrogative questions-cum-statements, "Would you like your photograph taken with Ivan?" "You can have your photograph taken with Ivan." "Ivan will sign your book." "You can have your photograph taken with Ivan." "If you'd like to buy a copy, Ivan will sign it." "Why don't you have your photograph taken with Ivan?" Lin has boundless, almost relentless, enthusiasm allied to the sunny demeanour of a synchronised swimmer (albeit without the nose plugs and cap) after they burst back to the surface following a particularly gymnastically complex underwater exercise.

One of the real joys of Cardiff – prior to the actual meeting itself – is the bonhomie and camaraderie of the speedway community as it gathers together drawn here from all parts of Britain as well as the farther flung outposts of the speedway world. A chance to catch up, renew acquaintances or shoot the breeze with similarly minded people whom you see regularly, frequently or intermittently always helps make the day. Wolverhampton club historian and compulsive results collector Mark Sawbridge arrives with his Poole Pirates supporting partner Sally Knight to soak up the pre-meeting atmosphere as well as hunt for bargains at the Fayre. Mark's quest for lost results continues apace, "I'm less than 200 away from having them all!" Jeff and Ann Dooley are on a well-earned break from their duties running the Sheffield trackshop but, though they're officially off duty, they're still sourcing merchandise to further distinguish their franchise. "We're going to buy some mini riders from Pawel. We'll spend £600 or £700. Last year the paint chipped and flaked off some of the riders when they knocked together but Nick [Barber] had a word and he's gone back to proper enamel paint again like the year before." Peterborough Panthers fans Graham and Hilary Rouse mingle with the wall of fans that still queue to buy the Mauger, Adams or Lee autobiographies. Hilary's reluctant to regale me with any more stories of Jason Crump's shopping exploits but is happy to offer advice to help improve the quality of my publishing output. "I'm not speaking to you! If you didn't use such big words in your books, you'd sell a lot more than you do!" Redcar fans couple Keith and Mandy Mason drop by. When I visit to South Tees Motorsports Park during my next northern tour for the King's Lynn Premier League meeting, they'll be away on a weekend in Anglesey. Keith hopes to ride over 200 miles on the motorcycle racetrack there. One of speedways most charming and photogenic couples, Barry and Alison Axtell, are here too and they proudly show off their beautiful baby daughter Nia Starr. Born on 17th August 2009, Nia's now almost 11 months and already a dyed-in-the-wool speedway baby. She shares her parents' good looks. Nia is also a calm and contented baby. Alison proudly tells me, "My beautiful baby only cries when hungry." No Cardiff GP would be complete without the Brown family from Sheffield, who've kindly read and supported my books from the outset. They stop by my table and – as is traditional – Philip (Mr Brown junior) kindly offers some nuanced corrections of misapprehensions I apparently hold about various matters to do with the world of speedway (particularly anything to do with the Grand Prix Series or BSI). Paul (Mr Brown senior) welcomes the arrival of Tony Olsson who's taken over curatorial and organisational duties this season from Ole Olsen "All the meetings have run quicker! Tonight will be the best because all previous Cardiffs have overrun!" [1] It's safe to say that Mrs Brown isn't a Nicki Pedersen fan. "What goes around comes around."

[Paul Brown] "Well that's what his compatriot Hans says!"

[Mrs Brown] "He used to knock everyone off and they got excluded! When he got knocked off, they got excluded! He was just lucky and now he has lots of bad luck and I'm pleased."

There are still many 'veteran' riders competing in the Grand Prix Series. Paul Brown gives some insight into Greg Hancock's probable tactics, "Greg has been protecting his shoulder ever since he injured it at Cradley. If he doesn't gate and find himself in the lead, he's more careful. We all hope Gollob wins." My theory that Jason Crump's transformation from Jason Grump to the more amenable character he now cuts on and off the track nowadays might have some direct connection to the financial incentives contained in the small print of his Red Bull contract are dismissed as balderdash by Mr Brown senior, "Jason was getting nicer ever since he won his first GP and nothing to do with the Red Bull contract!" Mr Brown junior is equally adamant, "That's irrelevant!"

After two hours, I've sold three copies. John Chaplin offers some tangential but possibly relevant sales advice, "Peter Lipscombe used to say 'If you can get it in their hands in the first 30 seconds they buy it!' [pause] then, what we were selling did cost £2!" After they've patiently queued up at the tables opposite, most fans gleefully blow the ink dry on Ivan Mauger's book or stash away the memorabilia they specifically brought along today for him to sign. According to a passing fan, apparently there might be some interesting insight buried in the Michael Lee book provided Tony McDonald decides to lift some juicy quotes from the director's cut version of the Michael Lee DVD. "Michael Lee says on his DVD, 'The people who used to run the sport didn't want it to get too big!'"

[2] 11.45 Meet the Grid Girls
12.00 Barry Briggs interview on the stage
12.30 Titan first show
12.30 Steve Johnston interview on the stage
13.00 – 14.00 Meet the Sky Sports team
Meet the presenters of speedway on Sky including Charlie Webster, Nigel Pearson, Kelvin Tatum, Sam Ermolenko and MOLEY!!!
13.30 Titan second show
14.00 Wonderbrass
14.30 Leigh Adams interview on the stage
15.00-15.15 Autograph session Chris Harris, Scott Nicholls, Tai Woffinden and Jason Crump
15.15-15.30 Fanzone closes Wonderbrass

Cardiff: "*Michael Lee says on his DVD, 'The people who used to run the sport didn't want it to get too big!'*"

When I compliment Martin on his resistance during the Guantanamo Bay inspired endurance exercise – against the soundtrack of his wife Lin endlessly enquiring, "Is anyone waiting?" – Martin's insouciant about both his strength and the incredible sales already achieved, "Three hours is nothing! This is nothing, come see me after six. It's going well!" As I wander back to my stall I hear Martin announce in a loud voice, "For anyone over 21 – Ivan's book!" Given the contents of the book have been extensively trailed, profiled and valorised in the pages of the *Speedway Star* I'm already well aware of much of the contents including the exciting innovation of Raye Mauger's own chapter and the lavish colour photographs that adorn the text. However, the pornography section that Martin's now so suddenly keen to advertise hadn't previously caught my attention. Lin Rogers eschews any unnecessary hint of salaciousness and, instead, enquires of persons unknown, "Is there anyone to see Ivan here? If you're not, don't worry!" The Rogers are so professional in their sales technique that any visual clue they spot is instantly seized upon and effortlessly integrated into their sales patter in order to try to sell yet another copy of the book. When a man in an Eastbourne Eagles replica team shirt dithers near their stall, Martin chimes, "Former Eastbourne rider Ivan Mauger." Martin has a simple sales philosophy, "You got to get the message across and keep repeating it! That's the way to sell a book or [pause] speedway! There's no magic to it, it's mostly perspiration!" Over on the ReRun stall Steve Girdwood looks on admiringly as a flood of cash rains down upon the Mauger stall, "It's like a printing press!" Steve's struggled to achieve his usual sales volumes, "You can't make people spend what they don't have!" Shortly afterwards, I realise I've obviously failed to make an impression on Lin Rogers since she asks, "Would you like to buy a copy?" I wouldn't.

A few streets away from the Millennium Stadium, Grand Prix organisers BSI/IMG have an agreement with Cardiff City Council to close off a street before the event so that it can be occupied by something they designate as "Fanzone". There's a "full schedule of events" from 11.00 until 3.30. Though it probably wouldn't be so attractive on a rainy day, the warm weather and bright sunshine attracts a large number of fans along to enjoy the inaugural schedule. [2]

Apart from sundry speedway riders and personalities, it's arguable that both 'Moley' and Titan the Robot from Channel 4's *Big Brother* might be slightly less wooden than Kelvin. Sensibly, or strangely, dependent upon your point of view, the organisers want to ensure only SGP official merchandise is sold there. It is also possible to apply for permission to give stuff away for free. That said, they give Leigh Adams special dispensation to sell his book (not a surprise given his contribution to the Speedway Grand Prix series). Barry Briggs's charitable fundraising venture also enables him to promote and sell his book. Ivan Mauger and Michael Lee are both precluded from a book sales presence in the Fanzone. Though I can't go myself, I'm told that ex-SGP supremo John Postlethwaite's new clothing empire – grandiosely titled Dig Deep also aren't able to display their merchandise. [3] This is probably fortunate given any casual understanding of the speedway demographic immediately indicates that Fanzone wouldn't be overrun with young men with chest size measurements in the range of 26-32 inches. Johnny Barber tells me that their garments are also a little pricey, "unfortunately the banks weren't open so no one can remortgage their house to buy one!"

Back at the Speedway Fayre, Eastbourne fan and *Daily Telegraph* sports reporter Ben Findon, soaks up the atmosphere but also keep out half an eye in case he can satisfy his own particular

[3] Dig Deep is a brand new sports-inspired line for (scrawny) men and speedway fans. "We support sport from the bottom to the very top, and we're supporting athletes who understand what it really means to really dig deep for the extra 10 per cent that makes all the difference …" is the verging on laughable copy that adorns many of the fatuous full-page adverts they regularly place in the *Speedway Star*. For reasons unknown, these adverts also include a rear view photograph of a Formula 2 racing car as well as some sample designs cleverly presented to look like they've been cobbled together by reluctant teenagers in the last half hour of art-class detention.

Cardiff: *"Michael Lee says on his DVD, 'The people who used to run the sport didn't want it to get too big!'"*

speedway memorabilia proclivity (for pre-war programmes). Ben looks admiringly towards the substantial queue of interested punters that still surround Ivan Mauger's stall. "Ivan is my real childhood sporting hero – a lot of people didn't like him. It was anyone but Ivan (ABI) then; nowadays, everyone says they loved him. I always did!" I'm not sure that is quite the case since, shortly afterwards, I'm told by someone on condition of anonymity, "Steve Brandon said when Tony Rickardsson was going for his sixth world championship that he hoped he won – not cos he liked Tony Rickardsson but only so it would stop Ivan Mauger flipping going on about being the only six-times World Champion!"

Though it's unlikely that charitable fundraising efforts ever manage the five-figure revenues each autobiography launched at Cardiff reputedly generated, nonetheless Oxford speedway fan Rob Peasley works tirelessly on behalf of speedway for purely altruistic reasons. Last night, once again, Rob went to the Premier League Pairs at Somerset to try to raise money for the Speedway Riders' Benevolent Fund – this time (rather unbelievably) dressed as the Ben Fund logo! "It's designed by some kid. I'm quite tall and, with the head on, I'm about seven foot. Loads of people want their photos taken with you! I even went on the parade truck last night with the Super7even girls – so there is a perk to the job! Some kids are scared of me, though. One boy at Lakeside was really frightened. I reckon it's those that watch *Doctor Who*. People kept asking last night if I was okay in the suit and I said I was. I thought I was until I took it off and I was soaked. I reckon I lost about half a stone. While I was sat in the pits with my head off a bloke wanted a photo because his son is frightened of mascots and he wanted one with my head on and another with my head off so he could see I was real and human!" Rob definitely is real and human but so are the speedway riders who, since they share our fallibility and fragility, sometimes sadly need to call upon the Speedway Riders' Benevolent Fund when career injuries cause difficulty in their post-speedway lives.

With the Cardiff Grand Prix nowadays scheduled to start at the so-called more "fan-friendly" time of 5 p.m., the Fayre empties much earlier than it used to do. Amongst the lesser performing stallholders, there's an undercurrent of dissatisfaction that their afternoon hasn't quite gone as they'd anticipated. Organiser Nick Barber also isn't on top of the world. "This isn't going to happen again! Some have come in and just monstered it cos they won't be here again. Kylie Adams was lovely – she couldn't be nicer – but others haven't even paid! I reckon Ivan sold, at least, 600; Leigh 600 (400 of them here) and Michael Lee 400 odd, I reckon. Then Leigh did have the Fanzone. Bob Tasker and Steve Girdwood aren't happy cos they had people queuing in front of their tables all day. It's something we're going to have to look at in future so we can properly look after our loyal stallholders." Though he's too polite to say, today's skewed allocation of disposable income at the fayre has some parallels with the annual impact of the BSI/IMG organised Cardiff Speedway Grand Prix upon the fragile financial ecosystem of the British speedway community. For some fans, Cardiff is the highlight of their speedway calendar and, consequently, they budget to splurge out on the day. Ludicrously overpriced tickets (a.k.a. market forces) thereby drain revenues away from the regular British speedway world for a month or so after the event. This would be fine if BSI/IMG actively support or help rider development within British speedway. Sadly, they don't. Nor do they directly help any club. They do continue to siphon substantial revenues back to their mother ship, partly to help fund the lifestyles their smartly dressed cadre of executives deserve. This is understandable, of course, since they're a commercial organisation with no duty of care or any real responsibility toward the sport that they've vaguely helped 'popularise' but now feed parasitically upon.

10th July Cardiff Speedway Fayre

Cardiff: *"Michael Lee says on his DVD, 'The people who used to run the sport didn't want it to get too big!'"*

CHAPTER 9

Redcar
"Chris Mills won't be on Tomáš Suchánek's Christmas card list"

15th July

Any Reading Racers fan on a visit the South Tees Motorsports Park can't help but have a twinge of nostalgia about the loss of Smallmead. Like the '70s version of the Berkshire track, the STMP is located in an industrial estate that mixes the newly built with the dilapidated. The car park is similarly rough-hewn (albeit bigger) while the track itself also sits proudly upon reclaimed land (a former steelworks in Redcar's case and in Berkshire a rubbish tip). The stadium infrastructure at Smallmead looked better from day one but, under various management teams, the buildings and facilities in use at the STMP improve with every passing year (and each time I visit) within sensible budgetary constraints. Those in charge of these developments have fashioned a club fans and locals alike can be proud of. It's St Swithin's Day and rain is forecast. However, incredibly strong winds ensure low clouds move past at such a pace that it's unlikely that the dark ones will manage to linger. Lit by bright sunshine and with a bowser driven by track curator Tony Swales slowly circuiting the shale, it's impossible to resist taking some photographs. They say that a man who tires of Middlesbrough is tired of life. I'm unable to contemplate my relative exhaustion or boredom levels because, almost immediately, a car pulls up alongside to find out why exactly I'm using my camera. The driver is Redcar speedway co-promoter Brian Havelock who, despite his 69 years, clearly still has excellent vision (though he confesses to having to wear glasses to read). Though we've met before, I have to jog Brian's memory. "When I saw you taking photos I thought, 'God, it's the council!' You got a mention on *Radio Tees* last night."
[Jeff] "Did I?"
[Brian] "Yes, I mentioned you! Dunno where to suggest you go. It's very windy. Why not go by the programme hut then you can operate out of the boot of your car. I can't stop I've got to go and do my [SCB] paperwork!"

With permission to roam, a trip to the centre green is difficult to overlook. Tony Swales continues to go round and round with the bowser. The strong wind hampers his work spraying the water far and wide. Through from the terraces you know that the STMP track is banked until you walk down from the pits gate to the centre green it's hard to properly appreciate how steep the incline of bends three and four really are. Typically, no sooner is the bowser empty than spits of drizzle supplement Tony's handiwork.

With nearly four hours before tapes up, the pits are deserted except for a foreign mechanic and his wife who build up a speedway bike in the home section of the pits close by to a nameplate that says "Stuart". They've parked another ready-to-race speedway bike nearby. From the letters JUUL on its saddle, it takes little deduction to deduce it must belong to the Redcar Bears newly recruited 19-year-old Danish rider Peter Juul Larsen. Peter rode last season for Glasgow in the Premier League. He presently rides for Esjberg in Denmark and arrives as a straight replacement for the injured (with a damaged knee) Stuart Swales. Thinking about it, I suspect Peter's hardworking mechanics are, in fact his, parents. They've too much work to stop and chat but both

78

smile warmly. Peter's dad adopts a serious expression to tell me, "It was dirty – now clean!" They both need no second invitation to eschew chitchat in favour of the task at hand with the chain and back wheel. [1]

For tonight's meeting against the King's Lynn Stars, Bears media-relations/programme editor Gareth Rogers arrives early. With few people to chat to on a windy afternoon, Gareth sensibly relaxes in the front seat of a Toyota that was previously loved by Dave Rattenberry. No sooner am I sat in the passenger seat than Brian Havelock's car pulls alongside. Gareth winds down his window to listen to Brian call across, "It's Peter YULE not Larsen! That's how he wants to be known when you announce him [pause] and in the programme." Invariably a meticulous researcher, this is precisely the sort of information that Gareth needs to hear only once. With bags of experience, Gareth enjoys numerous connections within the speedway world. "I've been speaking to Andy [Hewlett] about Bristol and that's going slower than he'd like. So much so that 2011 looks unlikely now! The council are supportive but they know somebody will complain because, they say, someone always does! So they allow for it." Unofficially Gareth offers the speedway equivalent of a speed dating service, albeit that the parties involved are usually speedway promoters, landowners and council officials. In light of the administrative hurdles that any new speedway track needs to overcome, perhaps Gareth's service should really be characterised as slow dating, given the glacial speed to consummation. "I've introduced two tracks now so I know all about that [objections]. Andy says all the delays have made him more determined not less! The objections can be quite strange! At the Isle of Wight, it was the bark coming off the trees! At Somerset, it was that it would cause asthma and, at Bristol, [according to Natural England] it's disturbing the birds flying up the Bristol Channel. Silly when you think they have wind turbines there anyway. In fact, people objected to the wind turbines saying they'd disrupt the birds!"

[Jeff] "Well it's been shown that wind turbines kill them."

[Gareth] "True they do but the birds have already been disrupted by the wind turbines and adapted."

[Jeff] "Maybe they're noise sensitive."

[Gareth] "Here it was a snail. Stupid when they've had motor sports at this location for over 20 years! I said,

Bowser

Victory Parade

[1] During the close, Brian Havelock commented on Peter's signing in the annual Redcar end-of-year review that appears in the pages of the *Speedway Star*. "Peter was another who approached me and I had nothing much to lose at that stage. He came with good equipment and good back-up and I was generally pleased with what he did". During the 2010 season, in ten meetings Peter scored 60 points for the Bears to finish with a 5.45 average.

Redcar: *"Chris Mills won't be on Tomáš Suchánek's Christmas card list"*

'They've had 24-hour events so surely the snails have adapted by now?' Some people just don't want speedway and will find any reason to stop it."

Despite many years involvement in speedway, Gareth still retains his love of the sport. He tries to get to meetings whenever his other commitments allow. "I went to the Wolverhampton versus Eastbourne meeting to see Trevor [Geer] and Deano [Dean Barker] and, I must say, the approach of Matej Zagar was most peculiar. He declined to race in heat 15 but you could see from the look on Trevor's face that he didn't know quite what to say to him. Barney Kennett – who used to be team manager at Eastbourne, when I was there – used to shout at all the riders when they came back if he thought they could have done better! If they were third when they could have been second he'd really bollock them. Still, they were young with David [Norris] and the Standing brothers."

Vastly experienced in media relations, Gareth tips me the wink that my sincere praise of the pies they provide here for (lucky) corporate sponsors – produced by A.P. Jackson's Butchers (10 High Street, Ruswarp, Whitby) – has been hijacked. Or, rather, taken out of context by the refreshment kiosk that also operates in the same building. While it's true that I praised Jackson's Butchers pies ("the best pies in speedway"), this definitely doesn't hold true for any pie and peas I've yet to taste. Apparently, I'll be disappointed when I do. Many years within speedway has given Gareth an iron constitution – probably similar to that gained during National Service, when it existed. His taste buds are so immune – due to the heinous assault on the senses that often comes as standard with speedway stadium catering – that the visual image of his tongue that springs to my mind is the proverbial rivet catcher's mitt. Though Gareth will eat anything, his brother Laurence is fussy ("Laurence never eats stadium food, but I don't mind!"). On the subject of good nosh, en route to the STMP, I treat myself to a late lunch at the wonderful McCoys restaurant at the Cleveland Tontine (near Stokesley). Last season staff at the 'Customer Information Centre' at Middlesbrough bus station hadn't heard of the Redcar Bears, yet the girl on reception at McCoys based 20 miles away envies me my trip to the South Tees Motorsports Park. "I haven't been to the new track but I used to go all the time to see them. I'm distantly related to the Swales so we had to go to the speedway! The things I most remember are the chocolate chip King Cones and the very loud music – lots of Queen songs, as I remember. I've just had my hours changed so I hope I can go along on a Thursday night to watch them now!"

Inside the Redcar clubhouse, the catering and bar staff prepare for the night ahead. In the adjacent trackshop, Dave Rattenberry and Bill Gimbeth finish laying out their merchandise. Award-winning columnist from the *Northern Echo*, Mike Amos, will tonight make his first visit to see the Redcar Bears at the STMP. Not only is Mike a legendary sports writer but he's also intimately involved at the grassroots level of football (Dave Rattenberry's real metier). Mike is Chairman of the Northern League and also entirely produces the monthly Northern League magazine (*Northern Ventures Northern Gains*). Since I know Dave is a football ground hopper, I'm suddenly keen to establish exactly how many grounds he's been to. The answer is 3,268 grounds! When I jokingly ask, "What? Approximately?" missing the 'humour' Dave replies, "No, that's dead on!" If Mr Rattenberry has a football obsession, then Mr Gimbeth has a speedway one. So much so that this winter – along with Selwyn Webb and John Rich – he's going to the far-flung speedway frontier of Argentina during January and February (2011) to see the Argentinian National Championships (though the fixture list was unavailable when they booked). Should he remain free of injury, the result is a foregone conclusion: Redcar Bears No. 4, Emiliano Sanchez, should – by all accounts – emerge triumphant. Then presumption is often the mother of all cock-ups. I suspect that Selwyn, John and Bill don't speak Spanish so this will add a further fun element to the complicated travel logistics they expect on their trip. Bill bats off my anxieties about language difficulties but, as a

Redcar: *"Chris Mills won't be on Tomáš Suchánek's Christmas card list"*

keen programme collector, he's already positively scandalised that the Argentinians don't see fit to produce a programme at any of the many venues where they stage these championships! When I wonder if they'll provide first-hand reports on the championships for the *Speedway Star*, Rat peremptorily dismisses the very suggestion with derision, "They couldn't write! They couldn't string two words together those three!"

Bears announcer Keith McGhie, also arrives early at the stadium to research and prepare for the night ahead as well as to check that all the equipment he'll use still works. Away from speedway, Keith takes a keen interest in Rugby League. During the recent close season, he was part of a five-man journalists' squad that attempted to row a marathon (26.2 miles or 42,195 metres) in four hours to raise money for Try Assist (the Rugby League Benevolent Fund). Held at Leeds Metropolitan University, the Carnegie Rowing Challenge is a stern test of endurance, physical strength and stamina but, obviously, pales in comparison to the amazing spirit and resilient approach to life taken by the many ex-Rugby League players who unluckily suffer life-changing injuries. Though I'm one of his sponsors, Keith can't tell me the time his team achieved (the record is an incredible 2 hours 15 minutes and 51 seconds). He's pleased he took part. "We raised about £15,000 in total! Not just us. It's funny but rugby and speedway attract the same kind of serious neck and back injuries!"

Hull speedway fan Janet and her husband Stan also arrive way ahead of the start time. "We used to be Vikings fans but they shut our track. We come here or go to Sheffield – it annoys me a bit there because they soup-up the bikes."
[Jeff] "It is a fast track."
[Janet] "Yes but Ricky Ashworth will have an advantage when they race the [PLRC] there. Do you know all the speedway managers? We had Dave Younghusband visit us two weeks ago. We like to see all the riders who are in wheelchairs. We went to see Garry Stead when he was first in hospital. Both hospitals. He looks really well now – he's courting!" Janet would buy one of my books but doesn't ("I've left my purse in the car"). Keith McGhie distracts us with an important announcement, "If anyone is in the stadium, well you are obviously, who walked past the grandstand? I've just picked up a nice blue pen with black ink – a very nice one with a rubber grip!" Moments later Keith corrects himself, "In actual fact, it's just been pointed out to me that it's not a pen but a propelling pencil!"

Dave Rattenberry's out of the trackshop for a brief constitutional walk rather than his usual trip to the burger van. He introduces me to the two ladies – Janice Jackson and Claire James – who work in the Redcar Bears programme booth adjacent to the turnstiles. Dave's incredulity is always quickly stirred when it comes to money matters, "Believe it or not, they had a do for Maks Gregoric and Tomáš Suchánek that made £850!" Janice confirms Dave's story, "We raised £850 from 50 people on May 11th at the Priory Social Club, Middlesbrough where we also held one pre-season for Stuart Swales and raised £455." When not behind the glass windows of the programme booth, Claire and Janice drive the Redcar Bears Speedway Consortium on all their various travels to speedway tracks round the country. Claire tells me proudly, "We've done 6,000 miles since June – Janice who's the navigator comes with me and my goddaughter, Hannah Charville, who's 14. We take the Consortium on all their travels." When I ask who exactly the exotic sounding "Consortium" are I'm told, "Eric and Brian Havelock." I'm not sure that I've met Eric. Dave Rat helpfully tells me, "He's the little one!" I ask the ladies where their favourite track is.
[Claire] "This one!"
[Janice] "We gotta say that."
[Claire] "Course we do."

They also travel internationally to watch their speedway and, so far this year, have also visited the

Grands Prix in Prague and Cardiff.

In the building close by to my display, Steve Harland and his wife Jan ready the corporate hospitality area prior to the arrival of sponsors and would-be sponsors at tonight's meeting against King's Lynn. Away from the track Steve is a community protection officer (and ex-editor of Darlington Football Club's Fanzine). [2] My latest book *Shale Trek* erroneously claims that Steve's community protection beat covers Middlesbrough whereas he's keen to stress that he only "covers Guisborough and East Cleveland." Though Steve works tirelessly on behalf of the club, things might change in future. "The hours of my job are changing – I've notified the club – so I'm having to think about what I'm doing. If you have hassle at work, you don't want to have any at the speedway. Brian knows me as community and protection officer so, obviously, he can trust me to pass the [sponsorship] money over!" Steve's status as the most smartly dressed man at Redcar speedway tonight immediately disappears when the *Northern Echo's* ace report Mike Amos MBE arrives smartly dressed (probably straight from the office) in jacket, collared shirt and tie. Despite the substantial time commitment that his duties as Chairman of the Northern League and as the dynamo behind *Northern Ventures Northern Gains* requires, Mike's also a prolific and elegantly witty writer for the *Northern Echo*. "I'm up at half-five every day. I produce six fact-based multifaceted columns every week. 'Gadfly' and 'John North – 2,000 words a time – 'Backtrack' (two of these on sporting memories), 'At Your Service' which takes me to a different church every week and 'Eating Owt' which is a smart-arsed Geordie column."

Given Mike's prolifically prodigious output, it's an honour he's found the time in his schedule to come along and savour a night at the South Tees Motorsports Park. Home performances by the Bears at home so far this season as well as last week's heavy home defeat against Berwick make it highly unlikely that Bears will best the silverware chasing King's Lynn Stars tonight. In fact, since the return of Redcar to Premier League speedway five years ago, they have yet to defeat King's Lynn home or away. Steve Harland jovially suggests that Mike Amos might be the lucky charm Redcar needs to transform their fortunes. Mike has an easy manner with people, so much so that I suspect they'll often say more than they intend or, afterwards, would subsequently wish. Like all old-school reporters, Mike has excellent shorthand and tactical discreteness. Nevertheless, in his columns he's unafraid to venture honest, plainly written (albeit witty) opinions. Frankness and honesty doesn't always win plaudits and so it proves with Mike's recent review of the Fox & Pheasant gastro pub at the Gates shopping centre in Durham. [3] The owner of the Fox & Pheasant is so upset with Mike's review that he rings up to ban him from the establishment with the

---

[2] "The Darlington fanzine was called *Mission Impossible – An Alternative View of Darlington FC* and ran for ten years between 1989 to 1999 and produced 72 issues. It was likened at the time to be a cross between *Private Eye* and *Viz* – hence the reason we received so many solicitors' letters! At its peak it was selling 1,100 on average gates of 2,500/3,000, which in hindsight is phenomenal. I stopped going the season former safecracker and ex-convict George Reynolds took over. I was one of the few who wasn't sold on his dream of having a new stadium hosting top-flight football. They got the new stadium – all 27,500 seats on average crowds of less than 3,000 – absolute madness. They've also got non-league football again. I've been twice this season against Newport County and Barrow and no, I won't be going to Wembley to see them play Mansfield as I will be down south watching the Bears at Plymouth and Leicester. It wouldn't feel right going down to support them but as a former shareholder I wish them well – they seem to have a chairman and manager who actually care, after two decades of abuse."

[3] Spelling mistakes on the chalk board outside – "It says 'Mediterranean' on one side of the board and 'Mediterranian' on the other" – immediately alert Mike to potential problems ahead. Mike's equally suspicious of claims to offer "fusion" food: "The word fusion presumably means that sausage and chips and a few basic pasta dishes share the same menu and the only thing stunning about the bar would be if someone banged his head on one of the ghastly chandeliers. It's not a popular place compared to the Café Rouge over the way and their beer selection isn't exactly extensive." Mike's keen insight something positive "the beer – let's be fair – was so drinkable that I asked for another". Though the arrival of Mike and his companion significantly boost the atmosphere of the Fox & Pheasant, it's still dire ("It was like having a picnic in a funeral parlour"). Grasping at straws, Mike continues, "The menu's commendably inexpensive." The Fox & Pheasant's press release made great play of the quality of the cuisine they serve. Sadly, the experience fell short of Mike's measured expectations. "The fish and chips came with sort of mushy peas which on another day might double as putty. There was no Spam on the menu. The dessert selection was varied but wasn't extensive". Mike took no consolation in the ready availability of waffles, baked American cheesecake and chocolate cake. On Mike's visit they also didn't take credit cards nor could they provide printed receipts.

Redcar: *"Chris Mills won't be on Tomáš Suchánek's Christmas card list"*

lligerent news, I don't want to see you in here again!" Mike shrugs philosophically, "I wouldn't like to go more than once."

Mike's modestly self-effacing about the quality of his work. He knows more people than many have forgotten but, despite his best efforts to disguise it, understandably Mike takes artisanal pride in his writing. Like all true craftsmen, he's served an extensive apprenticeship. "Backtrack is 25 years old on November 2nd and I will have been with this firm 45 years this August 30th. Well, they're the same firm but they've changed names. It used to be the *Northern Despatch* and it's been the *Echo* since 1978." Mike's a careful questioner and when I reveal that Frank Keating was the first national journalist to (excessively) praise my writing, he confesses: "The first time I won National Regional Sports Writer of the Year – Keating was a judge, so I like him!" Later on when I press Mike for more details about his sports writing awards, he remains extremely reluctant to blow his own trumpet, even when pressed for specifics and dates. Eventually he tells me, "If we're boasting, which I'm not, I've won the National Sports Writer of the Year Award three times. The last was in 2007 and the other two were in the '90s. I can't remember the dates. I've been North East Journalist of the Year seven times in the last 20 years so, you could say, I'm the Gary Havelock of North East Journalism!"

Though Mike is a first-time visitor to the STMP, it's astonishing how many people stop and speak to him! He's equally surprised, "It's amazing how many Northern League football fans follow speedway!" One of the people Mike also knows at the stadium is Sunderland-based *Northern Echo* photographer Dave Cook. Laden with photographic equipment, Dave confers briefly with Mike about his photographic requirements and exactly who or what Mike expects to see captured on film. After Dave completes the insurance coverage formalities (by signing-in with the friendly ladies in the office below the referee's box overlooking the start line) we make our way down to the pits. For safety reasons, Brian Havelock insists we immediately return to the catering and hospitality unit to pick up hi-visibility jackets from his wife in the Speedway Office there. Brian's happy for Dave to take photographs throughout the stadium albeit with one caveat about the centre green, "You can go out there after the parade".

The meet and greet over, Brian wanders away preoccupied with all the last-minute preparations that assail anyone with speedway management responsibilities 20 minutes or so before the tapes rise. On our way to collect the hi-visibility clothing I suggest that not initially being on the centre green should be okay. Dave's not so sure, "Tomorrow Mike will probably ask 'did you get the parade?' and it'll be the only thing I haven't!" Dave's a youthful looking 35 who earned his photography spurs at the *Northern Echo* after study at Sunderland College (A level), Newcastle College (HND) and Sunderland University (degree). I wonder what makes a good photographer? "Patience, good interpersonal skills, technical understanding (photographically), an eye for a good picture and a hunger to get it! Also a good sense of humour doesn't go amiss." Photography isn't all weddings, funerals, fetes and sports events. "When I first started I was asked by a town paper editor to got out and photograph dog poo after the paper started a campaign to crack down on dog litter in a number of the towns parks. My fellow snappers gave me the nickname of The Shit Photographer' ... it didn't stick. Another news editor asked me to get a photograph of a local farmer who had had a number of their rare sheep mauled to death. I was told to get a picture of the farmer with the sheep (all the dead ones had been taken away). Only problem being it was pitch black at night, in a field, in the middle of nowhere, the sheep were all over the place and they were black sheep and my flash was knackered! A challenge but I got a picture. I used a number of torches and a set of car headlights. ARTY! I haven't taken my best photo yet. There are a few of my wife and son that I've taken that mean a lot to me but as for my best photo professionally? I've taken loads that other people think are great and a few that I've had shortlisted

83

for awards but there are only a few that I think might be half decent. I think it's just me but I always seem to look at one of my pictures and go over it with a fine toothcomb. You name it, I'd probably pick fault at it! I'm lucky because having a job that is your hobby is really great. Photography has changed A LOT since I started as a press photographer. As a photographer you are always learning new techniques, styles and changes in technology. I have a list of things I want to achieve professionally, but there are too many things to list, needless to say they all include me taking pictures and/or video. As to what or who I'd really like to photograph – anything, everything and anyone but not necessarily in that order!" Working at the STMP is another small step (albeit to speedway fans a milestone) in what promises to be a long, varied and successful career.

There are two hi-visibility jackets in the Speedway Office, albeit one is more of a sleeveless vest. Mrs Havelock insists I take both for our esteemed press visitors from the *Northern Echo*. With this additional layer of reflective clothing, Mike's smart office clothes fit much more into the trainspotter chic of the speedway world's logoed anoraks and hoodies. With a strong wind, he'll be fractionally warmer though, as a native of Shildon, I don't expect he feels the cold. Keen to stress to Mike how far the club has come since they opened the turnstiles at the STMP, I wave my hand proprietarily at the stadium infrastructure and say, "When they started it five years ago, it was just a track and the pits but they've gradually invested in further infrastructure." With a faint echo of Monty Python's Yorkshiremen, Mike notes, "I'm used to the Northern League and, by their standards, this is palatial!" Mike's amiable and engaging company with a notebook to hand that he fills with intense staccato bursts of shorthand. He's happy to listen but also to prompt conversation with apparently casual (but perceptive) interrogative questions, "How do you justify the claim that speedway is the most popular summer sport? Compared to say, cricket?"
[Jeff] "Well, you could estimate numbers at 50,000 per week in a season that runs from mid-March till the end of October. Last week, according to the organisers, the Cardiff Grand Prix allegedly had 44,150 people there."
[Mike] "Oh!"

Mike's picked a fortuitous evening to come along to watch his only speedway of the 2010 season since some of the great and the good of the community are on hand in the pits. Wolverhampton supremo and Redcar Bears co-promoter Chris Van Straaten (along with his son Karl) stands close to pit lane. It's the ideal vantage point to study the race action and pits activity. After the second race finishes in a 5-1 for the Bears (with a paid win for Peter Juul in his first British speedway ride for Redcar), Chris kindly finds the time to share his thoughts on British speedway with Mike Amos. If conversations were tennis, then I start the evening with an unexpected foot-fault with my mistaken claim that Mike hasn't been to a speedway meeting before. He quickly disabuses Chris Van Straaten of my misapprehension, "It's not my first time at speedway, it's my first time at Redcar!"

With the hubbub in the pits and the action about to start on the track, I retire a modest firework safety distance away to allow Chris and Mike's conversation to wander where it will. They chat for some time. Mike takes copious shorthand notes while talking and attacking the page of his notepad like a bird pecking in the snow for worms. Out on the track the third race of the night – sponsored by Keith and Mandy Mason of Norton-on-Tees (who are away in Anglesey) – Casper Wortmann is the second King's Lynn Stars rider to win a race though Charles Wright and Emiliano Sanchez ensure the heat is drawn to retain the Bears 2-point advantage at 10-8. Prior to the meeting, few pundits – including myself – hold out little hope of a Bears win. Our pessimism appears justified when King's Lynn fire in successive heat maximums with wins for Tomáš Topinka – belying talk on the Internet forums that since his return from injury he's lost his nerve – and, for the second time in five heats, Joe Haines. My curiosity about the content and nature of the

Redcar: *"Chris Mills won't be on Tomáš Suchánek's Christmas card list"*

ongoing in-depth conversation enjoyed by Mike and Chris eventually gets the better of me. Though softly spoken and understated, Chris Van Straaten speaks articulately with both insight and passion. When quizzed about what use Sky Sports coverage is for British speedway, he's matter of fact, "Cos of the Sky coverage everyone has heard of speedway nowadays. Sponsors are putting money into speedway and more people are watching it on the telly. Converting them from the couch to get them to come on a regular basis is hard! For a Bank Holiday we've got 50% more of a crowd at Wolves than usual. They're not our regulars. People always used to say things like 'I remember Barry Briggs' or Ole Olsen and Ivan Mauger but we're getting through that nowadays. People say 'I've seen you on a Monday night' and – because people know us from the telly or think they know us from the telly – they're more likely to come along and try it." Out on the track ex-World Champion and Bears club captain Gary 'Havvy' Havelock shakes off the comparative cobwebs of his first-race second place (behind Joe Haines) to race to a heat 6 win over Tomáš Topinka. With Ben Wilson third, their heat advantage reduces the Bears deficit to a manageable 4 points. Wilson goes one better two races later (in combination with Tomáš Suchánek) to level the scores after eight heats.

Though it's his first time here, even in the pits Mike knows people! In this instance, the tanned and vibrantly healthy-looking track curator Tony Swales, ("I know his brother Tim Swales"). Mike and Dave take time out to confer about the photos taken and what else Dave should look out for. With slight incredulity Dave says, "They've announced you three times now!" Not all the comments have been without a certain edge. [4] After half a season of torpor and disappointment, Redcar suddenly ride with some confidence and self-belief. With Mike in tow, I need no second invitation to visit the centre green and, given Mike's here to savour the atmosphere and thrills, I'm hopeful we'll see some exciting races. While they've been competitive, so far they've just lacked that bit of sparkle. This changes in heat 9 when Emiliano Sanchez (apparently suicidally) rides through a nonexistent gap to aggressively overtake the highly regarded Stars No. 5, Tomáš Topinka. With Charles Wright third, the Bears restore the 2-point lead they last held seven races ago.

Quickly sated by the joy of the STMP centre green, news that there's a cornucopia of speedway merchandise in the trackshop along with an owner who's visited 3,268 football grounds sounds good to Mike. His "I'm sure I'll know him when I see him" echoes Dave Rat earlier, "I don't think I've met him though I'm certain I'll know him by sight!" I'm curious about Mike's reaction so far, "My first impression is how friendly all the people are!" Ever curious Mike asks, "Do you think many people come to see crashes? Is that part of the appeal?" Probably some people do but I reckon they're the exception not the rule. "Officially no, but, obviously, crashes are part and parcel of the sport. It's gladiatorial! However, the fans don't just see the riders as a helmet but know the rider beneath it and often their parents or girlfriends too. They follow their careers closely and take their injuries to heart." Another reason to return to the vicinity of the first bend is to check if there's any delicious pork and stilton pies (made by A.P. Jackson's Butchers of Ruswarp, Whitby) still left in the hospitality area.

Judged by the determination and ferocity shown on the track, many riders like their meat red raw. Predictably Gary Havelock and Ben Wilson race to an ecstatically greeted maximum ahead of Casper Workman and Kozza Smith. Delight is almost unalloyed but, with the score at 33-27, Gareth Rogers sounds a note of caution before Kevin Doolan and Joe Haines take to the track, "It's King's Lynn's most effective pairing". That's the theory and appears to be the practice when

[4] Earlier when presenter Gareth Rogers welcomes Mike he then goes on to say, "Martin Neal of the *Evening Gazette* who reports regularly on speedway here every week". At this comparison, Mike exhales "Oh!" Earlier Gareth told me, "I send the press release to the sports editor of the *Northern Echo* every week but they only put in something now and again! We're lucky to have Martin [Neal at the *Gazette*] cos he's such a fan!"

Redcar: *"Chris Mills won't be on Tomáš Suchánek's Christmas card list"*

Joe Haines fires from the tapes to the lead closely followed by Kevin Doolan. Unfortunately the path to glory isn't always smooth and, just when they appear set, Haines inadvertently blocks Doolan to allow James Grieves through. The experienced Scots rider is unable to capitalise on his lead since his engine failure almost immediately gifts back the 5-1 to the visitor's power partnership. Charles Wright wins heat 12 while behind him there's a battle for second notable for its ferocity. Tomáš Suchánek looks all set after an overtake on the last bend of lap two until Chris Mills rides him very very hard to the second-bend fence on the third lap. Self-preservation, let alone discretion, is suddenly the better part of valour. In an instant, Soosh finds himself last and temporarily becalmed out by the fence. Although it's only early July, Gareth Rogers looks ahead to the 2010 festive season, "Darren Mallett won't be on Tomáš Suchánek's Christmas card list!" Too keen to be Christmassy Gareth's excitement carried him away, "Correction, Chris Mills won't be on Tomáš Suchánek's Christmas card list".

In the notional battle of the big guns that is often the reality of heat 13, Gary Havelock bests Tomáš Topinka and Kevin Doolan to ensure a drawn heat. Emiliano Sanchez repeats his earlier daredevil bravery in heat 14 to fire aggressively through a nonexistent gap – that appears to exist only philosophically – to win a race for the finish line with Kozza Smith. This last-gasp dash converts an almost certain drawn heat into a 4-2 race advantage for the Bears. Mike Amos looks on approvingly, "What larks!" Buoyed by the adrenaline rush that the denouement of this race prompts, Gareth seizes the moment to remind various naysayers who doubt the commitment of the Redcar riders, the quality of the entertainment on offer or the amount of overtaking to be seen at the STMP as "Absolute sphericals".

With the score at 44-40, it's mathematically still possible that the meeting could end in a draw. That's before you factor in the Bears ongoing run of bad luck and injuries or their five years without a win against Lynn. Never short on confidence or belief, Havvy flies from the tapes to ensure a well-deserved and ecstatically greeted win. It's a night that definitively kills off the King's Lynn voodoo. Conscientiously, Mike Amos returns to the pits to snatch an interview with King's Lynn and Team GB team manager, Rob Lyon. Though he's probably keen to vacate the stadium as soon as possible, Rob honours his earlier agreement for an interview after the meeting. David Wood has enjoyed his first impressions of speedway. "As a photographer, it was really good. One of the bonuses of being a press photographer, like I said, is you get access to places where other people don't. As a first timer it took me a while to figure where the best places were to get some good pictures. Saying that, it's always a good idea to follow other photographers (who photograph speedway a lot) to see where they go for the best positions. However, because of the access to the action in the pits, stadium, and track side it made it a great venue for taking pictures and I would recommend it to other photographers." [5] Mike returns with his notepad crammed with yet more indecipherable shorthand impressed by the access he's received to the national team manager. "He was very honest and told me lots of interesting stuff! If I knew more about speedway, I'd have been able to understand it! I don't know whether it was new information or not?" Dave Rattenberry is quick to sing the praises of tonight's entertainment. "It was a good meeting! There was a bit of grip tonight – a bit of shale – and that made all the difference." Edinburgh Monarchs fan Maurice enjoys the action they serve up at the STMP that it's already his third 280-mile round trip this season so far. "That's how a meeting should be run. No falls and no reruns. No faffing about! John Campbell was fined once for telling the ref to get a move on. Sky should come and see it too!"

Time waits for no man though so, as soon as the formality of the victory parade is complete, then

[5] Upsides invariably have their opposite. "Only downside was I that I was finding track grit in my hair, camera bag and clothes for days, it got everywhere!"

Redcar: *"Chris Mills won't be on Tomáš Suchánek's Christmas card list"*

the action cracks on with a four-heat Northern Junior League meeting between Redcar and the homeless but itinerant Halifax Dukes. Up in the commentary booth, Keith McGhie waxes lyrical about the possible impact the mere appearance of the Halifax Dukes race tabard on a track in Teesside might have on their nascent campaign to return their club to competitive speedway. "You never know if they'll return! I remember it's not so long ago that Jason Pipe and Steve Hargreaves started running a Redcar team in the second halves!" Steve Harland must be delighted to know that he's made such a big impression on Keith McGhie. Further stream of consciousness commentary is cut short, "As I speak, there's one or two words coming from the pits!" They could well be swear words, paeans of praise or equally, since occupational gender stereotyping never really died out, they could be catcalls since the three-rider team tracked by the Halifax Dukes[6] features two lady riders (the experienced Montana Jowett and also Rachel Hellowell). Paul Burnett completes their triumvirate but suffers mixed fortunes with a second place first time out, soon followed by a massive rear from the tapes at the start of heat 3 that nearly cleans out James Cartmell. It's a surprise to find that so much grip still remains after 18 heats of racing! Nonetheless, Paul ignores his wild start to race determinedly until he falls on the last bend of the last lap (when placed second). Between these second half Northern Junior League races, we're treated to some exhibition laps from Arlo Bugeja, Jade Mudgway and Adam McKinna (at least Keith surmises it might be him, "I guess the one with the Diamond on his back was Adam McKinna!") The previous week, many disgruntled Redcar fans reportedly left during heats 13 and 14. Only seven days later, some linger after the victory parade to watch the bonus of more speedway action. Once the traffic jam subsides in the rough-hewn STMP car park, Mike Amos says his farewells enchanted by the friendliness of the crowd, their enthusiasm for the sport and the excitement of the final third of the meeting. Given that so many hail him as the club's new "lucky mascot" – with the wonderful red, blue and purple hews of the noctilucent clouds providing a magnificent backdrop – Mike wonders if he's going to have to come along more often in future.

15 July Redcar v. King's Lynn (Premier League) 47-43

Mike's *Northern Echo* article on his visit appears here:

http://www.thenorthernecho.co.uk/features/columnists/mikeamos/backtrack/8281307.Are_Bears_out_of_the_woods_/

---

[6] Three men behind the campaign to keep the Halifax Dukes name alive are Jeff Hayes, Peter Dyson and Dave Burnett. To add further lustre to their local newsworthiness, the Dukes 16-year old rider Rachel Hellowell comes from Halifax. Previous possible new sites for the club – at Greetland and Scammonden – fell foul of objections. So, although the stalwarts behind this Northern Junior League incarnation of the club continue their search – in *Secret Squirrel* fashion – they keep their cards close to their collective chests about other possible sites either within the Borough of Calderdale or on the Bradford side of Halifax.

Redcar: *"Chris Mills won't be on Tomáš Suchánek's Christmas card list"*

CHAPTER 10

Edinburgh
"On the track it's fantastic – off the track we're losing four figures every week!"

The strong winds that buffet the opening two days of the Open Golf Championships at St Andrews lessen slightly in their severity by the time they reach the Scotwaste Arena (home of the Edinburgh Monarchs). However, according to co-promoter John Campbell, the winds of economic change that blow throughout British speedway during 2010 threaten economic disruption and require future structural change. Though he's tanned and cheerful after a holiday in Malta, there's no disguising his anxiety. "On the track it's fantastic – off the track we're losing four figures every week! Our crowds are 20% down. You know the recession that's ended has finally started to bite! Though we run a tight ship, based on many years' experience we assembled an attractive team for the crowd and – from the first meeting – the crowds haven't come! I don't know of anywhere I've been where you can say they have big crowds or even the crowds you'd expect. I don't know about Glasgow and Berwick because I haven't been there – except when we're there (and that must be April) – but, people tell me, they're way down too! With a team like this, we can have 30+ meetings here. Tonight is the night – you'd like to think people will see this as number one versus number two and, if that doesn't happen, that really is it! They're bringing two minibuses. 25 fans. And, next week, we have the Scottish Open where we'll be charging so much that, on a normal crowd, we'll do okay. At the end of the month, Rye House will bring 35." Things are so bad, the only really significant crowd seen inside the Scotwaste Arena this season (so far) isn't human, "the programme hut is occupied by wasps – you can use it if you like, though the wasps might have other ideas!"

The near gale force wind that blows through the stadium rattles the slightly dilapidated Scotswaste Arena grandstand adjacent to the two hospitality cabins that overlook bends one and two. "It's a very hard time – we just hope the stadium doesn't blow to bits before the season ends!" On the subject of stadium infrastructure and future track developments, we're interrupted by an old pensioner fan who – ignoring the weather in these parts – commits the style crime of wearing dark socks with open-toed sandals. Close by, the track appears sodden and all around us you can see that it's rained within the past few hours. It hasn't escaped the attention of this keen-eyed fan, "It's been wet, hasn't it?"
[John] "It's normal weather for Scotland."
[Fan] "Where's the new track?"
[John] "It's over there [points] you can see it. It's a field at present."
[Fan] "So you won't be there next season?"
[John] "It doesn't look like it."

[Fan] "I like it here – the track – not the place!"
[John] "We'll have a good track there too!"

Satisfied to learn that there might be problems ahead he predicts, said fan saunters off. John confirms to me that the turnstiles have yet to open. Quite where this man came from I don't know?

88

Like promoters' phones the country over after rain, when it's forecast to rain, or when it's reported as raining or is raining wherever the fan is calling from, meteorological queries flood in. John's iPhone is no exception, "Yes the meeting is on tonight. It starts at 7.30 [pause] we do have a supporters' bus that leaves Edinburgh at 6.15 that costs £7 [pause] it goes from the east end of Princes Street – Waterloo Place." John politely goes into further detail describing the coach, the company that owns it and enough further distinguishing features about the location and the transport on offer that I'm surprised he makes no mention of tyre pressures, registration numbers or the star sign of the driver. Though results so far this season have been good, the shale surface itself doesn't measure up to John's expectations. "On the track we've been great but the track hasn't been up to much! Anything that's not normal British weather – sun or wind – plays havoc with it. We've had a couple of good weeks but the track hasn't been consistent and it's tended to catch our boys out early in the meeting before they get sorted and pull away. With Kalle riding – who's been tremendous – you'd expect us to win tonight. They're missing Aaron Summers but can use rider replacement – so won't be quite as strong. Graham [Drury] has been ringing up all day asking if it's on so, knowing him, there must be something behind it. At half-ten he said, 'If it's off we won't even set off so that will save you!' I told him it's on. It's definitely going to be on. The track looks a little wet and the centre green looks lovely but it's under water really!"

I went to Hertfordshire the night that Edinburgh monstered Rye House at their home track in Hoddesdon. Since then Edinburgh returned there and won again, albeit by a much smaller margin (44-45). "I'm not telling you anything that I haven't already said in the press but I knew the first time that if the rain had hit we'd definitely win! And, even the second, though it was drier – we can ride there and I knew we would win." It would be nice to come up with some helpful suggestion based on my travels as to how John could improve his crowds. The very idea that I could do so – particularly given that John Campbell is the longest serving promoter in British speedway – is (obviously) pretentiously self-delusional. Nevertheless, like fans everywhere, I don't let my lack of knowledge get in the way of an opinion. "You need to run an ugly team that attracts big crowds." With practised ease in the face of bonkers ideas, John maintains a neutral expression, "I'll settle for a couple of seasons of that but, the question is, how exactly do you do that?" Reports during the close season would reveal the Monarchs

2008 Roll of honour

Start line

Edinburgh: *"On the track it's fantastic – off the track we're losing four figures every week!"*

lost £40,000 during the 2010 season.

Despite numerous seasons at the speedway coalface, John retains a good self-deprecating sense of humour about the limits of his shale-induced fame. "I often say to my wife – as a joke – whenever we go out that I'm the most famous person in here. We were out the other Friday at our local pub (because we'd had a rain-off) and the barman said 'I know you, your face is in the paper!' Then he said, 'I know! It's bowls isn't it?' and I told him it was. Alex Harkess was at Cardiff helping with the track and someone said to him that two Glasgow fans – a man and wife – pointed to him and said, "That's the Edinburgh promoter – John Campbell". I read the Bert Trautmann story by Kate wotsit [Catrine Clay] when I was away. It was 80% about the war and 20% about football. He's 82 or 83 and lives in Spain now and, whenever he comes back, as soon as he arrives at Manchester airport – he gets asked for his autograph. I said to Alex we don't get asked now! Never mind, we'll be long forgotten when we're in our 80s!"

With the Mauger autobiography out this year, Ivan tours the tracks. Everyone has their own memories. Some of them might already appear in the book, others don't. "It was about 30 years ago when we were at Powderhall and I organised a meeting for Ivan almost completely singlehandedly. I broke every rule the Elite League, or whatever it was called then – the British League – but they let me get away with it because it was Ivan. At the end of the meeting, there was a pennant missing and Ivan argued and argued over 50p! In the end I told him to go away. If he was a promoter, I'd fall out with him! We'd all fall out with him. He's coming here in a few weeks. He's been emailing for six months saying put this and put that on the website. He must have forgotten!"

The great and the good of North British speedway inevitably find their way to the Scotwaste Arena on a Friday night. Glasgow co-promoter Alan Dick is a frequent visitor and so too is Berwick presenter Dick Barrie. For the first time since Peter Waite tempted him back into the sport (after he took a break from it in 1991), Dick struggles to find his usual high levels of enthusiasm. The reasons for this temporary loss of Dick's always perky mojo are many and varied including the lack of opportunity for young rider development in this part of the world but also extend to concerns about the absence of basic promotional habits. "The National League seems to have become a South coast competition. If you've got a speedway bike north of Buxton or Scunthorpe and you're not in a Premier League 1 to 7, you have no chance! I'm not exactly sure how far away they are geographically? It's a long way! If you have a 15-year-old son in Scotland who's mad keen on speedway, where is he going to ride and get competition? Twenty-three years ago we had the Scottish Junior League. It produced riders like Andy Smith, Martin Dixon, Kenny and Charlie McKinna. To help fill the gap, the Northern Junior League is going to have three-man teams and four heat meetings. Next year we'll run a bit bigger and attract more riders north of Scunthorpe and Buxton. Reevo [Graham Reeves] has been really supportive. He doesn't charge for rider licences and he doesn't charge for team manager licences. Though it seems unnecessary, they have to have them as best practice. He said he'll have a word with the refs and keep them in order if any of them insist on two-rider races and the like. He'll tell them what's what! People say it should be no foreigners but why? We need competitive races and, if British riders who are King of their Small Hill get challenged then they have to improve. We have a Hungarian [Tamas Sike] at Berwick. Actually he has a British licence and, if he's good enough, he'll go on to ride in the National League or Premier League. And, if he's not, then he won't! The main thing is to provide competition for them all to improve."

Everyone's well aware that the football World Cup disrupted speedway meeting schedules throughout its duration. However, not all of the gaps in the fixture list can really be laid at its door since some of these gaps were already pre-planned by the authorities. "The BSPA – in their wisdom – said no meetings for two weekends in June so they could run the Knock-out Cup semi-final and the Premier Trophy semi-finals. A good idea. Half to three-quarters of the teams can't be in either, can they?"

[Jeff] "They're doing to the Premier League what the GP and Poland does to the Elite League!"

[Dick] "They have an Elite League mindset. Continuity is the key! The fans come every week but the "customers" don't and they're the difference between profitability and not! Len Silver used to run every week and always started on March 15th. When the Hawks were away he'd put on a junior meeting for the continuity! Continuity is the key! People turn up at quarter to eight when the meeting is half over at Berwick and are happy to pay. They remember and come back another year. When they turn up and it's closed and the circus isn't in town, they don't usually ever come back!"

Not so many weeks ago Birmingham Brummies fans would fancy a close meeting or possible victory at the Scotwaste Arena. However, over recent months, the form they showed in the Premier Trophy has dipped. It's a situation compounded by injuries to key riders – Chris Kerr (riding to a 9.00 average in 2010 but, since his injury came before the completion of 12 meetings, Birmingham were stuck with his 2009 5.00 average for replacements) and, more recently, Aaron Summers. Tonight the Brummies have Kenny Ingalls at reserve (in place of Kerr) and operate rider replacement for Summers. The young Australian would have been a threat around the tight Armadale track since he used to ride for Edinburgh. Despite the potential weakness of the opposition, the first Monarchs fan to stop for at my book display chat isn't optimistic, "We've been winning but we've been dropping silly points early on. If that happens tonight, they could take advantage!" Speedway author Gary Lough is even more pessimistic, "We'll get hammered! It's a 4-point meeting!" Gary's dad Alan is incredulous at his son's predictions, "Are you serious? What are you on? Even the Birmingham team manager says they're going to lose!" Gary's adamant, "it's reverse psychology, isn't it?"

A small girl is interested to learn that each season I visit every track. She'd do it differently, "I'd like to go all the tracks but I wouldn't write it all down!" With the Open on at St Andrews keen trainspotter and speedway fan Steven Brykajlo is in his element. "I've been out at Queensferry for a few hours because of St Andrews. They're running all sorts of extra trains to get the punters up there and back." Like his father, Steven's a Berwick Bandits fan. He's gobsmacked Redcar beat King's Lynn at the South Tees Motorsports Park last night. "I can't believe Berwick – who can't win away – won there and yet King's Lynn lost! I'd have put money on the opposite. Mind you, Berwick did have Michal Rajkowski who got paid 19". Edinburgh fan Maurice is enamoured by the calibre of entertainment offered at the STMP, "Even if you don't get passing, you always get close racing on a small track."

With Scott Wilson away on holiday, Volkswagen Beetle driving John McGilvary steps into the presentational breech this evening. His duties start with a smoothly efficient rider parade. After their warm-up laps, the riders get down to the serious business. On the small terrace adjacent to the Scotwaste Arena hospitality units, the sight of Jason Lyons in the lead fails to delight the woman stood behind me, "Freaking come on Ryan! Freaking take him out!" It's an unusual request from any speedway fan and falls on deaf ears. With Kenny Ingalls third (ahead of Tobias Busch), Birmingham gain an immediate 2-point advantage. After the Monarchs pair of Cal McDade and their star Finnish reserve Kalle Katajisto both exchange elbows with Kenny on the first bend, they then opt to lead comfortably. At least they do until Kyle Newman falls on the second bend of the second lap when fourth. Kyle fails to clear the track quickly enough so leaves Clevedon-based SCB referee Ronnie Allan with no choice but to stop the race. A staff member on the centre green isn't happy with reluctant-to-rise Newman and, noticeably, gestures his disgust.

Understandably, Edinburgh fans delight in the form shown this season by Kalle Katajisto though fans at other clubs – particularly Berwick and Glasgow – are quick to cry foul. Edinburgh taxi driver and Bandits fan Jim Brykajlo is no exception. "Kalle keeps missing matches – cheating bastards – so he doesn't get the proper average! They keep signing 7-point riders to keep Kalle at reserve. First it was Tabaka, then Busch and now they're going to bring in Lawson." The rerun prompted by Kyle Newman's slowness proves tactically shrewd when Cal McDade falls on the third bend during his vain attempt to get under the comfortably second Ingalls. The apex of the third bend also proves problematic for Richard Sweetman in the next race when he comes to grief behind Ryan Fisher to earn a disqualification. In the rerun, Matthew Wethers bides his time behind Justin Sedgmen until he blasts past at the start of lap three to ensure the Monarchs take maximum points from the race. Though he's ostensibly here to watch this meeting, Jim Brykajlo's thoughts are elsewhere. Jim voices reservations about the level of ambition shown by the promotional team at his beloved Berwick Bandits. "They walk in after being a butcher and selling pies and that. They don't know all about speedway. They haven't planned their fixtures well either. There's six Saturdays in the height of the summer and they've only got three meetings! They're past their honeymoon period – it's nearly two years – and everyone has to pretend things are great!"

With the Brummies 4 points down after three races, they need a big ride from their marquee signing of the recent close season, Steve Johnston. Going into the third bend of the second lap, the experienced old stager Johno tries to employ track craft rather than sheer velocity to pass Andrew Tully. In his mind Johno is well placed to elbow his way past Tully but, as he tries to connect with his flailing limb, Johno misses and instead fishtails across the track. His hammy gamesmanship more or less guarantees the Monarchs their second successive 5-1 to open up an early 8-point lead that they look unlikely to relinquish.

Dave Rattenberry's taken a night off from masterminding his extensive and lucrative trackshop empire to savour the thrills of this Monarchs versus Brummies Premier League clash. Some could suspect that he's been sent under cover as a secret shopper. Thirty minutes before the rider parade, Rat eats a cheeseburger with gusto. He returns to the burger van 15 minutes later to savour-cum-wolf-down the chips that he'd earlier denied himself. It's not long until Rat joins us on the terracing to eat some fudge. He enjoys the scoreline almost equally as much as the Monarchs fans, "I hope Birmingham get thrashed!" Jim Brykajlo needs to understand his vehemence, "Cos I don't like Birmingham!" Jason Lyons temporarily staunches the situation with a win in heat 5 ahead of Katajisto. However, normal service resumes in the next race when Ryan Fisher and Tobias Busch combine ahead of a lacklustre Steve Johnston for the Monarchs third (and, possibly, meeting defining) maximum heat advantage in four races.

With Birmingham down by 12, team manager Graham Drury gives Richard Sweetman the black-and-white helmet colour for heat 7. It's a tactical move that looks to have gone desperately awry until Cal McDade messes up and, thereby, allows Sweetman through into third. With Tully sure to win the race, it's an important change of position since it allows Justin Sedgmen to slow on the run-in to the finish line and let his teammate pass. Though the ungainly 3-5 heat advantage temporarily reduces the Brummies deficit to 10 points, the Monarchs continue to dominate proceedings with successive race wins for Katajisto, Tully (in combination with Wethers for a 5-1) and Fisher. The Edinburgh No. 1 wins by the proverbial tyre knobble after he zooms from bend four to best the fast-riding but determined Justin Sedgmen. Stood in the pits viewing area, Dick Barrie quickly identifies why the Brummies trail 39-23 after ten races, "It's Johnno who's been disappointing this evening!"

The eleventh race of the night is one of those cut-and-thrust high-speed affairs that captures all that is compulsively entertaining about an excellent speedway race. I'm privileged enough to

Edinburgh: *"On the track it's fantastic – off the track we're losing four figures every week!"*

watch the action unfold from the prized vantage point of the sodden centre green. With Jason Lyons in a black-and-white helmet colour, Graham Drury further explores his tactical options to bring in Steve Johnston on a rider-replacement ride for Aaron Summers. Surprising, given his early evening torpor, as the riders exit the second bend it's Steve Johnston who leads. Though clearly faster than his teammate, Jason Lyons proceeds to occupy the inside line. Using his experience and, apparently, with eyes in the back of his head, Lyons manages to parry and repel every determined charge past that Andrew Tully conjures up. It's a master-class in defensive team riding. Andrew tests him with blasts round the outside as well as dashes up the inside (after feigning the opposite). All these manoeuvres get snuffed out by the wily Australian who repeatedly slows up the hard-charging Manx-born Scot on his tail. The amount of pressure exerted raises the possibility that, if Johnston slows on the run-in to the line, then Tully might still sneak through for the win. However, with thousands of hours of shale time under their collective belts, with electric almost telepathic grace Johnston and Lyons find time to swop positions on the run-in to the line to maximise the Brummies points haul from the race. The skill of the riders, the ingenuity of the thrusts and parries as well as graceful control of their machines is a thrillingly absorbing spectacle for everyone lucky enough to witness it. Though his team have just conceded an 8-1, Monarchs team manager and co-promoter John Campbell is magnanimously ecstatic. "That was fantastic! Newcomers wouldn't get the subtlety of that race – that's what great speedway is all about!" The proverbial blanket could have been carried round the Armadale track over the three riders for the duration of the race. Still 9 points to the good, it's easier for John Campbell to be phlegmatically philosophical. "Johno came here last season on a wet drizzly day and, I thought, he'd be moaning like anything to get it off. But he was, instead, like the bloke we see on Sky! When I asked him why, he said, 'I'm ok – I stopped in at Biggar and got my haggis so I don't care what happens!' He rode in the drizzle throughout the night. He hasn't done anything here until that race!" Between races John Campbell and presenter John McGilvary gather round a mystery man to draw riders' names out of the helmet colour for next week's Scottish Open. The crowd greet each name – as it's announced – with a sustained bout of controlled unexcitement. Matthew Wethers wins a drawn heat 12 though the result would have been different if Cal McDade hadn't fallen (and remounted).

The chance to watch the next instalment of the Tully/Lyons/Johnston battle from the centre green – with the additional ingredient of Ryan Fisher to pep things up – is impossible to resist. Despite the responsibilities of his positions as BSPA chairman and Edinburgh co-promoter, Alex Harkess still isn't inured to the joy of anticipation. "This race could be just as good [pause] but I'd hope with a different result!" Distinctly trepid from the tapes in his first three outings, Johno's gating mojo once again returns in spades. He fires from the gate with Ryan Fisher in close pursuit who's in turn chased by Jason Lyons. Exploiting the full width of the tight Armadale circuit with some verve, Fisher harries, probes and cuts between his rivals searching for the vital window of opportunity that never quite materialises. An equally exploratory Lyons shadows him throughout. When for all the world it looks like Johno will survive Ryan's attentions, he slightly locks-up on the very last bend to present Fisher with a fractional opening that he seizes with alacrity to zoom past. Though engaged in an intense harum-scarum dash for the finish line, Fisher nonetheless punches the air with both hands as he takes the chequered flag to loud acclaim from the Monarchs faithful. With his persistence rightly leading to last-gasp triumph, Ryan continues his 'look mum no hands' celebration in front of both Scotwaste Arena grandstands. If heat 11 was tactically spectacular then heat 13 is "fantastic" (as Mike Hunter notes afterwards in his meeting report). Presenter John McGilvary decides to highlight the value for money aspect of the entertainment on offer tonight in Armadale, "You're getting your money's worth tonight!"

With the result mathematically already beyond doubt Kalle Katajisto races to his fourth win of

Edinburgh: *"On the track it's fantastic – off the track we're losing four figures every week!"*

the night in the penultimate heat (taking his tally from the reserve berth to 15 points from seven rides). Kalle's closely followed home by Matthew Wethers and their 5-1 further enthuses the already excitable Monarchs crowd on the first and second bends of the stadium. Graham Drury fails to nominate Steve Johnston for heat 15. This isn't a surprise to Dougie Copland, "I think Johno is close to retirement." Though Jason Lyons bested Ryan Fisher in heat 1, the American is on a roll and his race win is never in doubt. After he dropped a point in his first ride, Ryan hammers home five race wins for a total of 17 points from six rides.

After the Monarchs victory parade, the entertainment continues with a Northern Junior League mini-meeting between two elegantly named and eloquently sponsored teams. With the American Dream team rider Gino Manzares in their side, it looks likely that the Redcar NEBT Stockton Van Centre Cubs will win, despite the minor blip of James Cartmell getting lapped after a fall and remount in heat 2. The real point of these second-half fixtures isn't the result but the opportunity it gives wannabe riders based in the North to get some shale time. To note that the Linlithgow Tyres West Lothian Wildcats comprehensively lose on home shale completely misses the point of the exercise. Various fans stop at my table for a few words as they leave the Scotwaste Arena. Glasgow fans in attendance at the hope of a Brummies triumph leave disconsolate, after witnessing a powerhouse performance from the Monarchs that bodes well for their later season pursuit of silverware. A large contingent of Birmingham fans wear their team colours with pride to gather in hope and genuine anticipation of greater success at Berwick and Glasgow over the next two days of their mini Northern tour. Amazingly Monarchs fans that stop to chat aren't universally happy. "Why does John Campbell go on the centre green complaining about the lack of fans to the ones who turn up? Recently they did some Ryan Fisher car stickers – you had to stick them to the outside of the car – to promote the speedway. He went on to the centre green and said, 'He'd been round the car park but had only seen three of them!' Isn't it his job to promote the speedway?" These Ryan Fisher stickers sound an exciting collector's item and are a piece of (promotional) memorabilia that I'd gladly stick on the outside of my car windows. Sadly the trackshop is closed so I can't lay my hands on any examples of this innovative promotional idea; Dick Barrie suggests I maybe try looking in one of the hospitality units once I've packed away. Glasgow presenter Michael Max pulls alongside my display table in his car as he exits the stadium. He sympathises with the tough sales environment that is the present lot of any speedway author on tour (ex-World Champion excepted), "No one has any money!"

On the decking outside one of the two hospitality units at the Scotwaste Arena, a crowd of voluble sponsors enjoy testing their reflexes on the speedway bike specially set up for that purpose. Dick Barrie draws my attention to this crowd of approximately 15 people who are unobtrusively supervised by (gifted commercial artist) Allan McDade. Dick is keen to sing the praises of this modest but hardworking hospitality manager for his public relations work. " Alan works really hard making sure everyone enjoys themselves. He gets a rider involved and makes sure they all have a good time. You never see an Edinburgh promoter up here. [1] Sometimes Alex Harkess does. I think they assume you just serve food and drink and that's it! Allan McDade is fantastic! He really makes it work. Hospitality income is vital but they don't know what they've got. Every club could do with an Allan McDade in hospitality!"

Monarchs rider Matty Wethers joins the throng but leaves almost immediately gulping down in almost one slurp the entire contents of a full-fat can of Coca-Cola. I'm absolutely certain that such synthetic drinks shouldn't form the cornerstone of the dietary regime required if you intend to be a fully functioning speedway rider for the duration of any speedway season. Nonetheless,

94

[1] Moments later, Mike Hunter – a member of the Edinburgh Monarchs management team – emerges from the hospitality unit next door and briefly comes over to watch the fun.

Matty drinks his Coca-Cola with gusto. It's his eighth consecutive season at Edinburgh and Matthew's second as captain. Given how athletic, bordering on skinny, he looks in the off-duty speedway rider uniform of T-shirt and scruffy jeans – clearly Matty has yet to reach the stage in his life where he has to consider his calorie intake or the nutritional quality of the fluids he enjoys. Moments later I nearly reverse into him while he stands and chats in the gloom outside the wasp-infested programme stall. With the lack of a Ryan Fisher sticker on my car it's clear I must be a visitor (or a Monarchs fan reluctant to promote the club), Matty shrugs off my apology ("Sorry I don't usually run over speedway riders") with a phlegmatic, "Don't worry, I'm used to it!"

16th July Edinburgh v. Birmingham (Premier League) 54-41

Edinburgh: *"On the track it's fantastic – off the track we're losing four figures every week!"*

CHAPTER 11

Northside

"One of the riders here today will go on to be a star! Trouble is, you don't know which one! In 20 years' time, we'll all say that we could see that today."

17th July

After a drive through the mining villages that line the A596 coast road from Maryport to Workington you get to a large roundabout on the outskirts of the town. You can turn left to the out-of-town superstores of the Dunmail Mill Retail Park, go straight on into the town centre or turn right for the Docks. I head seawards, cross the railway line and take the third turn right close to a gap in the fence that – from the sign attached – has some connection with Eon. Armed with directions from both Barry Stephenson (Workington Comets programme editor) and Tim Hamblin (Wolverhampton *Express & Star* speedway reporter and exiled Workington fan), it's easy to find the Northside Arena. Today they'll stage round 3 of the British Under-15 Championships. The heritage of the surrounding area is industrial – well, more post-industrial nowadays. That's definitely the feel of the track approach road edged with untamed scrubland. With jet-black clouds and giant wind turbines overhead, there are a substantial number of white vans already parked up outside the one-storey building that serves as the administrative nerve centre of the Northside Arena based at the Allerdale Motor Project at Old Side, Workington. Inside the one-storey building there are essential but basic facilities including showers, washing area, toilets and kitchen as well as a speedway office. The woman outside it calls to Judith Lomas, "Judith, there's a man here to see you!" Calling back unseen from her inner sanctum, Judith temporarily breaks off from the admin/preparations required to ensure that this round of the British Under-15 Championship goes ahead smoothly to check out the talent, "I don't care who he is so long as he's handsome!" There's a slight pause until Judith arrives in the doorway, glances me up and down, looks slightly crestfallen and exhales, "Oh!" Quick but crushing analysis over, Judith matter-of-factly welcomes me to Northside and points me towards the direction of the public entrance for this afternoon's meeting adjacent to a sea container. The first ever meeting at the Northside club was on 6th August 2002 and, after five years operating solely as a training track, for the past four seasons the club have staged open meetings on their extremely well cared for and professionally prepared 138-metre circuit. This afternoon will be the fourth successive year that a round of the British Under-15 Championship takes place in North Workington.

The facilities here are all you need to stage a successful close-fought meeting as well as test the skill and ability of the riders. There's a large pits area with a substantial open-fronted breezeblock-built covered section. It's more than enough to accommodate the bikes, assorted equipment and mechanics that accompanies today's 17 riders. This afternoon they'll race the 500cc British Championship, 250cc British Championship and the 125cc Support competition. It's hard to miss the substantial number of advisory notices stuck on the breezeblock wall of the covered pits area. Riders, mechanics and family members are reminded: "Strictly no smoking in the pit area",

Northside: *"One of the riders here today will go on to be a star! Trouble is, you don't know which one! In 20 years' time, we'll all say that we could see that today."*

"Valuables left at owner's own risk", "No smoking", "No mobile phones" and, possibly somewhat unnecessarily given the age group here this afternoon, "Strictly no alcohol or drugs at any time"! The pits are a hive of activity as the mechanics, helpers and proud dads ready bikes of varying engine size for the scheduled start in around 90 minutes' time. Riders of differing heights and ages return smartly dressed from the changing room and begin to psyche themselves up or ostentatiously supervise-cum-advise their mechanical staff.

Last year's 250cc champion, Brandon Freemantle this year graduated to the 500cc championship. He's the form rider and favourite this afternoon having won the previous two rounds at Newport and Weymouth. He's an extremely tall 14-year old. His proud father Richard is at a loss to explain his great height. "He just eats healthily. He doesn't go to the gym. On the 30th [July] Brandon has been picked to ride in the Under-18s at Somerset. I said to him if he just got a point it would be an amazing achievement!" Brandon's not the only rider to have taken his first steps in speedway on the junior track at Eastbourne since Jordan Hazelden's also here. He's stood by his bike and, like many other riders/mechanics, waits for the signal to fire his engine into life. Jordan's section of the pits is crowded with two more Hazelden generations – father Mark and grandfather John. Before he hit his teens, Jordan rode grasstrack and motocross. Nowadays he's switched codes to compete just as keenly on shale. He's a modest young man with a sunny disposition and ready smile. His father fusses around the bike while his grandfather John sits in a garden chair and considers his next mechanical intervention.

Inside the shelter of the pits, the riders and their staff escape the strong winds that presently batter and buffet this part of the northwest coast. It's an area known for its wind and, nowadays, its wind turbines. The track is more or less under the lee of five wind turbines that, viewed from close at hand, appear much taller and impressively monumental than from distance. While wind turbines are beloved of the government and environmentalists alike, sadly the electricity they create is, inevitably, intermittent. For safety reasons, most turbines have to be switched off when winds gust over 40 mph. Mysteriously, given this afternoon's strong winds, of the five wind turbines that surround us, the propellers on two move very quickly, another moves super quickly while the two others barely move at all! The same can't be said of the thick black clouds that scud across the sky. As predicted by the meteorological professionals and also the amateurs at the Northside

Pits pose

Crowds gather

Northside: *"One of the riders here today will go on to be a star! Trouble is, you don't know which one! In 20 years' time, we'll all say that we could see that today."*

training track, a very heavy 15-minute burst of rain lashes the area. Much closer to a torrent than a dousing, it forces riders, fans, mechanics and staff to dash for shelter. All except for two lone fans reluctant to vacate their prime position on the rough ground that overlooks bends one/two and serves as the public viewing area at the Northside Arena. One man sits damply stoic in his garden chair while behind him – on the raised scrubland that overlooks the tyre-reinforced wooden safety fence that encloses the entire circuit – another man in a Workington Comets anorak stands impassively apparently waiting for the heavy rain to pass. These two lone fans remain confident that this is only a passing shower. The man in the garden chair points in the direction of the sea and the black clouds that stretch away to the horizon, "When the afternoon tide comes in, this is normal for round here! It's brightening in the distance. The Isle of Man is only 25 miles away and the forecast from Ronaldsway Airport is very accurate. And not only is it sunny there (and they're playing golf) but it'll brighten up here. The worst we'll get is showers and sunny spells!"

Sheltered away from the wind but not rain in the lee of the sea container by the public entrance are ex-Peterborough programme editors Steve and Sarah Miles. They're here on a brief Northern mini-tour of Northside this afternoon, Workington tonight and Glasgow tomorrow. They stand with entrance gate man Barry Stephenson. Although it's widely held that nature waters speedway tracks better than track curators, Barry still forecasts that this torrential downpour won't completely dampen the shale, "When it dries, this'll all be dust!" While we wait for the rain to subside talk turns to the British round of the Speedway Grand Prix staged at the Cardiff Millennium Stadium last weekend. Steve and Sarah help at Nick Barber's Speedway Fayre before they go off to watch the action. Sarah believes 2010 was one of the best events yet, "For once, the racing matched the occasion and the spectacle!" While Steve's also positive, "The track was the best ever!" Sarah's positively evangelical, "I thought Cardiff was really excellent – the Fayre was good too. Lots of people came out with the Ivan Mauger book and the Leigh Adams. People kept coming down for more change so they did well but hardly anyone came past with the Michael Lee book."

[Jeff] "They say they all sold well. You couldn't put a Rizla between their sales figures."
[Sarah] "I won't mention the tumbleweed." It's probably best not to mention weed of any variety.

Speedway fan Richard Dalston visits the Northside Arena from another part of Cumbria and, like many others, is full of admiration for this facility created by Michael and Judith Lomas. "This is a lovely track but, just think, we need 30 or 40 of these tracks! My girlfriend is from Finland and, though there's no track in Helsinki, there's six to eight tracks in Finland and it's not even a speedway country! It's a tiny sport there but they still have more and better facilities that we do."

My display table of my books now looks sodden, despite my protective plastic sheets. Ex-Workington Comets programme editor, speedway journalist and die-hard Comets fan Tony Jackson surveys the scene, "You've cured our drought then! We haven't had any rain for four weeks. Last Saturday I was at Cardiff and this weekend I'm here. You couldn't ask for a bigger contrast!"
[Jeff] "I know which I prefer."
[Tony] "I like Cardiff and they have a good meeting here. One of the riders here today will go on to be a star! Trouble is, you don't know which one! In 20 years' time, we'll all say that we could see that today."
[Jeff] "Let's confer later so we can agree who that is then! Do you think there'll be any crashes?"
[Tony] "None at all."

98

No sooner does the torrential rain lash down than it stops. The riders leave the shelter of the covered pits for an inspection walk of the sodden track while spectators rush through the turnstiles to bagsy their favoured spots on the raised scrubland that overlooks the compact 138-metre Northside Arena circuit. Soon bathed in sunshine and, with the initial rush of fans now over, Barry Stephenson luxuriates in the warmth as it dries his anorak. "The sun shines on the righteous or the devil looks after his own – whichever you prefer! This is the only chance to see two meetings in one day in the North and the one time that Northside is officially open to the public this year. There's 50 paying customers today. Last year there was 80 to 100. Most of the people here are travellers rather than from Workington [points to the crowd] there's two from Kettering [Steve and Sarah Miles], Bill Gimbeth, Dave Rattenberry, Charlie McKay, there's a Bradford guy on his right and a bloke from Newport – I don't know his name [John Short], two sitting there from Ulverston, and there's two from Ipswich, there's Charlie's sister, there's Andy Reid from Edinburgh and John Turner, of course, from Belle Vue and our friend who's an exiled Cradley supporter. Steve Lawson is local, stood behind his father Keith, there's another traveller whose name I don't know, and you. Most of these travellers will go to the Workington meeting afterwards [versus Somerset] and they wouldn't have gone there but for this meeting at Northside this afternoon. Dick Jarvis isn't here. Have you noticed, like a lot of speedway supporters, he doesn't drive? Les [Drury] is away so he's missing it. Mike Hunter doesn't drive either."

[Jeff] "So the crowd is mainly family apart from that?"

[Barry] "No, they're in the pits."

[Jeff] "So there's approximately 50 in the pits too."

[Barry] "I don't know."

Twenty-five minutes after the scheduled start time, referee Jim McGregor – who occupies a side-less raised platform built from scaffolding poles and what appears to be corrugated iron to give it a look that's a cross between a bird spotter's hide and a prison security tower of the type often seen in World War II POW films – presses the tapes button. There's immediately problems with the start gate. It doesn't let all the riders evenly away at once. The flag marshal on the first bend hangs out his red flag promptly but the riders in the initial 250cc race of the afternoon are so focused on doing well that one starts his second lap before the race finally grinds to a halt. Barry looks on dispassionately, "I wouldn't like to be a flag marshal today out there!"

There are more competitors [eight] in the 250cc championship than either the 500cc [five after the non-arrival of Cameron Hoskins] or the 125cc [four] Support Races. The programme punctiliously lays out the heat schedule and also exactly identifies when there'll be track grades and/or demonstration races. The scorecard in the centre of the programme is laid out in a fashion I've not previously encountered. Vastly experienced in the world of programmes, Sarah Miles comments approvingly, "I like programmes like this. They're like this in Sweden. They're much simpler and you don't have to write in them so much!" Robert Lambert wins the rerun of heat 1 in a time of 49 seconds. It's not exactly a shock since Robert also won the first two rounds of the 250cc British Championship held at Newport and Weymouth. He looks smooth and stylish on the bike. Heat 2 features riders from the 125cc discipline. The house-style of these younger riders is to tentatively approach each corner as though on the lookout for unexploded mines before they zoom down the straight like police in hot pursuit of robbers. They then repeat this process with four laps of further tentative corners until completion. The first 500cc race of the afternoon (heat 3) only features three riders because Cameron Hoskins – though he appears in the programme – is a non-starter (throughout the afternoon) for reasons that remain mysterious. By the time the race finishes, three riders become two after a fall for Andrew Ross. The exotic-sounding rider in the No. 6 tabard, Tyler Govier, crosses the line ahead of Adam Portwood in a time of 53.5 seconds. Sarah Miles notes, "That Lambert did it in a quicker time on a 250cc than Tyler won heat 3!"

Northside: *"One of the riders here today will go on to be a star! Trouble is, you don't know which one! In 20 years' time, we'll all say that we could see that today."*

The fourth race of the afternoon stops almost as soon as it starts after Jack Jones showcases an elegant almost graceful slow motion fall on the second bend. Generously referee Jim McGregor allows Jack back into a rerun won by Nathan Stoneman who sports the kind of pink/purple-coloured kevlars that really should come with sunglasses as standard. Given how fashion conscious teenagers can be, perhaps, Nathan is demonstrating the hi-vis colour of the future (should fluorescent yellow ever fall out of fashion)? Exactly who will drive the Miles mobile back from Glasgow to Kettering is a matter of some terrace debate. Sarah explains, "When we last came to Workington it was a few years ago. I think it was the PL Fours and he [Steve] thinks it's the Pairs. We came with Nick and Johnny Barber. We had a marital bet, whoever loses drives back from Glasgow tomorrow night. The first text that came back said it was the Fours but Steve wants a steward's enquiry to double check."

[Steve] "I think it was 2000."

[Sarah] "I think you're wrong on that too!"

After a few moments thought, Steve returns to this topic of conversation when his mobile phone rings, "It was a really wet one and I think Powell and Stonehewer won it! [listens to reply] It was the Pairs!"

[Sarah] "It's not."

[Steve] "Can you text Sarah and tell her."

[Sarah] "Don't believe him: it's the Fours!"

Charles McKay likes to enjoy his British speedway but also goes overseas. He tends to go away on a Travel Plus tour for a week on the grounds of good value. "You pay £400 for a GP weekend and £800 for a week." Steve Miles is nonplussed, "It don't quite make sense how he [James Easter] prices them!"

After a scheduled track grade, Brandon Freemantle shows a healthy liking for the newly smoothed surface of the Northside Arena track and comfortably wins heat 5 in 51.1 seconds. The predicted dust-storms arrive from heat 5 onwards but, luckily, the direction of the strong wind blows the loose grit over the first bend and avoids choking the small gaggle of appreciative fans gathered to watch this particular round of the British Under-15 Championships. Jordan Hazelden features in the next race so it gets my full attention. Jordan gates slowly but sneaks up the inside to secure third place as the riders exit the second bend. Up front Robert Lambert wins extremely comfortably in the fastest time of the afternoon (48.8 seconds) although this is still three seconds outside the track record set by Jason Garrity in August 2008. Dave Rattenberry studies the second 125cc Support Races – once again featuring careful bends and exhilaratingly speedy straights. After the riders finish, Rat enquires, "What age are these?" Since it's the Under-15 Championships, I can't resist replying, "I'm guessing – under 15!" It's news that only confirms Dave's opinion, "I know! They're only children, they're all only children!"

After the first two rounds of the 500cc category, Brandon Freemantle leads with 36 points ahead of Adam Kirby on 32. Heat 8 reflects their rivalry in a microcosm. Brandon leads from the gate until he's surprised on the second bend by a big elbow from a determined Adam Kirby. As intended, it's a manoeuvre that discombobulates and gives Kirby the lead. Adam remains ahead until he exits the fourth bend on the final lap when, rather than zoom over the finish line, he instead clatters into the wooden fence panel a yard or so from the chequered flag. In practical terms, his bike crosses the finish line first but, since he isn't still in contact with it, Jim McGregor – in his referee's box cum hide and security turret – disqualifies him. Heat 9 (or the fourth 250cc race of the afternoon) sees Nathan Greaves lock-up on the second bend of the second lap to give Jordan Hazelden a gilt-edged chance to pass. He can't quite avail himself of this opportunity and, in the blink of an eye, the chance is gone and I'm deprived of seeing Jordan win his first

Northside: *"One of the riders here today will go on to be a star! Trouble is, you don't know which one! In 20 years' time, we'll all say that we could see that today."*

Under-15 Championship race. Given the age and inexperience of the competitors, falls are always likely but happen much less often than predictions beforehand. That said, each and every fallen rider is very noticeably offered words of wisdom and encouragement by championship organiser and SCB Co-ordinator Graham Reeve (who stands on the centre green during each race for this very purpose). There's drama on the fourth bend of the first lap of heat 13 but, again, no fallers. Brandon Freemantle straightens while ahead, slews across the track and, thereby, allows Adam Kirby to scoot past round the outside for the race win. Given that these two vie together at the top of the 500cc British Championship, it could be a vital point to claw back. Between races people banter and gossip. Apropos of nothing at all Dave Rattenberry expounds on Kirkmanshulme Lane, "Tell you what, that Belle Vue is the worst track in the country!"
[Charles McKay] "And, tell you what, you've been listening to that tosser Rossiter!"

Dave Rattenberry also has no doubts about who'll triumph in the Premier League. "Newcastle! They're coming good at the right time, they'll win the league!"
[Charles] "The racing is so naff there; no one seems comfortable round Newcastle."

To my mind Edinburgh shouldn't be discounted. Sarah Miles recalls her last trip to see the Monarchs. "We hadn't booked a hotel when we went to see Edinburgh at Armadale and we stopped in Bathgate. I went to the first hotel we found and said 'Have you got a room for the night?' and the man said, 'Yes, why?' I said, 'I'd like one for me and my husband,' and he told me, 'We have a room for him, but not for you!' When I asked why he told me, 'Cos it's an all-male hotel.' I didn't think they still existed?"

If there was a competition for the most exotic mobile phone call of the afternoon, then Dave Rattenberry wins hands down. "You'll never guess who that was? [pause] Ivan Mauger – he wants me to sell his book! John Rich rings me up right [from Stoke where he's on duty in the trackshop] and he says 'There's a man here who's got some Ivan Mauger books – do you want to speak to him?' He puts him on and the man says 'It's Ivan Mauger here!' John didn't even know it was Ivan!" Always well informed about other people's obsessions as well as his own, Dave wonders aloud about the programme collection mania of his travelling companion Bill Gimbeth. "Do you know anyone more obsessed with programmes than Bill?" Sarah Miles definitely does and nods towards her husband Steve, "Yeh, you're standing next to him!"
[Steve] "I'm not. He collects every programme from every meeting."
[Sarah] "So would you if you had the space."
[Steve] "I wouldn't. I only collect programmes from Peterborough."
[Charles McKay interjects] "Sky meetings; junior meetings."
[Sarah] "*Speedway Stars* going back to 1970."
[Dave Rat] "*Speedway Now*, you've got that."
[Sarah] "All the 5-1s; *Speedway Mails* from 1970."
[Steve] "It's when Peterborough started and I was born as well."

Out on the track, Tyler Govier makes a late bid (though there haven't been many entries) to win the 'Most Spectacular Fall of the Afternoon' competition with a dramatic tumble from his bike on the third bend of heat 17. The next race sees another fall albeit a slightly less spectacular one from Nathan Greaves who tumbles from his bike adjacent to the finish line (on the second lap). He remains on the shale for some time before he's eventually helped to his feet. Though disqualified as the cause of the stoppage, Nathan nonetheless amasses enough points to make it through to this afternoon's 250cc final. For the n-millionth time this afternoon – as the medical staff make their way back to their positions – Dave Rattenberry returns to his favourite theme, "They're only little boys!"

101

Joe Levi Courtney wins the 125cc Support Race final, "It's the first time Joe Courtney's been on a speedway bike – very impressive!" Kyle Bickley takes second place to warm appreciation from the crowd – possibly partly since he's local but also because he's only eight years old! Ignoring this achievement, Sarah Miles observes, "The 125s sound weird!" The initial attempt to run the 250cc final finds Nathan Stoneman ahead of the impressive and undefeated Robert Lambert. However, under the close attentions of the cumulative championship leader, Stoneman falls on lap 2 as he transitions from the first to the second bend. Nathan remounts but his lost chance of glory is greeted with a display of red flags. Steve Miles comments wistfully, "He gave it a big handful!" Dave Rattenberry (for once) discounts Stoneman's youth to observe, "Serves him right for being too clever!" Given a second invitation, Robert Lambert comfortably wins the rerun without challenge to end the afternoon with five wins from five races. The final of the 500cc Under-15 British Championship stops almost as soon as it starts when Adam Portwood clatters into Adam Kirby. Immediately behind them, Tyler Govier lays down with alacrity only to hurt himself. Nonetheless, though still barely into his speedway career, like riders everywhere Tyler dusts himself down to ride when the race reconvenes. The rerun fails to last even as long as the first attempt. This time Adam Kirby knocks off Adam Portwood in the run to the first bend. Jim McGregor again rules "all four back". On the third bend of the second lap of the re-rerun 500cc final, Adam Kirby completes a hat trick of falls, following close behind Brandon Freemantle joins Adam on the shale. Bizarrely, referee Jim McGregor adjudges Freemantle to be the cause of the stoppage (!) and disqualifies him. Tyler Govier also gains a disqualification since he wasn't under power at the time of the stoppage. Charles McKay's mystified, "I thought Kirby went too hard into the bend and lost it so that's not quite right!" Dave Rattenberry has seen it all before with this particular official, "He's a bugger McGregor. When he's not a ref, he's nice but, in the box, he's a twat!" After a delay for a bustle of activity and the sound of hammering (some wooden panels of the fourth-bend safety fence get repairs) Adam Kirby remains on his bike throughout to beat Adam Portwood in their match race and emerge as the third-round winner of the 500cc class of the Under-15 British Championship. Despite his exclusion, Brandon Freemantle remains the cumulative leader of the competition (4 points ahead of Adam Kirby).

The crowd are quick to leave the stadium or join the riders, parents and mechanics in the pits for some post-meeting analysis and congratulation. It's been a grassroots meeting to savour and – without the hard work and dedication of Michael and Judith Lomas as well as their unsung band of volunteers – the next generation of young British speedway riders wouldn't have showcased their talents this afternoon in the Northwest of England at the Northside Arena.

17th July British Under-15 Championship Round 3
125cc winner Joe Levi Courtney; 250cc winner Robert Lambert; 500cc winner Adam Kirby

Northside: *"One of the riders here today will go on to be a star! Trouble is, you don't know which one! In 20 years' time, we'll all say that we could see that today."*

CHAPTER 12

Workington

"He told me that for the first time ever as a referee he had awarded a track 10 out of 10"

17th July

Most of the fans that specially travelled to Northside to watch the British Under-15 Championships then travel on into a sun-kissed central Workington to boost attendance at the Comets versus Somerset Dickies Rebels Premier League clash at Derwent Park. When I arrive at the Speedway Office Workington co-promoter and team manager Ian Thomas is in conversation with Graham Reeve. Ian's keen to know how the meeting went, "How was it?"
[Graham] "It was excellent. There were less incidents than last year."
[Ian] "How many were there?"
[Graham] "I dunno, about 80."

Joking aside, a smooth well-prepared Northside track kept crashes and incidents to a minimum. The reshaped and reinvigorated Derwent Park track has also been transformed since the arrival of Keith Denham. In so many areas of the club, no metaphorical stone has been left unturned and, indeed, many actual stones were shifted from the shale here. So as much so that the track was singled out for praise by experienced SCB official Mick Bates after the Birmingham meeting a fortnight ago. Ian Thomas proudly notes this in the programme, "He told me that for the first time ever as a referee he had awarded a track 10 out of 10. So congratulations to the guys who do the track. Mick Bates is a former speedway rider who you may remember riding for Mildenhall. I look forward to seeing a few congratulatory emails on the forum."

Speedway is a numbers business – points on the track, rider averages and fans through the turnstiles as well as the nowadays all-important sponsorship revenues. As a curious man and an author himself Ian always takes an interest in the sales success of my books, "How did you do at Cardiff?"
[Jeff] "11! Ivan did 600."
[Ian] "I don't believe that! What about Briggo?"
[Jeff] "Dunno he was at the Fan Zone not the Fayre. They say Leigh Adams and Michael Lee sold similar quantities to

Ian Thomas at work on race night

Craig Cook and his dog

Ivan."

[Ian] "Why don't you get Michael Max to say you're here and wander round with your book? The Alan Wilkinson book sold about 20 that way!" Ian glances inside the copy of *Shale Trek* that I've given him. He studies my signature with a quizzical look on his face, "What does that say?"

Because of tractor movements, the sea container that serves as the Workington trackshop has relocated from inside the Derwent Park Stadium walls to the outside edge of the rough ground of the car park. The shop is positioned at a point equidistant between the grandstand and first-bend turnstiles, albeit some distance removed from the stadium perimeter wall. Ian suggests I base myself adjacent to the shop and, when I check if this is okay with the hardworking trackshop manager Liz Fleming, she advises, "Don't stand on the grass as the dogs use that." The trackshop sea container and a phalanx of riders' white vans flank my display table. Many Comets fans don't go anywhere near the shop. Some do come along to survey the stock or stop in for a brief chat. Bristol-based John Short darkens the entrance of the trackshop filming with his video camera. He gets short shrift from Liz who explosively demands that he immediately cease, "Stop filming, please! It's against the law and BSPA regulations!" As a keen (stills) photographer of trackshops myself I jokingly reassure Liz, "I promise not to film". Liz reiterates her position, "It's not polite, let alone it's against the law without permission and it's against BSPA rules."
[Bill Gimbeth] "Watch it, or he'll write it in his book."
[Liz] "He can't do that either."
[Bill] "He can."
[Liz] "Well I want a cut of the profits! Where is Dave Rattenberry?"

I'd only be too happy to share a small percentage of the profits, if there were any! Later, during the meeting, I question gentlemanly wrestling and speedway fan John Short about his cinematic activities. "I was filming because of rumours that Workington might close. I don't do it for commercial purposes. It's the first time I've ever been asked not to do it. I always film tracks that might close. Or are abroad and I'm only going to go once. I've been to 203 tracks in 22 countries. I'm not boasting because there's people who've seen more tracks and been to more places (including Selwyn). I've been to all League tracks in Britain since 1965 and also all Open ones, like Northside today. We need more training tracks. There's Sittingbourne and Lydd – and I know Malcolm is a bit of a rebel but the Lydd track is excellent! There was more passing two years ago at Northside but it was a good meeting!" John isn't so keen on the Northern Junior League as a route to young rider development. "It's got a Hungarian – I saw him at Berwick – and a 48-year old and, apart from that, it's largely professional second-halfers. I haven't seen Halifax yet and they've got a new woman rider – not Montana Jowett – she's been around for ages!"

Two of the few fans that do pass by my table are Chris Butterworth and his 6-year-old son Glen. They travel to Workington each week to watch the Comets from their home in Grange-over-Sands. Chris is highly appreciative of my latest book (bought as a surprise gift by his wife for Father's Day), savours the time he spends with his son at speedway and football as well as delighting in the quality of the entertainment they regularly serve up on the Derwent Park shale. "It's my best ever Father's Day present! The racing has been fantastic here this season but the crowds are down. There's been some really bloody good meetings here. Craig Cook has been amazing! Chris Schramm is Chris Schramm! The biggest disappointment is André Compton – he's dropped 2 points off his average. We're missing a real No. 1. The Workington public are used to real heat leaders: Stoney, Kauko, Daniel Nermark. You never quite know what the management are up to. They're sticking with André. I nearly emailed you last week – I rate the meetings now, and the one against Birmingham a fortnight ago was a 10! The people who've stayed away have missed some awesome racing! The racing has been fabulous and the track has been good. There's

104

been a lot of rain this week, though the track should ensure it's still a good meeting. We're not going to be top four but there's quite a good balance about us. I don't think there's any love lost with Birmingham. We were 6 points down and then won. It really was a good advert for speedway!"

Trackshop entrepreneur Dave Rattenberry knows a bit about the importance of location when it comes to maximising sales. He's mystified by my positional backwater. "Why are you outside?"
[Jeff] "Ian suggested I stand by the trackshop."
[Dave] "I don't agree with that. You should be inside!"

After I achieve the sum total of nil sales, the lure of the meeting proves irresistible. As luck would have it, I immediately bump into Ian Thomas. When I tell him, "That must be the worst located speedway trackshop in British speedway!" he agrees. "It is! What can you do when you have no room for it?"
[Jeff] "If I stand at one entrance, I miss the other – there I miss both!"
[Ian] "If we built a bridge that would solve it but it's impossible!"

Ian loves his work at Workington (though recently he finds the drive from Yorkshire to the Northwest coast tiring). Without a meeting last weekend (because of the Cardiff Grand Prix) Ian took a well-earned vacation. "I just came back from a cruise to Corfu last night. It was 105 most days. We went because my wife [Dot] hasn't been that well. She's had three operations and general anaesthetics but we're flipping alive and that's the main thing!" Away from the shale Ian has a successful and ongoing show business career. "I've done Showaddywaddy in Yorkshire, Ilkley – you've heard of them – they were kicking the doors down – the fans not the band! I'm doing them in Barrow in October – its 50% sold already and I haven't spent a penny on adverts. I've been round the tourist information offices and the book the theatre produces comes out next week, so they'll sell more. It's on the Showaddywaddy website. I'm doing the Drifters just after that – the only thing that could disrupt that is a BSPA meeting. I went to the Whitehaven Festival last week and saw Katherine Jenkins [at the Whitehaven Marina]. Fifty quid a ticket but a printer I know got us tickets for £20 each. VIP seats, food and drinks for an hour beforehand and row three seats! I missed Status Quo the next night because of the speedway [Workington v. Berwick] but I didn't go on the Sunday when they had some flipping Asian hip-hop band!" [1]

Craig Cook's meteoric rise up the Workington Comets averages nowadays sees him race in the No. 1 race tabard. Unfortunately for the assembled Workington faithful, before heat 1 can get underway Craig touches the tapes and is disqualified for his trouble by the referee that Comets presenter Michael Max describes as "Big Cheese – Graham Reeve". Rather than race off 15 metres, yet another Workington rider with a grasstrack and motocross pedigree, reserve Richard Lawson, takes his place. Son of the legendary Steve Lawson, it's only natural that there's a pressure of expectation that some of Richard's Premier League performances at reserve belie. Though it's early days in his speedway career, Richard has already scored paid 12 points at Derwent Park against both Stoke and Scunthorpe. When the first heat finally gets underway, Rusty Harrison flies from the tapes to win with such great speed that Michael Max forecasts, "I reckon that could be Rusty's fastest ever time!" When confirming the results, Comets announcer John Walsh notes, "Actually it's Rusty's second best ever time." With former Comet Ritchie Hawkins second and Cory Gathercole third, Lawson's participation effectively serves as an extended warm-up for heat 2. It proves useful since Lawson applies his first-hand knowledge of tonight's track conditions with

[1] Interviewed over the winter in the *Speedway Star*, with his keen eye for any promotional opportunity, Ian would tell Richard Clark about the Barrow gig, "[it] was a sell-out with a waiting list of 30 or 40. I even had to stand myself! ... I'm going back to Workington to put on Showaddywaddy at the Carnegie Theatre on April 29. I've made that a Friday on purpose so I can stay over and go to Derwent Park for the speedway on the Saturday." Sadly, Ian died on February 17th 2011.

Workington: *"He told me that for the first time ever as a referee he had awarded a track 10 out of 10"* some aplomb and, better still, flamboyant race partner Kenny Ingalls follows him home. Though it's his debut season in British speedway, judged by the stylish way Peter Kildemand wins heat 3 you'd be forgiven if you thought last-placed André Compton was the junior member of their partnership. Christian Hefenbrock's cut back on the second bend of the first lap briefly gave him the lead until Kildemand sweeps past as they exit the next corner. Steve Miles savours the Derwent Park racing from a vantage point that overlooks the first and second bends. He can't quite believe the size of the audience, "This is the worst crowd I've ever seen here, I think!"

The riders manage a smooth departure from the tapes at the start of heat 4 but they're soon called back for additional homework by referee Graham Reeve. From the centre green, Michael Max gives us his gloss on the situation, "I suspect, perhaps, somebody might not have been sitting still – no names [pause] Chris Schramm." When the race gets run to completion, Shane Parker becomes the first Somerset Rebel to take the chequered flag tonight. Very familiar with the Australian after his long service with the Glasgow Tigers, Michael Max gurgles approvingly, "Shane Parker's 40 and he rides like he's 21!" The fifth race of the evening looks likely to end in the second Comets maximum heat advantage of the night up until the moment André Compton succumbs to an aggressive passing manoeuvre on the last bend of the second lap by Ritchie Hawkins. In almost the identical place, the third lap sees André passed by Cory Gathercole to relegate him to last position. Luckily, from a Comets perspective, Peter Kildemand wins easily.

With a lack of race winners, it's something of a surprise that the Rebels only trail 17-13 after five heats. However, from this point on in the meeting, the Comets riders collectively kick on to assert their home-track advantage and evident superiority. Heat 6 sees both Comets best Shane Parker of the Rebels when Rusty Harrison races to his second win closely followed by Craig Cook. Christian Hefenbrock offers some resistance to Richard Lawson in heat 7 but not enough. Rusty Harrison settles for a paid win in heat 8 won by Kenny Ingalls. Rebels stand-in team manager (and press officer) Ian Belcher sensibly refrains from any use of the black-and-white headgear colour until Shane Parker can race from gate 1. The Somerset captain doesn't disappoint but, with Peter Kildemand and André Compton in the minor places, the three additional points the Rebels claw back only vaguely massages the (34-23) scoreline. The gulf in commitment and pizzazz between the two teams then showcases in miniature when Craig Cook and Rusty Harrison determinedly combine to hammer home the Comets third maximum heat advantage in six races. Rusty Harrison's paid win secures his deserved paid maximum.

In an ideal world, temporary team manager Ian Belcher requires Cory Gathercole to win heat 11 in the black-and-white helmet colour to stem the flow of points. Unfortunately, Chris Schramm wins instead and, with Richard Lawson victorious from his third-place duel with Ritchie Hawkins, this heat is drawn. In the pits Ian Belcher remains phlegmatic. "I'm helping out because Bish [Steve Bishop] is ill. I haven't missed a Somerset meeting this season! So Shane, Ritchie Hawkins and myself are the ever-presents! We haven't been lucky this season. If you look at the team of riders we could have had if fate hadn't intervened, we'd have a much different line-up. There's Brent Werner, Steve Boxall, Jay Herne and Luboš Tomíček. Also you have to wonder if whoever wears the Rebels No. 1 jacket is fated? Let's think: there's Emil [poor sod], Shane [he wasn't the same], Luboš, Hefenbrock and Cory!"

Perceptions that tonight Shane Parker is the only really competitive rider in a Rebels race tabard take a slight dent in heat 13, after the Derwent Park stadium track slickens. Despite four laps probing for a possible route past the back wheel of Chris Schramm's bike, Shane is completely unable to find sufficient traction to pass round the outside. Although lacking the requisite velocity, nevertheless, Shane makes a determined dash for the finish line in an attempt to snatch second place but, narrowly, comes up short. Lawson and Kildemand combine in heat 14 to further extend the scoreline to 57-32 and, in so doing, gain the sixth Workington 5-1 of the night. Heat 15 is more or less a repeat of heat 13 from Shane Parker's point of view. The Australian continually probes for a way past the back wheel in front (this time Peter Kildemand's) but, once again, he's unable to find sufficient shale on the outside line to provide the traction he requires to convert his third place into something more meaningful. The final 62-33 scoreline arguably belies the comfort of the Comets win. The Workington faithful greet this victory with customary triumphalism. It's the first time since September 2008 that the Comets pass 60 points in a home meeting. Sadly, though it has one of the best views from its balcony in speedway, the corporate hospitality area remains resolutely shut. A Comets fan laments its unavailability, particularly since he believes that the manner and style of this victory would definitely prompt even the most reluctant would-be sponsor to put their hand in their pocket. "It's only been open a few times this season – the 40th bash and someone's birthday, I think."

As usual, it's been fun for Chris and Glen Butterworth, "It was a good meeting. We just need to get rid of one rider but I'm not naming names!" There's little demand for my books or for the speedway memorabilia in stock at the trackshop. Liz Fleming remains philosophical, "People are skint after Cardiff."
[Jeff] "It sucks all the money out of the speedway economy."
[Liz] "It's a big weekend for everyone and you try telling the fans about that." Despite flaccid levels of demand, the Workington fan in Liz dictates that she savours tonight's victory against Somerset, "It's a while since we scored 60 but our riders are riding well!" But for his first race exclusion, the Comets No. 1, Craig Cook, could (possibly) have had a paid maximum. Nonetheless, locally he's still a hugely popular talismanic rider. Indeed, it takes Craig about 10 minutes to negotiate the distance from the pits gate to his van (parked adjacent to my display table). Craig patiently poses for photographs, signs autograph and chats affably to any and all of the many Comets fans that wait to hang on his every word. Eventually free of adulation, Craig opens the passenger side door of the van to enthusiastically kiss and pet his rather cute Jack Russell (guard) dog.

Enthusiastic smokers unofficially police the doorway to the undercroft bar that's located in the main grandstand of Derwent Park stadium. Inside, it's crowded and noisy. Assorted prizes for the raffle lay out on the stage ready for their soon–to-be lucky owners. Close to a jam-packed but convivial bar – Steve and Sarah Miles, Dave Rattenberry and Bill Gimbeth stand round and chat to a youthful man who dresses in the speedway rider's civilian uniform of choice: T-shirt and shorts, albeit (in this case) with sunglasses perched on a Tour de France style cap. It remains one of the joys of speedway that – particularly at the Premier League and National League levels – throughout the country fans, riders and officials mix together afterwards for a drink in handily placed bars. Familiar with the Derwent Park track from his time here, Ritchie Hawkins happily talks about his evening's work. It starts promisingly but ends with 5 points from four rides. "There was only one line in the first corner and it was rutty! I found a pound coin on a track walk [smiles broadly as he proudly produces a dusty.and weather-beaten coin from his wallet] it made my night!"
[Steve Miles] "What do you do on a night off?"
[Ritchie] "I've got my clubs in the van but my wrist isn't so mobile!" He shows us all an impressive-looking scar.
[Steve] "Is it plated?"
[Ritchie] "Yeh but I'm gonna get it taken out!"

I lose track of the conversation during Dave Rattenberry's explanation of the best route from Buxton to the M6 motorway. He warns about speed cameras and also the overzealous policing that you can apparently expect in Staffordshire. "George Andrews got done last year for eating a banana in his car! It was front page news in Stoke!" Ritchie's popular everywhere he goes this evening including the gents, "Some bloke talked to me in the toilets. We got on okay but I couldn't understand a word he was saying!"

17th July Workington v. Somerset (Premier League) 62-33

Workington: *"He told me that for the first time ever as a referee he had awarded a track 10 out of 10"*

CHAPTER 13

Newcastle

"If knowing that has annoyed you, remember it when you go out on the track and score a few more points!"

25th July

After a powerful end to the 2009 season, over the close season the Newcastle Diamonds retain many of the key riders who contributed to that success. The 2010 team prompt the notoriously unreliable *Speedway Star* pundits to predict third place in the Premier League. But, as they say, speedway is raced on shale not on paper. Tonight's meeting is actually a cup competition, namely the first leg of the Premier Trophy final against the Birmingham Brummies. Earlier in the season few speedway fans would be prepared to bet against the Brummies making a clean sweep of all available silverware. However, speedway is a notoriously capricious sport and, though there are factors behind Birmingham's comparative decline that are easy to identify (Chris Kerr's broken leg, Aaron Summers's broken collarbone and Justin Sedgmen's loss of form), they've definitely stuttered over the last month or so. While Birmingham stumble, Newcastle soar as have last year's champions the Edinburgh Monarchs.

Ensconced in the Speedway Office away from the gusty wind and dark clouds that scud overhead, Diamonds co-promoter and team manager George English studies his laptop intently "watching" the World Cup Final from Vojens via the Speedway Updates website. If George is optimistic about success tonight in pursuit of the Premier Trophy silverware (or, indeed, about the Diamonds prospects in the PL or other competitions), he's carefully guarding his optimism. Perhaps it's his natural inclination or the result of following his local football team but, sat behind his desk smartly dressed in his BSPA regulation jacket and tie, George sports the pained, slightly quizzical look usually adopted by detectives in a Euro thriller wondering why someone has such a murderous grudge against zookeepers. "Things aren't so good for us! I lost two riders at Scunthorpe on Friday night through injury. Dak [Dakota North] only had three of his seven rides and Kenni Larsen

Brum faithful

Old school

three of his six. The track was crap. There was so much dirt that Carl Wilkinson didn't go on the outside until heat 15 and he spends all his time there usually! Kenni's gonna ride tonight – although he shouldn't really – but we've lost our high-scoring reserve, which isn't what we want. Birmingham have got Lee Smart who got paid 17 at Stoke last night and wasn't bad here a couple of weeks ago." I'm not so convinced of his threat, "Doesn't he like to ride each track as if it's a Polish one?" George possibly also has his doubts, "He's too tall to be a speedway rider, really."

A stocky blond man interrupts our conversation. He's the Diamonds low-scoring reserve, Anders Andersen, brought in at the start of June to replace the injured Adam McKinna. [1] George glances down at his laptop to double check the latest score in the Speedway World Cup Final on the updates and then says to Anders, "Your lot are doing crap."
[Anders] "What?"
[George] "The Danes aren't doing very well in the World Cup."
[Anders] "Ah, ah, don't tell me anything – I want to watch it later!"
[George] "If knowing that has annoyed you, remember it when you go out on the track and score a few more points!" It's advice that completely passes Anders by, if his complicated discussion of recently driven miles as well as payments made and payments owed is anything to judge things by.

After Anders departs to the pits to start his preparations for the important meeting ahead, George refreshes the updates page. England – or Team GB as they are known nowadays – actually make it to the World Cup Final, improvement after a few seasons when even this proves beyond them. However, if the Danes are doing "crap" then the Brits fail to hit those standards. Other matters temper George's natural patriotism, "I don't mind how Team GB get on because I've an issue with one of the riders." Like London buses, world cups of all varieties impinge upon British speedway fixture lists this season. The football World Cup in South Africa ensured a number of fixture changes and delays in all the British speedway leagues. "When the fixtures came out in November [2009] King's Lynn and us immediately made changes. We went there on a Tuesday but Len [Silver] who'd switched to Saturdays to avoid the *X-Factor* didn't realise until two weeks beforehand that there was a clash with the England game! It's not like there'd been any talk about it?" Standing in the corridor outside the Speedway Office, George's mum, Joan, is dressed very smartly as if about to go to a dinner dance. Joan looks youthful and must feel excited by the meeting ahead, judged by the way she hops from foot to foot in her dress shoes as she considers the Diamonds prospects. "We haven't got Dak tonight." Unlike Joan, I've yet to see him ride in the Premier League. "He started the season very well and, then, he went through a poor patch. I don't know why exactly? His dad was here and then he went back and also he had to move from Peterborough to Milton Keynes, so that could have been something. He's missing tonight though."

After the whereabouts of the Premier Trophy is decided, the next really important meeting on the PL calendar is the Four Team Tournament that takes place in mid-August at the East of England Showground. The return there pleases Joan, "The Fours always used to be held at Peterborough,

---

[1] If Anders also reads the programme later he might notice George English's weekly column "In Black and White". It might give him some pause for thought vis-à-vis George's almost lawyerly comments apropos of last week's comfortable 61-33 home win over Somerset. "Anders who has been really struggling of late found a little form that will hopefully boost his confidence. He made a couple of reasonable starts that must help him and hopefully he can build upon that. He knows that Adam [McKinna] has been given the all clear to ride a lot sooner than expected and that news alone must surely send alarm bells ringing in his head and give him the added determination to make sure he stays in the team. At the end of the day it comes down to points scored on the track so the ball is in Anders' court. ... Adam is desperate to get back into the side and I can honestly say that I thought very long and hard about whether to bring him back into the fold. He was pushing to be included this evening but in the end he accepted my decision with good grace and he knows he will have to bide his time... it's been a remarkable recovery as he gets nearer to racing fitness he will be pushing Anders hard to hold onto that No. 7." Shortly afterwards, Newcastle would loan McKinna to the Weymouth Wildcats in the National League in order to help him get back to race fitness.

Newcastle: *"If knowing that has annoyed you, remember it when you go out on the track and score a few more points!"*

then they changed it. It's nice to be back there again!" In gusty winds overhead there's the distant roar of old military planes en route to the Sunderland Air Show. This season I contribute a monthly article to the award-winning Newcastle Diamonds official race-day magazine. The latest contribution was about the cloistered world of speedway memorabilia collectors. George notes, "I didn't know if your article was about me? A few years ago that would have been me definitely." Reserve choices play on George's mind, "one reserve is excellent and the other is [blank]". George mouths the word that's probably a reference to their raw potential. George searched widely to secure a suitable replacement for Dakota North, eventually securing Jade Mudgway. He'll wear the Diamonds No. 6 tabard for Newcastle's most important meeting of the season so far. "If Berwick had ridden last night I'd have had Michal Rajkowski. I rang him from the pits at Scunthorpe [on Friday] to ask if he was here but he was in Poland!"

Preparations for the meeting ahead continue apace on both sides of the Brough Park pits area that overlooks the first and second bends. Also setting up nearby is Bob Tasker of GRT Media. He's well prepared with his own stepladder that he uses to climb on top of the metal sea container that's really the track staff hut and storeroom but also – when you're on top – provides a panoramic view of the circuit ideal for his film work. Bob went to the Cardiff Grand Prix and can provide an *ad hoc* estimate of the numbers inside the Millennium Stadium, "I'd say it was up a couple of hundred." Though ongoing doubts exist about the veracity of the figures, officially it was supposedly up 150 people to a suspiciously rounded new record of 44,150. "There you are! Dalbers [Andrew Dalby] kept saying it was down. Because of where they put the Sky booth on the second bend this year, they had to rearrange the crowd – so it's hard to compare. They had a packed home straight. What I want to know is how can they have a track so dry and have no dust? As you know, I get to see tractors four nights a week and, although they appear to have a grader on the front of the back (if you know what I mean), it appeared just to pack it down rather than smooth it out or rip it up! There wasn't a great deal of passing during the meeting though." A recent letter in the *Speedway Star* claims that it's not passing that counts during a meeting but, instead, the metric we should admire is the skill of a rider as they hold the position in the first bend and how they subsequently repel advances. Like many old-fashioned fans, Bob's sceptical, "They must be Lee Dicken fans then! Anders Andersen is a bit like that too! If he gets out in front, he's impossible to pass – although he's going no quicker than two farts a fortnight. There's nothing wrong with that, of course. Lee just gets in all the awkward positions and there's no way past at all! It helps he's bigger because that makes it harder again."

Bob's GRT Media work means that he gets to see a lot of speedway, "The most impressive team I've seen at Sheffield was Newcastle. I'm not just saying that. How they only won by 4 points I don't know as they absolutely humped them! And Newcastle winning there was a miracle in itself, if you think about the past. Not that Sheffield did anything wrong. The next week Sheffield rode exactly the same if you only look at the red-and-blue helmet colours – hard to do (but you know what I mean) – they rode the same but got 61 points! Something I want to know – and I don't know if you can tell me – is about the Sky graphics? Sad, I know, but I can't help noticing them! I do have a professional interest, of course. Sometimes they have to cut and paste the head of a rider onto some team colours but they pasted Jason King's tiny sized head on the body of Matty Weathers with the neck brace thing he wears. Jason's head could fall right down inside the neck brace. Another thing, I'd like to correct their graphics so that you can fit in the word "disqualified" rather than keep using the word "excluded!" When they cover football, they don't use old terms or invent their own – how come they think they can do that at speedway? If they could change the white helmet colours to green (and change them back) to suit themselves, why can't they use disqualified?"

Newcastle: *"If knowing that has annoyed you, remember it when you go out on the track and score a few more points!"*

Over by the turnstiles, presenter Andrew Dalby is smartly dressed in his Newcastle Diamonds anorak. Establishing a good lead tonight is crucial if the Diamonds are to gain some silverware from the return fixture on Wednesday at Perry Barr Stadium. It's a prospect that should lure out wavering or lapsed Newcastle speedway fans, despite the dark clouds overhead. "We're expecting a big crowd and, obviously, you want to entertain them! The weather is going to be like this – spitting on!" Moments later, the turnstiles open and cup fever officially hits Newcastle stadium. Initially there's a big influx of Birmingham Brummies fans, many resplendent in bright red-and-yellow clothing to proudly proclaim their allegiance. This particular cohort of Brummies quickly occupy as their own a central section of the covered home-straight terraced stepped grandstand. These Birmingham diehards still travel in force, despite last weekend's Northern tour of successive losses at Edinburgh, Berwick and Glasgow. It's a sign of their overall diminution in form that they didn't even beat Glasgow. These recent performances recalibrate Brummies fans' expectations if judged by their pre-meeting conversations. "I'd be happy if we did as well as we did at Edinburgh."
[Fan] "What lose by 13?"
[Fan] "Yeh, that was good."
[Fan] "Dunno. We've got the same ref – Craig Ackroyd – as we had last Sunday at Glasgow. There were six controversial decisions and all six went against us. You know it's bad when Glasgow fans come up and commiserate afterwards!"

After the initial Brummie rush, there's a steady stream of Newcastle fans into the stadium. Inside their official race-day magazine, the club reproduce a letter (received on House of Commons headed paper) from the Right Honourable N. H. Brown MP, Member of Parliament for Newcastle-upon-Tyne East. Nick knows his speedway onions and is a comparatively regular visitor at Brough Park. Unfortunately he's unable to attend tonight's important meeting but writes to George English to both apologise and pass on his good wishes. [2]

Sussex-based Alex Raby nowadays views the Newcastle Diamonds as his adopted home club, at least for the duration of his Durham University degree course. Similar to his contribution to the Eastbourne programme, Alex provides an overview of visiting riders. So often trumpeted that you'd have to be based on a remote island not to know it, most speedway fans long ago internalised the news that Birmingham have a strong Australian presence in their team! In Alex's notes the exact birthplace of Jason Lyons (VIC, Australia), Justin Sedgmen (VIC, Australia) and Richard Sweetman (NSW, Australia) retain an air of mystery. Generally packed with interesting comment, insight and news, the official race-day magazine even goes so far as to thank club photographer Steve Brock for his shale donation!

Thirty minutes before the scheduled start time, Edinburgh fan Maurice arrives in a disguise that wouldn't trouble the least-observant wannabe detective. Given his love of the Monarchs, it's nevertheless a shock to see Maurice resplendent in his Newcastle anorak! This surely is speedway's equivalent of cross-dressing? Maurice professes no embarrassment but refuses to have his picture taken. While the bowser slowly circles under dark skies, Maurice chats amiably about his personal speedway allegiances. "This is my 52nd meeting of the season. Last year, I only got to 74. I must get a Berwick jacket soon as I'm a Berwick season ticket holder. I don't go on holiday, I go to speedway. Last night's meeting at Workington – if I was writing a report – I'd say it was better than the scoreline suggests." Some things about speedway defy explanation, even to the initiated but especially to the casual uninformed. "I tried to explain to a non-speedway friend of mine how Newcastle and Birmingham could race in the Premier Trophy final when Glasgow and Edinburgh

[2] The letter reads: "Dear George, I'm delighted to see the success that the Diamonds are having this season and I'm particularly pleased to see that they are riding against Birmingham in the final of the Premier Trophy over two legs starting this Sunday at Brough Park. I will be grateful if you could pass on my best wishes to all concerned for both the final and the rest of the season. As you know I try to visit the speedway as often as work commitments allow and look forward to seeing you shortly."

Newcastle: *"If knowing that has annoyed you, remember it when you go out on the track and score a few more points!"*

are racing a Premier Trophy qualifier this afternoon. Technically, as Ray the gateman pointed out, that qualifying group will be finished before this one starts as it starts at 4 p.m. It's already 43-23 after 11 heats. Nonetheless, it's still like playing the FA Cup Final and a third round match on the same day! By the way I started reading your book [*Shale Trek*] last night and I'm sure it's David Nimmo not Derek Nimmo. Have you ever chatted to the first-aiders? David wasn't there at the meeting on Friday and there were lots of fallers so he missed out! A pal of mine once said 'paracetamol for Danny Bird' – Ha! Ha! – when he was up for his drugs test!"

Tonight's meeting definitely catches the imagination of the Newcastle public. With five minutes to go before the scheduled start time, there's still a substantial queue on the wrong side of the entrance turnstiles. It impresses Peebles-based Maurice, "That IS quite a big queue!" Middlesbrough *Evening Gazette* ace speedway reporter Martin Neal arrives to savour the action but has some hard-won but practical advice, "You have to stand in just the right place to hear things here!" He's soon off on a brief jaunt down memory lane to recall the speedway travel schedules of his youth. "When I lived down south – before I married – it was Milton Keynes on a Tuesday, Wimbledon on a Wednesday, Arena Essex on a Thursday, Hackney on a Friday, down the pub on a Saturday and Rye House on a Sunday!" Demand for my books remains poor, though some passers-by who view me as some sort of authority figure (or information centre) continue to delight with random questions like, "Can I book a coach trip?" and that hardy perennial, "Have you got a 2010 *Yearbook*?"

Exactly on 6.30 p.m., both teams' riders go on parade and are greeted with a riotously loud welcome. The packed grandstand terraces enjoy a vibrant (cup final) atmosphere. Presenter Andrew Dalby attempts to start his rider introductions only to have the grandstand crowd – in pantomime fashion – shout three times in unison, "We can't hear you!"
[Andrew] "Do we want a sound check before we proceed?"
[Crowd] "Yes!"
[Andrew] "Let's proceed anyway!"

After their intermittently audible introductions, the riders pose amiably for a commemorative photo joined by the diminutive Diamonds mascot with his customised pushbike (recently pictured in the letters column of the *Speedway Star*). On the subject of speedway coverage, Mike Amos's recent visit to Redcar speedway delivered a full-page article about the club in the *Northern Echo*. It's the first time that this regionally important newspaper has covered the Teesside club. According to Martin Neal, mixed reactions ensued, "The fans were evenly split. Half liked the full page and the other half though it was condescending and that he shouldn't have made mistakes."

A loud roar of appreciation from a partisan home crowd greets the Diamonds riders on a possible 5-1 as they exit the second bend. Jason Lyons and Lee Smart immediately pass either side of Derek 'Deek' Sneddon to calm this enthusiasm until Lyons suffers an engine failure on the second bend of the third lap. I'm stood with a large contingent of Brummies fans. At the instant of Jason's mechanical difficulty a Newcastle fan to my right celebrates this misfortune with some zeal. One middle-aged lady Brummies fan retorts, "How nasty is that?" only to be told, "Tell him to get another mechanic!" After the race, discussions continue. This voluble Diamonds fan is unabashed, "You dinnae cheer when he pops off but when his bike breaks down you do!" Over the loudspeakers we're told Jason lost a primary chain though, afterwards, the Australian explains, "A little bit of mud or dirt got in the breather hole of the fuel tank which wasn't good, but there's a first time for everything." In the world of Internet forums, trolls are posters who seek to provoke others with extreme opinions. If acknowledged, this abrasive Newcastle fan provides a similar service for visitors at Brough Park. The second race of the first leg of the Premier Trophy final starts unsatisfactory according to referee Craig Ackroyd (after Diamonds guest reserve Jade

113

Newcastle: *"If knowing that has annoyed you, remember it when you go out on the track and score a few more points!"*

Mudgway moves). Effortlessly partisan, our nearby chain-smoking Diamonds fan finishes his second supermarket own brand can from his first four pack to loudly offer words of encouragement to the New Zealander, "Go on Mudgway!" Locked in a battle for third place with Kyle Newman, Jade nearly falls on the second bend of the second lap. His wannabe number-one fan offers words of tactical advice, "Cut the inside off, son, that's the one!" Jade's unable to make headway but Newcastle's under-pressure reserve Anders Andersen manages to secure second place behind Lee Smart. Leaning against the fence in the pits viewing area, with his chin in his hands George English looks on with a disconsolate expression.

Richard Sweetman appears to get a heat 3 flier to the annoyance of the Diamonds uber-fan. He reacts by thrusting both arms melodramatically in the air in an evocative but unheeded appeal to Craig Ackroyd to order a rerun. These anguished cries of foul quickly die on his lips as Rene Bach monsters then eludes the Australian on bend two. Soon joined up front by Jason King, the voluble fan draws deeply on his cigarette and exult, "Keep it tidy, son!" before directing further goads to the nearby large contingent of middle-aged Brummies fans resplendent in their brightly coloured anoraks, "Shouldn't he be trying to chase back? Oh dear me, that's rubbish!"

Andrew Dalby's post-race congratulatory words indicates that the Jason King/Rene Bach partnership is often productive, "It's Newcastle's 4-3 combination in heat 3!" After Barry Wallace formally confirms the race result, Andrew Dalby gives vital housekeeping news, "Unfortunately the outdoor toilets are closed here this evening at speedway." Without any race action requiring his unique brand of provocative running commentary, the Diamonds uber-fan slurps from his third can or draws melodramatically deeply upon his cigarette in the manner of an under-aged teenager by the school gate keen to impress his mates. Dressed in a slightly oversized Newcastle anorak, it's hard to guess his age. His appearance suggests mid-20s, while his conversation – if you ignore the swear words – suggests arrested adolescence. With thinning hair and hormone-light bum fluff bristles, he could be mistaken for Charlie Brown's recalcitrant brother.

With every point vital, wily team managers George English and Graham Drury make tit-for-tat changes prior to heat 4. Simultaneously, they both send out their weaker reserve riders to get their allotted three rides out of the way as quickly as possible. Steve Johnston makes his only promising start of the night but Mark Lemon soon overtakes him. Behind them, there's a mini-duel of the weaker reserves. Jade Mudgway finds himself slightly ahead but travels on a trajectory towards the back-straight fence that sees his back wheel clip the front wheel of Kyle Newman to ensure his immediate contact with the Brough Park shale. Kyle's demise prompts cheers in the grandstand, ecstasy from the provocative wannabe and outrage from a middle-aged Brummies fan ("He took him out!"). From what I've seen of him, Jade Mudgway certainly isn't a shrinking violet. He's unafraid to mix it on the track but, in this instance, while he's slightly at fault, it's just one of those racing incidents that afterwards will be seen as part of the rough and tumble of both of these young riders' speedway apprenticeships. Not that that is how the Newcastle fan interprets the incident, "He couldn't ride his bike! He hoyed his-self off the bike!" Bound by the rules to disqualify at least one rider, Craig Ackroyd lights the blue exclusion light to boos of disbelief and a screech of "You are flippin' kidding me!" from the lairy Diamonds uber-fan.

To both fill the time and calm the situation, Andrew Dalby decides that this is the right moment to conduct the weekly competition to win a prize from the trackshop. "I dunno if Rachael's got the music ready for the mini-basketball – we'll do it now!" The object of the exercise sees the mini-basketball thrown into the crowd and, whichever lucky youngster catches it or grabs it first from the subsequent scrum, wins the prize. I'm advised that the competition doesn't always go to plan, "He's got such a weak throwing arm it often goes on the greyhound track!" While the Thunderbirds introductory music blasts out, Andrew Dalby lobs the mini-basketball with all the

Newcastle: *"If knowing that has annoyed you, remember it when you go out on the track and score a few more points!"*

power and grace Terry Hall brought to skimming stones in the promotional video for 'Ghost Town'. As predicted, the ball falls short of the terraces and, instead, lands on the greyhound track tarpaulin. A larger gentleman leans over to rescue it and passes it to his own child. To the neutral observer this doesn't appear to be the fairest way to allocate the prize but, in the confusion, Andrew Dalby makes an executive decision, "I didn't see what happened there but – we have a winner!" While we wait the contingent of Birmingham fans launch into their "Gives us a B, give us an R…" Brummies chant while the balding provocateur in the Newcastle anorak attempts to drown them out with a shouted tuneless rendition of "Diamonds are forever". Fielding an intricate knowledge of speedway regulations to match the intellectual rigour of his insights, said fan laughably claims that the absence of the disqualified Mudgway won't be a problem in the rerun, "They'll replace him with Andersen off 15!" If it's possible to be doubly wrong, then this claim is a textbook example. Re-living an imaginary version of the incident on his own personal big screen, said fan chunters on, "He was past him and he dumped it!" When the rerun of the race gets underway, Kyle Newman is subject to provocative volleys of expert analysis. Highlights include: "Watch he doesn't take a dive ref!", "He cannae even ride a bike" and, possibly betraying confusion better dealt with by Freudians, "He took a muff dive, man!" Out on the track, Mark Lemon again easily bests Steve Johnston ("See you, Stevie boy!"). Kyle Newman's rough-and-ready riding style suggests that the third-place point for just finishing the race is by no means a certainty. Kyle rides with wholehearted brio. He mixes bursts of acceleration with wobbles and near falls, "Look at him – he's shit, a danger to his-self!"

The first attempt to run heat 5 ends on the third bend of the second lap when Rene Bach drives fast up the inside of Jason Lyons with sufficient speed to overtake him. Contemporaneous with this manoeuvre – and at the farthest point of the track away from the referee's box – Jason Lyons tumbles from his bike and hits the fence. It's another incident to greet with unabashed delight by the Diamonds uber-fan. His reaction proves to be final straw for a Brummies fan in his early 50s who channels the spirit of Victor Meldrew and has strong words (without swearing) about the unsportsmanlike attitude of his would-be interlocutor. The outspoken gentleman fingers his precious Newcastle anorak as if he briefly but theatrically toys with taking it off to properly address the situation. He thinks better of it. Instead, with gestures and full-beam smiles, he luxuriates in the white disqualification light lit by referee Craig Ackroyd. Though we're also some distance away, Jason Lyons did appear to "put down" his bike. There's barely any murmur of objection from amongst the Brummies fans at his disqualification. The rerun delivers the Diamonds second easy maximum heat advantage of the evening to take the scoreline to 19-11. Life's too short to endure the lava flow of mindless piffle that pours forth from the mouth of the cartoon Diamonds fan so, instead, I retreat to one of the pub beer-garden style benches adjacent to the grandstand. Redcar pits gate man Jim Elsdon and a relaxed Ray (fresh from his pre-meeting duties on the Brough Park entrance turnstiles) are already sat there. They're dedicated long-time speedway fans that – like so many genuine people who love the sport – definitely have their favourite riders and teams but prefer to savour the race action with equanimity rather than jingoism.

If Birmingham want some silverware for their trophy cabinet this season, they're going to collectively have to buck up their ideas over the remaining two-thirds of the meeting to restrict the scoreline to manageable levels for a possible second leg fight-back. Their newfound determination needs to start immediately in heat 6 with a big performance from Steve Johnston. Sadly for the Brummies, Andrew Dalby's pre-meeting comment ("a half-fit Larsen is okay because he's half a lap ahead most of the time") again proves prescient. Nevertheless, you'd still expect Johno to beat Deek but, as the riders enter the second bend for the second time, Johno simultaneously loses traction, race position and control to slither from his bike. It gifts the Diamonds successive 5-1s, despite a pacey last lap from third-placed Kyle Newman. Though their

Newcastle: *"If knowing that has annoyed you, remember it when you go out on the track and score a few more points!"*

12-point deficit notionally gives Graham Drury additional tactical options, it's hard to believe that he welcomes or would engineer such a situation so early in the meeting. With the always threatening Mark Lemon off gate 1 in heat 7, the Birmingham black-and-white helmet colour remains unused in the pits. Jade Mudgway again rides in lusty whole-hearted fashion but comes to grief as he transitions from the third to the fourth bends after he hits the kerb and bounces back for his bike to then crumple underneath him. Commendably Jade quickly clears the track probably unaware that (with Birmingham on a 4-2) George English might prefer he linger on the shale. With their initial use of the black-and-white helmet colour kept back until the strategically most advantageous time, Graham Drury sends out Johno for Aaron Summers's heat 8 rider-replacement ride in said helmet colour. Unfortunately, the best-laid plans often go awry. Apparently mounted on a lead bike, Johno takes until the back straight to overtake under-threat Diamonds reserve Anders Andersen. Amazingly, they then proceed to exchange positions until Anders dives underneath Johno over-ambitiously and clips the Australian. Johno's core resistance instantly deserts him and his theatrical tumble ensures the disqualification of the stocky young Dane. Ahead by the proverbial mile when the race stops, in the rerun Derek Sneddon then does it all over again.

Between races, 72-year-old Jim Elsdon chats amiably about some of his speedway memories. "I've been doing it since I was seven-year-old. The lady from across our road took me – to Norwich I think – I lived then where I live now [Connaught Road, Middlesbrough] just over the road from Cleveland Park. I got really involved in 1960 – I started as a track waterer when I first started and the promoter then gave me the security job and looking after the pit gate and that. We always went to Cleveland Park until the stadium owner sold it over the speedway club. My sister Julie Lewis ran the speedway office – she does now! She's been the same time as me – over 40 year! In 1946-1947, we used to come straight from school and sit outside the track. If we didn't do that we wouldn't have been able to see because so many people came. [3] There were 14,000 spectators in them days in Cleveland Park. There were long queues and buses came from both Stockton and Middlesbrough. We had to run down to the front straightaway. Speedway was different in the 1940s – they were leg trailing from behind and used to put a pad on their knee to put the bike down. In 1946 we had a rider killed – Blondie Wilson – not at our place but in Norwich. He went up in the air and hit a light post. There was no motorways in those days. In 1947 we were winning everything and they applied for the big league but they wouldn't let us in the National League cos we were off the beaten track. The crowds died and died until we shut in 1948. We were opened again for three years by Reg Fearman and another chap called Parker from 1961-1963 before the licence went to Halifax in 1964. Ah, it opened in 1950 for a couple of [pause] a very short, very short period. Another team I can recall from those days was Frank

[3] The *Speedway Star* dated 21st August had sad news. "Everyone connected with speedway on Teesside has been deeply saddened by the death last Saturday of longstanding officer manageress Julie Lewis. Julie had been a stalwart of the Bears for a period spanning no fewer than six decades, originally taking charge of race-night administration at the old Cleveland Park circuit in 1968. She ran the office right until the track was closed for redevelopment at the end of 1996, but was immediately reinstated in the position when Chris Van Straaten, Glyn Taylor and Gareth Rogers reopened the club at the South Tees Motorsports Park ten years later. Julie had been suffering poor health for a number of years, being periodically forced to miss her beloved speedway on Thursday, and spent the last few days of her life in Middlesbrough's James Cook Memorial Hospital. Paying tribute to her, current Redcar promoter Brian Havelock said: 'She was a workaholic for speedway, yet I don't think she ever had the chance to watch many races as she was always in the office. At Cleveland Park she wouldn't have been able to see anything because there was a little embankment between where the office was and the track. And you couldn't see much from the door of our old office behind the crowd at the South Tees Motorsports Park. That's why, when they moved the office forward at the start of this year, I made sure we had a window in the side that faces the track. I've known her for 40-odd years since I began riding and was trying to break into the team in the early '70s, and she became very much part of the furniture.' Chris Van Straaten added: 'Julie's local knowledge and history with previous Bears' promotions made her invaluable, particularly in the initial years of Redcar speedway. She was fiercely loyal and committed to her beloved Bears with an energy that belies her years. Julie epitomised the qualities of many fine people I met while establishing Redcar – loyal, hardworking and outspoken. She will be sorely missed.'" Julie's funeral took place on Friday 20th August at St Martin's church, Whinney Banks, Middlesbrough – less than a mile from the site of her beloved Cleveland Park.

Newcastle: *"If knowing that has annoyed you, remember it when you go out on the track and score a few more points!"*

and Jack Hodgson, Kid Curtis, Wilf Plant, Ed 'Crusty' Pye, Jack Gordon and Jeff Goodwin. Harry Whitfield – a fruitier who had a fruit-and-veg warehouse that supplied all the shops – and another chap called McKinna were the promoters in those days. Did you know the council built the track at the South Tees Motorsports Park? Not many people do. We could have been where we are in the 80s in that spot but then it was going to be called 'Wheels'. A Cleveland Borough Councillor was going to do it but he lost his seat. The promoter at the time was Tim Swales and he was gonna have everything. The lot! Like some other people, I helped get speedway back. We used to meet once a month with the dog people." Apart from his passion for speedway, Jim has other strings to his bow. "I'm also a singer – all sorts. I'm involved with a male voice choir and a mixed choir. I've sung at the Albert Hall and sang at the City Hall here. I did the clubs and the pubs when I was in my thirties. I had a tenor voice like Mario Lanza – he was a top tenor, like Pavarotti – and I had a voice like that. I come every week to Newcastle with a friend from Redcar (Ian Jackson) who's the pit marshal. The original race night was a Monday but they had to move it to a Sunday. The tannoy is awful here but they have to keep it down because of the complaints. This is the best side Newcastle have had for a very long time. They look awkward here because they have tight corners and they have to ride it differently! Middlesbrough was like it too. Small track with tight corners and we had to really ride it and we had good racing!" Unlike some of his fellow Redcar speedway fans, Jim enjoyed Mike Amos's recent article in the *Northern Echo* following his visit to the STMP. "He's a lovely man. He's what you call a dedicated man. He stutters when you talk to him but he doesn't when he gives speeches!"

In need of some lightning reflexes from the sunshine-bathed tapes in heat 9, instead Johno brushes them. Penalised by 15 metres, the rerun of heat 9 is something of a collector's item for any Kyle Newman fans inside the stadium. Kyle rides Jason King legitimately hard into the first corner forcing him wider and wider up until the moment he appears to caress King's bike. This touch thrusts Jason towards the fence and off his bike. Untroubled by the carnage behind him, Kyle races very quickly down the back straight in pursuit of Rene Bach but, unable to control his own velocity up the inside, tangles with his rival as they zoom into the apex of the bend. This contact sends both off on close inspections of the safety fence and shale. With only the slow-starting Johno still on his bike, there's a trackwide catalogue of mayhem that's tricky to adjudicate! Passionately strong opinions are held on the terraces as well as both sides of the pits. Cognisant of the importance of this meeting, referee Craig Ackroyd orders a rerun with all four back to a rumble of grumbles from the crowd and an ear bashing from both Graham Drury and George English. Fortunately I'm out of earshot so don't hear the opinions of Brough Park terraces self-nominated, "Mr Newcastle". Both gate men – Ray (Newcastle entrance) and Jim (Redcar pits) – greet this peculiar decision with studied impassiveness. They've seen it all before and, when it comes to voluble fans with wild opinions, Jim has heard it all before, "You get nutters at every club!" Already over 90 minutes into the meeting with only eight races completed, the re-rerun sees Jason King avoid a wild fling of Kyle's back wheel on bend two. King proceeds to resist Newman's close attentions throughout the length of the Brough Park back straight until, possibly distracted by his own efforts, Kyle gets totally out of shape. Though Kyle shows good skill to recover rather than fall, inevitably his challenge falters as the Diamonds power partnership of Bach and King secure another yet Newcastle maximum heat advantage. Given a third chance to shine, albeit off 15 metres, Steve Johnston trails home last.

Heat 10 sees Diamonds Kenni and Deek comprehensively best the Brummies Sedgmen/Sweetman pair to take the score to 39-23 and take the tally of Diamonds maximum heat advantages to five. In attempt to resuscitate their challenge, for heat 11 Graham Drury sends out Jason Lyons in the black-and-white helmet colour and Lee Smart as rider replacement. George English responds with Anders Andersen in place of Jade Mudgway. With a win for Mark Lemon

Newcastle: *"If knowing that has annoyed you, remember it when you go out on the track and score a few more points!"*

and an engine failure for Lee Smart, this drawn heat double underlines the Brummies quest for damage limitation over the closing heats if they're to put up any sort of meaningful challenge in the second leg at Perry Barr. Like many Birmingham riders this evening, Justin Sedgmen hasn't enjoyed his finest hour. Justin hasn't even flattered to deceive and, with only 2 points from three rides, it's no surprise to see Lee Smart take his place for heat 12. Though it's sensible to choose the more in-form rider, sadly (with no one near him) Smart slides off on the first bend. Lee stays down on the shale looking for an 'all four back' decision that referee Craig Ackroyd eventually answers with the red stoplights and Smart's disqualification. Jim Elsdon shrugs, "He said bollocks!" I'm not so sure, "Or something else." "No, I said he's hurt his bollocks!"

If the police were to arrive and seal off the Brummies side of the pits, it would be a fruitless search for their collective mojo. With the possible exception of their reserves, no Birmingham rider really performs with the determination you'd ostensibly expect the occasion (and their large contingent of supporters) to demand. The heat 12 rerun sees Newman and Andersen enjoy a slightly wild first bend. Rene Bach avoids the traffic with a cut up the inside to zoom away to victory. On the second bend of the third lap, Kyle Newman overtakes Anders Andersen and probably seals the end of his Newcastle career. Disappointed and self-critical, Anders denounces himself angrily as he crosses the line. The Brummies power partnership of Jason and Johno then toothlessly concede ground in a one-sided heat 13 won by Mark Lemon. In the penultimate race, Lee Smart fires up inside Anders Andersen on the third bend of the second lap to gain a third place that makes him the Brummies top scorer with paid 10 from seven rides.

Off gate 2 in the final race of the night, Kenni Larsen rears slightly at the tapes and proceeds to play bumper-cars down the straight. After rebalancing himself with a foot on Sweetman's bike, Larsen veers over to sweep under but not really touch Jason Lyons on the first bend. Nevertheless, Lyons comes to grief and angrily leaps to his feet. The usually taciturn Australian waits for Larsen to return to the vicinity of the pits gate so he can wave his hands in wild gestures of dissatisfaction. To the chagrin of a partisan crowd, Kenni Larsen is disqualified. Nimble fleet-footed Diamonds fans rush over to the pits fence in anticipation of further drama in the pits but have to content themselves with the sight of Graham Drury ostentatiously holding Jason Lyons back from going across to the Newcastle section of the pits. Rene Bach wins the rerun to complete an almost effortless five-ride 15-point maximum that deserves the bumps his team mates then administer by the pits gate. The meeting closes at 21.10 after 160 minutes of Premier Trophy entertainment. The Birmingham riders briefly venture out onto the tarpaulin-covered dog track to wave to the healthy contingent of their fans who continue to wait patiently on the home-straight grandstand terraces. Some Diamonds fans banter with a laughing and smiling Jason Lyons who ignores shouts of, "Put your dummy back in!"

Andrew Dalby interviews the victorious Newcastle riders while the Diamonds fans who remain inside the stadium glory in the 22-point lead they'll take to the Midlands. En route to the car park Brummies co-promoter Mick Bratley is informed by a Birmingham fan, "That was really embarrassing!" Sometimes, even if you're a member of the management team, emollient words of corporate speak just won't cut it. Sensibly Bratley replies, "I know! I know!" Shortly afterwards, Emma Lemon catches a few words with Newcastle team manager and co-promoter George English, "Imagine how it would have been if Dak [North] had ridden!" George nods in agreement, "Yes we were weaker without him!"

George would later tell the *Speedway Star*, "I thought the referee had an abysmal night and some poor decisions cost us a few more points. Still a lead of 22 is very handy, though we are not taking anything for granted." Plain speaking is the order of the night and Jason Lyons provides some *ad hoc* feedback on the performances of Kenni Larsen and Rene Bach for the magazine too. "It was

Newcastle: *"If knowing that has annoyed you, remember it when you go out on the track and score a few more points!"*

typical young little Nicki Pedersen's. Nicki has learnt his lesson over the years and these kids are gonna go down the same road. They've got talent and they've got everything going for them but you lose respect very quickly riding like that. What comes around goes around." Emma Lemon enjoyed the victory but her mind is really on her chickens. "When Mark went to the cricket with Jason Crump – I'm sick of hearing about it – invited by Justin Langer, he had a pass out that night so I got two chickens!" [4]

25th July Newcastle v. Birmingham (Premier Trophy Final, First Leg) 58-36

[4] In his rather wonderful Twists and Turns column from the Wolverhampton speedway programme for their meeting against Coventry, luxury transport entrepreneur and club sponsor Dave Parry reveals more about this particular trip to the cricket. "I cannot really call myself a cricket fan but I was sat watching a test match on TV between Pakistan and Australia. The game was being played at Lords when out of the corner of my eye I thought I saw Mark Lemon and Jason Crump. I saw Lemmo last week and asked him if my old eyes had been playing games, gladly he reported that they were in working order! It turns out that Lemmo is an old pal of former Aussie test player Justin Langer and what a day the speedway duo had. The cricket finished early so the boys jumped on the team coach and went back to the cricketers' base in Kensington. Now cricket and drink usually go together and it would appear that night went along those lines!!! Joe Bugner junior (son of the guy who fought Cassius Clay) is another friend of Lemmo's (is there no one he doesn't know??) and he arranged the evening's entertainment. Suffice to say a good time was had by all."

Newcastle: *"If knowing that has annoyed you, remember it when you go out on the track and score a few more points!"*

CHAPTER 14

Isle of Wight

"He said he'd stop the race in case a rider went over the fence and hurt themselves on the brambles!"

3rd August

Huge queues of cars, lorries and vans wait patiently for the slightly delayed 3 o'clock ferry sailing from Portsmouth Harbour to Ryde on the Isle of Wight. After the giant craft slides into dock, ferry staff load the boat with expert casual nonchalance. Since it's the height of the holiday season, large numbers of vehicles want to go over to the Isle of Wight. During the summer months, the Island population of 135,000 swells to a quarter of a million. The six or so weeks of the summer school holidays is the key period for the Isle of Wight speedway club to generate substantial revenues through the turnstiles to help eek out their leaner months.

Tonight's meeting pits the Islanders against their local rivals Bournemouth Buccaneers. Many riders, volunteers and fans cross on the 3 o'clock sailing. Without Dave Croucher to assist, I'm in need of a lift and Steve Hill – father of the Islander's 23-year old reserve, Thomas – kindly volunteers a lift in their van. After a brief struggle with the faulty lock on the side door, Steve ushers me into the customised space behind the front seats. It's fitted out with a number of home comforts including a bed on a ledge (that's the width of the van), passenger seats, a small primus and kettle for a refreshing cuppa should the need or inclination strike them. The Hill family live in Glossop. Steve makes light of the journey down to the Isle of Wight they take every Tuesday (and some Thursdays) during the speedway season. "It's three and a half hours to Portsmouth from Glossop and three-quarters of an hour over on the ferry and ten minutes to the track. We share the driving. Sometimes we sit together and other times we sleep for an hour on and an hour off in the bed. We've been finishing all season at 9.20-9.30 (unless there's crashes), so it's not been a rush back to the ferry. Thomas even has time to change before we leave or, if not, like the rest of the riders he does it at the Ryde ferry terminal. The Isle of Wight [club] is the friendliest. We really like the people. He's been all over – Buxton, Scunthorpe, Belle Vue – lots of places. He started at Peterborough when they had a junior team but that folded after about four months and then he rode at lots of other places. They have their favourites so it's hard to get a team place. We kept going to the training schools at Scunthorpe every week and they kept saying 'come along'. But, when I asked Malcolm Vasey if there was a place, he said they were full already. So we stopped going as £35 a week is expensive. Tom's got a good job with training but he had a chat with me and the wife and said he wanted to go for it. You can always get another job but you can't always get to be a speedway rider! I work nights on two different shift patterns so I'm always off on a Tuesday. When I can't do it, he goes with Henning Loof who lives in Lincolnshire. You need someone who knows about speedway! I think Henning would like to ride but he has a good job with Lincolnshire Library Services – in the library, I think – plus he's getting married in October, so it's a regular wage and he has his responsibilities. With speedway you need all the components to be right – the bike, the track, the rider – if one of these is slightly off it's a nightmare! It's such a delicate balance. One thing can throw everything out!" Islanders No. 7 Tom is a quiet, fair-haired gentle giant of a man. He drives us from Ryde to the track. Father and son chat in staccato short sentences. Tom's feeling a bit under the weather and debates with his dad what he can take for a splitting headache? Unfortunately, speedway regulations dictate that riders can't take any medication to treat their ailments (whether temporary or serious) if they wish to ride. As they open the back door to unload his bikes and equipment, I wish Tom success, "I'll look forward to you winning a few races tonight!" Ignoring his symptoms, Tom smiles confidently, "I intend to!"

Inevitably there's a friendly welcome in the upstairs bar of the clubhouse cum sports centre that's adjacent to the entrance turnstiles at Smallbrook Stadium. I join a couple of smokers out on the balcony that overlooks the second bend of the Islanders 385-metre racetrack in one direction and the cricket pitch in the other. We sit and savour the warm shade along with the wasps brought out by an intermittently sunny afternoon. I'm clearly a stranger and this prompts one gentleman to ask, "Are you the ref?" Today's Speedway Control Bureau official is Darren Hartley.

It seems peculiar that Dave Pavitt is now no longer involved at Isle of Wight speedway. Dave 'Crouch' Croucher still works behind the scenes at the club but prefers to remain in the background. "I don't go over to the pits because it's not my show anymore! I've had my time – in fact, I was looking through some old photos and found one with me and the England U21 team at Wolves. It brings back memories. If they want me to do anything in the background, I do but I don't walk round. I don't want to be seen with my stick for one thing. I'll tell Big Tim [Helm] that you're here. I usually make a list for them to read but I haven't this week. It would help if he read it more than once. Last week, I did a long list and he said 'we have an ice cream van here. I don't know where it is? Oh, there it is on turn one!' I rang him the next day and said 'I'm gonna have a bellyache with you.' 'Why?' he said, 'I mentioned everything you said!' I told him, 'If you don't know where it is keep it to yourself till you do. It's hard to miss, it's big and white like an ambulance and with a giant ice cream cone on top that makes it about 12ft tall!'"

Another recent change at the club sees another long-time Tuesday night stalwart, Bryn Williams, relieved of his club press officer/programme editor and announcer duties. Though we'll no longer hear his dulcet tones over the stadium speakers, he's still come over as usual with club incident recorder, Chris Golding. "I'm here cos I'm the reporter for the *Speedway Star!*" [1] Bryn has a close eye for

Fundraising

Gardening

Isle of Wight: *"He said he'd stop the race in case a rider went over the fence and hurt themselves on the brambles!"*

detail. "Did you see that Tim Helm in his press releases gives the full teams out? I said to him 'even if it only costs five lost programme sales and people making their own racecard that's still five lost sales which, in the present climate, is vital!' It's definitely not the sort of thing you should take casually!"

Chris and Bryn took in the recent Speedway World Cup semi-final held in King's Lynn at the Norfolk Arena. Chris reveals, "It looked smooth and professional to the public but I can assure you that behind the scenes it was anything but!" In the flesh, last night's televised Lakeside versus Poole meeting impressed Bryn. "It was a great meeting – did you see it on Sky? I've never seen Lee Richardson get annoyed because he's so laid back but he tried three or four times to get past their Pole – wot's his name, Mroczka! He kept weaving from side to side. You don't do that! Fair play to Darcy Ward, he raced properly and left a handlebar width for Stuart Robson to get past and, somehow, he did. They shook hands afterwards. I did the phones last night and four different people rang up who hadn't been to speedway before. They said they'd turned on Sky Sports 1 on the telly to see the cricket and seen the Speedway World Cup instead and decided they wanted to come and see it live!" This contradicts the commonly held opinion of some naysayers. It's so much of surprise that I can't help but exclaim, "Just shows that Sky does make people go to the speedway!" Bryn remains uncertain whether the ongoing Sky Sports speedway coverage really is the magic bullet its advocates claim, "Well, those four anyway!"

Potentially exciting though this local derby fixture is, the Bournemouth Buccaneers aren't the powerhouse team they were in 2009 and, since it's rumoured that Matt Ford has fallen out of love with them, they might well be here today and gone tomorrow. In terms of tonight's contest, so far this season the Islanders have shown their usual variable form – mostly strong at home and poor away. From a future-of-speedway point of view, both clubs (and, indeed, the National League) are needed for and are important to young rider development. Elsewhere in the country today, senior speedway figures meet to thrash out possible (hopefully robust) ideas for the future of the sport and, doubtless, propose rule changes that disadvantage others. Aside from obvious economic pressures, 2010 crowd levels indicate ongoing fan disinterest and should, you'd like to think, give these discussions greater urgency and creativity. "There's the big management committee meeting in Rugby today. They've got to sort things out. The Elite League is f***ed and this League [NL] is too! There's talk of not working with Sky so they don't have to give Terry Russell his 10%! But what is that, really, compared to the impact Sky has?" Though with astonishing regularity, the rules and regulations of British speedway are discarded, amended or ignored – unless Sky also really want to walk away, it's highly unlikely that they'll ignore the three years left on their contract. Especially when some rule changes appear to happen at their (implicit) behest.

With only a few minutes to go before the turnstiles open there's a small queue outside the stadium gates. Inside the perimeter fence, some delights await. There's my book display; the traditional programme and raffle tickets stall run by sexy Sue and her colleagues plus – for one night only –

---

[1] As befits any competent press officer, Bryn released a statement about his situation. "It is with deep regret and much personal sadness that I can confirm that, since June 2nd this year I have no longer been acting as the Wightlink Islanders press officer, programme contributor and meeting announcer. I was briefly taken ill on the ferry back to Portsmouth following the home match the previous evening but matters in that direction were quickly sorted following a telephone call to my doctor next morning. I was therefore astounded to receive a phone call on the night of June 2nd from one of the club's directors telling me that my services were 'no longer required!' I have been given NO real explanation other than the club's current chairman saying to me during a brief conversation that the directors were apparently 'concerned about my health.' I would willingly carry on the above duties especially as my own doctor says I'm perfectly fit to do so but alas the Isle of Wight Speedway's Board of Directors obviously think differently! Never mind, I will continue to travel from Kent to the Island on Wightlink Islanders race nights and provide match reports from the Wightlink Islanders home matches for the sport's weekly magazine – the Speedway Star – AND continue to help out "behind the scenes' as I do, at various other clubs in the UK. I hope you enjoyed and appreciated the service I provided to you by way of Press Releases etc whilst I was the club's press officer announcer etc for in excess of ten years and indeed thank YOU for the superb coverage you afforded the club during that time. Should you require any further information whatsoever, then please do not hesitate to contact me."

Isle of Wight: "He said he'd stop the race in case a rider went over the fence and hurt themselves on the brambles!"

Ros Parsons and Dani Johnson with their collection buckets. They've also come along with a box of eye-catchingly distinctive large-sized bright yellow sunflower badges sold for a bargain £3 to help raise money for the Earl Mountbatten Hospice in Halberry Lane, Newport. The dynamic duo behind T2TV – the Isle of Wight speedway's official film company (with bargain priced DVDs at £7 per meeting) – Jackie and Ken Burnett wander past having set up their equipment on their film platform perched high above the referee's box and start/finish line. Ken jokes, "There's a ferry sailing at 10 tonight – did you know that? The difference between this promotion and the last one is that these want you to come and enjoy the speedway rather than run it so people can't make the 10 o'clock sailing and have to stay in the bar! I suppose it's because they come from the mainland and understand that people might want to leave to go back there." Those in charge of the club finances are also keen to see a big crowd flood through the turnstiles to see Bournemouth ride. The man inside the entrance booth declares, "Let's hope they get 500 tonight!"

With an hour before the tapes rise, the dark clouds overhead could discourage waverers from venturing along to Smallbrook Stadium. If they could see the bowser dousing the track, they'd know how confident the Islanders management must be about the weather this evening! After a few circuits the bowser retreats to the pits to leave the track soaked and smooth on the inside and, to my untutored eye, rough and rutted on the outside. One of the centre-green marshals also studies this handiwork, "I'm only a marshal here and I have no standing but, looking at the track, I think it should be smoother on the outside and there should be more dirt on the inside. But what do I know?" Many of the initial burst of fans through the turnstiles buy programmes, raffle tickets and, pretty regularly, some make donations. Nonetheless, we're soon collectively becalmed. Volunteer fundraiser Ros Parsons wonders, "Where is everyone? It's usually much more crowded that this!" Ros and Dani (who's not a volunteer but formally employed as an Event Fundraiser for the hospice) are friendly, persuasive and very enthusiastic about their work. Both hold collection buckets and seek to engage people in conversation about their work – or the talking point of their distinctive sunflower badges – rather than alienate would-be donors with aggressive rattles of their buckets. Ros studies the lettering on her bucket, "It should say 'Earl Mountbatten Hospice' – this is the new bucket too – I don't know why it says 'The Island Hospice'. We sell everything in yellow. We have a thing called 'Go Yellow Day' in October and people go round the bars dressed as giant peeled bananas. Every day there's an event going on – particularly in the summer – because there's so many extra people on the Island. They say during August it gets to a quarter of a million people. It's amazing what people do to help the fundraising!" Dani interjects, "We do special Cowes sunflower badges for Cowes Week and those are £2 rather than the usual £3 for the big sunflower." Apparently amongst the 135,000 regular inhabitants, there's still a marked divide between those considered to come from the Island and those who move there. Ros Parsons is a Caulkhead, "We go back to the 1720s – my parents, grandparents and great-grandparents come from here". While, nowadays, Dani and her family live on the Island, it's only been for the past year since their move from London. They love the life and definitely won't go back. Nonetheless, Dani knows her place, "I'm an overner and I'll be an overner till I die. Even my children – including Harry, who's four – because he wasn't born here is an overner and his children will be too! Oh, and tourists are grockles!"

Weymouth fan Allen Boon (senior) regularly visits Smallbrook. He's come over tonight with 2010 season Wildcats and Islanders announcer, Tim Helm. Allen's already read *Shale Trek*. His feedback remains similar every year, "It would be better if you had bigger type and bigger photos." Albert Shepherd arrives in his Islanders anorak laden down with food and a large flask of coffee for the evening ahead. As usual, he'll stand by the section of the pits fence that overlooks bend four and the access pathway that runs between the pits and the track. It still feels peculiar to see him here without his lovely wife Eileen (who, sadly, passed away in April). "It's the loneliness that drives me

Isle of Wight: *"He said he'd stop the race in case a rider went over the fence and hurt themselves on the brambles!"*

mad you know. I go out. I do the gardening. But there's no one to discuss it with! I was here on Saturday with Kevin [son and co-team manager] cutting down all the brambles by the back-straight fence. The ref [Dave Robinson] a few weeks ago said we had to cut them down – they were three or four feet high – or the next time he was here he said he'd stop the race in case a rider went over the fence and hurt themselves on the brambles! That's speedway riders with kevlars and crash helmets on – how are they gonna to hurt themselves on the brambles? I ask you?" FIM referee Pavel Vana's on another speedway holiday in Britain. He looks very summery in his shorts, "When I ref'd in Siberia it was 32 degrees freezing". He's come to the Island with Hove-based Eastbourne programme editor, Mick Corby but really he's from a small village called Kratonohy near Hradec Kralove (located in the Eastern Bohemian county area of the Czech Republic). Pavel first went to speedway in 1975 with his father to see the Czech Golden Helmet. Pavel's officiating duties take him to numerous countries (UK, Germany, Italy, Poland, Norway, Denmark, Sweden and the Czech Republic to name but a few) but he also likes to see as many meetings as he can each season as a fan.

Prior to the start of the meeting, there's a centre-green presentation of £50 to Brendan Johnson from the late Eileen Shepherd to recognise his achievement as the first Isle of Wight rider to win a trophy since her death. Brendan won the British Under-18s Championship at Somerset. Earlier Ken Burnett reveals that his DVD work over the years enables him to know some riders and their families so well that they're good friends. Like many others, Ken's chuffed to see Brendan full recovery from last season's life-threatening injuries, let alone riding again. Brendan's one of Ken's favourite interviewees, "Brendan is one of those riders whose interesting and intelligent answers you can really feed off!" During the centre-green presentation, Tim Helm makes no attempt to exploit this chemistry option and, instead, asks a pro-forma question, "So what was it like to win the Under-18s at Somerset?" Banal questions get platitudinous answers, "Yeh, I really enjoyed it. It is a great achievement and it's really nice to bring something back for the fans!"

Buccaneers and Islanders fans react mutedly to the first drawn heat of the night. I take a keen interest in the reserves race – a.k.a. heat 2 – since it features Tom Hill. He gates confidently and flies round the track leading from tapes to chequered flag. Tom rides with an all-action racing style. There's a slight flamboyance to his love of the outside racing line – an effect emphasised by the old-fashioned tassels that flap from the arms of his kevlars. Stood cigarette in hand on the balcony of the bar, Crouch looks on admiringly as Tom celebrates, "He's a very popular and likable young man!" Talk of young riders improving prompts Crouch to come over all wistful. "I used to do the second halves at Poole and Chris Hunt [Islanders co-team manager] was always there. Tom Brown was if he could and Danny Gifford and Glen Philips, if he fancied it! Chris wouldn't be here without me and, now, I wouldn't be here without him. When we started at Wimbledon, I would have understood it if he'd given up but he never did and never complained and always gave everything. He might not have been the best in the world as a rider but he had the best attitude."

It's a shame that the rules and regulation of the sport preclude Danny Warwick from wearing his distinctive dreadlock hair extensions outside his helmet. Tonight he positively flies round the circuit – closely pursued by teammate Brendan Johnson – as they record the Islanders second successive maximum heat advantage. Danny's hair flowing behind him would definitely add to the visual impact of their triumph. The Bournemouth Buccaneers include the Baseby brothers – Mark and Aaron – in their team and they ride together for their first and only time tonight in heat 4. Sadly an engine failure for Mark on the second bend of the last lap instantly transforms the race and expands the Islanders heat advantage into a 5-1. Race winner Ben Hopwood looks an exciting prospect as he races with high-speed dynamism and confidence round the large Smallbrook Stadium track. Dean Felton – riding in place of Tom Hill – follows his partner home

Isle of Wight: *"He said he'd stop the race in case a rider went over the fence and hurt themselves on the brambles!"*

for a paid win. Back in the pits, Tom Hill is too ill to take this programmed ride and, shortly after, withdraws from the meeting. His father Steve reloads the van. It's a long way from Glossop for only one race but Mr Hill senior remains philosophical. "He was feeling funny on the way over and then it went off but it came back again. It's a shame because the track is just right for him. It's nice and moist on the outside. He likes it moist!" Tom looks pale and is politely apologetic. "When I took the chequered flag I didn't feel that good and when I took my helmet off I felt dizzy and thought this isn't good. I'd like to have gone out for some more wins but it's not to be! I'm sorry about that!"

Buccaneers team manager Garry May gives his only race winner (so far) James Brundle the black-and-white helmet colour for heat 5 but it's a decision that only claws back 2 points in a race won by Danny Warwick. Further indication that it isn't to be the visitors' night arrives on the last lap of heat 6 when BoMo race leader Mark Baseby falls on the second bend. Islanders captain Nick Simmons lays his bike down wonderfully to minimise the carnage. Though it would make little difference to the Islanders pay packets or the maximum heat advantage, referee Darren Hartley strangely decides to award the blue-helmeted Lee Smethills the race win. In his traditional spot by the fourth-bend pits fence with the vista of Smallbrook Stadium laid out fully before him, Albert worries about Tom Hill's withdrawal and reports of his vomiting. Albert's concern for others is touching, particularly given his own difficult emotional circumstances, "I can cope with the washing and ironing but not the loneliness! I've got four wardrobes full of [Eileen's] clothes I haven't touched yet!" Islanders co-team manager Kevin Shepherd takes a slightly circuitous route to trackside in order to briefly linger by his father. With the scoreline at 26-12 my comment, "It's going well so far" get superstitious short shrift, "Shush!" News from the pits is that Mark Baseby's second spill of the night sees his right wrist to swell massively. With a possible cricket score in prospect, the withdrawal of a wholehearted and entertaining rider like Mark Baseby is a body blow to the Buccaneers chance of a fight-back. [2]

The brief respite of a drawn heat 7 gives way to the second awarded race in three heats when a fall for Dan Halsey results in yet another awarded maximum race advantage for the Islanders. Heat 9 sees John Resch, Aaron Baseby and Brendan Johnson cause a veritable logjam of riders as they race into the second bend three abreast. Brendan Johnson leans heavily onto Aaron Baseby and, unable to resist the pressure, he crashes with such velocity into the wooden safety fence that some panels dislodge. Disqualified from the rerun, Brendan Johnson then takes no further part in the meeting because of this fall. Aaron Baseby participates in said rerun but the hip injury he sustained also then prompts his withdrawal from the rest of the meeting. If it was originally unusual enough for both teams to field a full complement of riders only to find that, after nine races, there haves been four rider withdrawals to reduce each team to only five riders. Last season Bournemouth scored 5-1s home and away for fun. Still massively short of anything resembling a concerted fight-back, the tenth race of the night provides the collector's item of a rare Buccaneers maximum heat advantage from Karl Mason and Kyle Howarth. They're helped in no small part by the fact that an unpredictably wayward Lee Smethills manages to maroon his race partner Nick Simmons back in fourth place for the first three laps of the race.

[2] Interviewed afterwards Mark would make light of his injuries but bemoan the unusual nature of his mechanical woes, "I can't quite believe it. I usually only suffer one snapped chain a season. Now I've snapped two on the same night. In my first race before I fell, I had just gained on Ben Hopwood to pass him. I'd done all the hard work. But unfortunately the chain snapped. I borrowed one off Kyle Howarth for my second race and it was the same again, it snapped. My chain came off, threw me forward and I went over the handlebars, landing face first before falling on my hand. I've had a problem with my hand since [a fall at] Mildenhall [in June]. It's one of those niggling injuries that takes time to heal, so you just try to ride through it. It's a shame really because I was feeling good. Usually I only have one chain go a season, I've never had two go in the same year before. I can't believe my bad luck. To be fair, I was making good starts, but just messing it up on the first corner, the same as I did at Poole in my last meeting there. I have a good engine which is working very well. I'm getting used to it because it's so fast."

Isle of Wight: *"He said he'd stop the race in case a rider went over the fence and hurt themselves on the brambles!"*

At each and every Islanders meeting, T2TV's Ken and Jackie Burnett enjoy a panoramic view of the track from their eyrie that overlooks the start line. Though it's an exposed position, on a cloudy late August evening it still feels comparatively warm. Their camera position is an area out of bounds to the public but, between his races, Buccaneers diminutive No. 4, Kyle Howarth joins them ("It looks differently from up here"). Clearly a conscientious apprentice, Kyle realises and wants to solve a specific problem, "I can't hold the line!" Ken Burnett's only too happy to pass on some tips and tricks. "I told him 'you don't want to hold the line on bend three, instead go wide to avoid the bumps and chase the dirt'. Then he went out and got a paid win in his next race and I said to him when he came back up 'you listened, didn't you?' I told him it's easy for me I don't ride but Holder, Shields, or Danny Bird never touched the white line. That was when it was real speedway!"

Before heat 11 starts, the Islanders Ben Hopwood protests to the start marshal that the Buccaneers James Brundle – programmed to race off gate 1 – is too far across. His protests are dismissed. In the black-and-white helmet colour, the Buccaneers Dan Halsey fires away from gate 3 until a very fast-looking Dean Felton expertly picks him off round bends three and four of the second lap. It's a manoeuvre that requires skill, nerve, speed and local knowledge. On the next lap Ben Hopwood also exploits the contours of this section of the Smallbrook track to pass Halsey, again on the transition from bends three to four. James Brundle trails off so far behind the rest of the pack that he's able to safely remove his goggles on the first bend of the last lap. With Tom Hill indisposed, Dean Felton's a busy man. It's extra activity Dean clearly relishes since he races to consecutive paid wins – this time accompanying Danny Warwick home. Experienced enough to apply a psychological element to his race-day armoury, James Brundle (this time off gate 2) goes out of his way to again line up much too close to Ben Hopwood. This takes some doing since Hopwood rides off gate 3 in heat 13. With elbows out wide as the riders come under orders, James Brundle fires from the start line, deliberately sweeps wide through bends one and two to block the run he anticipates from Ben Hopwood. However, the youngster has the bravery, savvy and speed to blast round this erstwhile blocking manoeuvre to take the race lead as they exit the second bend. In lusty pursuit, Brundle unfortunately falls on the third bend. Behind him, Nick Simmons for the second time this evening shows lightning reflexes to immediately lay down his bike. With Brundle disqualified from the rerun, the Islanders proceed to hammer home their third successive post-interval 5-1. Kyle Howarth wins heat 14 to become the third Buccaneer to take the chequered flag tonight by riding the wide outside line (previously favoured by Smallbrook luminaries of season's past) that he earlier identified from the T2TV camera position. Kyle fully deserves his heat-15 nomination but isn't able to make much impression upon Ben Hopwood or race winner Danny Warwick. In what proves to be a one-sided contest, the Islanders get nine maximum heat advantages as they romp to a comfortable 60-32 victory for the second week running.

With the 10 o'clock sailing dictating action stations in the pits area, riders and mechanics race to pack up their equipment. Mark and Aaron Baseby's dad had the luxury of packing up slightly earlier so, instead, relates a tale of woe on his mobile phone, "We've got two battered bikes and two battered blokes!" On the way to the ferry terminal, Ken Burnett recalls when he used to provide some film for Sky Sports' speedway coverage on a relatively regular basis. The advent of HD means that Sky nowadays employ freelancers with the relevant gizmos. Sadly, while these people know their technology, they often exhibit a highhanded approach towards the regular speedway press and rarely, if ever, understand the real dynamics of the sport. "Sky just want to make money, they don't care about speedway! They used to take film off me but now they want it wide screen and HD. I chat to the TV people at BBC and ITV and they say 'why would we want to advertise the Sky Sports Elite League' on our channel? Did you see the Speedway World Cup on Sky when Niels-Kristian Iversen blasted brilliantly round the outside to win a race? After he'd

Isle of Wight: *"He said he'd stop the race in case a rider went over the fence and hurt themselves on the brambles!"*

celebrated and got back to the pits, the first thing Charlie [Webster] says to him is 'Did you mean to do that?' He's a very polite bloke but you could see that even he struggled with a question like that!"

3rd August Isle of Wight v. Bournemouth (National League) 60-32

Isle of Wight: *"He said he'd stop the race in case a rider went over the fence and hurt themselves on the brambles!"*

CHAPTER 15

Coventry
"How many other trackshops provide pens for the away fans?"

6th August

Any Midlands derby clash between Coventry and Wolves invariably attracts substantial interest in the region irrespective of its location or the comparative league position, strengths and weaknesses of the two teams. In Elite League racing terms, there's no doubt that (so far) with little over a month of the regular season to go Wolverhampton eclipse Coventry. However, since the arrival of Krzysztof Kasprzak (for Rory Schlein) in May – and to a lesser extent the decision to replace Filip Šitera with Lewis Bridger – the Bees have generally delivered robust performances on the track much more in sync with the strength of their line-up on paper. Those in the know suggest that the signing of elusive Pole Przemyslaw Pawlicki could also be a masterstroke but, with only six appearances so far, it's hard to authoritatively comment. The highly respected trackman Terry Chrabaszcz has recently taken over curatorial duties at Brandon and this is also seen as a factor in their burgeoning resurgence. To further help the Coventry cause, tonight's Wolverhampton line-up enjoys a make-do and mend quality. They operate rider replacement for Nicolai Klindt, bring in guest Grzegorz Zengota for the injured Adam Skornicki and select ex-Coventry rider Ricky Wells to race for them at reserve.

Stood in the doorway of the Speedway Office, Colin Pratt prefers to look towards the big picture. Colin's got concerns for the future of the sport in Britain. Throughout all the British speedway leagues in 2010 crowds have mainly dwindled but, arguably, it's at the Elite League level that the structural problems are seen in sharpest relief. "It's terrible for everyone this season. Even Poole probably isn't as good as they think it is. They're winning and that and getting big crowds but that's why. They have to sort it out! We need to tell the GP riders and that, that these are the terms for riding in the British League. And, if they can't ride on a Friday, then they have to ride on the Continent in Poland and Sweden and that. New stars will come up in their place and then they need to go on into the GPs, then the other riders who used to ride here can come back. They can have their average assessed so it's fair and then they can go back to the club that owns them. If they don't want them, they can go back to somewhere else. Something needs to change – has to change – they have to sort it out! I hope they will." Colin's lifetime of service to the sport means that he's old enough to have lived through the last root-and-branch British speedway revolution that was the amalgamation of leagues in 1965. "In '64 I, like Eric Boocock, was a Provincial League rider but by '65 we were lining up against the likes of Fundin and Briggs and that. By the next season, we were beating them and I finished third in the averages! And in '67, I was in the World Final with three others. [1] That took two and a half seasons! Malcolm Simmons took seven years and Terry Betts took ten. If you give young riders the chance, new stars will emerge!"

Though the turnstiles open on time, there are initially no programmes on sale at the programme booth. A raffle ticket man quizzes Lynn, one of Britain's most glamorous programme sellers,

[1] Ray Wilson (Long Eaton), Rick France (Coventry) and Eric Boocock (Halifax)

"Where's your programmes then? Why's Ty Proctor got them?" Lynn isn't exactly sure, "Dunno – last-minute alterations?" The raffle man remains perplexed, "They're usually here by now!" Over at the trackshop fans mill around, make purchases or chat to the always friendly track staff. Trackshop manager Joyce Blythe wonders how my book sales have gone so far this season. When I tell her my sales have been poor her husband Malcolm interjects, "Tell me about it! I only sell 50 *Stars* now." I'm curious to find out how many it used to be. Without hesitation, Malcolm replies, "80!"

Sales have fallen off so much that the trackshop no longer operate the satellite stall they previously ran at the entrance of the home-straight grandstand undercroft passageway. Though in recent weeks the Bees woke from their early-season torpor, it looks highly unlikely that the club will contest the end-of-season Elite League play-offs. Like many Coventry fans, Malcolm is disconsolate at this prospect, "We've hardly got any meetings left because we're not going to get into the play-offs. I think we have four home meetings and then there's the Knock-out Cup, of course." Malcolm's wife Joyce hasn't yet completely given up all hope of a turnaround that could – if the results go with them – see Coventry sneak into the playoffs. While there's still a faint mathematical glimmer, Joyce remains guardedly optimistic.

Diehard Peterborough fans Graham and Hilary Rouse arrive in ecstatic mood after last night's Panthers win at Swindon. The always affable, Graham confesses, "I'm still on a high from last night! It's our first time in 26 meetings after 17 years of trying!" Hilary reckons the Robins got off lightly, "It would have been more but they doctored the track." According to Graham, there could be something in this viewpoint. "Chris Harris put on the Peterborough website today that Swindon's best rider was the tractor driver! We were winning easily – it had lots of nice grip – and then they thought 'Hello' and then the tractor went round for 15 minutes and made it all slick. We still won though! We've got 42 points and home meetings left against Eastbourne (twice) – not being funny we should beat them – Coventry (you don't know which side will turn up) – and Swindon, who'll look to do us what we did to them!"

Graham and Hilary travel to speedway tracks throughout the country, "We went to Buxton that day when you were supposed to be there [18th July]. We got there at 2 o'clock and the track was lovely! And dry. But it was off. We then drove to King's Lynn. We only live 75 minutes from King's

Karl, Alec and Olly Roberts

Programmes on sale

Lynn but went there via Buxton!" Every time I see Hilary nowadays, she's got the hump for reasons I'm not exactly clear about but has something to do with the fact that Jason Crump shops where she works. As if it's a state secret, Hilary still refuses to reveal the exact nature of the products sold at her store, nevermind reveal its name. For all I know it could be Ann Summers, Poundland or Lidl? Tonight Hilary adds some literary criticism to her usual repertoire of insults. "I've got Michael Lee's book. It's much better than yours! Have you ever thought if there was less fancy words you'd sell more? Speedway people are just ordinary people." My protestations fail to convince Hilary "Not with all those fancy words!" Graham and Hilary's favoured location in the home-straight grandstand overlooks pit lane and also provides – like every other seat in the Brandon grandstand – a panoramic view of the track. In their case, the first and second bends are closest. Hilary's adamant, it's somewhere I'm not welcome, "I don't want you sitting next to me!" No matter where I sit, I can't imagine that I'll block Hilary's favourite speedway view – Fredrik Lindgren's bottom. Hilary takes particular delight in Fredrik's extensive enthusiastic pre-meeting regime of calisthenic exercises and stretches!

Always polite, friendly Wolverhampton club historian Mark Sawbridge gives his take on the slightly suboptimal line-up Wolverhampton have for tonight's meeting. "It's a Wolves select tonight. Nicolai Klindt's in the Danish Championship, Adam Skornicki is missing due to his adventurous donut injury. 'Stormy' Wethers – he's a gutsy rider – is riding for Edinburgh and, as I understand it, Joe Haines has been sacked at King's Lynn and, therefore, can't double up. Chris Kerr is out with a broken leg – I think he rode for Birmingham much too early and now they've replaced him. We've got Grzegorz Zengota – presumably for Klindt, but I don't know. We have rider replacement but I don't know for who and Ricky Wells at reserve. It's lucky we won here earlier in the season because it doesn't look like we'll win here tonight. Ty Proctor passed Rory Schlein in the last heat and Schlein went bonkers, he wasn't too pleased at all. It was terrific! We won by 2 points. Their Pole Przemyslaw Pawlicki isn't here tonight. I think he's riding in the World Under-21 Championship. Some people have suspicions he might only do 11 meetings for Coventry this year. By the way, they've got Auty and Sweetman at reserve tonight. Ludvig Lindgren is flying at reserve for us but, the last time he was here, he fell off and got only 2."

Karl Roberts from WildKaRD and Meth Designsz (inventor of the oft-delayed 5-1 Speedway computer game) arrives early with his sons Alec and Olly. Fanatical young Bees fan Alec wears his favourite heavily autographed junior-sized golden coloured old-fashioned Coventry race tabard. Alec features in *Quantum of Shale* and is delighted that he also appears in *Shale Trek*. Karl tells me, "He's practically worn that book out. He's spotted himself three times in the photos. When he got the book he wasn't reading but he is now." It's hard to believe that my writing could inspire ("What? Reading my book?"). Karl isn't surprised, "When you're really interested in something you want to learn and it's easier!" Mark Sawbridge admires Alec's Bees tabard. "I've got a tabard like that one in my loft from round then – the '70s. I shouldn't admit this but I've always liked the Bees logo! It's much better than ours. When I look at my old school books, I've drawn bees all over them!" Again Mark briefly outlines his concern about the likely performance of the Wolves select. Karl is happy to confirm his fears, "You've got Ricky Wells so I think we're going to do well!"

Speedway fans like nothing better than a gossip about recent results, regulatory scandals or rumours of sharp practice. However tonight, despite our location, the unusual topic of traffic jams on the M25 (near Lakeside's Thurrock home) is a cause célèbre. Many times, I'm told breathlessly that traffic news on the radio as fans drove to Brandon Stadium warns local drivers of the closure of the Queen Elizabeth Bridge over the Thames because of a lorry fire. Traffic in both directions now uses the Dartford Tunnel. Traffic reports alert drivers to the dangers of the ten-mile tailback from Junction 27 and estimate that it presently takes around three hours just to cross the river. It's the kind of news that makes you glad to be elsewhere.

Out on the centre green (or possibly in the pits), Coventry Bees roving presenter Peter York collars Alun 'Rosco' Rossiter for their weekly chat. It's the aural equivalent of a warm bath of speedway insight, "We've got a little featurette – Alun you thought you could get away!" The glare of the media spotlight doesn't frighten Rosco and, such are the unkind rumours put about by Robins fans of his love for any microphone, that (apparently) trips to any karaoke bar in Rosco's company are ill-advised. Preferring to shoot from the hip rather than waste time on reflection, Rosco invariably makes a refreshingly honest interviewee. Last week's 58-35 home victory in the Elite League 'B' fixture against Eastbourne gave Alun guarded grounds for celebration. "It was the proper Coventry speedway that turned up against Eastbourne!" Despite the innate thrill that the Eastbourne team usually engenders on their travels, attendance levels failed to reach historic or budgeted levels, "Some of them [the crowd] stayed away and it's got to be addressed. It's something we've got to address seriously. Friday night is Coventry speedway night." Amongst the fans that do bother to turn up, some haven't got the right attitude according to Rosco. "Chris Harris is on fire but there's a certain little section here at Coventry that seem to get on Chris's back, I dunno why! Okay, he's not a Leigh Adams – Chris Harris is a very good team captain and I'm pleased to work with him." Derby meetings with Wolverhampton are still a comparatively fresh experience for Rosco, "It's a new one to me. They beat us last time but this time we'll see. Hopefully the REAL Coventry Bees will turn up here tonight!" Quizzed about his own performance so far this season in the various roles he occupies at Brandon Stadium, Alun speaks with trademark candour, "It's been a big learning curve. I had six years at Swindon as a team manager – after being a rider – but it's totally different here. What you see behind the scenes you wouldn't believe, if you've been a rider. You think they're making tons of money but they're not! Telling them [the riders] what to do is part of the job. Some people don't like it but that's the way the cookie crumbles. If they don't like it, then don't ride! It's as simple as that! I also do behind the scenes while someone like Middlo [Neil Middleditch] sticks purely with the team managing and doesn't do behind the scenes."

Rosco's honesty makes Peter York anxious, "Sometimes I think, oh, you can't say that over the tannoy." Rosco remains unbowed, "What you're saying – you can't say the truth? The truth hurts some people!" Asked to review likely qualifiers for the end-of-season Elite League play-offs, Rosco states that he considers that Coventry continue to have an outside chance of qualification that isn't solely mathematical because "Lakeside are still vulnerable". Rosco warns that this feeling in his waters will only come to fruition if, "All the Coventry boys – seven riders – stand up and be counted!" Rounding up their conversational featurette Peter York confides over the stadium speakers, "I've known you since you were a rider, sometimes I've seen you in a rage because someone hasn't done something you've told them!" Unusually Alun's almost lost for words as the ever-professional Peter York segues into an appeal to the Brandon crowd, "Yeh – go on – make him feel at home, let's show him what you think about him [muted reaction] we've booed him for years!"

It's not often at a speedway meeting that you get to learn traffic information about another track. However, Peter York is keen to gleefully update us, "I know Lakeside have had to cancel their meeting as there's 22 and a half miles of tailbacks on the M25! It's definitely not on because Adam Shields is here." Contrary to expectations, Wolverhampton take an early lead when Ty Proctor wins heat 1. It's a disappointment that Fredrik Lindgren finishes third but, then, last place for Krzysztof Kasprzak isn't exactly ideal for the Bees. Hilary Rouse does deign to let me sit next to her but, sandwiched between her husband Graham and me, she remarks, "I'm squashed in here!" The visitors' not-so-secret weapon Ricky Wells finishes last in heat 2. With not much action on

---

the track to enthral her, Hilary keeps a close eye on my notepad. In all seriousness, she's also keen to emphasise that, should my writing not meet with her approval, then she reserves her right to take her case (whatever that is) to the European Court of Human Rights. "I will take you to court next time! I will! I'm allowed!" When I joke if she doesn't tell me about Jason Crump, then I'll just have to make it up about his noodle habit or haemorrhoid cream addiction, Hilary stroppily reiterates her legal threats, "If you write that bit, seriously, it will go to court!" In heat 3, Ty Proctor falls on the last bend of the second lap when fourth so SCB official Mick Posselwhite awards the race as a win for Tai Woffinden with Ben Barker second and Edward Kennett third. I could have sworn at the time of the incident that Ben Barker led? That's an opinion also shared by some fans behind me who exclaim, "That's not right!" If the awarded race order reflected this perception, then this drawn heat would, instead, be a heat advantage to the Bees.

Coventry's surge into a lead that they don't relinquish arrives soon enough via Chris Harris (followed home by his team mate Richard Sweetman). Grzegorz Zengota's last place isn't good news for Wolverhampton's fans or management. Fredrik Lindgren shows off the tightly kevlared backside that Hilary Rouse so admires to lead the rest of the field for most of the first two laps until, without pressure, he clatters into the airfence. Such a loss of concentration would end the race for lesser riders but, somehow, not only does Fredrik stay on his bike but he still manages second place behind Edward Kennett. Heats 6 and 7 see Coventry reinforce their dominance with race wins from Kasprzak and Harris. However, it's Josh Auty's last-lap second-bend pass of Tai Woffinden that gets the most ecstatic reaction from Hilary (and the rest of the crowd). As the race ends she casts aside the warmth and security of her lap blanket and leaps up to exalt in Bomber and Josh's achievement. Lewis Bridger's heat 8 win fails to spark similar enthusiasm. Slightly unnecessarily, Hilary confides, "I can't stand Bridger". Peter York's praise for Lewis over the tannoy indicates that he must still have some bridges to build with the Brandon faithful. "He's really starting to shine – it's taken him some time to find his feet or find his wheels – come on, give him some praise!" Lewis celebrates with some trademark wheelies while the banks of video screens dotted throughout the stadium replay the [big word warning, Hilary] *denouement* of his race win. Trackshop man Malcolm Blythe can't quite believe that canny Wolverhampton team manager, the wily Peter Adams, has missed a trick. "I thought they could have given the black-and-white to Proctor in heat 8 as he's been flying!"

The meeting proceeds at a brisk pace, "Mindful of the weather conditions in Warwickshire, the interval has been moved until after the completion of heat 12." With the Zengota/Wells partnership out in heat 9, Peter Adams sensibly keeps the black-and-white helmet colour in his pocket. It looks a shrewd decision, particularly since Barker and Kennett combine to win comfortably. Ricky Wells earns his only point of the night, after a fall for Zengota. Peter Adams continues to eschew any use of his tactical options. In the next race, Kasprzak wins his second of the night ahead of his fellow countryman Zengota. In the mini Battle of Variable Form Riders, Lewis Bridger is third ahead of Tai Woffinden. The wait to see a Wolverhampton rider actually win a race ends with Fredrik Lindgren in heat 11. He shows the rest of the field (including Chris Harris) a clean set of wheels and the taut glutei muscles that get Hilary Rouse so pumped up. In an ideal world, Wolverhampton would gain more points but, unfortunately, Ty Proctor finishes last. After 75 minutes and a drawn heat 12, there's an interval with the score at 45-32. Peter York reminds us to dig deep in our pockets for the Speedway Riders' Benevolent Fund collection, "In case the unthinkable happens – which it has in the past before!"

My interval trip to the trackshop allows Joyce Blythe to raise the philosophical question, "How many other trackshops provide pens for the away fans?" The literal answer is everywhere (provided that the away fan is prepared to buy one emblazoned with the home team's logo). The

Coventry: *"How many other trackshops provide pens for the away fans?"*

highly focused customer friendly approach that is the watchword of the Brandon Stadium trackshop *modus operandi* under Joyce's friendly management means that they also stock Wolves pens for Wolves fans unprepared to be seen with or using a Coventry pen. Well-travelled and oh-so-well-connected speedway fan Brian Oldham provides some feedback on my development as a speedway writer. "I still think you're much nicer in your books now – in your first book, you criticised everyone!" Back in the grandstand, while we wait for the action to get back underway Hilary recalls her introduction to the wonderful world of speedway. "The first track I went to was Berwick. The old track near a farm. Graham said 'Come along, you'll enjoy it!' All I saw was riders following each other! I said, 'I've seen more exciting races on the M1!' But, then, I went to Peterborough and it wasn't just riders 1-2-3-4 and I was hooked!"

Though it makes very little difference to the result, Fredrik Lindgren follows up his heat 11 victory over Chris Harris with further examples of the genre in heats 13 and 15. The last race is arguably the best of the night. Both Grand Prix riders vie for supremacy before Fredrik snatches victory in the final yard or two before the finish line. Peter York conducts some post-meeting interviews. Apparently channelling the spirit and voice of the late Alan Ball to communicate with the dogs of the neighbourhood, Ben Barker informs us, "Yeh, we let ourselves down at the League!" That's pretty well the sum extent of his revelations. Sensibly Peter York is quick to wrap things up ("Thank you, Spudo"). There must be good team spirit in the Coventry camp – at least, between Bridger and Barker – since Lewis then treats those still within earshot inside the Brandon Stadium environs to an interview conducted throughout with his own unique version of Ben Barker's accent. It's definitely a light-hearted moment, albeit that it's unlikely to lead to an alternative career in show business. Unluckily for his long-term prospects as an impressionist, Lewis speaks with too low a pitch to convincingly hit Ben's trademark falsetto notes. Also he occasionally lapses into a voice that sounds like his impression of an old age pensioner with a cold and badly fitting dentures. Nonetheless, it's funny. Workington Comets speedway fan, Tony Jackson (and also ex-Comets team manager and ex-Comets programme editor nowadays) relishes his time on the terraces. "We're on a Midlands tour of Birmingham – Eastbourne ("it was quite good but there was no passing") – Coventry – Workington and Glasgow." An obvious feature of my last trip to the Derwent Park Stadium was the noticeably reduced number of people there, ("What surprised me was your crowd"). Tony furrows his brow, "It surprises us too! The problem with speedway being a family sport is that when times are hard families have to look and ask what are we spending our money on? And, if you go as a family, speedway isn't cheap. If it's football, it's usually only one bloke and they're every other week not every week. If you're honest – if they go regularly as a family – they'll be spending a lot!" It's been a strange season for the Comets but Tony accentuates the positive. "We won't make the top four but we'll finish strongly and that's better than finishing with a damp squib. It keeps the fans happy and we could do well in the Young Shield. I had a wry smile at that Redcar article [by Mike Amos in the *Northern Echo*]. It was very well written which is unusual nowadays. It could be read on a number of levels which shows how good it was!" Talk of speedway invariably involves mention of the Speedway Grand Prix and of course the Speedway World Cup. "They say BSI means Bull***t Incorporated but, then, there's a lot of that in speedway!"

Quite a few Coventry fans continue to linger by the pits area or the trackshop. And, as the VIP car park slowly empties of riders' vans, Ben Barker is the life and soul of the party. Amongst friends and admirers, he pretends to sign the face of one of his lady fans with a felt marker pen. Just like his first and second rides, Ben isn't quite fast enough to achieve his ambitions but tries wholeheartedly and with some gusto.

6th August Coventry v. Wolves (Elite League 'B') 52-43

CHAPTER 16

Berwick

"I don't know if you remember when riders just used to turn up with a second-hand bike on the back of their car with a small toolbox?"

7th August

I'm so early at Shielfield Park in Tweedmouth – home of the Berwick Bandits – that the only signs of life is the tractor that slowly circles the football pitch that on speedway night is the centre green. Reminding me that this stadium is really the home of Berwick Rangers FC, a large group of footballers amble round the track perimeter. There are high dark clouds overhead with nearly three hours to go before the scheduled start time. Close to the referee's box in the main-straight grandstand, I bump into Ian Rae who just this week became the Bandits team manager (replacing Dave Peet) in addition to his existing responsibility as track curator. Ian's temporarily parked the tractor and lifts the magic wheel so that he can dismount to, apparently, rush purposefully in all directions trying to complete the endless round of pre-meeting preparations that is the lot of speedway management everywhere prior to any meeting. Ian modestly bats off my congratulations, "Oh, aye!" Like people everywhere, he's keen to talk about the weather, "On a day like today [glances upwards] you just don't know how to prepare the track. We had some rain earlier and it's do you or don't you water it? We have! It's not going to rain more. Last week, wouldn't you know, it rained nearly at seven for five minutes and spoilt things. This week it won't or I hope so." Nodding towards the two large plastic football dugouts that occupy the inside lane close to the start/finish line, I wonder if these obstacles are to be the Bandits secret weapon against tonight's in-form visitors the Edinburgh Monarchs (who've yet to lose away in the Premier League this season, so far). "Oh, aye! They're the bane of my life. We drag them onto the centre green during the meeting. They're very heavy, though."

In the deserted pits area a staff member in blue overalls stops for a brief chat. Since the start of the John Anderson and Lynda Waite promotional era in 2009, there have been changes throughout the club, whether basic housekeeping or infrastructure development. For example, the track's been smoothed and new shale applied. Taken together, all these various changes, tweaks and improvements make the overall Berwick speedway race night look much more slickly professional. Apparently typifying this newfound attention to detail, another small but significant customer facing initiative is to issue every Bandits member of staff with a name badge. My surreptitious glance at the man in blue overall's badge reveals that he's called Raymond Thorpe. He tells me that the footballers who amble about the place are the "Under-21 players coming back from playing on the second pitch over there."

[Jeff] "The first team pitch doesn't look as immaculate as usual!"

[Raymond Thorpe] "You can see that the new drainage [points to a roughened area behind both sides of the goal]. They only just put some fertiliser down so they'll have to leave it till Monday."

[Jeff] "They've got new toilets next to the [home-straight] grandstand."

[Raymond] "They're not finished yet – they're taking ages to do!"

Later, closer inspection of the new restroom facilities reveals that the urinals work but the

134

cordoned off trio of toilets lack privacy since they've still to fit the cubicle doors or walls! Even more excitingly (and hygienically), we'll soon all be able to wash our hands since there's a line of basins (also not yet plumbed in). There are also hygiene-related changes elsewhere in the stadium, "There's new changing rooms over there [points across the pits] the old ones were condemned. It had a communal bath but they're not allowed those nowadays because of Health & Safety! They have to have showers. We're not allowed to use them because they're the football club's. About 30 years ago, when the riders used to go in there and clean their leathers, it started a fall out with the football club." [1]

Good queue

At the other end of the stadium inside the programme booth, the Queen is in her Counting House – a.k.a. Davina Johnston, who carefully checks the exact numerical content of each box of tonight's programmes. She glances upwards out of her window at the jet-black rain clouds that scud in over this part of Tweedmouth, "With Edinburgh being rained-off last night, maybe more of them will come along? We've known that they're coming. No one likes them and, with [William] Lawson at reserve, he can have seven rides. Did you see Monday [on Sky] at Lakeside? I liked Lee Richardson when he stood in here once at the Brandonapolis or something but he had to be held back by two or three saying that 'he' – the Pole [Mroczka] – 'wouldn't let me past!' He's in the lead so it's up to Lee to get past! The Pole's a bit wild – all over the track like [Michal] Rajkowski is here [pause], except Rajkowski is slower! Michal [Makovský] says it's like riding with the handbrake on! He might be slow but he's hard to pass! It

Start line team

might be track craft – whatever it is – he goes from side to side and he's difficult to get round! With what's his name [Alex Harkess] from Edinburgh being chairman [of the BSPA] it just shows what a mickey-mouse sport speedway is. He could be in charge of the Elite League but all of speedway?! First Edinburgh get rid of Tabaka and then that Busch and now they've got William Lawson. He was excellent for us at Newcastle." Tonight's meeting is effectively a warm up for Edinburgh's top-of-the-table clash at Newcastle tomorrow. Davina's fellow programme store operative, David, isn't convinced Lawson will be able to repeat his contribution, "They didn't have Lemon or Bach then!"
[Davina] "True. They didn't have Lemon or Bach then but the tapes lifted and he was gone! You could mark the win in your programme before the race finished!"

[1] The refurbished toilet block was opened fully for 2011, to general approval.

Berwick: *"I don't know if you remember when riders just used to turn up with a second-hand bike on the back of their car with a small toolbox?"*

[Jeff] "You have one of the best views in speedway here."

[Davina] "It's very nice but you can't really see the first bend or the second bend at all. I just mark my programme for the first few races on the results Dennis [McCleary] gives out." Light drizzle flecks the programme booth windows, "Have they watered the track?"

[Jeff] "Ian said they did."

[Davina] "They'd watered it last week when the sky was dark and then it rained, really rained. People complain about Peter Waite but then some people can do no wrong!"

Phil Newton the friendly trackshop man (and much more than that – Phil is Commercial Manager, and together with wife Julie is a huge power behind the throne) is excited by prospects ahead. "It should be a big crowd! Edinburgh are flying. They've got a new rider – [William] Lawson at reserve and we have a new rider, that should bring out our fans – [Marcin] Rempala. [2] He had a ride here for the first time after the meeting last week [v. Rye House]. The tapes went up and there was none of that settling in for a lap – he just really attacked – on his bike set up for small tracks! He looked great! He'd only ever been here before to watch with his brother."

After the turnstiles open, stood close to the first-bend fence Edinburgh co-promoter and Monarchs team manager John Campbell meets and greets a good number of travelling Edinburgh fans. Smartly dressed in a very snazzy-looking almost fashion forward Edinburgh jacket, John's happy to shoot the breeze with all-comers prior to his work in the pits. One of the real delights of speedway is the direct and unmediated access that fans can have with management and performers alike. John tells me that Ivan Mauger recently sold 64 copies of his book at Armadale (Ivan repeated, even bettered this achievement at Berwick the following evening, selling 65 copies). These are the kind of sales figures I can only dream of. Though tonight's meeting is important for the Monarchs, arguably one of their season-defining fixtures actually takes place tomorrow night in Newcastle. It's certainly on the mind of Edinburgh programme vendor Margaret who, typically, plays down the possibility of success, "Newcastle is going to be the difficult one!"

Bill Gimbeth and Dave Rattenberry are again out and about on yet another speedway tour together to see key meetings (and share a room afterwards). Dave survives the arduous trek from the substantial grassy parking area outside Shielfield Park but continues to clutch his emergency rations of a half-eaten pork pie. He swiftly transfers this to his pocket for later when he spots how short the queue is at the refreshment kiosk. It's been a hard season to run a trackshop even if you have the array of merchandise Rat displays throughout his empire. "It's hard, it's flipping horrendously hard this year! Last night, John [Rich] took £100 at Scunny. I don't pay any rent for the Conference League but there's still the petrol and paying John out of that!" Should Dave's burger come without enough relish, luckily he's already taken an onion from his pocket. Though John Campbell's rather deluxe anorak stood out, in actual fact there's quite an outbreak of relatively fashionable speedway clothing inside the stadium. Notable in this shale-inspired fashion parade are the rather spiffy 'Andrew Tully Racing' navy-blue hoodies. At the moment there's not much need for the additional warmth I suspect this line of ATR clothing might provide because, with 30 minutes to go before the scheduled start time, the clouds clear to bathe the stadium in bright warm sunshine. Lifting my spirits, a man looks interestedly at my book display and, with a rising note of excitement in his voice, asks, "Where did you get your table – it's really nice!" He admires my table for its sturdiness, looks and the measurement feature printed on the tabletop surface.

Though this Edinburgh season has mostly been one triumph after another, all true Monarchs fans

[2] Marcin Rempala is the younger brother of former Berwick rider Jacek Rempala from Poland. He rides for Tarnow and comes into the Bandits side as a direct replacement for the injured Craig Branney. The 25-year-old has previously ridden for Poland in the World Cup.

Berwick: *"I don't know if you remember when riders just used to turn up with a second-hand bike on the back of their car with a small toolbox?"*

reveal themselves by keeping their delight held in check to only alloyed levels. Obviously that's along with the obligatory numerous sideways critical comments about Glasgow speedway that come fitted as standard. "At Glasgow they hardly put any dirt on it nowadays and there's only one racing line which is too close to the fence for it to be conducive to good racing! To get past there nowadays you have to be a kamikaze!" Indeed, tracks everywhere away from Armadale are subject to intense critical analysis. Berwick's reinvigorated surface is no exception. "The track is crap. There's lots of grumbling. We don't pay to go to see tractor racing for 40 minutes, like when Workington were here. The riders refused to ride." Dick Barrie later tells me, "Untrue the grading actually came *après* the deluge mentioned by Ian Rae." To my untutored eye, the Shielfield racing surface looks manicured and well prepared. The third and fourth bends still slope but – under this management – the Wall of Death has mellowed into the Bump of Death. This season many clubs struggle to race competitively at home every week. This is partly because of the football World Cup but also (in the Premier League) the authorities planned the fixture list to accommodate the Premier Trophy semi-final staging's. Despite tacit acknowledgement of these influential factors, some incomprehension still exists amongst the fans about the lack of regular racing. "There's been lots of Saturdays when they didn't have a meeting!" Batting off my suggestion that it might be due to circumstances beyond the control of the promotion, I'm told, "On June 19th they didn't have a meeting cos it was John Anderson's son's wedding. But if you're running a speedway club, you should do that sort of thing in the winter!" In tandem with this undertow of critical comment about the lack of fixture continuity, sympathy definitely lies with the riders since this lack of meetings interrupts their stream of earnings and, consequently, makes budgeting expenditures difficult. "Speedway riding is a terrible job and often a hard life. Just a few moments of aggressive riding can change your life forever – well, 20-30 seconds can – it can leave your life handing by a thread. What other jobs do people take such risks in?" Even rider Adrian Rymel – despite being on a two-year Berwick contract – codedly shares his opinions, albeit in nuanced form via the pages of the *Speedway Star*. "I was very positive and optimistic at the start of the season that we could do very well, but it just hasn't happened as we thought it would. There have been changes at the club both in the team and in the promotion and I am pleased with some things and disappointed about others." [3]

Long-time Bandits fan Jim Brykajlo is here with his son Steven and Jim's younger brother George in tow. Over on the back-straight banking, there's a parp from the latest fad to hit the world of sporting instrumentation: the vuvuzela. Speedway already had its own version of the vuvuzela – the air horn! The Bandits terms and conditions regarding their use of this stadium prohibits of air horns at Berwick speedway meetings. Steven notes, "Officially vuvuzelas aren't banned here – yet – but air horns are!" Despite all he's done for the club, George Brykajlo isn't yet a John Anderson fan, "He should stick to selling pies!"

With a strictly enforced 9.30 p.m. curfew in operation for speedway meetings at Shielfield Park, running an efficient meeting is a key requirement. Unfortunately at 7 p.m., just as the meeting is about to get underway, there's a "medical emergency" on the back straight. The ambulance and stretchers along with the medical staff are quickly and visibly into action (apparently treating a keen fan with a serious stroke). Information is scarce but, luckily, veteran speedway presenter Dick Barrie keeps us advised and regularly updated as far as it is possible while we collectively await the arrival of the "County Ambulance".[4] Unsure how long a delay this will actually turn out to be,

[3] Sadly, Adrian's career was abruptly ended at Edinburgh in September, when a simple crash left him with a broken neck and spinal damage. Although now able to walk again, he still requires regular therapy to restore full mobility to his right arm. A well-attended benefit meeting at Berwick in March 2011 offered appreciation and compensation for his long service to the club.

Berwick: *"I don't know if you remember when riders just used to turn up with a second-hand bike on the back of their car with a small toolbox?"*

Dick Barrie effortlessly fills dead air with *ad hoc* opinion and comment as well as various interviews. According to one fan, delays waiting for the arrival of the County Ambulance aren't unknown in this neck of the woods, "This has always been a problem at Berwick. It's just one of those things. When Lee Complin crashed and broke his arm in the first meeting of the season, there was about an hour delay." Though I'm a reluctant interviewee, Dick calls me to the centre green to help raise local awareness of my latest book *Shale Trek*. Before the interview starts, I want to avoid surprises so check with Dick what exactly we'll talk about, ("What shall we discuss?") only for Dick to advise with trademark rapier wit, "It would be best to talk about your book otherwise you're not going to sell many!" Dick really knows his medium and instantly puts me at my ease. So much so that I'm able to advise any partially sighted members of the crowd that they shouldn't ever teach their guide dog to swim.

My interview over, I take advantage of the proximity of the start gate staff who'd, otherwise, usually be busy supervising the riders and the racing. Probably the only staff member in the stadium without a name badge is the start marshal who, I'm going to guess (looking at the Bandits Who's Who listing in the official programme) is Tom Anderson. He stands with Alan Easton and an apprentice member (Andrew Blair) of the Berwick Bandits start marshalship staff. Alan and Tom have donkey's years involvement with speedway.

[Alan] "We've both been going 30 years. We helped build Berrington Lough and then just carried on."

[Tom] "Trouble is the bikes are too powerful for humans to control nowadays. They're okay until they hit a bump and they get out of shape."

[Alan] "They used to be out for 72 hours when they fell off. Nowadays it's three to four weeks – at least! I don't know if you remember when riders just used to turn up with a second-hand bike on the back of their car with a small toolbox? Have you seen what they come with now? Mechanics, managers, motor homes and toolboxes! When we had the police radar gun here, they got up to 75 mph on the back straight! Paul Fry, it was. The real problem is the management of the sport – you've got the Edinburgh man and the Sheffield man in charge. Look at Lawson: when he rode at Belle Vue he finished on something like a 4.9 average. Yet [gets out a programme exasperatedly] look he's down as 6.39! All right you have to allow for bonus points, probably, but it should be doubled to around 9? How can that be?

[Tom] "I really blame Sky in introducing the black-and-white helmet colour because they want close meetings! When we started here, the Canterburys and the Eastbournes used to win 82-18 or the like, you know what I mean. Speedway is like that! The racing was still good! Canterbury used to have seven riders and six of them would be back the next year. Do you know Josef Franc? He's a Berwick rider on loan to Sheffield who rode at Armadale last Friday for Rye House against Edinburgh and then rode for Rye House here against his own team! How can you explain that? If you decide to read the rulebook – this laddie here [points to Andrew] it's his first year – after about 20 pages he glazes over. It's too complicated! Still we're both retired and it's nice to be able to put something back into a sport we love!"[5]

To continue to wile away the time Dick Barrie collars Edinburgh Monarchs captain Matthew Wethers, "Have you ever seen anything like this before?" Matthew replies confidently, "Yes, I have! It's a bit of a disappointment but the ambulance isn't here yet. It's lucky that speedway was here to take care of them!" At 7.55 p.m. a sound of a siren outside the stadium is audible. Dick ignores this aural signal to concentrate upon our collective mortality, "Each and every one of us realises it could be you or I!"

[4] Thankfully the patient received treatment and has even been back to meetings at Shielfield Park since.

[5] Tom, a robust 82, retired from flag-waving in 2011, handing on the pennants – and the trademark black-and-white striped starter's jersey – to young Andrew. Alan remains on duty as first mate.

Berwick: *"I don't know if you remember when riders just used to turn up with a second-hand bike on the back of their car with a small toolbox?"*

The meeting eventually gets underway at 8.05 p.m. with a win for Adrian Rymel ahead of Ryan Fisher. On his first official ride at Shielfield Park, Marcin Rempala finishes third helped in no small part by engine failure for Kalle Katajisto. William Lawson's return to the Borders starts ignominiously with a heat 2 last place. Keen to educate newcomers Dick Barrie helpfully observes, "As long as you keep an opponent in fourth place, they can't get a heat advantage!" This is oh-so-true but, judged by its repetition, must also be Dick's own Buddhist mantra. The sight of Paul Clews in full flight round the outside at Smallmead was one of the occasional thrills of that era. Nowadays, Paul plies his trade as Berwick captain and, though he takes his responsibilities seriously, he wears them lightly. Paul certainly knows his way round the Shielfield track. He's also added some steel to his riding repertoire. The first lap of heat 3 showcases this when he passes Kevin Wölbert on the outside of the first corner and then proceeds to ride Matthew Wethers much closer to the fence on the next corner in order to take the lead. Part Buddhist monk, part Mystic Meg, prior to heat 4 Dick Barrie forecasts, "Personally I expect there's going to be a change, William Lawson is doing an impression of someone who wants to be excluded!" King's Lynn based referee Mick Bates does indeed disqualify Lawson under the two-minute time allowance (to be replaced by his fellow reserve with the exotic name, Arlo Bugeja). Under the rules and regulations, each rider has to take a minimum of three rides during the meeting. Dick helpfully reminds newcomers and grizzled fans alike, "Lawson's exclusion doesn't count towards his rides."

For the fourth race in succession the race is won by a Berwick rider and finishes 4-2. Luckily, Dick's on hand to remind us, "As long as you keep an opponent in fourth place, they can't get a heat advantage." Heat 5 sees Ryan Fisher become the first Monarch to win a race but, with Kalle Katajisto last, the race is drawn. William Lawson secures last place in the next race with an engine failure while Marcin Rempala rides with noticeable speed and grace to record the first win of his Berwick career. Though Matthew Wethers wins heat 7 in black and white, the real action takes place on the third bend of the first lap, where New Zealander Jade Mudgway gives Wölbert a huge shove to gain third. Jade's physical approach lacks sophistication but, if you can amass points as a rugby player on a speedway bike, who's complaining? Berwick fan Steven Brykajlo admires Jade's progress, "He's gone off the boil a bit recently but, for his first season, he's been excellent!" After confirmation of the official results, Dick joins in the delight over Mudgway, "If you have a third place ahead of an opponent, you can't get a heat advantage." Actually, if tactical rides are involved, you can actually get a heat advantage as evidenced by the 3-6 scoreline in favour of the Monarchs. Though it won't trip off the tongue quite so easily, clearly this truism should come with an elegantly worded caveat about the black-and-white helmet colour.

One of the stars of the Monarchs season so far, Kalle Katajisto, wakes from his torpor to lead heat 8 until the fourth bend where Marcin Rempala passes him in industrial fashion. William Lawson continues an evening to forget with yet another last place. Jim Brykajlo certainly isn't impressed, "4.47 was his average at Belle Vue after 13 meetings yet he's on last year's [Premier League] average! The Edinburgh chairman gave them permission so to do!" In case any riders and fans have inadvertently lost sight of the importance of the need to gain at least one point every race, Dick Barrie reiterates, "As long as you keep an opponent in fourth place, you can't get a heat advantage." It seems this oft-repeated message still hasn't quite percolated through to the Monarchs side of the pits. Given the scoreline, the Edinburgh riders now need to occupy first and second places for the remainder of the meeting, if they're to maintain their unbeaten away record.

Marcin Rempala's run of consecutive race wins effectively ends when he fishtails away from the gate at the start of heat 10 and arrives fourth into the first corner. Ryan Fisher wins heat 11 but, with Katajisto fourth, the heat is drawn. A maximum heat advantage from Paul Clews and Michal Rajkowski ends a mid-meeting sequence of drawn heats and takes the score to 45-30. An

Berwick: *"I don't know if you remember when riders just used to turn up with a second-hand bike on the back of their car with a small toolbox?"*

incredible 12 races are run to completion in 55 minutes! A determined Ryan Fisher then screws it on round the outside of bends one and two to pass through the proverbial absent gap to storm away to win heat 13 in a black-and-white helmet colour. Unfortunately, Andrew Tully's last place ensures the Monarchs slim mathematical chance of snatching a draw disappears and, thereby, ends their unbeaten Premier League away record. William Lawson caps off a poor night with a last place in heat 14 and races (if that is the word) to a five-ride minimum. Dick Barrie celebrates as only he knows how, "As long as you keep an opponent in fourth place, they can't get a heat advantage!" Adrian Rymel bests Ryan Fisher to the chequered flag in the nominated race to close the meeting at 9.17 p.m. Fifteen races in an incredible one hour 12 minutes! If only all meetings could run this efficiently![6]

Edinburgh fan Dougie Copland is magnanimous in defeat, "Berwick have ridden very well. We've been a bit of a two and a half man team and Lawson hasn't done so great. I think the momentum is with Newcastle now!" Many Monarchs riders disappoint tonight but, to my mind, Kevin Wölbert's drop from first to third place by the third bend of heat 12 encapsulates the lack of application shown by some Monarchs riders. Dougie doesn't agree with my analysis, "Clews rode him really hard in the first bend." By the refreshment kiosk one drunken Berwick Bandits fan celebrates loudly and over-exuberantly. He emotes in a partisan accusatory fashion that indicates he isn't a genuine speedway fan. Stood in the doorway of the trackshop, Phil Newton isn't surprised by William Lawson's performance. "Lawson was hopeless when he rode here. He doesn't like it at all. He never left the white line all night!"

7th August Berwick v. Edinburgh (Premier League) 54-42

6 Not to be outdone they then also run a three-heat Northern Junior League mini-match before the 9.30 p.m. curfew!

Berwick: *"I don't know if you remember when riders just used to turn up with a second-hand bike on the back of their car with a small toolbox?"*

CHAPTER 17

Buxton

"You go to speedway but you don't see old riders! They're not made welcome!"

8th August

The Buxton versus Isle of Wight National Trophy meeting lost to the weather on 18th July is quickly rescheduled for three weeks later. At the booth that serves as the paypoint-cum-entrance turnstiles into Hi-Edge, Buxton club chairman Jayne Moss deals with a steady stream of fans keen to park their cars with as good a vantage point as possible. Local climactic conditions dictate that some meetings are better appreciated from the warmth and comfort of your own vehicle. "Some of the crowds have been very poor this year." This sounds ominous. My anxious question, "What, below three figures?" Jayne quickly allays, "Not that bad!" It's almost warm enough to verge on the barmy. So much so that I tell Jayne, "It's feeling so warm I'm going to have to take my coat off!" Such over-confidence isn't sensible in these parts, "Don't say that, this is Buxton!"

Tapes rise

Notoriously, Buxton pride themselves on their careful husbandry of their finances. But, like many other clubs throughout British speedway, in the time of a downturn each and every fan through the turnstiles is vitally important. This season, like last, Buxton continue to cast off their reputation as a club more concerned with rider development than trophy success. Instead they've exchanged it for a mixed regime where rider development runs hand in hand with vaunting ambition. The key rider behind this recent resurgence is Craig Cook. He surprised many experts with his decision to continue to race in the National League (particularly after an exceptional 2009 season). Unfortunately, he's unavailable this afternoon and, instead, Tony Atkin will guest. In addition to watching the pennies, success on the track inevitably dictates an increase in the Buxton Hitmen's cost base, "It's been an expensive season winning so often!"

Tactics

[Jeff] "It would be best to win 46-44."
[Jayne] "Nah, we need the extra bonus point."
[Jeff] "Ok, 48-42 then!"
[Jayne] "Things are going well but the trouble is we don't have all the riders when we really need them. Nick [Morris]

is out but we don't need him at home so there's no need to replace him because anyone we get wouldn't be as good! We still use him away. With so many of our riders going well, it makes other clubs want to use them! That's always been the way when riders start going well. But, then, that's how we see ourselves as a club – giving riders the chance to improve and better themselves!" Isle of Wight Islanders co-team manager Kevin Shepherd draws up at the booth in his light metallic green Ford and quizzes Jayne, "You're not going to call if off again are you?" News that "We left it as long as we could to see if we could get it on" fails to reassure Kevin, "We were 20 minutes away when we heard!"

Jayne and Kevin discuss the restaging of the National League Fours meeting abandoned earlier in the season at Mildenhall. Or, rather, whispers of its restaging at Hoddesdon. Kevin notes, "They haven't said officially but, seemingly, it's the day before the NLRC." One of the more Internet-savvy promoters and a relatively regular poster on the British Speedway Forum, Jayne's investigated, "Rye House put it on their website that the practice was cancelled and the Fours was on. I don't think they meant to let the news out." The abandoned 4TT took place on June 6th. Kevin asks a question he knows the answer to already but checks anyway, "Have you been paid for that yet?" Jayne confirms, "We haven't!"

Buxton regular Charles McKay is also an early arrival. "There's been nothing in the *Star* about Tyson [Nelson] either in the news or in the Rye House section. They published my letter in this week's *Star*, though I sent it in a month ago. [1] Using a rider without a permit can't be right –

---

[1] Charles wrote a two-topic letter "wondering if the [National] League has a future". After discussing Charles Wright, this letter continues, "The second worrying development was the inclusion of Australian Tyson Nelson in the Rye House Cobras team at Scunthorpe. Tyson is set for a PL place at Sheffield on an assessed CMA of 5.00 when the necessary paperwork has been obtained from the UK Border Agency in the form of a GBE Sponsorship, the replacement for a work permit. The fact that he needs this paperwork suggests that Tyson, unlike other Australians riding in the NL, does not have any British partiality and so one assumes he is not riding on an ACU licence, but one issued by the speedway authorities in Australia. If that is the case, it would appear his riding for Rye House went against Regulation 13.1.2, which states that 'Holders of a foreign FMN (Federation Motorcycliste Nationale) licence are not permitted to ride in the NL'. On the Internet forums, it was claimed that Tyson was allowed to ride for Rye House without the necessary immigration paperwork and against Rule 13.1.2 because he was riding as an amateur. Did anyone from the Rye House promotion or the SCB check with the Border Agency to see what their view was of Tyson riding as an amateur and if that did, in fact, mean he didn't need any immigration paperwork? If the Agency now decides that riding as an amateur alters the need for necessary paperwork, what would have been the position of the various parties if Tyson had been seriously injured? Also, if the 'amateur' move is judged to be unacceptable by the Agency, what will be the effect on Tyson's current application for GBE sponsorship and, more importantly, what will be its impact on other riders' applications in the future? Will it mean that speedway has lost any goodwill it has built up over the years with the Border Agency for what appears to be the short-term gain for one team?" Rye House speedway promoter Len Silver wrote a letter of response in the next week's *Speedway Star*. "Tyson got in touch with me to ride for the Kart Cobras after being very frustrated by the inability of Sheffield to obtain permission for him to race. He had been in the country for many months waiting and he was getting fed up. In order to get the permission of the UK Border Agency to ride for Sheffield, he would need to return to Australia first as permission cannot be obtained for persons already in the UK. I discussed the situation with both Peter Morrish, co-ordinator of the National League and with the chairman of the BSPA, Alex Harkess of Edinburgh. I suggested that the professional aspect was the item that needed consideration and then if he rode as an amateur, then it would be legal (I was wrong). There was a misunderstanding during my conversation with the chairman and he believed that I had claimed that Tyson had a "working holiday" visa. He did not – he had a normal holiday visa. This misunderstanding led the chairman to suggest that he was eligible to ride at Scunthorpe. He rode, and demonstrated his huge talent, which I'm sure, was worth watching. Subsequently, I personally obtained the information from the Border Agency that riding as an amateur is not permitted and passed that information to the BSPA and the SCB. As a result of that information, Nelson's points were deducted from my team's total and the result amended – a decision I did not like but accepted with good grace." Since then Tyson's 17-point contribution to the Rye House Cobras score in their 40-53 away win in the National League at Scunthorpe has been amended to 40-36. Though on the surface this appears to address the situation and resolve it, Scunthorpe promoter Rob Godfrey isn't happy with this solution. "Nelson's points have been taken off but not given back to us, which I'm not amused about as it gives Rye House a point they wouldn't have got had they had a "normal" reserve in. We're not happy about it because we should have all three points, not just two. We did everything by the book that day, we told the referee but we allowed that rider to ride knowing full well he did not have a work permit. The outcome is not satisfactory because I believe either the meeting ought to be rerun or we should have all three match points."

Buxton: *"You go to speedway but you don't see old riders! They're not made welcome!"*

particularly when they fine riders for speaking out about the referee at the British Final! [2] Worse though, if I was the immigration people I'd start to think that speedway promoters would say anything to get what they want! If, another time, the immigration people decide not to grant someone a visa because of what Rye House have done – then all of speedway will suffer due to their actions! I hope it isn't ever the case." Charles's concern about the administration of National League matters is thrown into sharper relief by recent events at Mildenhall speedway where their promoter Ray Mascall found himself in a position where he couldn't financially afford to carry on. "They say Ray Mascall put his life savings and pension into Mildenhall but that isn't the way speedway should be run! They also say that no one has been paid yet from the Fours!" Though not exactly his cup of tea, Charles also keeps a close eye on events within the Speedway Grand Prix Series. He wonders that if, as publicly stated, the BSI blueprint for the future is supposed to see state-of-the-art stadiums staging important Grand Prix and World Cup events, then what's with the continuing excessive use of Ole Olsen's Vojens? "Ole the Wally's stadium was built in 1975 and, although they've made a few changes, it's still a difficult location to access and notorious for its wet weather. Nonetheless, BSI just can't get enough of the place! This season Vojens will stage a round of the Speedway Grand Prix, GP Qualifier as well as the Play-Off final and actual final of the speedway World Cup. That can't be right!"

Not all speedway clubs allow dogs into their stadiums but Buxton do. Guy Allott's here with his dog Shadow. He's the grandfather of Buxton rider Adam. Guy has a lifetime's involvement with speedway. "I first went in 1928 when I was about 6 years old. I've ridden them all! We lived in Yorkshire, my brother Tommy Allott – have you heard of him? – he's been dead a number of years – started at Barnsley. I've been to speedway all my life and I can honestly say speedway is the worst bloody run sport in the world and the best sport in the world to watch! Where you're sat now I've seen 75,000 people. They had a festival in 1975 here."
[Jeff] "Who played?"
[Guy] "I've forgotten. Modern ones! It was full of tents for three or four weeks at a time. I know a lot but I forget a lot, I can't remember me. I'll be 88 in another month. I do one or two engines still. I did young [Jason] Garrity's here. He's starting to go well!"
[Bob Granley] "You know him? Someone needs to chat to him – he's so wild."
[Guy] "Once he knocks his head a couple of times, he'll calm down."
[Bob] "What's going on in speedway is a scandal! Charles Wright should be able to ride. There's nothing in the Rules but he's banned!" [3] After Bob wanders off, Guy surprises me with the news that Ivan Mauger actually gave (rather than sold) him a copy of his latest autobiography, "Well, I worked for Mauger for about 15 years!" Despite very successfully tuning Ivan's, Ole Olsen's and many other top riders' engines in from a shed in his garden in Buxton, Guy professes that his engine-tuning business is more of an interest than a living. "I don't make a business of it – I do it

[2] The SCB fined Jordon Frampton £300 for comments he made about referee Ronnie Allen during the British Final at Wolverhampton in June. Jordon wrote a letter of apology to the referee and also said publicly, "I would like to apologise for the comments I made about Ronnie Allen following this year's British Final at Wolverhampton. The interview was conducted immediately after my races for the evening had finished when I most frustrated. I realise this is no excuse for what was printed but I hope it shows it was not my real intent, only a 'knee jerk' reaction to what had been a rather disappointing night for me personally."

[3] Charles Wright's case is also addressed in Charles McKay's recent letter to the *Speedway Star* about the future of the National league. "Charles Wright was stopped from riding at Buxton after signing for Redcar in the PL following complaints from certain nameless NL promoters. The official reason for this ban is that, according to the Regulations, his PL CMA of 5.36 obtained in 2009 while riding for Workington means that he can't ride in both the PL and the NL. Reading the relevant Regulation, 17.4.7.2, this decision would appear to be correct as the Regulations states 'No PL rider with a PL CMA of 4.00 or above may ride additionally in the NL'. Charles is banned because of 17.4.7.2, yet at least four other riders with PL CMA's of above 4.00 continue to ride in the NL as well as the PL. The reason given for this apparent inconsistency is that the Regulation was meant to say 'at the start of the season', something the Regulation hasn't said since 2002. So now we appear to have three Rulebooks – the published rulebook, the unwritten rulebook and the meant to say rulebook."

Buxton: *"You go to speedway but you don't see old riders! They're not made welcome!"*

to amuse myself and to work every day. I'm at work at 9. I do a lot of talking – rubbish mostly – every day. Sometimes I think I've been doing it too long. Did you see the World Cup? I'll tell you why it went wrong – England didn't have any older riders there – people like Mark Loram and Dave Jessop. Whereas Denmark had many experienced riders they could call on for help and advice. One of the best mechanics in the world is the Polish team manager [Marek Cieslak] and who did we have as a team manager? A bloody programme marker, that's all! The Speedway World Cup was never mentioned in the national news or on the telly! Lots of minority sports – trotting and hound training in the North East – don't get coverage. Nobody wants to know the promoters who run this business! You go to speedway but you don't see old riders! They're not made welcome! Lots of them live close but the promoters don't want to hear what they say (if they're trying to be helpful). What other sport wouldn't welcome people who used to play and know so much about it?"

Out on the centre green the flag marshal on the first bend looks suspiciously like Charles McKay. "Have you noticed how quiet it is on the Buxton terraces here today? Charles McKay has been dragged to the centre green to work the red flag – don't worry, he's paid. He's alleged to be on bend one after he's been back to the car to get his yellow [fluorescent] jersey." Jim Sanderson stops by for a chat. Like many fans, he's gone to speedway for years. "If you go back to the Scottish Junior League in 1977 you'd have seen my brother Mike, ride."

Staying in a holiday cottage that's midway between Buxton and Bakewell, knowledgeable speedway fan and Reading club historian Arnie Gibbons is in the Dales for a week of relaxation. "My husband did say you can go to Buxton and I said 'Not only there but Belle Vue, Stoke and Sheffield!'" Though delighted to return to Buxton, a track he rarely visits since moving down south, Arnie's greater concern is the warp and woof of the everyday British speedway world. "Is Charles McKay claiming responsibility for Tyson Nelson's points being deducted? Only hours after his letter appeared in the *Speedway Star*, the SCB issue a statement/ruling (which appears on the BSPA website mid-morning) that said Tyson was ineligible to ride and his points had been deducted. Rye House's win at Scunny is now a defeat there!"

Jim Sanderson makes the point that in football (when Sheffield Wednesday reserves, say, want to give a player without a permit a run-out) they ensure that the match is truly considered to be "amateur" by not charging any admission to see it! Asking a question he already knows the answer too, Jim wonders if Scunthorpe charged for admission and, if they did, will they be giving a refund? This is precisely the kind of nuanced response to a situation that appeals to Arnie. "The Rye House line was that Tyson was an amateur so eligible to ride. They can say or think whatever they like but the immigration definition of an amateur would be, amongst other things, that he wasn't getting paid. As a work-permit issue – to keep on the right side of the immigration rules – Tyson mustn't appear as a professional. So it's not solely just a matter of him not getting paid but, in order to avoid any complications, no admission should be paid by the fans as that indicates they come along to see performing professionals. As Jim says, Sheffield Wednesday reserves charge no admission when they have an amateur from abroad performing (having a trial). That said, Rye House do blood a lot of young riders and do run proper second halves which is much more than pretty well every other track in the country!"

If Arnie could pick his ideal National League final to decide the whereabouts of the championship silverware, then, "Personally, I'd like a Buxton versus Dudley final!" Arnie recently went to the Oak Tree Arena to see the British Under-18s championship. "I tell you what really impressed me – 24 races finished by 9.45! Then it did start at 7.30 on the dot. It was lovely to see Brendan Johnson win after all that happened last year!" I quiz Arnie about Brandon Freemantle's performance, "Brandon started slowly but ended up with a race win and 5 points, I think." The first speedway meeting of Arnie's holiday in the Dales saw him take in the last night's Stoke versus Sheffield Premier League encounter at Loomer Road Stadium. "Stoke last night had less passing than any meeting I've ever seen except Reading versus Exeter about eight to ten years ago. That meeting was completely devoid of passing and Stoke last night was almost devoid of passing! The real highlight of the evening was when the lights went out after another generator failure at Stoke! So we had 40 minutes when nothing happened! Then Stoke had Frank Facher at No. 1. I assume it's because he's on an assessed average of 7.00. The Stoke rider with the highest average was Taylor Poole with a green sheet average of 6.23. When you look at the averages, you have to wonder why Sheffield didn't win by more and, though it was technically a last-heat decider – with the unbeaten Ashworth and Franc out – it was a little unlikely! Then Sheffield did choose the "mighty" Soosh [Tomáš Suchánek] as a guest and he failed to beat a Stoke rider all night!"

Though not fancied to excel at Hi-Edge, the Islanders open the meeting with a heat advantage via a win for Nick Simmons and third for Lee Smethills. The initial attempt to run heat 2 ends with a theatrical fall from the betassled Tom Hill. With fellow reserve and team partner Dean Felton – star of the opening meeting at Buxton in 1994 – in the lead, this stoppage is suboptimal from an Islanders point of view. Prior to referee Stuart Wilson's decision, Arnie wonders aloud, "It'll be interesting to see if red [Lewis Dallaway] is excluded for not being under power when the race was stopped as he was coasting!" In fact, Tom is the only rider disqualified. In the rerun, race leader first time out, Dean Felton leads until the start of the third lap. Arnie then shouts, "Go on, Deano!" just at the moment Jason Garrity passes stylishly underneath him with a cutback. Last in heat 1, Garrity possesses the kind of all-action style that simultaneously suggests great effort fighting his bike but also significant speed.

Joshua Moss stops by my table to show off his new Nike 'miracle' football boots, "They were £30 in Denton – my friend paid £69 for his and that was in Long Denton!" The third race only lasts as long as it takes Brendan Johnson to land on the first-bend shale. It's all four back, albeit with an admonishment from referee Stuart Wilson who (we're told), "warns the rider in white [Danny Warwick] to stay still at the start."

Between races I'm told about tracks elsewhere in the region: "The lights failed in heat 8 at Stoke last night! When we went there last season, all the floodlights failed on bends one and two – you'd think they'd have got it fixed by now!" In the rerun, second-placed Brendan gets discombobulated before getting further out of shape on the back straight. It appears his front wheel is suddenly too heavy for his bike and, by the time he gets to the third bend, he's ready to fall under minimal pressure from Jason Garrity. Brendan leaps to his feet with a speed that suggests petulance. It's an impression quickly confirmed – despite his karate blackbelt – by wild, almost kung fu style, gestures to persons unknown, just prior to confirmation of his inevitable disqualification. In the heat 3 re-rerun, Danny Warwick stands out for all the wrong reasons: namely, his lacklustre approach. Robert Branford wins but it's Jason Garrity – racing his third race on the trot (after Jonathan Bethell fails to beat the time allowance to take his first programmed ride). The slightly peculiar shape of Jason's sweeping rather strenuous broadsides that he executes for all the world as if his back wheel were temporarily too light for his bike, only serves to further highlight his unique eye-catching all-action style!

Tom Hill gates and wins heat 4 comfortably ahead of Lewis Dallaway and Buxton captain Adam Allott. On my brief trip to the hallowed confines of the referee's box, I admire the view enjoyed by Speedway Control Bureau official Stuart Wilson, "You really have the best view here!" Stuart's also appreciative, "I do until I make the wrong decisions and then everyone lets me know I can't see." So far, this reaction isn't necessary, "I'm sure that won't happen!" Stuart remains on his guard, "And the Derbyshire people are too polite to say!"

Buxton: *"You go to speedway but you don't see old riders! They're not made welcome!"*

Almost immediately afterwards, for the second time in three races, Jonathan Bethell exceeds the two-minute time allowance and is disqualified. This afternoon's stand-in announcer tells us, "So Jonathan cannot be replaced as he has to have three rides – so it'll be three riders only [pause for five seconds] or he can go off 15 metres as the referee has just told me!" From back there, Jonathan's unable to make any impression on the riders ahead. The Islanders numbers 1 and 2, Nick Simmons and Lee Smethills hammer home a maximum heat advantage to level the scoreline. Sadly, this is good as it gets for the visitors. Recent heats see eddies of shale dust blow over the parked cars and away onto the Fells so, prior to heat 6, the Hi-Edge circuit is watered intensively. While the bowser circuits, there's a serenade of intermittent but loud squeals from the car tyres of the stockcars racing on the track adjacent to the speedway stadium. Whether it's the wet condition of the shale or a momentary lapse in concentration isn't exactly clear but, after Brendan Johnson fires from the tapes to lead, he then rides a grunky first bend that loses him position. Slightly overriding in order to make up for lost ground, Brendan executes a pretty graceful 180 degree pirouette before his fall gains another third-bend disqualification. Experienced enough to genuinely appreciate that discretion is the better part of valour, the rerun of heat 6 sees Dean Felton take it extremely easy. So much so that Robert Branford and Tony Atkin race to an untroubled maximum far ahead of him and restore Buxton's 4-point lead.

Out on the centre green, with great concentration, between races temporary first-bend flag marshal Charles McKay assiduously fills his programme. Heat 7 sees Lewis Dallaway's enthusiasm run away with him to the extent that he moves ostentatiously at the tapes just prior to the start of the race. Although Stuart Wilson immediately illuminates the red lights, it's not until they've begun the second lap that the race actually stops for some riders! Via the temporary announcer, the ref has some polite but firm advice, "Can the start marshal warn the rider in blue about moving at the start and can the start marshal also look out for the red lights!" Adam Allott wins the rerun while Brendan Johnson manages to complete his first race of the afternoon (albeit in fourth place). Tom Hill soon collects his second disqualification in only three rides in heat 8 after a touch of the tapes at the start. While we wait for the rerun, I snatch a few words with Jonathan Bethell in the pits, "Nice to see you riding again." Jonathan is taciturn about his renaissance, "I wish I could say the same." His non-appearances today seem mysterious, "Why do they keep excluding you under the two minutes?" but aren't, "I've blown two engines today so far!" Injuries continue to plague Jonathan but, in true speedway rider fashion, he battles gamely on. "It's nearly two years since I rode with my wrist and knee. I've had two ligaments replaced – the ACL and medial ligament – but the knee still isn't right. Today it's okay but, on other days, it swells up and I have pains in my [upper] thigh and ankle. They've been inside three times. They [the surgeons] say there's nothing they can do and don't know why it's like that! There's a bit of arthritis but that shouldn't cause this! I can't even run ten yards, if I wanted too."

Jason Garrity wins heat 8 in impressive fashion. He certainly looks an exciting prospect. Arnie Gibbons gazes on from the slightly raised area close to the gents toilets. "Until you stand on the back straight, you don't realise how steep it is here. The first time a rider races here they're bound to be a bit tentative! They'll know it's strange. When it's wet, it's clearly very tricky plus there must be some bumps!" Next time out, Jonathan Bethell races to a paid win behind his teammate Robert Branford. Tom Hill had third until an engine failure on the last bend gifts Lee Smethills this position. Heat 10 takes a couple of attempts to run after Lewis Dallaway picks up drive between bends three and four (on his second lap) to hammer straight into the safety fence. After three scoreless races, Brendan Johnson wins the rerun and, with Danny Warwick third, they contain the Buxton lead to a mere 8 points.

Jason Garrity's never-say-die attitude gets another showcase on the run to the line at the end of

Buxton: *"You go to speedway but you don't see old riders! They're not made welcome!"*

heat 11. Sadly his last-gasp blast gets nowhere since he locks up and remains third. Fans savour the racing along with the comparatively balmy conditions. "We've been here four times this season and it's the first time it hasn't rained! Every time we come, Tony Atkin rides instead of Craig Cook so we've only seen him once – when they rode against Newport. That's the problem with doubling up! Now 10 points to the poor, Isle of Wight send Danny Warwick out in the black-and-white helmet colour. Sadly he only gets two yards from the tapes before a glance down at his sickly engine. Jason Garrity – the rider with the most flamboyant back wheel in British speedway – needs no second invitation to exit stage left, closely pursued by teammate Jonathan Bethell who finishes his afternoon with two paid wins (from four rides) to go along with the expense of his two blown engines. With a bonus point still a vague outside possibility, Nick Simmons dons the black-and-white helmet colour for heat 13. It's an eventful race throughout. Tom Hill falls on the second bend of the second lap but clears the track with commendable speed (particularly helpful since Nick Simmons leads). The Islanders No. 1 takes the chequered flag and slows knowing that his race is run. Tony Atkin stops immediately after nursing his bike round the last two laps with a noticeably flat tyre. Oblivious to the usual obvious signals, Buxton captain Adam Allott proceeds to ride lustily on in his own imaginary race. After an ostentatious glance around on the fourth bend of his fifth lap, Adam slows on the run-in to the finish line to warm ironic cheers from the knot of fans there. Stood in the pits, Jonathan Bethell reflects on his exertions and explains that racing speedway isn't conducive to a full recovery for his right knee. With the cost of a knee brace £500, rehabilitation isn't a cheap option either. Just walking down the street Jonathan has suffered a number of embarrassing falls. "When you think about it you're okay but, as soon as you don't, it bites back! You lose stability, it locks up, you get shooting pains and tingling nerves. That's why I'm not so bothered about riding. When you're doing this, you have no time! If I did, I could help it recover!"

The initial attempt to race heat 14 ends for Tom Hill in another fall and disqualification after Robert Branford challenges him. The rerun penultimate race of the afternoon then becomes an impromptu exhibition by Lewis Dallaway of slow motion almost surreptitious falls from his bike. Dallaway's nemesis is definitely the second bend. He falls and remounts there on the second lap and, for good measure, then repeats the exercise on his third lap. I remark approvingly to Jonathan Bethell, "He gets up quick!" Jonathan retorts, "He's had lots of practice!" Sadly Lewis gets no more practice this afternoon since the referee disqualifies him and awards the race as a win for Brendan Johnson with Robert Branford second. The Isle of Wight Islanders Nick Simmons wins the nominated heat 15 – ahead of the impressive Jason Garrity and Buxton team captain Adam Allott – to take his points total to 17 from five rides. It's hard to be effective opposition on your own especially against a team where Garrity, Branford and Allott all finish with double figure scores.

8th August Buxton v. Isle of Wight (National League) 51-41

Buxton: *"You go to speedway but you don't see old riders! They're not made welcome!"*

CHAPTER 18

Wolverhampton

"When he gates, he wins. If not, he can't be bothered. He'd be on the list of riders I wouldn't have in my team!"

9th August

With just over a month before the Elite League cut-off date, second-placed defending champions Wolverhampton comfortably nestle in the warm metaphorical bosom of the play-off places. Derby meetings with local rivals Coventry invariably attract good crowds irrespective of comparative league positions. This is just as well since Coventry currently languish down in seventh in the Elite League table. Familiarity apparently also doesn't breed contempt since tonight's Elite League B fixture is already Coventry's fourth visit to the Monmore Green stadium. Compared to both last season and also Poole, Wolverhampton aren't quite as rampant but have, nonetheless, already beaten Coventry three times at home and once away. It would be a surprise if there were to be any other outcome than a Wolverhampton victory.

Presentation team member Shaun Leigh arrives early and, when he passes the trackshop, Dave Rattenbury is quick to quiz him. "Are you doing the announcing tonight?"
[Shaun] "No, Peter [Morrish] is back."
[Jeff] "Last year he said, '250,000 words I wonder who counted them?' Obviously he doesn't know about the functionality of Word documents."
[Shaun] "He still uses a typewriter! I know he does cos he sent me a condolence card when Sheffield Wednesday went down."

Smartly dressed in a Speedway Control Bureau jacket, most recently qualified referee Darren Hartley is also an early arrival. His involvement with speedway goes back many years, "I spannered for Joe Screen from '93 and Jan Stæckmann from '96. I sometimes helped Jason Lyons out too. I rode as a junior until I got this [points to stomach]." I suspect talking about his background rather than stomach, *Wolverhampton Express & Star* speedway journalist Tim Hamblin interjects, "That gives you a unique perspective!" Darren continues, "Well, it's funny when I go down to the pits now as a referee because the riders do treat me differently, Jason calls out 'Hey, Fudge! Do I have to call you *Mr Hartley* now?'" When not in charge of meetings, Darren also travels widely with his refereeing colleagues. The recent Newcastle versus Birmingham Premier Trophy Final first-leg clash at Brough Park sticks in his mind, "I've never seen a crowd like it. I was in the referee's box with Craig Ackroyd and they were banging on the windows and gesturing. It could be quite intimidating but Craig is his own man. I don't think he got any of the decisions wrong. Perhaps, the only one there could be any debate over was the one with the [simultaneous] incident on bends two and bends three but, once he'd put on the red lights, it didn't matter anyway! Things don't happen there on the track unless something unusual has happened." Like many there that night, I noticed, "Jason wasn't very happy in heat 15." Darren jokes, "He was probably frustrated because he wanted to get on, get changed and get to the bar!"

Any referee gets a unique perspective upon the sport and Darren is no exception. "None of the riders tend to ring you up from the pits phone! Mark Lemon likes a chat but it's the managers who call up. " Apparently some pre-warn Darren that they might ring up during the meeting apparently highly annoyed but say that they'll only do so for show to appear supportive of the riders rather than because they want a decision changed. Others make no such promises and ring up for genuine reasons. Sat in the referee's box you see all sorts, whether you're in charge of the meeting or not. "I was there [Brough Park] last night [for Newcastle versus Edinburgh] with Graham Flint and he said, 'If that happens [banging on the windows and gesturing] I'll call George English.' I think René Bach is the more polished performer and Larsen is more unpredictable! I had an interesting reception at Glasgow recently when I'd excluded their rider in heat 15. The security man came up to the box and said he'd escort me to my car but I said 'It's alright.'" Darren's travels as an SCB official have yet to take him to Lakeside, Ipswich or Eastbourne, "This is my first full season, I did half a season last year!"

Bathed in sunshine

Sittingbourne Speedway's pits marshal and itinerant Edinburgh Monarchs fan with the distinctive originally eggshell-blue coloured anorak, Dick Jarvis, also saw last night's Newcastle versus Edinburgh clash. "Wölbert was flying last night. The problem with a track like that with bumps is, that if the opposition gate (like he did last night), then it's hard to get back! Sneddon only rode one race and Larsen injured his elbow when he fell off on his own. As he went back to the pits a big fan came down from the back of the grandstand and told him what he thought. That's just what you want to do to your Number 1! It was quiet after heat 5 last night, which is just how you like it there! I think that has ended Newcastle's hopes of winning the Premier League. Looking at the table, Sheffield could be the team to beat, it's definitely not Birmingham!"

Library display

Laurence Rogers lingers and needs no second invitation to take his own brief trip down memory lane. In this instance about Wolverhampton speedway's main sponsors Parry's International ("International Coach Tour Operators") since Laurence goes back a long way with the owner, "When was Dave Parry at Crayford? Was it the '70s?" Dick Jarvis knows his speedway onions, "1968." Laurence continues, "We used to meet up at the Royal India in Walsall. He only had a mini bus then! It was before mobile phones and he used to say 'See you there at 11.30!' It's not there anymore." Laurence Rogers is a keen observer of people. Even more so when they visit Newport speedway in flamboyant dress, like Weymouth's Phil Bartlett did earlier this season,

Wolverhampton: *"When he gates, he wins. If not, he can't be bothered. He'd be on the list of riders I wouldn't have in my team!"*

"Remembering he's got ginger hair, he turned up to our place wearing a really bright pink shirt!" Speedway inspires many long-term friendships, both on and off the track. Some change, mature or fall apart with time; others remain pickled in aspic. "I was having a pee at Stoke with CVS and we looked up at the paint and I said 'It's the same as 1973 when we started here!' Then we looked at the toilets and they were the same too!" The toilet hygiene standards at Stoke are a topic close to my heart. I joke, "They say it was 1973 when they last had soap or paper towels there too!" Dick Jarvis has his own insights, "Isn't it Stoke where they rain off meetings in the sunshine and run them in the rain?" Sight of Peter Morrish passing interrupts Laurence Rogers's reminiscences about his trips to the Stoke toilets with Chris Van Straaten, "Peter said after the [National League] Pairs at Newport on Saturday, 'You know that was a good well-run meeting – I can't think of anything wrong with it at all!' I told him to tell the BSPA that!" Graham Reeve passes too. His nod and cheery greeting ("Hello, John!") indicates I'm nowadays almost part of speedway's charmed inner circle.

The speedway grapevine pulses and echoes with factual statements and rumour alike. Tonight the talk is of dramatic team changes in Norfolk, "Have you heard about King's Lynn sacking five and signing six!? One of them is a Dane who rides on a Wednesday and what night do King's Lynn ride?" It's no surprise to Dick Jarvis, "I thought Chris Mills might be leaving. When there was a long break because of Paul Cooper's injury, they interviewed him and he said 'I got out of riding at Newport today' and just after he said 'I'm going to be riding a lot more grass track next year', as that's on a Sunday that doesn't make Premier League that easy!"

On the crowded home-straight terraces prior to the start of heat 1, a morose Coventry fan presciently observes, "It'll depend on which Krzysztof Kasprzak turns up!" He doesn't identify exactly what versions are available. Any club, obviously, needs a Number 1 who wishes to race and compete to the limit of his machinery and ability. Wolverhampton's Fredrik Lindgren certainly fits that particular bill and, when he's followed home by Ty Proctor, centre-green announcer Ian 'Porky' Jones can barely contain his hair-trigger delight, "The first 5-1 of the night, and you know what that means, don't you?!" Porky's an acquired taste. So much so, many people would probably pay good money to see him reprise writhing on the track in agony like he did last season. Others evangelise about Porky as an essential part of a proper evening's speedway entertainment at Monmore Green. Either way, celebratory music blares out over the stadium loudspeaker system until Peter Morrish switches on his microphone to share the race results and an observation ("very quick winning time for Freddie Lindgren in heat 1"). Wolverhampton speedway historian Mark Sawbridge nods at news of the 54.59 seconds winning time and echoes Morrish's sentiments, "Very quick!" Many Elite League speedway fans who are not of the Bees persuasion, hold the opinion that Coventry's Polish reserve Przemyslaw Pawlicki won't rush to achieve the 12 meetings milestone that will ensure his assessed average increases to the level his current performances on the track in British speedway dictate. Glancing at his programme prior to heat 2, Mark Sawbridge notes, "Aaron Summers is in for Przemyslaw '11 meetings' Pawlicki! I have a chart on my desk and his number of meetings is slowly creeping up." On the subject of creeping, there's a hint of movement at the start line that the referee ignores before Ludvig Lindgren becomes the second member of his close family to win a race this evening. With Joe Haines second, 'Porky' gesticulates exuberantly on the centre green in celebration of Wolves successive maximum heat advantages. Coventry fans don't need the loud blare of the music to appreciate that, with the score at an already forlorn 10-2, it could be a long night ahead.

The day before his 20th birthday Tai Woffinden takes to the track for heat 3. I ask Mark Sawbridge, "Did you know tonight is Tai's last night as a teenager?" It's news to him, "I didn't know that, actually!" and some delight for me, "I can't believe I'm telling the Wolverhampton speedway historian facts about Wolves!" Mark's much too polite to highlight the disparity between his

150

Wolverhampton: *"When he gates, he wins. If not, he can't be bothered. He'd be on the list of riders I wouldn't have in my team!"*

knowledge of speedway and mine, let alone – if this were *Mastermind* – his specialist subject of all things Wolverhampton speedway. To further my education, Mark suggests that if I've got time tomorrow morning, "You should go and see the Wolverhampton Photographic Society exhibition on the top floor foyer of Wolverhampton City Library. They've got two bays of historic rider photos, programmes borrowed from the collections of various speedway collectors." Mark's Poole-supporting partner Sally Knight works at the Library but says that, even if she didn't, she'd recommend this exhibit. Built from distinctive red terracotta stone, the Central Library in Snow Hill, Wolverhampton opened in 1902. At the top of the building underneath an ornate ceiling, the Wolverhampton Photographic Society's Speedway Exhibition occupies two large glass-fronted bays. It runs until the 28th August and covers the period from 1949 to 2010. The materials displayed instantly catch the eye, whether you're a neutral or speedway memorabilia aficionado. John Adams, Mick Foster, Jon George and Mike Piper have kindly given the Wolverhampton Photographic Society the use of their collections for this display. Capably produced by Gerald Hanrahan (LRPS), ably assisted by Joan Madeley Griffiths with additional continuity work undertaken by Tony Price. There are programmes from many clubs including Oxford, Crewe Kings, Leicester, Halifax, Wimbledon, Peterborough, Hackney, Wolverhampton and Coventry as well as a smattering of World and British Finals programmes. Understandably rider photographs take centre stage and these include action and/or posed images of Pete Jarman, Johnny Grant, Brian Shepherd, Graham Warren, James Bond, Derek Braithwaite, Bengt Anderson, Ivor Brown, Graham Warren, Terry Betts, Harry Ward-Ropper, Keith Mantle, Adam Skornicki [doing his trademark Donuts], Ole Olsen, Gary Petersen and an excellent Erik Gundersen photo. Speedway, however, isn't solely about the riders so St John Ambulance members, start line staff, machine examiners, tractor drivers, mechanics and even Lewis Bridger's granddad (Tony Thompson) also feature. Pride of place is also given to the scorecard from a keenly fought Wolves versus Cradley meeting (one that saw a heat 12 race maximum for Cradley move the score to 35-37 only for Wolves to reply in kind to snatch victory – and happiness – at 40-38). There's a photograph of Ian Jones with the caption "Long Serving Mobile 'continuity announcer' known affectionately as 'Porky'". Also included is a Redcar Bears advert that suggests that people should rush down to the South Tees Motorsports Park on Dormer Way, Middlesbrough to savour some shale action. News of the exploits of Wolverhampton speedway headlines some front-pages chosen from the local *Express & Star* newspaper. This also features a masthead photo of their speedway reporter Tim Hamblin in his debonair Eastern European spy persona. The quality of the materials on display is such that only a very hard-hearted speedway fan could fail to feel envy or be seized by some degree of covetousness.

Edward Kennett gates with alacrity at the start of heat 3 but soon finds himself in a battle for the lead with Tai Woffinden. On the fourth bend of the first lap Tai uses his local track knowledge to cut back sharply up the inside to take a brief lead that he soon concedes. His manoeuvre prompts me to ask, "Is that legal putting both wheels on the centre green?" Mark Sawbridge shrugs, "Technically not!" Edward's victory isn't a shock for Tim Hamblin, "Edward Kennett has been the Wolves default guest for the last one and a half years." Sadly with Ben Barker last, Coventry can't capitalise upon this Kennett race win nor do they build on Chris Harris's victory in heat 4. The Wolverhampton faithful on the home straight react with indifference, so much so that 'Porky' demands greater response from them, "Come on! Show your appreciation. He's a really nice guy!" John 'Fozzie' Hendley isn't a fan of the smooth-talking Terry Wogan of speedway, "You go round to a lot of speedway tracks, are we the only club to have an imbecile like this on the centre green?" Good speedway presenters add to the enjoyment with their insight and repartee. Others merely demand to be noticed. It's a job some (appear to) do effortlessly while others struggle to excite their own enthusiasm, let alone that of the fans. Still, in the absence of universal acclaim it's better

151

Wolverhampton: *"When he gates, he wins. If not, he can't be bothered. He'd be on the list of riders I wouldn't have in my team!"*

to inspire strong emotion rather than studious indifference.

Heat 7 sees Edward Kennett fail to gate but, with a shrewd blast round the outside, he'd have the lead as the riders exit the second bend if teammate Ben Barker didn't hold him back. It's a distraction that nearly allows Joe Haines through until Edward zooms off with Ben Barker in trademark wholehearted but ugly pursuit. In contrast, Edward looks smooth, comfortable and elegant on his bike. At least until the back straight of the last lap, where his engine splutters and he slows to a serenade of cheers from the Wolves faithful. However, with a substantial lead already established their cheer of joy is short-lived since his engine splutters back into life. They greet this Coventry Bees 5-1 with a loud burst of "Ladies Night" over the stadium speakers. I'm told they see this as Ben Barker's signature tune around these parts. Coventry's Aaron Summers gets a flier from the tapes at the start of heat 8 that 'Porky' greets with his own shale version of a Dadaist chant, "Red lights, red lights, red lights, red lights!" The rerun looks likely to give the Bees successive maximum heat advantages until Ty Proctor overtakes Aaron Summers down the back straight for second place behind Lewis Bridger. This Bees heat advantage nearly declines to a drawn heat via an unlikely dash to the finish line from the fourth bend by Ludvig Lindgren. It's blocked at the last moment by a mid-track broadside across the line by Aaron Summers. Deprived of the 5-1 that would restore tonight's meeting to parity, 'Porky' playfully demands greater fan engagement, "Come on you Coventry fans, that should keep you happy!" Mark Sawbridge wonders, "Did you hear when Rosco was asked about their Elite League play-off credentials? He said, 'Peterborough did us a favour beating Swindon' when, if you look at the table, it put Coventry further behind!"

Though ostensibly merely a drawn heat, the ninth race is one of those intense speedway spectacles it's a joy to witness. Joe Haines gates and Tai Woffinden proceeds to team-ride cum chaperone him from the ongoing attentions of Chris 'Bomber' Harris. Speedway's equivalent of a fencing duel showcases a shale repertoire of lunge, parry, defend, as Bomber repeatedly probes the outside line for the real or imaginary gap he requires to find a way round the Wolves riders. For three and a half laps, Bomber seizes every opportunity to probe the outside line only to find his erstwhile advances repelled. There's a heady mix of discretion, backing off and lack of the required speed that's also Tai skilfully predicatively blocking these attempted passing manoeuvres. It's a team-riding master-class right up until the riders exit the second bend for the last time when, with a telegraphed feint to the outside, Bomber surprises Tai with a burst up the inside for the first time to find fresh air as the riders arrive at the third bend. As he crosses the finish line to win, Harris celebrates with an exuberant display of short jabs-cum-rabbit-punches. Mark Sawbridge simultaneously manages to celebrate the spectacle of this race and appear downcast at the result, "Tai should have won that one. He should have just been away! You knew he could go up the inside, but he thought he wouldn't be able to turn, but he did!" I can't help but marvel at Harris's skill too, "He knows the PK lines he did it there in a much narrower space close to the white line!" During his post-meeting pits interviews, Tim Hamblin asks Tai about this race and his reaction to Bomber's repeat attempts to split them. "Joe Haines rode a brilliant first two laps but then started drifting in and getting narrower and getting slower and slower until we both weren't going fast!"

Mark studies the score chart closely and though it tells us that Wolverhampton lead 28-26, the pessimist in him notes, "If you ignore the first two races, they're winning!" Though always studiously modest about the wealth of insight and subtly of his elegant speedway writing, understandably Tim Hamblin has many admirers. When recently in conversation with Nigel Pearson, an old age pensioner interrupts their chat to say, "I've rode speedway and I've been going for 60 years and I just have to say I enjoy reading your stuff and you're the best speedway writer I've ever read!" Mark needs no second invitation to second these sincere words of praise,

Wolverhampton: *"When he gates, he wins. If not, he can't be bothered. He'd be on the list of riders I wouldn't have in my team!"*

With Freddie Lindgren out in the next race with Ty Proctor, Mark believes the tide is about to turn, "Ty is one of those who absolutely hates losing. He kicks the toolbox and everything!" Predictably enough Fredrik Lindgren leads comfortably throughout though, behind him, there's a battle royal between Edward Kennett and Ty Proctor for second. Although it's always likely to be hard to out-think Edward on a track he knows so well, Proctor rides resourcefully. On the last lap, from around about the vicinity of the start line Proctor broadsides early into the first bend to create the opportunity that enables him to force his way up the inside on the transition from bends two to three to grab second place. It ensures Wolverhampton race to a maximum heat advantage in a hard race that Edward Kennett salutes afterwards with a wave towards Ty Proctor. Perched high above the track in the referee and announcer's box, Peter Morrish luxuriates in the warm glow this spectacle induces, "It doesn't get any better than that! What a fabulous heat of speedway!"

With a race win in heat 11, Krzysztof Kasprzak doubles his points total to 6 points (from three rides), despite an enthusiastic four-lap chase from Nicolai Klindt. Mark Sawbridge questions Krzysztof's temperament, "When he gates, he wins. If not, he can't be bothered. He'd be on the list of riders I wouldn't have in my team!" During the interval, the small world that is speedway means I bump into Pete Lawrence who's a music business friend of Britain's leading blues musician Billy Jenkins (a.k.a. the bard of Bromley). Like Billy, Pete has a lifetime love of speedway, "I started a festival – the Big Chill – have you heard of that? I've not been too involved these last few years because I've been starting a social networking site (www.picnicvillage.com). It's going to be owned by the community and have no advertising. At the moment we've only got up some teaser forums because we're still talking to the lawyers. It starts on September 7th. It's lots of work and it's really exciting. We're still looking at funding but I still find time to go to speedway!"

With the scores relatively poised at 35-31, as the interval ends and the riders line up at the start line ready for heat 12, it starts to rain. Nicolai Klindt carries on where he left off to win. Indeed, Nicolai's dander remains up next time out in heat 13 (his third consecutive race), so much so that he leads Krzysztof Kasprzak into the first corner. It's a challenge the Pole takes in his stride with a pass up the inside but, as he does so, Fredrik Lindgren goes round both to lead. Klindt continues to give very fast chase and even attempts a back-straight overtaking manoeuvre on lap three that's all the braver because of the increasingly slippery conditions. Eight points to the good with two races to go, Wolverhampton's historian gives a half sigh of relief but doesn't quite yet assume victory, "I'd have taken the win halfway through. Now we look okay." Though Edward Kennett wins the penultimate race of the evening, it's without any support since Aaron Summers finishes last. This drawn heat retains the Wolverhampton advantage and ensures their victory. Mark Sawbridge is now finally able to bathed in the warm glow of another local derby triumph, "I'm really pleased with that because we were really struggling!"

The initial attempt to run heat 15 gets no further than a first-corner clash between Fredrik Lindgren and Edward Kennett. With conditions somewhat slippery under tread, Tim Hamblin gives a typically fair-minded assessment, "Wolves fans would see that as all four back whereas Coventry fans wouldn't! I'd say – with the track as it is – Freddie needed to attack the track and be assertive!" The rerun of heat 15 sees 'Bomber' Harris re-find his gating gloves to vie at high speed with Fredrik Lindgren for prime position in the first corner. This time out Edward Kennett sensibly decides discretion is the better part of valour so enters the first-corner fray much more sedately. Harris and Lindgren battle but it's Fredrik who shows the speed, strategy and tactical

Wolverhampton: *"When he gates, he wins. If not, he can't be bothered. He'd be on the list of riders I wouldn't have in my team!"*

edge required. Tim Hamblin savours the tactical nuances, "Did you see Freddie already knew that Harris would pull the high locker and cut back so he drifted in as they raced the line?" Perhaps Bomber should stick with his intuition and flamboyant high-speed racing style rather than indulge in a battle of minds with Freddie? Tim Hamblin's quick to recall that this is the second time in four days that the more thoughtful version of Chris Harris has come unstuck. "Did you see in heat 15 at Coventry? Harris rode the only racing line for three laps but out-thought himself by cutting to the inside on the last bend (predicting a similar Lindgren manoeuvre to the famous 2009 second fourth-bend race on the last lap) only to see Lindgren sail past him on the outside! With pretty well any other rider, Harris would have ridden his own race and ignored him and stuck to the fast line." Wolverhampton win by 10 points in a meeting notable for a number of close fought and notable races that should please partisans and neutrals alike.

9th August Wolverhampton v. Coventry (Elite League) 50-40

Wolverhampton: *"When he gates, he wins. If not, he can't be bothered. He'd be on the list of riders I wouldn't have in my team!"*

CHAPTER 19

Belle Vue
"Am I Chris Morton?"

16th August

Last week's demolition of Elite League championship would-be contenders Peterborough ensures the Belle Vue Aces remain undefeated at Kirkmanshulme Lane since their loss there to Poole on 2nd June. Monstered would be a better word or, perhaps, crushed. In addition, Poole have lost the burning urgency for league points they held back then while the Aces nowadays show greater belief in their home-track advantage. Echoing the programme front cover headline ("all to play for still"), club co-promoter Chris Morton really can't be faulted for his positive forward-looking outlook. "I was never one to give up in my racing days and I'm still not. I know the odds aren't brilliant about us making the top four and a place in the play-offs but, at the time of writing this column, it's between us, Lakeside and Swindon for the fourth and last play-off place. If we can get some away points and win our last three home matches, starting with tonight's big test against league leaders Poole, we have got a chance of making the play-offs. It's still a reality and I have talked about it with the lads. We know it's a big ask at this stage of the season but it's not impossible and we are up for the challenge." Advising fans and riders alike that the Aces have to "take the matches one step at a time", the minimum requirement is to win meetings at Kirky Lane by seven or more points, "so we can take all three match points". At the same time, results must go in the Aces favour.

Apart from the racing, the highlight of last week's meeting was with the arrival of Peterborough Panthers owner Rick Frost in a helicopter! It certainly saves an early evening journey on the 201 bus from the city centre. On the upper deck, on my way to the stadium, a dishevelled tattooed man lolling across the aisleway with a dangerous dog at his feet had a nice line in coarse language, racial epithets and boasts-cum-chat-up lines: "I bet my giro is bigger than your giro!" Rick's mode of transport certainly stands out from the norm in speedway circles and Luke Jameson's Point of Vue column in the programme admires the skill of his helicopter pilot and his efficient use of the makeshift landing pad a.k.a.

Poster

Pit gate

155

"the motorbike park by the dog kennels". If there's a better-produced programme in British speedway, I have yet to see it on my travels. It would be no surprise if Belle View won the *Speedway Star* Programme of the Year for the second year running. I'll leave others to talk about technical matters but (to the lay user) it feels nice, rests easy on the eye, uses lush photographs plus it's packed with interesting columns and articles. One of the big themes this week is centre greens. Torrential rain in the hours before last week's meeting with the Panthers saw Belle Vue track curator Tony Swales blade-off the top layer of wet shale. With an evocative description that takes some beating, Luke Jameson describes the pile of shale Tony Swales created as "looking like 13 tons of forlorn and abandoned chocolate angel delight." Steve Casey's always-readable Anoraknaphobia column makes some bizarre comments apparently prompted by the World Cup qualifier at the Norfolk Arena. "The racetrack at King's Lynn has been widely regarded as one of the best in the country for a few years now, but didn't the stadium look a bit grim? When the TV cameras focused on the riders on parade I just thought it all looked a bit too 'Industrial'. With no centre green on show I just felt the appearance of the stadium for a 'Showpiece event' looked anything but inviting." Luckily Steve isn't subject to visual disappointments on a regular basis since, on a weekly basis, he enjoys regular sight of the elegantly manicured vista that is the Kirkmanshulme Lane centre green and, of course, the visual splendour of the Aces own stadium infrastructure.

Vue ("the official race day magazine for the Belle Vue Aces") is so compelling that it even includes the "Brolly Blog" written by the "Brolly Girls" a.k.a. the start gate lane identification management team. Like British speedway teams the country over, the line-up has to change from time to time and, as a result, the girls didn't take to the track against the Panthers last week. "Several problems had taken place in the lead up to the meeting which must be kept between the girls, but have unfortunately led to Danielle leaving the line-up and being replaced by a new start girl in the line." Initially, this change has been made for the rest of the season. Karlie Johnstone from Cumbria takes Danni's place with immediate effect. She started watching speedway at Workington and came along to Belle Vue for the first time "several weeks ago as a treat for her birthday with her fiancé Adam". Away from her track duties, we learn brolly girl Karen decorates her house. She also issues an advisory warning for local drivers since she's "starting driving again after a few years off". Frankie "has been working as normal", while Cat's been "working in the Little Premier Inn from Cumbria as well as going on a surprise mystical magical tour with her partner Ewen".

At the pits entrance, the gateman takes a commendably stringent approach to his work and, rightly enough, refuses admission to anyone whose name doesn't appear on his list. Obviously this applies to strangers but it also applies to those who've gone to the great length of wheeling up a speedway bike to his table in order to try to blag free admission to the Kirkmanshulme Lane stadium. With a sparkly clean speedway bike by her side, Jason King's mechanic stops and attempts to sign in. Her presumption gets her nowhere without some additional more meaningful form of identification (in addition to the speedway bike). "I'm Jason King's mechanic!" The gateman's incredulous at the gender incongruity, "Mechanic?!" she retorts, "Yes, his mechanic!" Still unable to quite believe that women are capable of such activities it's only the intervention of Don Walton the Belle Vue track doctor ("she's his mechanic!") that prompts the gateman to reluctantly relent ("Ah, okay then!") and allow entry to the inner sanctum that is the away section of the Belle Vue pits. Shortly afterwards, Gareth [Parry] – listed in the programme as clerk of the course – arrives, clutching a white carrier bag.
[Don] "Have you got your pie?"
[Gareth] "Yes. I won't be doing anything till I've had it."
[Don] "Make sure there's something to do."

[Gareth] "You mean let's hope it's covered in crimson so you've got something to do." [wanders off]

[Don] "Do you know who that is?"

[Jeff] "Is he the Parry who sponsors Wolves and owns all the coaches?"

[Don] "Nah, he runs a travel agency. All the riders use him. They're always ringing up at funny hours saying 'I've lost me passport!'"

Belle Vue's recent away trip to Arlington stadium is precisely the sort of meeting that they needed to gain something from but, sadly, instead they went down 57-35. Apart from the Eagles total dominance, the real talking point of the meeting is Peter Karlsson's 2-point haul from five rides. Usually a difficult-to-pass rider on his visits to East Sussex, PK looked a shadow of his usual self. So much so that I rang Tim Hamblin – the Wolverhampton *Express and Star* speedway reporter – to check if this lacklustre display might mean it's time for the Swede to retire. Tim dismisses my talk as premature (citing a rare off night) while noting that PK remains a highly skilled rider with many more laps left in his tank. Nonetheless, given that no one can recall the last time PK only got 2 points from five rides, it's still a hot topic of conversation. Track doctor Don has his concerns but, as you'd expect from someone well versed in medical emergencies, he prefers a calm analytical approach. "Were you at Eastbourne last week? I asked Chris [Morton] how it was and all he did was grunt and then he said 'we didn't gate'. It doesn't stop people gossiping. Some of the wilder conspiracy rumours – how people can say this with a straight face I don't know – has it that the two and a half grand PK loses getting down to a 6-point average will be sorted when Wolves have him back next year for one final season. That sort of nonsense is beyond belief! However, if I had my way, he wouldn't be riding for us after the last time Poole were here. We'd lost our No. 1 and No. 2 before the meeting had hardly started. PK pulled out after half a lap. If I was the promoter, I'd have told him to get on his bike then! He only came over for the appearance money. I'd have said 'If you'd told us you were injured, we could have got a guest!' Hans [Andersen] only did a quarter of a lap." Patrick Hougaard's arrival interrupts our conversation, "Oh, Patrick, they've ripped up bends two and three so remember that! Bear it in mind! [Hougaard wanders off] I like him he's a thoughtful lad. Ulrich [Østergaard] is a nice guy too, I like him. He's exciting to watch round here but that's probably because he's not in control of his bike!" In answer to my question, "Have you had many crashes or injuries here this season?" Don replys, "Nothing much to speak of. What I want to know is what injury has Jason got? Jason had another operation the other week [after the Speedway World Cup] so I'd like to know what was going on there? Really. I was with him after the crash last season. After the paramedics had seen him and he'd come back, they said he was running round the [medical] room. He was too! When I asked him to raise his arm, he could, so that meant he hadn't broken his collarbone or really damaged his shoulder area. Otherwise it would have been really too painful for him to lift without holding it! When someone has a heart attack, we give them 10 milligrams of morphine for the pain. We just gave Jason a little to take the edge off it and still let him know what he was doing. You could see that the burn was getting worse and worse by the minute! As he climbed into the ambulance to go to Manchester Royal for a thorough check up I said, 'Jason, you must remember for every day you delay before a skin graft adds a week to your recovery. If you want to get treated here [in Manchester], it's potluck – like it can be anywhere – so you might want to go back to your doctor in Northampton but that extra time will delay your recovery'. Many people prefer their own doctor because you don't know what you're going to get when you go somewhere else. There is a rumour – why is it that rumours are only ever wild ones? – that I don't think to be true. But I will ask him about his arm, when he comes here next week – that he had a pin put in? I can't see that he needed that! Never mind, they wouldn't have let him ride in the World Championship, if they'd known!"

If Belle Vue performed poorly at Arlington then Eastbourne did similarly on their last visit to

157

Manchester in mid June. "When Eastbourne were here last time, Žagar tossed the coin for heat 15 and said 'we'll have gates one and three'. Then their manager [Trevor Geer] said 'What are you doing, Matej? You're not in the race!' Phewp! He was packed up and gone just like that!" If seeing Matej Žagar close up is an education, then visits from the Coventry team manager are even more special. "The best one who comes here is Alun Rossiter. He was just a reserve or a poor second string yet now he's an expert on who's a good rider and who's not!" Billed as Eastbourne's No. 1 rider, Matej Žagar's absences from the Eagles line-up has ceased to be a talking point and, often, become a given. The Aces will also be without their No. 1 tonight for their important clash with the Poole Pirates. The reason for Hans Andersen's unavailability is independently verifiable since television viewers saw him injure his hand during a crash with Nicki Pedersen during the Scandinavian Grand Prix held at Malilla. When I ask, "Who is your No. 1 then tonight? Don nods towards the sparklingly pristine speedway bike – parked close to the entrance gate – liveried in the colours of the Peterborough Panthers and emblazoned with the badges of an impressive number of sponsors. "Kenneth Bjerre?"

[Don] "Nah, his average is too high! Rory Schlein."

[Jeff] "Isn't he the one who the Belle Vue fans threw beer over a while back?"

[Don] "It is. He didn't like it very much!"

[Jeff] "I didn't know that you could have No. 1s with too high an average! I thought you could just bring in one No. 1 for another No. 1. Yours has too low an average, obviously."

[Don] "It seems that way."

[Jeff] "Perhaps the ones you wanted are riding elsewhere tonight?"

Away over inside the main grandstand's reception area, adjacent to the shuttered turnstile's entrance, a disorientated lady fan from Somerset asks programme vendor John Thomas, "Are you Chris Morton?"

[John] "Am I Chris Morton?"

[Lady] "Are you Chris Morton?

[John] "Have you ever heard of Chris Morton?"

[Lady] "No!"

[John] "He won the World Pairs Championship."

[Lady] "Oh!" [Looks unimpressed]

[John] "If you go down to the pits – the entrance is down there [points] – you should be able to find him." Barely able to contain his disbelief beyond the second of her departure, John Thomas turns to the security man and asks rhetorically (with his hands held at about chest height), "Am I Chris Morton?" John's so anxious about the future of British speedway that he believes we should immediately adopt a template of a bygone era – so long ago that even Chris Morton wasn't riding – in order to rectify the situation. "We need to do what they did in 1965 and blitz the sport. Split it into two leagues and give everyone the same averages, no plus this or minus that! Having a small [Elite] League is no good for anyone! Riders not riding on Saturdays is what has ruined the sport in this country! How can 16 riders [in the SGP] decide what we all do?"

[Jeff] "What's worse is BSI dictating."

[John] "Well they have – and they do get whatever they want! And also the TV people, who have to see the winners on the telly, which is why we are finishing on September 6th! When did we ever finish on September 6th?"

[Turnstile man] "If we'd done better, we'd be in the play-offs."

[John] "That's just two more meetings and we don't want Mickey Mouse meetings instead. They don't need to bring in a Lord Shawcross, like they did last time, and pay big money. It's commonsense to start again and split it into two leagues! A little [Elite] League is no good to anyone. The clubs can have GP riders, if they want, but – if they're away – they have to run rider replacement! The problem is the BSPA people are just looking after themselves. The team with the biggest snout gets their way. The club with the biggest crowds gets its own way. It's Poole now but they depend on the rest of us to get the big crowds! Belle Vue used to get all the big crowds and, now, it's them. They need us – and clubs like us – so they win and get the big gates."

This season the Belle Vue Aces have a 50-50 raffle that, as the name suggests – after administration costs – gives half the money they raise at any meeting to the riders and the other half to the lucky winner. The 50-50 stall is prominent just after the entrance turnstiles and, prior to the arrival of the public, long-time Belle Vue Aces fan Lou Northey sets up their stall. "God, yeh, I'm a Belle Vue fan since I was that long [gestures like an angler, albeit (unusually) one whose caught a very small fish] and I'm not exaggerating. I first came in August 1988 when I was 6 months old and I've been coming – probably since I was about three – in 1991. Me and me dad have been ever-presents pretty much since then. I was on the first aid team for three years but, then, we had a rejig and I started here. The 50-50 draw is a new thing this season. It's gonna be quiet tonight. With no Hans and we're gonna get battered plus United are at home! I've seen Rory Schlein in the pits and he's in a good mood, if that makes any difference? He's here every week at the moment. He was here for the Peter Craven meeting, rode against us last week and he's here at this! So he should know his way around the track. Shame we couldn't get Chris Harris but he's injured with his knee or something." Talk of rider injures prompts John Thomas to recall past injustices, "I think Nicki Pedersen has a thing against Belle Vue."

[Lou] "He's a tosspot, I don't like him!"

[John] "He badly fenced Kenneth Bjerre in his country and we couldn't get a replacement for him because we let him ride there. We only got a PL rider for the play-offs."

[Lou] "He wasn't the same next year; he's just about over it now!"

Lou's likes what she's seen of Glasgow rider Josh Grajczonek's when he appears in the Elite League for the Aces. "He's lovely Josh – we need to sign him – fancy there being speedway riders younger than me!"

[John] "On July the 28th, we had the Belle Vue Junior Championship here. The people who didn't come to that meeting really missed something! Close racing, lots of passing, better than the Elite League and only a second slower!"

[Lou] "That's cos they're of a similar standard."

[John] "We hardly own any assets – Jason is owned by Poole. I think we only have Andy Smith and Joe Screen. I tell you what, it would be good if there could be a list of the assets of who owns who."

My note-taking catches Lou's attention: "I hope you're not blackening my character."

[Jeff] "No, you're doing it yourself."

[Lou] "Everyone has picked on me since I came here tonight!"

Buxton co-promoter Jayne Moss is a trusted behind-the-scenes staff member at Belle Vue. Quite what her responsibilities are here exactly I don't know but – along with Lynn Wright – she clearly has some regular supervisory responsibility each week for the cash takings generated at the turnstiles. Her Manchester City supporting son Josh no longer comes along to watch the Aces. "Joshua used to come along all the time when James [Wright] and Simon [Stead] rode here but, when they left – I know James is back now – he lost interest. It's Buxton and Man City only for him now!"

[Jeff] "He told me all about his football boots."

[Jayne] "They're so expensive and they don't last at all as their feet grow so quickly. He wanted a £150 pair but there's no way I'm paying that when he wants the Man City kit too!"

Club physio Steve F Williams MCSP arrives laden with boxes. In addition to his medical work,

159

Steve also helps run the Belle Vue trackshop franchise (part of the Nick Barber speedway memorabilia empire). With some stock still yet to be laid out on the tables close by the (downstairs) grandstand bar, he doesn't have time to stop and chat. Neither does tonight's Speedway Control Bureau official, Chris Durno. He wonders what my impressions are of crowd sizes this season as I travel round many outposts of the British speedway scene. Chris furrows his brow, "You'll have been seeing what I've been seeing then? The fall-off in the crowds – particularly in the Premier League – is incredible!"

[Jeff] "I haven't been but they say Dudley has big numbers."

[Chris] "They're the exception – the only exception though!"

Aces fan Peter Fitcroft does stop by my table for a chat. "I bought them [Belle Vue] a tractor last year. They don't need it this year so it's back at home. So I'm in her [wife's] bad books. She's the speedway anorak – she reads the *Speedway Star* from cover to cover each week – and won't believe me that Jeff Scott is actually here! She's got a pile of books by her bed – including the Alan Wilkinson and Ivan Mauger books – so this will keep her happy. I got the tractor at a good price from a certain online site."

Denise Thirsk and Hilary Battersby are the very personable raffle ladies on the 50-50 stall. Some fans stop for a chat as they purchase their tickets, others rush past looking off into the near distance as if they've just seen something vitally important (and must have x-ray eyes since two sets of double doors obscure the near and middle distance). One fan doesn't want any tickets but stops to air his opinion, "Hans Andersen has let us down tonight!" Denise has no problem with his unavailability, "He's broken his bloody finger!" Though the 50-50 draw only started this season, it's already been won three times by the same lucky winner!

[Hilary] "Last week, he won £63."

[Denise] "I think he's called Eric Gordon Weaver."

[Hilary] "Jammy so and so, as I know him."

[Denise] "He gives half the money back to Belle Vue every time!"

[Hilary] "They spend £8 a week so they deserve to win."

Shortly afterwards, the lucky winner or should I say winners, stop to get their weekly fix. "It's Gordon Weaver, I don't use the Eric. We buy them between us [gestures to man at his side]. Can you put Michael Dilworth's name in too?" Gordon and Michael chat affably before they wander off to enjoy the imminent rider parade. Denise and Hilary leave for a birthday party on the back straight. Hilary tells me, "It's the best view – the best place to watch! I've got me Cheddars." Lou Northey takes over their duties on the 50-50 stall until just before the tapes rise for the first race. Lou faffs about for a moment or two putting on her money pouch, "I looked attractive until I put this bum-bag on, even if I say so myself!" An impressive number of people have come through the two open turnstiles tonight already and there remains a substantial queue. I question Lou's earlier prediction, "You said there wouldn't be a crowd!" "Okay so I was wrong!" A fan stops to playfully complain that the tickets Lou identifies as 'lucky', apparently haven't been so, "As I say to everyone – drawn at random! Good luck anyway." Lou's dad Ian is yet to arrive, "His shift is nine till seven but he can lock up at quarter to seven – but he still has to get here from Warrington!" Lou greets her friend Joy, "Happy Birthday!" and then chides the gentleman stood next to Joy, "Fancy forgetting your own daughter's birthday?" During a fractional lull in raffle ticket sales, I quiz Lou about her favourite all-time Belle Vue rider. "If you'd asked me who my favourite rider was when I was five, I would have said Carl Stonehewer but, now, it would be Jason Crump! It was Jason Lyons after Carl left to Workington but, as a personal preference, it's Jason or Carl!"

160

To my mind no trip to Belle Vue speedway is complete without sight of Lynn Wright. I greet her with the words, "James has done well this season!"

[Lynn] "He hasn't! It's his confidence."

[Jeff] "It was a scandal about Charles."

[Lynn] "It was!"

[Jeff] "Were you at Eastbourne last week?"

[Lynn] "Nah, the only place I go now is here. I've changed jobs and I finish at five so I can't!" We both head in the same direction and, as we go through the double doors that lead out onto the home-straight terraces, we're confronted with the sight of the riders making their final preparations up at the tapes prior to the start of heat 1. Lynn tuts, "I called the pits and told them to delay it but they haven't!"

If forced to make a wager on the result of the first heat, most neutral fans would favour the Pirates young Australian partnership of Chris Holder and Darcy Ward to best the Aces Rory Schlein and James Wright combination. Any cursory study of the formbook and current averages would confirm this supposition. Though rarely much longer than 60 seconds, each speedway race is a formal exercise in discipline that requires varying portions of skill, experience, bravery, luck, fault-free equipment and good judgement to perform successfully. Even if you factor in speedway's supposed notorious unpredictability, it's still nonetheless quite a shock to see Chris Holder finish last! This immediately prompts those dark whispers of average manipulation that so unfairly continue to dog the Pirates. Rory Schlein wins and with James Wright third, the Aces take a 2-point lead. Rather distinctively stadium presenter Natalie Quirk stands behind a lectern on the centre green close to the start line. It's the kind you'd expect vicars use to deliver sermons or professors to lecture from. Natalie speaks quickly, clearly and enthusiastically and, in contrast to other parts of the stadium, on the home straight she's also audible! When Ulrich Østergaard wins the reserves race with his race partner Filip Sitera third, the Aces double their lead. Filip recently replaced William Lawson in the Belle Vue line-up. It's not a staff hire met with universal acclaim on the various speedway forums. So much so that veteran sports journalist Richard Frost uses his (Frosty's Vue) column to defend this selection of a "nice young man – he's 22 – who was desperate to succeed. We should be helping him out to do that at the moment and, if it doesn't work out, then it's the end of the season next month anyway." Though in recent seasons Filip's been let go by Coventry and Peterborough, he's enough of a prospect to ride for Mseno in the Czech Republic and Lublin in Poland. Perhaps, giving credence to "critic fans" that rush to criticise him in kneejerk fashion on their laptops, this would be Filip's only point tonight.

Following a close season move from Lakeside, until July, Leigh Lanham's home (and away!) form for the Aces is a revelation. Though still not exactly a powerhouse on the road, Leigh quickly masters the Kirkmanshulme Lane track to handily rack up double figure scores on a regular basis! However, since his end of June paid 13 haul against Wolverhampton that prompts his promotion into the Aces top five, Leigh nowadays fails to scale the heights he's educated the home faithful to expect. Further evidence of his struggle arrives in the form of a last place behind the Pirates promising young Pole Artur Mroczka with Bjarne Pedersen (or "Pederesn" as the programme compilers christen him for this race). Poole's heat advantage reduces the Aces overall lead to a slender 2 points. Contradicting the conspiracy theories of anonymous Internet posters, Peter Karlsson imperiously wins heat 4 ahead of his teammate Ulrich Østergaard (paid 6 from two races). It's another maximum heat advantage that confounds expectations and also features a last place for SGP wannabe Davey Watt. Closeted away from any sight of the racing during each and every Aces home meeting, in the trackshop Matt refuses to get carried away at my incredulous news, "Belle Vue are winning easily!" Studiously downbeat, Matt remains calm, "Well, we'll see when it comes to heat 15!" He enquires about tonight's (nonexistent) book sales. At least I've been sharp

161

eyed enough to keep shrinkage to a minimum, "Someone tried to nick a book while I was stood there next to them! Do you get that much, here?" Again Matt isn't surprised, "Last week [points behind him] someone tried to walk off with a fleece!"

A scorching hot Manchester summer's afternoon gives way to a glorious sunset. Sat between small knots of fans on the crumbling concrete terraces (set back a short distance from the dog track that separates the crowd from the third- and fourth-bend airfence), there's a distinct chill in the air. This slow but noticeable change of the seasons also confirms that yet another speedway summer heads towards a close. Second time out, the Pirates Chris Holder rediscovers his mojo and, indeed, the Pirates were assured of an easy maximum heat advantage up until the moment second-placed Darcy Ward (under no pressure at all) slithers off on the second bend of the second lap. A heat 6 race win for James Wright, while his race partner Rory Schlein sees off the lacklustre Eastbourne 2009 version of Davey Watt, gives the Aces their second 5-1 in three races and extends the score to 23-13. Though those with a more suspicious cast of mind probably pause to question if tactical calculations enter into any Pirates riders' heat performances here tonight, it's nevertheless still a peculiar world where Neil Middleditch resorts to use of the black-and-white helmet colour in an away meeting, let alone as early as heat 7! Artur Mroczka's so keen to impress that referee Chris Durno has no choice but to immediately stop the initial attempt as an unsatisfactory start. After the start marshal reminds the yellow-helmeted Mroczka to keep still at the tapes, viewed from my elevated position behind the riders, the rerun looks more akin to bumper cars or rollerball than it does to speedway. The black-and-white helmet coloured Bjarne (off gate two) barely travels two bike lengths before (off gate one) PK clatters him from the inside. A fraction of a second later, Bjarne's clattered again – albeit from the other side – by Filip Sitera who's off gate three. Though in reality it's just the usual rough and tumble of speedway racing, these jostles in traffic immediately relegate Bjarne to third place until he voluntarily (but temporarily) decides to maroon himself back in fourth! Luckily, Filip Sitera is eminently catchable – and so it proves – even if PK is long gone. Afterwards, reviewing an untroubled meeting from his referee's perspective, Chris Durno comments, "It was an uneventful meeting except when Neil Middleditch rang up about Sitera when Bjarne was on a tac ride. I told him if we stopped every race where there's an elbow we'd never finish any speedway meeting!"

Heat 8 sees Darcy Ward gate brilliantly closely pursued by yet another Australian, teammate Jason Doyle. Even better from a Pirates perspective, Ulrich Østergaard keeps James Wright back in fourth for well over a lap. Over the next three laps Wright gradually makes up ground, close enough to attempt a last-ditch outside dash to the finish line. He still finishes third and, beside me, an Aces fan remarks *sotto voce*, "It's the first time he's been round the outside this season!" Davey Watt continues his disappointing but average-amending night with his best ride of the evening in heat 9 – third place behind Leon Madsen. We're only 54 minutes into the meeting as the riders line up prior to heat 10. Such speed prompts speculation that SCB official Chris Durno wants to see the second half of Manchester United versus Newcastle United on the telly. Though the heat is drawn, results over the 2010 season so far suggest that over the closing heats the Pirates will now kick on for victory or, dependent upon your point of view, the Aces fall away. Such a scenario looks likely after Chris Holder sneaks past PK through a nonexistent back-straight gap with an elegantly executed swerve and weave. With only two laps to go and, apparently, with choice of only one racing line, PK's track craft, guile and local knowledge enables him to regain the lead by the first bend of the third lap. Chris Holder's immediate attempt to go round him takes him over the berm and ends his challenge with the grief of a visit into the bend-two airfence. Commendably, Holder clears the track with alacrity no doubt marginally influenced by Ward's position at the front. The second fall of the night arrives in the next heat: Ulrich Østergaard comes

162

to grief in a race won by Bjarne Pedersen (to narrow the scoreline to 38-36).The racing looks fast to the naked eye but the actual times remain something of a mystery at my end of the track due to the muffled, barely audible loudspeaker system. Nearby householders definitely won't be disturbed by race-night speedway announcements!

With three high-pressure heats to go, off gate three Peter Karlsson intuitively but majestically sweeps wide to the apex of the first bend to block Davey Watt's attempted outside run. This instantly subdues Watt's challenge. Continuing his own poor performance this evening, Chris Holder only manages third place. This Aces 5-1 gives them the psychological comfort of a 6-point lead with two races to go. Leon Madsen wins the penultimate race and with Jason Doyle third, the heat advantage sets up the possibility of a drawn meeting if Poole take a 5-1 from the last heat. However, it's 16th time lucky when PK ends his heat 15 voodoo to finally win a nominated race in an Aces tabard. Speedway fans are rarely brashly exultant but there's definitely a spring in many Belle Vue fans' steps as they leave the stadium building. Peter Fitcroft stops for a few words, "This is my long-suffering wife!"
[Jeff] "The naysayers were proved wrong."
[Sue] "Some people type before they think!"
[Peter] "There was a good bit of dirt on there tonight. It's not normally like that! Tony [Swales] was using the wonder wheel and he doesn't usually like to do that!"
[Sue] "There was some really good racing."

50-50 saleswoman Hilary Battersby is equally ebullient, "We never expected that! My husband said they were looking at their averages!" Lou Northey also passes so I raise with her the remarkable coincidence that last week's and this week's raffle prize are both for exactly £63! Given I understood they sold over 200 tickets tonight, this seems strange. Lou bats away my suspicions, "It's a coincidence it was £63. It was £100 the other week for a big meeting. They take off 10% and then it's half to the riders of whatever we take!" Roving speedway reporter Paul Burbidge is in Manchester, instead of Phil Chard, to file the Pirates match report for the *Bournemouth Echo*. He's in a rush to get back to his room inside the Diamond Lodge Hotel directly outside the Kirkmanshulme Lane stadium perimeter fencing. Paul sees more speedway meetings than most people have hot dinners. He also reports regularly upon Dorset's other speedway club, the Wildcats. "Things appear to be picking up at Weymouth. Phil Bartlett seems a bit more positive about things since he has got rid of some of the people he didn't get on with off the track – like Jem Dicken. But it will be interesting to see whether the club can cope without someone like Jem, who put a huge amount of time and effort into the Wildcats. The racing has been incredible in the meetings I've seen. Lots of last-heat deciders." Paul is also a major contributor to the BSI Speedway Grand Prix website and a regular visitor to the various European locations that make up the backbone of the SGP Series. He's just back from last weekend's Scandinavian Grand Prix in Malilla, "From two miles away it looks just like a field in the middle of nowhere but, when you get there, it's brilliant! It's a great stadium with fantastic racing and a party before hand and afterwards with lots of Swedes!" Aces fan Charles McKay savours tonight's unexpected victory. "I enjoyed that but some of the more cynical crowd members thought they [Poole] might be looking at their averages. Speedway is a good honest sport run by good honest people, so I doubt that!" Some feel that the omens aren't good for those who allegedly pick and choose their wins. "Reading did it a few years ago when they came here cos they didn't want to finish top of the league and then they threw it away in the play-offs!"

It's been a smoothly managed night at the office for SCB official Chris Durno. "They had a temporary clerk of the course here tonight. He's involved at Leicester and he says everything is going to plan and, with seven day a week UK operations, they could be the saviours of British

163

speedway! Something needs to happen! If the promoters keep bringing in any Pole, Dane or Swede, then in three years' time there'll be no Brit capable of riding in the Elite League, let alone a Grand Prix! The fans need local riders to support – claiming they're seeing the best in the world won't make any difference!" Despite regular exposure to speedway, Chris continues to enjoy most meetings, "I was saying before that with a bit of dirt on the track, the riders are often going too fast into the corners. Bend two certainly caused them some problems tonight!"

16th August Belle Vue v. Poole (Elite League B) 48-44

CHAPTER 20

Birmingham

"The future is bright – the future is red and yellow"

The August Bank Holiday sees Birmingham to run on their off night of Sunday for their Premier League clash with the King's Lynn Roger Warnes Transport Stars. The Brummies need the points against a much-changed Stars line-up to cement their place in the play-offs. However, their most important meeting of the season took place on Thursday away from the speedway track in the offices of Birmingham City Council. Since the Brummies reincarnation at this venue, the club have thrown themselves into an energetic campaign with the City Planning authorities to acknowledge, address and mitigate potential noise issues that could result (or be seen to result) from staging speedway at Perry Barr Stadium. Birmingham talk the talk but also walk the walk to behave as responsible members of their local community. Given the complexity of the regulations, their vested interests and, of course, the ongoing possibility of capricious decision making, the senior management of the club waged their campaign with great diplomacy ably supported by their own passionate supporters as well as speedway fans from around the country. Inside the Birmingham Brummies Speedway Office on the far side of the stadium adjacent to the pits area behind the back straight, I congratulate club co-promoter Graham Drury on the successful outcome of the campaign. "I'm very pleased but I'm even more pleased for Tony Mole because he's put a hell of a lot of work into it! He's invested a lot of his money into Birmingham Speedway. He could have had an asset he could invest in further or he could sell on or he could have had nothing! So a lot rode on the decision with the Council."

[Jeff] "You must have the gift of the gab."

[Graham] "I left all that dealing with the Council to Tony as he loves that sort of thing! His business is aggregates so he knows all about planning. Paragraph 34(b) section C Part 4 or regulation P33 and that – I don't know! Tony does. He speaks the same language as they do and really goes into it. He could talk all night with them."

Early arrival

Bright sunshine

165

It's my first ever visit inside the Speedway Office at Perry Barr. The trackshop franchisee Nick Barber doesn't come over much either. "Looks nice inside here!"

[Denise] "Haven't you been here before?"

[Nick] "I rarely come over."

[Denise] "Well, I've rearranged it because he wanted his desk behind mine so that, when people come through the door, he's a little bit away from them initially." Unlike portacabins everywhere, Denise ensures the Brummies office mixes functionality with home comforts. In addition to their desks, there's a refreshment table with kettle, tea and coffee, paper cups and a water filter. I'm at the stadium tonight with Graham's kind permission. "I've put your advert under 'Patch's Piece' – it's one of the better read columns in the programme." There's serious men's work to be done if judged by the way Graham ostentatiously thumps a heavy boxed lever-arch file of paperwork onto his table. He expertly thumbs through it before his discussion with Nick Barber starts.

The Brummies programme is a full-colour affair. They must have a very capable commercial manager given the substantial number of (mostly local) advertisements inside. These adverts take up 16 of its 32 pages. Apart from columns by Graham Drury, Gary Patchett, club captain Jason Lyons and Brummies historian Brian Buck, regular readers are treated to the joy that is Mick Bratley's often thoughtful and sometimes witty 'Bratley's Bulletin'. No longer part of the Peterborough Panthers management set-up, Mick Bratley brings his insider's view of the Elite League to bear in a discussion of the many possible future options for the top tier of the sport in Britain, should it be restructured. Though it's a well-worn theme, Bratley cuts to the chase and slaughters some sacred cows. In speedway, as in life, context is all, "You could argue that things have gone from bad to worse and problems have been exacerbated. ...it's going to be a brave man who moves to champion the changes that the Elite League is screaming out for. And surely changes do have to be made, for the current EL, business model simply does not work and its actual continuance in its present format could have much wider implications throughout the sport as a whole in this country and obviously there could be a knock-on detrimental effect to the Premier and National Leagues." Fans, media and pundits alike coalesce around four possible future scenarios. Mick carefully discusses each one of these in turn. [1]

[1] "1. *The Elite League and Premier League should merge into one big league.* It was tried before with disastrous consequences. It very nearly killed the sport as many clubs were on the verge of financial collapse. There would be far too many fixtures to encourage enough top riders back to the UK and I suspect even if they could be tempted back, few clubs would be able to afford to pay them. For the majority of the clubs the season would be over by May as the cream would rise (and stay) at the top. Rather like the Elite League this season.

2. *The Elite League and Premier League should merge into two separate leagues, north and south, with play-offs between the top two clubs from each league.* Although this would be slightly better and would encourage more local(ish) clashes, thereby generating clubs more income, my comments in 1 above would still apply. And besides, why would the Premier League want to even chance their arm with this? The Premier League works, the Elite League doesn't, I am afraid.

3. *The Elite League should race on one fixed night a week with a reduction of fixtures in that only the 'A' fixture should be contested, plus play-offs.* For me this is the only near sensible solution and one I have suggested many times previously, but there are a lot of hurdles to overcome. For a start, many tracks are committed to race a certain number of times a season in accordance with their tenancy agreements and can only race on certain nights due to other regular events at their stadiums. I know of two clubs in the EL who have to race at least 25 times a season and, if they don't, I believe they still have to pay the rent and a penalty to boot. However, it could be argued that for some clubs it would be cheaper to pay rent and not stage a meeting and actually save some money! I am pretty certain this option would entice all the GP stars to ride in the British league, the maximum meetings would be 20 (10 home, 10 away) for the winners/runners up. But what of the teams that don't contest the play-offs? 16 meetings (8 home, 8 away) would be it. Whilst good for the top line riders in the world, what about middle order riders who don't regularly get a ride in Poland or Sweden and rely on the UK for their main income? How will they make up that financial deficit?

4. *A league should be created that is of Premier Plus standard to include the current EL and any current Premier clubs who would like to join.* It's being floated that this could be combined with 3, but I can't see the fans supporting this. Steak and Chips one week fish and chips the next, the fans will not go for it and it could be a financial disaster for those clubs. The option on its own, though, could work. A Premier Plus League and a Premier League, but would the Elite clubs be willing to not employ the better riders and keep wages low and would any Premier League want to increase their wages to join them? My answers in 1, 2 and 3, will all apply.

Birmingham: *"The future is bright – the future is red and yellow"*

Slightly disappointingly, Mick concludes by sitting on the fence, "Well as I wrote elsewhere at exactly the same time last year, I don't know. One year on, Elite clubs are mostly all still losing lots of money, crowds are not getting any bigger and sponsors are not exactly beating down the doors wanting an association with them. Alarmingly, the Elite product is now being based increasingly on fragmented fixture lists, where British clubs have to give way to Poland's Extraliga and an increasing number of (ridiculous in my opinion) FIM fixtures and not only that, the racing appears to be suffering as well." The fare served up on a regular basis by Sky Sports on a Monday night is of such poor quality that *EastEnders* and *Corrie* both take priority in the Bratley household. The oft-muted independent enquiry ("think tank") will actually have to convene and, when they issue proposals, these will actually have to be implemented! "Huge concessions will need to be made and if that means certain clubs have to leave the top league sphere then they will have to accept that for the future success of the sport." [2]

Arguably the Premier League is the only robustly performing tier of British speedway. According to Nick Barber, off the track it's also been a struggle. "It's been awful this year and awful this week. We should have had seven meetings this week but this is the first we've had on, so far. Five got called off. I don't like being negative about speedway, as I said to Bev on the way up, but I can't wait for this season to be over. Over the winter, when I chat to the promoters, I'm gonna have to tell them that I can't pay what I did this year. They'll be amazed but the promoters always don't really mind anything until it affects them – then they complain! I wish I could have a decade off not just the winter!" Birmingham is one of the very few clubs not to welcome Ivan Mauger during his recent extensive promotional book tour. Ivan's no longer in the country. Apparently, he's returned to New Zealand without he or his representatives settling the table charge levied on all exhibitors at the annual Speedway Fayre (staged prior to the Cardiff Grand Prix). Nick remains phlegmatic about the lack payment. "Did he heck! It's great that he's left the country. I haven't been sold any stock – not that I'd sell them anyway!" Over the past few seasons at Birmingham, Nick operated two separate trackshop stalls in the downstairs bar and refreshment area of the modern sleek Perry Bar Stadium home-straight grandstand. However, this season all speedway merchandise is now consolidated into the one location. The other area where Nick used to display his merchandise looks forlorn apart from a solitary gaming machine that we used to call one-armed bandits until technological advances made them push-button affairs. "It's supposed to be a gaming area but they've taken all the slot machines away, except one. [wistfully] It would make a lovely area for the shop!" The configuration and location of the trackshop isn't the only noticeable change. The majority of fans now enter the premises through a fully secured proper turnstile area so nowadays no longer arrive through the double doors previously used to access the downstairs area of the grandstand. Nick explains, "They don't use those doors so much since they had the robbery because they no longer come into that entrance. Well, the disabled do but everyone else comes through a proper enclosed turnstile area nowadays. It's more secure. Earlier in the season just before tapes, a gang came in just took all the money!"
[Jeff] "I didn't know about that, was it in the *Star*?"
[Nick] "It was only a small piece, if it was!"

Though it's the way of the modern world such events make everyone question their current safety and security arrangements. Nick certainly adopts the precautionary principle, "I'll show you where you can park your car so it's nice and safe. I've never had any trouble when I've parked outside

[2] Mick's column also includes a welcome to the visitors, praise for the supporters and statements of great respect for the Brummies "wonderful sponsors". One of these highly respected supporters of the club are GH Moore & Son who hail from the heart of the city ("part of Birmingham's world famous jewellery quarter"). They're based at Vyse Street in Hockley. Given Mick Bratley sports no visible face furniture of any description, his enthusiasm for the product range at GH Moore & Son ("they cater for all jewellery requirements, male and female, and in every material imaginable") boggles the mind about the real basis of Mick's personal requirements."

Birmingham: *"The future is bright – the future is red and yellow"* but it's best to be safe!" Nick does have a question for me, "Do you know who won the GP?"

[Jeff] "Is there a GP on then?"

[Nick] "You're as interested in it as I am then!"

[Jeff] "Is there?"

[Nick] "Yeh – at Gorican – it got rained off yesterday."

[Fan] "Pavlic's dad said if they guarantee him x number of GPs, he'll put a roof on! He's one of the richest men in Croatia too!"

[Nick] "I wonder if Travel Plus Tours will stay to see the GP? Did you hear what happened at the World Cup Final? They left on the Saturday night and missed the final that had been rearranged to the Sunday!"

Bev Barber proudly points out the new car sticker they have at the trackshop to commemorate the planning permission approval. They're in pride of place at the centre of the merchandise display. "Me dad did a sticker for me on Thursday when I was over there helping him with his stamps!" The sticker features an unnamed rider in Birmingham Brummies colours along with the slogan "The future is bright – the future is red and yellow". Nick's earlier visit to the Speedway Office was by request. "Graham sent Nick a message saying 'Could you come to the office'. I said, 'Have you been a naughty boy then?' [mimes slap on wrist] and he said, 'Naw, he just wants me to value a collection!'"

When the turnstiles open, the ReRun Productions stall is abandoned as if it were a speedway version of the *Marie Céleste*. It's unfortunate since there's a deluge of fans keen to buy DVDs of the recent Brummies Fours victory at the East of England Showground. All the action from the most recent Premier League meeting against Rye House is also in high demand. In a matter of moments I've taken £82, something I've yet to experience this season with my own books! Shortly after the initial rush subsides and the Rye House DVD sells out, stallholder Tony returns, "Apart from the filming I don't have anything to do with the production."

[Jeff] "Everyone went mad for them when the turnstiles opened!"

[Tony] "It's the Fours, usually there isn't a queue!"

[Jeff] "The Rye House meeting has the wrong date on it."

[Nick] "That it has. Last week someone stopped me on the stairs and said 'What day was the Sheffield meeting?' And I said, 'I don't know?' He took great pleasure in telling me it was wrong, probably the same one who spoke to you. You just happen to be here on the one week when my salesman, interviewer and commentator are all away!" Brummies fresh-faced announcer and programme editor David Rowe arrives. His ease with a microphone means that he's much in demand. Yesterday his football duties took him to Blackburn, while his speedway responsibilities bring him to Birmingham this evening and take him to Coventry tomorrow. David is in a hurry to get to the pits but is also reluctant to talk. "I'm going to be careful what I say to you. These really used to be fire and brimstone meetings but won't be today."

Keen Brummies fan Mike shares his impressions from the various recent Birmingham Northern tours. "The Glasgow fans were so lovely! Really, really nice. I think we were robbed though. The Glasgow fans said so too! Afterwards, I asked Travis [McGowan] about the incident but he was noncommittal. When I said, 'If that had happened to you would you be happy?' He was about to answer when Jason Lyons said, 'He's not going to say, is he!' I thought Berwick was nice too and Dick Barrie is very good. The Newcastle fans weren't that friendly to say the least. Their fans banged on the referee's window. My wife couldn't believe their attitude. Even at the Fours one of them said to me (beforehand) when I asked who he supported, 'We're the team that stuffed you in the Cup!' You expect that at football but not at speedway! Not that it matters but I said, 'Have you forgotten we scored 60 against you at ours at the start of the season?' I didn't see him after we'd won the Fours! The Edinburgh fans weren't that friendly either and I thought their [relief] announcer just wanted to wind us up – or try to – rather than inform everyone. He could definitely learn a thing or two from Dick Barrie."

The lure of a sun-dappled Sunday evening meeting brings a good crowd to the stadium including a recent returnee fan. "I used to go in the '70s so I don't know many tracks now."
[Jeff] "Some of them haven't changed much."
[Fan] "King's Lynn has from what it used to be. Stoke looks terrible! We live in Skegness so we go to King's Lynn and Scunthorpe. We're going there tomorrow."
[Jeff] "Is Craig Cook riding?"
[Fan] "No, Simon Lambert."
[Jeff] "He's gone off the boil a bit this year."
[Fan] "Yeh, he's got a really funny riding style. He should get a few points tomorrow though!"

Riders from both teams circuit the Perry Barr track side by side in pairs – in true Noah's Ark fashion – as they're introduced over the loudspeaker system to the crowd. Nowadays it's custom and practice for many speedway teams to make almost monthly changes to their line-ups based on the latest set of BSPA averages. However, even in a sport well used to such tinkering, the promotional team at King's Lynn shock many when they made wholesale changes to their line-up on the 9th August. Five riders left! Some changes were due to injury (Kevin Doolan) and also the "current illness of Darren Mallett". Nonetheless, this Norfolk night of the long knives – ostensibly to refresh things and, the club claim, build for the future – is characterised by the club in positive terms as "an almost completely new line-up after taking the decision to rebuild their team in mid-season". Stars promoter Keith Chapman observes, "I feel we have been so successful for such a long period that we all started to take winning for granted." After some mixed results – a poor season by their own high standards – rather than make minor adjustments, the promotional team opt for root-and-branch surgery, "We felt it was beyond a quick fix so we decided to replace a total of five of the seven riders". Tomáš Topinka and Kozza Smith keep their places but the Stars decide to release Chris Mills, Kasper Wörtmann, Joe Haines, Kevin Doolan and Darren Mallett with immediate effect.

At the start of a season, it usually takes time for any team to hit their stride. Understandably, many observers don't expect the new-look Roger Warnes Transport Stars to run the BRC Roofing Brummies that close. Irrespective of the opposition on display, the talk that animates the terraces is the favourable Council decision that guarantees the immediate future of the Brummies. With his wife and daughter also in the crowd, Tony Mole takes to the microphone to delight at this positive outcome. Tony's at pains to stress that the Council was influenced by what Birmingham speedway "had done for the image of the City of Birmingham". After he carefully thanks all parties involved, Tony notes his "agreement with the GRA to be here for a number of years to come!" Tony also offers thanks to the boisterous Brummie faithful, "You've been solid as a rock as ever – we look forward to your continued support at Perry Barr – hopefully increasing – and at away meetings!" Perhaps giving away more than officially confirmed, Brummies presenter Chris Simpson greets the riders onto the track for the first race of the evening in ebullient fashion, "Great news about Birmingham being a permanent fixture in British speedway! Be it Elite League or Premier League!"

Arguably the most exciting aspect of the Stars recent transformation of their team is the arrival at No. 2 (on an assessed 7-point average) of 16-year old Lasse Bjerre. He's younger brother of the eponymous Grand Prix star rider Kenneth. Lasse is so keen to do well on his first visit to Perry Barr that he moves at the start of heat 1. Definitely hard to miss in his brother's superseded but still incredibly bright fluorescent kevlars. If you dressed like this as a breakdown repairman, you'd minimise any chance that you'd accidently get run over on the hard shoulder of any UK motorway, day or night! Trackshop man Nick Barber looks on with expert eyes as Lasse struggles at the rear of the field. After he again rears unexpectedly on the back straight, Nick muses, "He rides like his brother." Birmingham's Jason Lyons and Justin Sedgmen deliver an untroubled 5-1 that doesn't bode well for a close contest but, nonetheless, still sends the Brummies faithful into paroxysms of joy when their riders cross the finish line. If it's going to be thin pickings on the track (for King's Lynn), then similar applies off it too. "ReRun have been taking all the money tonight. That's why we've done so badly. That's how brittle it is! Before we'd do well and they'd do well – nowadays, it's not like that!" The hardworking Brummies commercial team have heat 2 sponsorship from the exotically named "Mercia Detective Agency – International Private Investigators". This all sounds very Austin Powers and their name immediately conjures up in my mind a heady brew of exoticism, surveillance and mystery. Sadly, there's absolutely no mystery about the likely result of this meeting, after the crowd witness another Men versus Boys style race in heat 2. Second-placed Kyle Newman is so far ahead that he can briefly but safely falter, content in the knowledge that Cal McDade won't make up enough ground to overtake. The third 5-1 of the night arrives quickly in a processional third race won comfortably by Aaron Summers. After only a lap and a quarter, there's already a huge gap between the Brummies partnership and their King's Lynn rivals. Co-promoter Mick Bratley is on hand for me to complain too directly, "This is pitiful!"

[Mick] "Yes, it is, but brilliant to see!"

[Jeff] "Not as a neutral."

[Mick] "King's Lynn have done this to so many teams over the years – it's brilliant!"

[Jeff] "Their line-up looks like cost-cutting rather than building for the future at the moment!"

[Mick] "I'm enjoying it whatever it is!"

With the score already 15-3, prior to heat 4 a Brummies fan wonders aloud, "I'm amazed they haven't brought Topinka out in black and white!" By the standards of the first three races, Tomáš Topinka's second place is a minor triumph since it limits the Brummies to a mere 4-2 heat advantage. Said quizzical Brummies fan takes a philosophical view of the situation, "I think we've won only once here against King's Lynn since we started – so this is most unusual!" Over the speak system, David Rowe highlights exciting aspects of tonight's programme in a vain attempt to distract the Brummies faithful from the one-sided nature of the encounter. "Just to draw your attention to Mick Bratley's column – as I usually do – it's a great read!" Earlier in the Speedway Office, Graham Drury courteously told me, "We're really going to plug your book tonight!" News of this plan doesn't reach David Rowe or, else, he decides my books don't have the verve of Mick Bratley's column.

Adopting his usual positive outlook on life, Nick Barber shrugs in the face of the Stars poor performance. "Hopefully they'll sharpen up a bit now they've had a ride on the track." There's definitely an element of increased sharpness in heat 5 signalled by the way Olly Allen and Lasse Bjerre pass either side of Aaron Summers at the end of the first lap. Their reward is a drawn heat. Sadly this nascent fight-back is a false dawn since it's followed by a ridiculously easy but processional Brummies 5-1. Things look slightly better for the visitors in heat 7 when Kozza Smith finds himself placed second as the riders exit bend two. Unfortunately, Kozza immediately appears to then simultaneously struggle with both his bike and the track. Drawn ineluctably towards the safety fence in a manner that suggests he's magnetised, Kozza's challenge fades though, fortunately for King's Lynn, Adam Roynon shows some sparkle to finish ahead of Kyle Newman. There's then a brief interruption to proceedings. David Rowe explains with a hint of amazement in his voice, "Just to let you know – very unusually – we're taking a ten minute interval now because of the sun – the setting sun!" Enforced sunset glare break over, the racing resumes with Lasse Bjerre out in the black-and-white helmet colour. It's a helmet colour that serves to further emphasise the industrial strength brightness of his elder brother's discarded kevlars. Fortune favours the fluorescent if judged by referee Jim McGregor's decision to call all four back after Bjerre suddenly parts company from his bike on the first bend. After years of practice, the pronunciation of the Bjerre surname is meat and drink to most speedway announcers and presenters. However, his given name is going to be much more of a linguistic and pronunciational test. In this particular part of the Midlands, the presentational team decide to settle upon the "LASS-SAY" version. In the rerun, it looks like Lasse misunderstands the function of the black-and-white helmet colour, apparently under the impression it's an invitation to a bike-throwing competition. Lasse rears impressively at the start line and flings, with some aplomb, his bike away so it can go somersaulting down the track. Other riders are genuinely fortunate to escape being clattered by his riderless machine. Channelling his inner AA patrolman, Bjerre sportingly rushes over to clear his bike from the track to try to ensure the race doesn't stop again. The Birmingham crowd appreciate his gesture and, though they don't really need his help, you'd expect the reaction of their team management to be similar as the Brummies race to their fifth maximum heat advantage of the night.

Continuing his one-man campaign to massage the scoreline (and despite being the first to arrive in the pits this afternoon), Aaron Summers suffers an engine failure at the start line. Sight of this mechanical mishap prompts Bev Barber to sigh deeply, "Poor old Aaron!" Until the end of the second lap, Tomáš Topinka appears likely to become the first King's Lynn race winner of the evening until Johno rushes past with some ease. While we wait for the tenth race to get underway, speedway fan Paul alerts me to the popularity of Dudley in the National League. "The crowds at Dudley have been brilliant this season. I hope they make the top two – I think that they could win it! The problem here is the view isn't so great at the start line and [points at the grandstand windows] up there it's brilliant but you can't hear anything! That's what all the people behind the trees over there [points in the direction of bend one] would like but, when you think you can hear the M6 motorway three miles away and the A34 is nearby as well, it makes you wonder what they were complaining about!" Out on the track, Adam Roynon gets a flier from the gate only for Justin Sedgmen to power past him on the back straight. Reluctant to relinquish the lead, Roynon regains supremacy on the fourth bend only to lose balance in the next corner and crash out of the race. Adam is the second King's Lynn rider to sportingly clear his bike with haste.

As the riders line up at the tapes for heat 11, possibly randomly, the *Red Dwarf* theme tune blares over the speakers in the grandstand bar. Possibly operating under the auspices of a little-known Space Corps directive, black-and-white helmeted Olly Allen rides Kyle Newman really hard (but fair) on bends three and four of the first lap to gain a lead he looks unlikely to relinquish. Well, until a last-gasp effort from Richard Sweetman on the run-in to the finish line. Now the dam's broken, there's suddenly a positive avalanche of Stars race winners. A superfast-looking Adam Roynon wins heat 12 (after comfortably seeing off first-lap pressure from Aaron Summers) while heat 13 sees the Stars threaten their first proper – rather than tactically induced – heat advantage through Olly Allen and Tomáš Topinka. However, they reckon without a brilliant ride from Jason Lyons who executes a hard but fair overtake past Allen for the lead. The penultimate race of the night is arguably the most entertaining from a pure speedway point of view since Kozza and Kyle regularly swap position throughout all four laps. Birmingham's seventh 5-1 of the night wraps up the evening and Brummies faithful leave with the council induced smiles they arrived with.

Brummies fan Paul expresses disappointment with the gumption levels of the King's Lynn riders as well as the fecklessness of their fans. "They've got a poor team who are going on a bad run but, I tell you, it's disappointing to see how few fans they brought with them! Particularly as it's a Bank Holiday. Usually it's packed with them but, clearly, they only come out when they're winning!"

The result (along with the whole Birmingham experience) excites and rejuvenates Mick Bratley. "Coming here was the best thing I ever did. It's rekindled my love of speedway and reinvigorated me! I wish I'd done it years ago! It helps racing every week rather than every five. The people are lovely but you can't pull the wool over their eyes because they're very knowledgeable – no sly stuff because they'll know!" Tony from ReRun is keen to share news of their success tonight with Mick Bratley, "We've sold as much as we've sold all season in one night!" Mick's politely curious, "Really?" so learns, "It's the Fours." Mick Bratley cuts short his conversation to say "Alright" to a young Australian in a peaked cap. After he's out of earshot, Mick tells us in a pantomime stage whisper, "He's going to be a star – Micky Dyer rides for Dudley."

Over by the parking area for the riders' vans, Shelly-Ann Willetts lingers for her man with her arm in a sling. Though the extent of his efforts aren't reflected in his 5 points, Adam Roynon battled throughout rather than cede position easily. "He rode really well tonight – he was flying!"
[Shelly-Ann] "Yeh, his confidence is really coming back!"
[Jeff] "Did you know that people search on Google for your name and, sometimes, end up coming to my website?"
[Shelly-Ann] "Sorry."
[Jeff] "I'm sure they're disappointed when they see my stuff instead. Though there is a photo of you."

Adjacent to the half-packed trackshop stall, physiotherapist Steve Williams congratulates Adam on his performance and advises that physiotherapy might be the way to ameliorate some of his injuries. As I head off into the night I hear Adam say, "I so wanted to beat Sedgmen cos he's such a cock but I knocked off the power..." Over at the staff car park, Steve 'Johno' Johnston stands by the open door of his transit van at the end of another relatively successful day at the office (paid 11 from five rides). Holding the canister up inside his T-shirt, Johno applies industrial quantities of fancy-smelling spray deodorant to the required areas. My "That's it!" elicits a trademark cheery riposte, "Yeh, that's it!"

29th August Birmingham v. King's Lynn (Premier League) 61-32

CHAPTER 21

Scunthorpe

"Everyone remembers the Moran brothers – Kelly and Shawn – but all of these lads are going faster than they did then because the bikes have moved on!"

30th August

Lunchtime at the Eddie Wright Raceway in Scunthorpe on a Bank Holiday Monday finds club founder, owner and promoter Rob Godfrey on a brief but well-earned break from his preparations for the double-header meeting versus Sheffield and, then, Buxton. In the Premier League the Scunthorpe Scorpions have, like many other clubs, endured a stop/start fixture list. Between June 4th and the end of August, the Scorpions only race six home fixtures. Their dominance round the Eddie Wright Raceway hasn't quite been what it was. Though there's no disgrace losing to Edinburgh, going down to the Newport Wasps here is altogether a different matter. Ignoring results on the track, Rob Godfrey has the slightly careworn preoccupied look of a man keen to refresh his own business model and that of speedway generally. "It's been a poor year everywhere! Last August [2009], my crowds fell off a cliff and I thought they'd be back but they're not! We're lucky that the stockcars have been so brilliant. We get 3,000 and they drink the bar dry and eat all the food! It's £10 to get in and I've lost count of the number of people who've come up to me to say 'That's the best £10 I've ever spent'. I'm independent and the nearest rival tracks are Skegness – they run on tarmac – and King's Lynn. There's a bloke in Rotherham who I've put out of business who's not too happy. I have them lining up here to take part. They make a mess but people love it! We were doing Formula 1 but I'm stopping that after the next meeting because I have to pay them too much. I'm saying it's the last meeting and that should get a big crowd – 4,000 or so. Have you seen *Tears and Gears* on a Monday night [on BBC1]? The first two were a bit slow but it's brilliant. It's about two drivers and their families going all out for glory. The drama is brilliant! They showed the World Final at King's Lynn and they had

Rider walk

Start line shadows

10,000 there. It was fantastic to see it full with 10,000 people. In future we're not gonna do Formula 1 but we're just going to do stocks and that. It's got me going so much I've got my own car and I'm gonna drive in the next meeting! What I want to know is how come that the stock-cars can have smash ups where the cars go in the air and the bloke is badly injured – and when you go to see him to ask how he is he says, 'I'm okay!' and puts his thumbs up – and, at speedway, we can't do anything like that? We've got lots of silly, silly rules that stop us having what people really want to see – crashes and clashes! The stocks and Formula 1 people love the track because they can ride it flat out, like they can at speedway. I'm biased but we have the best speedway in the country here but we still can't get the crowds to come! If it was only speedway, I'd have closed by now, we just couldn't survive! I've been to many other tracks and some of their crowds aren't there. I just don't know how they can survive."

"I've been worried here but the one thing I'm not going to say is we're going to close down because what can you say after that? Next year, some people - business people, who are gonna be prepared to put their own money into it too – are going to help me with the promotion. I've not done all I'd like before because I've been trying to do too many other things and, maybe, I've been too proud to ask for help. We've got a lot of good ideas I can't really tell you about. One of them is to develop our appeal in Hull. We're going to do a promotion there. We pay their bridge toll – which is £6 – provided they bring a full car, which is four extra people we wouldn't otherwise have. A few years ago we did a free meeting here and got 1,500 yet, when we did it last year, we got 800 – so we can't even give it away! Another problem is that many promoters are in denial. I've tried to inject some needle and controversy into the [Sheffield] meeting by saying stuff about them. We could say 'Neil Machin is gay' but it doesn't work! All the things that would get people talking and writing excitedly on the Internet costs £300! Look at Scott Nicholls last year [at Cardiff SGP], they probably got more interest and coverage from that than anything – yet we're not allowed to in the modern version of the sport! The old days, when you could, have gone. There's rules, rules, rules! We need drama and crashes to get people talking! Speedway has been very poor this year. We haven't had enough fixtures – no, it's they haven't been every week. I was in favour of bigger breaks [between meetings] this year but, now I've got it, I don't like it! We can't go on without a regular fixture list. I'm lucky because I've been able to put on extra stock car meetings but if I didn't have that I'd have to seriously think about what I'm doing." [1]

Before internet rumour-mongers turn nuances into news of club closure, Rob Godfrey discusses future fundraising for stadium safety furniture for the Eddie Wright Raceway. Nowadays, the club have an Armco wall on site. "We're having a meeting here, before the end of the season, to raise funds to buy the other half of the airfence. I'm hoping Leigh Adams – he doesn't have to ride flat out, just turn up – will come. It's the day before the ELRC and Leigh has his finale meeting at Swindon around then so he should want to come along." I suggest, "You could sell his book." Rob's surprised "Has he got a book then?" Someone else with a book to sell who didn't come to Scunthorpe on his recent UK tour is six-times World Champion speedway rider Ivan Mauger. "Ivan Mauger's been here to run a training school a while back and he hasn't been here since! I

[1] Interviewed by Andrew Skeels in the *Speedway Star*, Rob Godfrey later echoes these comments. "Speedway crowds have been very poor this year but it isn't just us, that's everyone across the board. I need all the money going into the pot I can get to keep the whole Raceway thing going and the crowds for the stock-cars have been really good…the only problem with the stock-cars now that I'm running it myself is that it's so time consuming. Against that, though, the financial rewards are way up there, there's no comparison between speedway and stocks, so it does go through my mind to pack the speedway in and just run stock-cars every fortnight. We're not closing yet, we're alright, I'm a speedway man, I don't mind the stock-cars but I love speedway. But when it becomes an obsession and you end up bankrupt running speedway just for other people to come and watch it, then you wonder what you're doing … hopefully the recession is coming to an end and I don't think Scunthorpe as a town has fared too badly so far. The steel works seem to be taking people on again, they're at full production and they've just got some new contracts, it's pretty much the major employer and it's a major factor in the town because everything feeds off it, the speedway included."

Scunthorpe: *"Everyone remembers the Moran brothers – Kelly and Shawn – but all of these lads are going faster than they did then because the bikes have moved on!"*

have his photo in the bar!"

People closely tied or linked to Scunthorpe speedway aren't always blessed with the best health news in recent years. Their affable and curious car park supervisor Richard Heasman takes an optimistic and philosophical view of his own unwelcome news. "I've got the old prostate cancer and, what with the limp, I'm walking round like an old man. When the doctor told me, I had no reaction because I've had 62 wonderful years. I've been very lucky so why complain or look gloomy? I have to take the tablets to control my hormones – testosterone – so you know what that means. I've got a friend who has it too and we compare notes – but everyone's treatment is different – we have a real laugh! If anyone looked at us, they'd never guess what we were falling about laughing about. When he asked his doctor how long he'd got, his doctor said 'My ambition is to keep you alive long enough to die of something else!' When he pushed him about when he was going to die the doctor said, 'I promise that you'll be the first to know!' I've been so privileged to come and work here since the first meeting as Rob's built it up – he's done a brilliant job!"

GRT Media supremo Bob Tasker parks up his car adjacent to the compact covered home-straight grandstand. "If you get the chance to see Berwick away – go and see them! It's like at Newcastle last year when they brought in René and Lemo – they had a poor team then and that transformed them! They've done so well because they kept them together this year. Well Complin – if you count him as a new rider because he crashed in his second race at the first meeting, he is really – plus Rempala are the two riders who transformed Berwick. You saw Rempala at his first meeting [versus Edinburgh] but he gets better and better every week. He's something else to watch! There should be a big crowd today but it's fallen off from what it was. There's only been four Scorpions meeting here in June, July and August and – once people get out of the habit or come along and find it's a National League meeting on a Friday – they don't come back so often. Plus, they tried to run one in the rain when it was forecast to rain and abandoned it after six heats." Fresh-faced SCB official Craig Ackroyd arrives from a surprisingly sunny Preston. Craig and Bob soon fall into the kind of staccato shorthand conversation often employed by the speedway cognoscenti to discuss goings on within the inner circle of the British shale community. This afternoon's topic of conversation are the problems that unsuspecting visiting riders can find if they're not familiar with the third bend at Newcastle speedway. Craig explains, "It's tight going into that corner and, if someone comes inside you, you add a little bit on not knowing you're now on the outside and then come off!" Bob Tasker's seen enough incidents on that particular bend to investigate their cause. "Someone explained to me that many riders don't realise that when someone comes up the inside, they've been moved to the outside not mid-track. So, as it funnels into there, they get in the loose stuff and fall off, when usually they wouldn't! Jason [Lyons] fell there when you were there and Ricky did last week. Actually I saw a first then because René bumped Ricky before the corner and it moved him to the outside and it caused him to come off when he didn't, if you see what I mean! Ricky went back to the photographer Dave Lowes and was holding his camera up to referee Barbara Horley showing her he was bumped! It's the first time I've ever seen a rider try to use photographic evidence to appeal against his exclusion." Highly fancied, Newcastle's recent substantial defeat at Berwick prompts much Internet speculation. "On the forums everyone says how poor Newcastle were but no one says how good Berwick were! They're in form and I wouldn't be surprised if they win the Young Shield. Dalbers [Andrew Dalby] said Berwick would get 55 against Newcastle but they got 61 because Newcastle was so poor."

Each speedway club Bob visits every week (to film action DVDs) enjoy their own particular excitements and special appeal. Not only is Sheffield the country's fastest track but also fans get the regular treat of the come-from-behind daredevil manoeuvres from both Josh Auty and Richard Hall. Recent seasons have seen Newcastle perform to a very high standard and also track

Scunthorpe: *"Everyone remembers the Moran brothers – Kelly and Shawn – but all of these lads are going faster than they did then because the bikes have moved on!"*

star of the future, René Bach. Speedway at Berwick has shaken off an element of torpor since the arrival of Marcin Rempala while, by common consent, Scunthorpe usually serve up exciting speedway on a weekly basis, irrespective of the team riding. When you get to see top quality on a regular basis it's only human nature to become inured to the thrill of the experience. "Last season you'd see 12 races here every week. They were brilliant! Now they're still good but it's definitely lost something. I don't know what it is – the riders, the stockcars taking it out of the track, something else – but it's definitely not what it was!"

Over in the pits, notoriously the tallest mechanic in speedway – Hull-based Paul Harvey – already has the preparations of Magnus Karlsson's bikes in hand. As usual, he's affable and dry-witted, "What do you find to write about? I suppose there's always stories in speedway!" Sheffield Tigers reserve and ex-Scunthorpe Scorpion Simon Lambert arrives and is immediately quizzed by Paul, "So what's happening? What news do you have for me?"

[Simon] "Nothing [smirks] I've been good."

[Paul] "What we want to know is how to chat up a blonde 19-year old Swede?"

[Jeff] "If you find out can you tell me?"

[Paul] "I've been looking for years so I don't think we'll find out today! But you never know! It's only a few weeks to go before the season ends – thank God – then, a bit afterwards, you can't wait for it to start again! Tell you what, you should do a feature in your next book of riders with money – with Simon at the top and Magnus Karlsson at the bottom!" Simon bites, "I haven't got any. Magnus has lots more than me!" Paul laughs, "I wish he'd give me some then!"

Speedway fan Charles Wright wanders round to the trackshop. One issue that continues to get the focus of his attention is the question of work permits for Australian riders. "Newport's Laurence Rogers has been quoted twice in the *Star* saying Mark Jones's 6-month permit has run out – but that's only for holidays and not for working! You can get a Sports Permit to take part in a specific event, say like Wimbledon, but you can't have a season-long event! Jones could ride as an amateur but, then, you'd have to ride in an Amateur League, which the National League isn't nowadays! If you were being intelligent, you would say Mark Jones went back to Australia for family reasons or because he'd run out of money or got a job! When it comes to Rye House's use of Tyson Nelson, the Rye House website says one thing and Len Silver's letter to the *Speedway Star* says something slightly different. On 17th July, the full and true story given on the Rye House website was that his use was illegal but they said something like 'used with our best knowledge at the time'. Then Len provided what he called his 'true and honest account' in a letter to the *Speedway Star*. It's hard for me to comment on something when I wasn't there but I would ask: how can Alex Harkess and Len have such a misunderstanding? Either you know or you don't! If you don't, you don't blag it. Or you say, 'I don't know.' Len has been in speedway since 1953 but I'm surprised at what he did over that weekend and thought he could get away with it! Someone will end up in a wheelchair and the insurers will walk away plus the Border Agency will go through every application tooth and nail! And I heard about someone else who might be riding illegally without a permit, as well. But I don't know! You were lucky you weren't at Buxton yesterday to see Weymouth ride or the Weymouth 'Tosspot' Wildcats as some people now call them. Most of their riders just didn't want to know. A couple of them took three races to complete four laps. They were atrocious! It was a double-header too. In the first meeting, they were appalling and never used a black-and-white. Phil Bartlett was manager. If you're riding crap, you use the black-and-white to give them a chance. The story was they wanted to get home! Phil Bartlett was parked next to me in one of those people carriers with what looked like a personalised number plate. The plate didn't match the age of the car put it that way. If you think he's a promoter that's allegedly losing money, his car didn't have a sticker promoting Weymouth speedway anywhere on the vehicle! So you wouldn't know he had anything to do with speedway, let alone he was the

Scunthorpe: *"Everyone remembers the Moran brothers – Kelly and Shawn – but all of these lads are going faster than they did then because the bikes have moved on!"*

promoter!"

North Berwick based Jim Dow has come to the Eddie Wright Raceway to savour the race action at this afternoon's double-header. "I don't like Berwick because it's a big track and, if you make the gate, it can be very boring to watch. So I don't go there but I do go to Armadale (it's roughly the same distance but quicker to get to). [Berwick owner] John Anderson is my local butcher in North Berwick. The Elite League has too few teams and, I hate to say it, but when I watch on a Monday night [on Sky], I get bored very quickly. I prefer the Premier League – there's more teams and more tracks! I must say I enjoy coming to this track. I came to the first meeting here and it's one of the best in the country (along with Somerset, which is great too). Sheffield is also good because it's full throttle." Scunthorpe's regular presenter Shaun Leigh isn't available this afternoon because his Elite League commitments take priority (similar to how riders Polish contracts trump EL ones). Instead Sheffield's Dave Hoggart kindly steps into the breach for centre-green duties. He faces a long afternoon ahead as a clash with the Buxton Hitmen follows the Sheffield Premier League meeting. If any superstitious Sheffield fans lurk in the Bank Holiday crowd, then initial omens look good after their captain Ricky Ashworth "calls tails and it is tails" in the toss for gate positions. Dedicated and well-travelled speedway fan Robert Peasley is at Scunthorpe this afternoon to savour the action rather than fundraise on behalf of the Speedway Riders' Benevolent Fund. Robert ponders how best I can increase my book sales. "Maybe you need a mascot? Now I'm pratting about as the mascot [for the SRBF], it's really made a difference! Will you be using Derek Barclay's suggested title for your book next year?" "I don't know – what's that?" "*Tedious Tome of Shale.*" Derek's such a card, "That's quite exciting but I don't know if it quite suits."

Thrust into presentational duty, Dave Hoggart leavens his usual mix of erudition and expertise with the kind of conversational bonhomie you'd expect from a favoured distant relative. For the neutral observer it's a delight to see that Josh Auty – as usual – fails to gate. Scunthorpe's exactly the kind of place you'd expect his 'round the boards from the back' racing style to suit but, sadly, he settles for third place behind his teammate Hugh Skidmore. Dave Hoggart's probably as disappointed as the rest of us but, since this afternoon he's notionally the home presenter, he's got to monitor his own conversation for obvious and/or unintentional Sheffield bias. "Josh didn't make the gate as usual. Am I allowed to say that? Sheffield put on a great show at Newport yesterday and let's hope they do so here today!" Rob Peasley studiously fills in his programme at some length with great concentration. Glancing at his handiwork, I can see that he records the race result and time but he also, in neat tiny handwriting that wouldn't disgrace a professional calligrapher or doctor writing prescriptions, records the key manoeuvres and dramas of each race! Surfacing briefly from his handiwork, Rob comments, "I've realised now that, if you have a notebook, you might be writing something. I was going to be doing a column in this year's Scunthorpe programme but Richard Hollingsworth told me they were going to be doing a £1 programme this year, which is a good idea to save the fans money!" It's difficult to know if Jan Graversen's unusual helmet colour really saves him any money on helmet covers? Notionally red in colour, Graversen's particular choice of hue ensures he stands out from the crowd. Heat 2 is rerun and, when it finally gets properly underway, Sheffield's guest reserve Alex Davies rides a wide line to press Jan Graversen throughout the race. Alex looks fast and his all-action style showers the fans stood close to the start line with shale. Each time he passes there's a pitter-patter as lumps of shale strike every nearby available surface. Simon Lambert wins the race to Dave Hoggart's approval, "Simon had a point to prove – it would have been nice if he'd come round to take your applause or whatever you have to give him!"

The third race of the late afternoon early evening is an eventful affair. Exotically named Tero

Scunthorpe: *"Everyone remembers the Moran brothers – Kelly and Shawn – but all of these lads are going faster than they did then because the bikes have moved on!"*

Aarnio – who sounds part speedway rider and part homeopathic tincture – goes from fourth to first in the space of time it takes to transition from the first to the second bend. On bends three to four, Josef 'Pepe' Franc nips up inside Carl Wilkinson. However, it's the battle for third place on the final corner that provides the real excitement. As they dash from the crown of the last bend to the finish line, Carl Wilkinson and Richard Hall tangle and grind to a collective halt a yard or so from the finish line. Linked together, like a bizarre sculpture, bikes and riders judder in slow motion to stationary. Both Richard and Carl are known to be combative riders. Luckily too, one of the lifelong joys of speedway is our close proximity to the action and, of course, the competitors. Carl Wilkinson's instantly aggrieved with Richard Hall, remonstrates angrily and shouts, "That wasn't me that was your freakin' teammate!" Track staff intervened to quieten their animated discussion. A nearby lady fan adds her tuppence worth, "Freak off, Richard! Go back to the pits!" From his vantage point on the centre green, Dave Hoggart verbally rubs gleeful hands together, "This promises to be a cracker – always entertaining when these two sides meet!" After the bikes and riders properly separate Richard Hall pootles back towards the bend-three pits gate area before deciding better of it and, instead, starts to head back towards the tapes area to remonstrate with referee Craig Ackroyd and his disqualification decision. Dave Hoggart kindly advises newcomers on the minutiae of the regulations that underpin the referee's decision, "As the first rider had crossed the line … the rider in yellow – Richard Hall – was disqualified." Though the incident took place directly in front of my position, without the benefit of replays let alone my instinctive reaction to flinch as the bikes head in our direction, nonetheless it did appear to me that Richard Hall knocked off Carl Wilkinson. To make doubly sure I consult the lady fan who'd earlier given Richard the benefit of her forthright advice. "I saw it as – and I'm a Scunthorpe fan but I know Richard's family – Richard cut under him and he drifted out wide so Carl cut back under him and then Richard turned inside on him so it was his fault! I'll tell him that later too!"

It's an afternoon to spot the great and the good of British speedway. Rob Peasley appears to know all in sundry, "That's Paul Ackroyd who, until he retired, used to be a ref who now runs the Ben Fund and his son is the referee here today!" Magnus Karlsson starts his afternoon with a race win heat 4 while, in the near distance, eight slowly moving wind turbines tower over the Scunthorpe pits area. To some people wind turbines are an eyesore, others view them as a vital energy source of the future. Erected in a light industrial area on the outskirts of Scunthorpe, they possess a harsh industrial beauty.

Heat 5 features an impromptu bike-throwing exhibition from Hugh Skidmore. After he rears towards the end of the first lap, this surprise manoeuvre prompts Hugh to throw his bike in the air and, amazingly, it somehow eludes the fractionally ahead Carl Wilkinson as he zooms by on an outside line close to the fence. Hugh scuttles after his bike in an attempt to clear the track, though he's nearly mown down by the other riders after they fail to see the red light. Josh Auty fails to gate in the rerun but powers round the outside from third to first on the first corner prior to a comfortable win. Speedway fan Joe from Halifax wonders if I ever got to visit The Shay, "Did you ever go there? It were brilliant! I went from '75 until it closed in 1985. A friend brought me here a few years ago; it's a great track! People say there's no passing in speedway but they haven't been here, if they say that! Hopefully, Halifax will come back soon." Richard Heasman returns to buy my latest book. He might soon relocate with his wife Sally. "We might move away from here. Once you've lived by the seaside, you really miss it when you move away. The North East coast just isn't the same [as the South coast]! That said, when you get to my age what matters changes – as long as you have enough, you don't care about money. It's all the other little things that you often take for granted." Scunthorpe music man Barry 'Bazza' Preston is here without his daughter Chloe. He's got exciting news, "Me girlfriend Sue just found out she's pregnant and, next year, there'll be another speedway fan here! Whether it's a boy or a girl, we're going to have Robin or

Scunthorpe: *"Everyone remembers the Moran brothers – Kelly and Shawn – but all of these lads are going faster than they did then because the bikes have moved on!"*

Robyn as a middle name in honour of Tai's dad. I've told his mum – Cynthia – but I haven't told Sue yet!"

The knot of Tigers fans who cluster by the start line greet Sheffield's first maximum heat advantage of the afternoon with ecstatic cheers. It gives the visitors a lead that they fail to relinquish for the rest of the afternoon. Vaguely convincingly, on the centre green Dave Hoggart suppresses his inclination to smile, "I'm impartial here today, don't you worry!" Viktor Bergström's so keen to do well in heat 8 that it takes him until the third bend to notice the red light illuminated by referee Craig Ackroyd for an unsatisfactory start. Hugh Skidmore (or "Skiddy" as Dave Hoggart calls him) wins the race ahead of Bergström who's pressured throughout the final two laps by a fast looking, outside line riding Simon Lambert. Always ultra-professional, Dave Hoggart conscientiously promotes the products of those who cover, help or support speedway through sponsorship, heat sponsorship, fundraising, merchandise, books or DVDs. Dave bigs up GRT Media who provide, "the best value speedway DVDs – £6 – no fancy packaging but the best production values in speedway. Bob Tasker covers all the Scunthorpe home meetings and the away ones at the tracks he does: Newcastle, Sheffield and Berwick." Heat 9 sees Ricky Ashworth tuck up Tero Aarnio by the bend-two airfence. So much so that Tero slows almost to a complete halt and then, in comedy fall fashion, somehow snags his bike on the edge of the airfence panel and collapses to the floor. It's done in such a theatrical manner that Rob Peasley bursts out laughing. In their fluorescent clothing, the centre-green medical staff jog-cum-trot over to the stricken rider to soon be joined by the ambulance and another paramedic in a black Volvo. Dave Hoggart stands by, guardedly anxious, "Obviously there's a bit of concern by Tero Aarnio – let's hope he's okay!" With so many medical assistance options on hand, recovery looks likely. The rerun of heat 9 also ends on the second bend – albeit on the second lap where second-placed Carl 'Wilko' Wilkinson clips Ricky Ashworth's back wheel. The close following Alex Davies somehow manages to evade the fallen Wilko. It's so close a shave, fans and Wilko almost flinch in unison as he tries to move aside as Davies bears down upon him. The referee disqualifies Carl Wilkinson. Rob Peasley approves of this decision "The ref got it right. He was going round the outside trying to dive into a gap that wasn't there! The same as was done to him [by Richard Hall] ironically!" Ostensibly a match race, the re-rerun sees teammates Ricky Ashworth and Alex Davies race but safely complete all four laps to register a 5-0 heat advantage for the Tigers.

With Sheffield ahead by 11 points Rob Peasley wonders, "Is it safe to put David Howe in as the tactical ride now?" When the riders take to the track, clearly Scorpions team manager, Richard Hollingsworth, thinks similarly. Heat 10 barely starts before it stops after Richard Hall falls under pressure from Viktor Bergström. His reward is disqualification from the rerun. Again Craig Ackroyd's decision meets with Rob Peasley's approval, "That's fair enough – Hall missed the gate and put it down. You've picked an incident-packed meeting! It's kind of building up nicely to the next Hall versus Wilkinson clash!" David Howe combines with Viktor Bergström to win the rerun of heat 10 and their 8-1 narrows the Scunthorpe deficit to only 4 points. We then luxuriate in a 15-minute delay prompted by paramedic unavailability. I wonder if parking up all those emergency vehicles could be a factor until Rob blandly notes, "There's an accident down the pits, apparently." Indeed, the paramedic treats Viktor Bergström after, peculiarly, he's run over by Richard Hall. Since the demise of Oxford speedway, Rob Peasley's thrown himself still further into fundraising activities on behalf of the SRBF. He still misses speedway at Cowley Stadium as well as his reporting responsibilities. "Once when I went to Monmore to report on Oxford for the *Oxford Mail*, I naively assumed that there'd be an Internet connection – which there wasn't! It was when reports had to be filed by a reasonable time – 11 p.m. – before it went silly. I'd written it already and thought that if I rushed I could get home in time to file it but Tim Hamblin said, 'Come to my house and do it'. Another time at Oxford for the Under-15s – it turned out to be the last

Scunthorpe: *"Everyone remembers the Moran brothers – Kelly and Shawn – but all of these lads are going faster than they did then because the bikes have moved on!"*

time I went to a meeting there – I didn't know how much they wanted but I interviewed all of the top three. James Sargeant was 13 at the time and was a bit shy and didn't want to be interviewed. It was quite tough getting two words out of him. Afterwards his mum asked, 'Did he speak to you at all?'"

The meeting finally restarts with a bizarre heat 11 that features Magnus Karlsson going out of his way to pin his teammate Jan Graversen to the airfence on the crown of the first bend. They both slow and, as a result, are unable to make up their lost ground on Josh Auty and Hugh Skidmore. It's the way of the world that maximum heat advantages often follow each other. So it proves here when the Tigers immediately ram home another to balloon the cumulative score to 31-43. Prior to the second appearance of the black-and-white helmet colour, Dave Hoggart issues a request over the loudspeaker system, "Can we put an appeal to all the riders racing in the National League meeting? Can you get changed and make your way to the pits?" Sadly for the Scorpions, Magnus Karlsson trails in last in this tactical helmet colour. The small knot of enthusiastic Tigers fans at the start line cheer every race win and 5-1 with gusto. According to Rob Peasley, the throaty sound of Ricky Ashworth's bike prior to the race indicates he might not be an obvious race winner, "That don't sound good!" If appearances are deceptive then, in speedway circles, sound is too. David Howe provides the real drama after he winds it on during the last two laps to somehow burst from third to second past Josh Auty on the run-in to the line. His last-gasp effort is such that he nearly also catches a slightly overconfident Ricky Ashworth. Rob Peasley exclaims even louder than the Sheffield fans, "Yow! I think he got one of them!" It's been a sufficiently dramatic finish for Rob to spend extra long concentratedly writing with his red pen in the programme. He covers his document in very detailed and small handwriting ("it's the over-takes and incidents! It's small but I can read it.")

News that Simon Lambert appears in the penultimate race of the Premier League meeting prompts an indistinct crowd murmur from over by the bar area. Rob Peasley notes, "Simon isn't popular with someone in the crowd. When he won heat 2, they shouted out lots of swear words!" This race is a treat and something of a delight to witness. Up front, Carl Wilkinson and Richard Hall battle with such intensity that you'd think the world championship rides on this race. Carl gates determinedly off gate 4 and brilliantly evades the other riders through the proverbial nonexistent gap. Richard gives lusty chase throughout but isn't able to overtake. Behind them, the battle for third between Lambert and Graversen is even more intensely and energetically hard fought. No quarter is given and their contest only really ends when Graversen falls on the third bend of the last lap. Dave Hoggart knows what he's seen, "Thrilling stuff – two races in one there!" Rob Peasley agrees, "The problem with that race was what you decided to watch! They were all over the place." With one race to go of part one of this double-header meeting, Dave Hoggart's thoughts turn to the attraction that is the National League clash between the Scunthorpe Saints and the Buxton Hitmen. "Do stay for the National League meeting. It's always exciting at Scunthorpe! The café is open, the bar is open and the trackshop is open." With no need for the track curator to worry about opening hours, there's a brief delay for a touch of track grading. Dave Hoggart remains keen to excite us about the forthcoming NL spectacle, "Simon Lambert will ride at No. 1 for Buxton unless there's been a change in the meantime."

Under referee's orders, the riders up at the tapes for heat 15 rev their bikes to a crescendo and Rob Peasley calls out, "Go on Richard [Hall]" only to then exclaim, "Oh!" when, off gate 4, Ricky Ashworth obliterates the tapes! Dave Hoggart verbally shrugs, "and…there he was gone! I'm told the only choice we have is Ricky going off 15 metres. I expect his clutch has gone." Usually at this stage of a speedway meeting, Dave would embrace his inner Steve Johnston and take a much-needed libation. "Do stay for the National League match – I always enjoy the National League

Scunthorpe: *"Everyone remembers the Moran brothers – Kelly and Shawn – but all of these lads are going faster than they did then because the bikes have moved on!"*

here but I usually watch from the bar – tonight, I'll make an exception! Now the sun has come out, it's warmer than when we got here!" Bob Tasker reminds me that 15 metres isn't so much of a handicap at the Eddie Wright Raceway, "Scunthorpe is one of the few tracks you could win from 15! Did you hear when Joe Screen touched the tapes in heat 1 last week that the Glasgow management preferred to put in a reserve rather than let Joe start off 15? Just shows how likely they actually think it is to pass there! You always kind of assume that there is one racing line – if you can find it – but, maybe, there, there isn't! Imagine how hard it is to pass Joe Screen and Lee Dicken anyway!" Contrary to expectations, Ricky fails to make any impression on the riders ahead of him. Josef Franc on the transition from bends two to three on the last lap briefly charges for second place only to see Carl Wilkinson aggressively block the inside line to immediately end this manoeuvre. The first meeting ends in just less than two hours. However, disaster nearly strikes the Sheffield team on the Scunthorpe parade truck during their second victory lap when they swerve dramatically to avoid the agricultural-looking bowser hugging the first-bend airfence line driven by Scunthorpe promoter Rob Godfrey.

Halifax Dukes fan Joe reminisces about the recent Buxton versus Isle of Wight Premier Trophy encounter at Hi-Edge. "I like that Tom Hill – he reminds me of Dougie Wyer! I'm looking forward to seeing that [Jason] Garrity again!" Off-duty referee Darren Hartley is in the crowd with his partner, "We're looking forward to seeing Jason Garrity."
[Jeff] "He's exciting – it looks like his back wheel is too light for his bike."
[Lady] "He's too fast you mean."
[Darren] "We're off to get somewhere safe."
[Jeff] "Somewhere safe?"
[Darren] "Away from the flying bikes!"

The National League meeting is quickly underway. Buzz Burrows' first race of the night lasts until his third-bend engine failure. It promises to be a long night ahead for him but also the team if the ease with which Simon Lambert and Jason Garrity (taking a rider-replacement ride in place of Nick Morris) power to a maximum heat advantage. While we wait for the riders to come out for the second race of the NL fixture, Dave Hoggart conducts a couple of trophy presentation ceremonies. David Howe wins the trophy for the fastest rider of the meeting while Carl Wilkinson takes the trophy for the most exciting rider of the afternoon. Dave Hoggart enthuses, "and I think we all can agree that he is the most exciting rider. Another trophy for your trophy cabinet then Carl – you can put that in your trophy cabinet along with Richard Hall's wheel!"

Released from the formal obligations of his promotional duties, Neil Machin remains at the Eddie Wright Raceway to enjoy surveying the up-and-coming new talent. His eye's caught by the performance of Buxton's Lewis Dallaway in the second race, "Who's this No. 6?" Neil's guardedly optimistic about the Tigers hopes of progress to the Premier League Play-off semi-finals. "Whether we'll make the top four depends on the results of others! Obviously, we want to finish above Rye House cos they're Southerners! Actually, I've always had the greatest respect for Len but one or two things have made me doubt that this year."
[Jeff] "Do you mean his 'fair, honest and true' recent letter in the Star?"
[Neil] "Going into the public domain [about Mr T. Nelson's visa] has made it look like we were the ones who faffed about when that is not true and not the case because we have facts that contradict that! I won't go into them but, suffice it to say, that isn't the case and going into the public isn't on that's for sure!"
[Jeff] "There's a rumour that permit problems might also apply to certain other riders?"
[Neil] "You have to remember that people like me have seen young riders coming up through the system for years when we've been visiting Oz. Closer to home, look at this race, Jason Garrity

Scunthorpe: *"Everyone remembers the Moran brothers – Kelly and Shawn – but all of these lads are going faster than they did then because the bikes have moved on!"*

started on our training track when he was eight, so I've known him for years."

Jason Garrity's an exciting rider to watch but an overworked one at reserve. He's soon out again in heat 4 after a first-heat paid win and second-heat victory. Until the last corner of the third lap it looks like a win for Ashley Birks – whose style on the bike and bobbling hand movements draw the eye – until Garrity blasts through on the inside for the lead. Ashley gives lusty chase. So much so that he does an extra couple of bends after the race finishes until he finally realises it's over. Book purchases are few and far between this season, "I've got all your books but I won't be getting the latest just yet cos I have Briggo's, Ivan's, Michael Lee's and Leigh Adams's to read yet!" Very smartly dressed Nigel Hinchliffe ("I have responsibility for the second halves at Sheffield now"), like his promoter, keeps a close eye on the action. "A lot of the Scunthorpe lads started in second halves at Sheffield. Lots of people are funny about racing in the National League but everyone remembers the Moran brothers – Kelly and Shawn – but all of these lads are going faster than they did then because the bikes have moved on! If you have four riders of roughly equal ability on a well-prepared track, you have a recipe for good racing! As the GP track preparation has proved this year, where the racing has been much, much better now the tracks are!" While we speak, close by to us on gate No. 2 Jason Garrity digs industriously ahead of heat 8. So much so it could well turn out to be a trench rather than an aid to acceleration. Nigel ignores Jason's curatorial propensity to comment, "He's gonna get his clutch hot that way." It's all part of his apprenticeship to my mind, "He'll learn." "Never knock enthusiasm."

Once again Jason Garrity fails to gate and so spends two laps racing very close behind second-placed Adam Wrathall. Jason hugs the inside white line on a bike noticeable for power to spare. With each passing circuit Garrity slowly manoeuvres Wrathall into a position he can ease past. The Scunthorpe Saints feature the Worrall twins Steve and Richie. Both look accomplished on their bikes. Richie triumphs in heat 7 while Steve follows up his heat 5 race win with another in heat 9. Nigel Hinchliffe sings his praises, "Steve Worrall's looking very good tonight. He's only got 12 months on a bike and his brother, his twin Richie, has only got two months!" Heat 10 is a peculiar affair in both of its incarnations and finally puts to bed that old canard that referees never change their mind. The initial attempt to run this race sees a win for Mark Burrows some distance ahead of Jonathan Bethell and Robert Branford with Adam Wrathall left becalmed at the start line. After we've all marked our programmes Dave Hoggart informs us, "Sorry ladies and gentlemen, you may have gathered something went on in that race when Adam Wrathall sat at the line. One of the green start lights didn't come on – the one he was totally focused upon! So, in consultation with the referee, team managers and the pits staff, we're going to rerun that one. If you, like me, have all filled in our programmes, we're going to have to do it again and get the green light fixed. The riders will be taking their starting instructions from the green light in the first corner." Whoever Buzz Burrows takes his starting instructions from knows their onions since he again wins the rerun of the race with similar imperious ease. Robert Branford and Jonathan Bethell reverse their final positions but the drawn heat remains a drawn heat after Adam Wrathall – despite his reprieve – again fails to trouble the scorer.

SRBF fundraising totals aren't usually publicised but the generosity of the Scunthorpe crowd prompts an exception, "We don't usually put the figures out but you've been fabulous raising £718." By heat 12, Jason Garrity is already on his sixth ride. Once more he fails to gate and has his work cut out to pass the two Scorpion Saints ahead. On the third bend of the second lap, Jason pushes Ashley Birks wide from behind and, shortly after, passes Steve Worrall. When Jonathan Bethell joins him up front, Buxton's second maximum heat advantage of the afternoon gives them a convincing 31-41 lead. Rob Peasley's impressed, "That Garrity's something. He bashed one out of the way and he nearly had his leg run over by his teammate when he stuck it out on the last

Scunthorpe: *"Everyone remembers the Moran brothers – Kelly and Shawn – but all of these lads are going faster than they did then because the bikes have moved on!"*

bend. He's been great but that one was his most spectacular!"

Saints team manager Stuart Parnaby sends out Mark Burrows in the black-and-white helmet colour in heat 13. Initially third, in the increasing gloom, Buzz appears to overtake Simon Lambert on the last bend of the second lap by virtue of sheer willpower alone. This manoeuvre prompts Simon Lambert to race neck and neck with the Yorkshireman. Up front, Gary Irving is tactically aware enough to realise that he has to let Buzz past but, in the process of doing so, the hard-charging Simon Lambert also takes advantage of this sacrifice. The 7-2 heat score narrows the Buxton lead to a more obtainable 5 points. Rob Peasley savours the action, "They did lock up a bit there – the key is, if you're gonna let your partner through, don't let the other through too!" Buzz suddenly appears appreciably quicker than earlier. It's not an optical illusion as Dave Hoggart explains, "We must pass on Buzz's thanks to Viktor [Bergström] for the use of his machine." Jason Garrity completes his seventh ride with a win in the penultimate race for an overall contribution of 17 paid 20 points. The nascent Saints fight-back then hits the buffers through a retirement for Benji Compton and mechanical difficulties for Richie Worrall (who limps home third). Critical Scunthorpe fans moan that rather than replace Luke Chessell with Benji Compton (who scored 1 point from four rides), the club could have won this meeting if, instead, they'd used rider-replacement facility! Ifs and buts and maybes are the *lingua franca* of speedway fans everywhere. Since this meeting represents the end of an era for Benji a look at the bigger picture is the real order of the day. Dave Hoggart effortlessly segues from presenter to master of ceremonies after Benji completes a helmetless lap of honour and an enthusiastic series of donuts. "Benji Compton has come out of retirement today – he's already started a new career. He was hoping to complete his last ride. Throughout his career he's shown flashes of brilliance, plenty of action, plenty of falls and he's given sterling service to British speedway!" Donuts over, Dave jovially enquires, "How long have you been practising that? Benji, you've had some tough times in speedway?"

[Benji] I've enjoyed it – the social side sometimes more than the racing! It's a wicked lifestyle and I wouldn't have changed it for the world."

[Dave] "What are you going to do next?"

[Benji] "I'm going to be a builder."

[Dave] "I heard something different. Tell me again."

[Benji] "Hairdressin'!"

[Dave "It's a sad day."

[Benji] "Just a bit, I'm starting to fill up now!"

[Crowd] "Ah!"

With extensive calligraphy all over his programme, Rob Peasley adopts a quizzical look, "Strangely that heat 14 was quicker than the Premier League heat 14. The times have been comparable." To cap off this double-header meeting, Buzz Burrows and Simon Lambert indulge in another harum-scarum, full-blooded, fast and exciting duel for shale supremacy. Both riders fully explore the multiple racing lines of the Eddie Wright Raceway. They ride lustily but fairly. No quarter is given throughout. It's a watershed moment for myself since I finally get to fully appreciate the contention that the inclusion of 'experienced' riders at the NL/CL level provides real apprenticeship benefits on the track for the racing development of younger riders. Here Simon Lambert races someone over two decades his senior who, thereby, provides precisely the sort of ongoing high-speed on-the-job apprenticeship he continues to require if he's to further advance his career and become an even more accomplished rider. As the riders cross the line, Rob Peasley takes a joyful mini leap of celebration with a smile and his eyes ablaze. Dave Hoggart echoes the feelings of many lucky enough to witness this particular heat 15, "That was a fabulous race – we'll let the ref call that one!" Rob's thoughts turn to absent friends cum Internet sparring partners, "I tried to persuade Derek [Barclay] to come cos Buzz was riding!"

Scunthorpe: *"Everyone remembers the Moran brothers – Kelly and Shawn – but all of these lads are going faster than they did then because the bikes have moved on!"*

A good-sized crowd rush for the car park. I catch a few words with Buxton presenter Graham Tagg, "Sorry to miss you at the Isle of Wight meeting but my mum was taken ill. It's been quite a season – Garrity is very exciting now he's learnt to ride!" Bob Tasker packs away his camera and various bits of recording equipment back into the boot of his car, "Four hours is too long for a meeting with no incidents except Hall ran over Bergström in the pits." After a successful day at the office, referee Craig Ackroyd departs with a warm sense of satisfaction of a job well done. "That was a cracking meeting – particularly the National League meeting – there was some brilliant racing!" Thrust into last-minute presentational service, Dave Hoggart savours his afternoon on the centre green, "Jason Garrity – he's another Josh Auty, if he could trap he'd be world champion at 19!"

30th August Scunthorpe v. Sheffield (Premier League) 41-51
Scunthorpe v. Buxton (National League) 43-50

Scunthorpe: *"Everyone remembers the Moran brothers – Kelly and Shawn – but all of these lads are going faster than they did then because the bikes have moved on!"*

CHAPTER 22

King's Lynn
"I try to watch it like a fan"

1st September

Already inside the pits area of the Norfolk Arena three and a half hours before the scheduled start time is casually dressed SCB track inspector, Colin Meredith. He carries the type of measuring wheel favoured by surveyors. "I'm here to do a track inspection. I'm gonna get changed in a minute. I've been looking at new ideas for fencing. Nothing's perfect so it's good to look at other ideas! Airfences are very good but you have to blow them up, let them down, fold them and put them away. With polystyrene or foam fences at somewhere like here, you could attach them [to the permanent Armco wall] and throw them over when needed and throw them back when they're not. It could work very well but, you don't know, so best to think about it and investigate!" Should he succeed in developing and then homologating an easy to use but economically priced clip-on fence, Colin will also face objections from the manufacturers of expensive airfences. Colin's clearly a man who likes to consider practical solutions but he's also got a keen attention to detail given how quickly he notices my front nearside tyre, "That tyre is slightly flat or not as inflated as the rest of them!"

Each time I visit the Norfolk Arena, it's clear that the Chapman family have made further investments in the stadium infrastructure to improve the overall experience for staff and spectators alike. They've reconfigured the entire programme and snack stall area just inside the turnstiles. The trackshop now has an easier access open-facing layout, while the Mad Hatters relocate from their chalet on the fourth bend to a more convenient unit adjacent to the trackshop. The hospitality area on the fourth bend is dramatically different since sponsors and their guests now enjoy a swish glass-fronted elevated panoramic view over the Norfolk Arena stockcar and speedway circuits (rather than the pine sauna-cum-shed effect previously in favour at the club). Inevitably on any race day, Buster Chapman works hard on his track preparations. The club have an extensive range of mechanical equipment to use ranging from diggers to

New look trackshop

Young fan

185

tractors. Buster uses them all industriously. On a brief break from his curatorial activities Keith tells me, "We put up our numbers through the gate year on year. Sales fell in the bars and cafes last year but they're picking up again. I used to try and give people [other promoters] advice but no one listens so I gave up and I just run my own business!" Tonight's SCB official Barbara Horley arrives. Buster immediately apologises to her, "Sorry about last time, I didn't mean to be like that but, to put it politely, I was upset! It was nothing to do with you. I think I'll just lie and cheat like the rest of them in future!" They confer about a variety of matters before Cambridge-based religious education teacher Barbara notes, "This is my second nearest track, Peterborough is the closest." As Barbara makes her way up the external metal staircase to the referee's box perched high above the grandstand building adjacent to the start line, Buster resumes his brief analysis of British speedway. "I don't go to other tracks much cos I'm sick of how they prepare the track. I'm sick of shitty tracks with holes and bumps and inconsistent surfaces. I've offered them to come here and spend time seeing how we do it. For nothing! Just come and see but no one can be bothered. Amazing! So, we still get tracks with bumps and holes and shittily prepared. Many don't do the basics off the track either. I went to Edinburgh – and this was before the meeting remember – I went to the toilets and the toilet seats were off, there was no toilet paper or soap. Before the public came in! And this is the chairman's track too! The one who's saying we must all improve. So I just get on here and ignore the rest of them and they ignore me. It's better that way!"

Johnny Barber and Phil Hilton draw up in a white van laden with speedway merchandise. Phil suddenly catches sight of the back of Johnny's head as he leans forward to pick up some boxes from inside the van, "Let's have a look – who cut your hair?"
[Johnny] "My mum. I've given up caring what it looks like."
[Phil] "Did she learn at Rampton? What does she use to cut it with?"
[Johnny] "An electric razor."

Their banter about tonsorial matters is cut short by King's Lynn Stars reserve Adam Roynon wearing a pair of garish yellow multi-patterned Converse All Stars trainers. Keen to ensure health and safety within the environs of the stadium, Phil ignores Adam's fashion statement to warn of potential off-track accidents ahead, "You do know you've got no laces in them, don't ya? You know how accident prone you are!"

Once the turnstiles open, Jonathan Chapman lingers in the vicinity to meet and greet the fans as well as make himself available to answer their questions and concerns. He's got a keen eye for business, "You've got your table the wrong way round!" Jonathan is eager to stress that King's Lynn speedway continue to buck the trend in a difficult trading environment for British speedway, "Everyone says their crowds are falling but ours haven't been. I reckon it'll be a really good meeting tonight. A good crowd and sunny – we can't go wrong, even if we lose by 10! People are eating before they get here and not buying so much from the shops but they're still coming!" No stone remains unturned or business practice uninterrogated if Jonathan is involved. This analytical approach is symbolised by the transformation of the club programme from last year's unfairly derided fold-away version into this year's A4 format they call the 'Official Raceday Magazine of the King's Lynn Roger Warnes Transport Stars'. "Whatever anyone says, the sheet programme we did last year was hugely successful. In the *Star* they didn't like it but they have a biased programme editor in charge of that. We did what was right for the public. In order to keep sales up we've gone to a magazine format this season. We've added 50p and given them extra quality! Okay, it's left some black marks tonight because of a problem with the printer. The problem is you've got to invest to start with. We've got our own printing machine for five years and now we've found the format we're gonna use that for the football club and the speedway! Unlike a lot of promoters who say – officially – everything is wonderful, even though crowds are falling and riders and fans are complaining. I don't ever think we've got everything right. I try to watch it like a fan and I know that if I'm bored watching a rider then, probably, everyone else is too and now it's time for a change! At a few places I've been the crowds have been down. Maybe, even here I think is a little bit down. Last year people ignored the recession but this year they have to be selective!" Jonathan didn't get off on the best foot with Ivan Mauger on a book-signing visit to the Norfolk Arena during the recent Speedway World Cup semi-final. "Ivan Mauger came here for the World Cup and parked in one of the disabled bays and I said, 'Can you move?' He said, 'What does it matter?' I said, 'It's a disabled bay so they're close to the stadium!' He wasn't happy so we didn't get off on the best foot. I didn't know it was him though until they introduced me to him in the pits. I'm not his era so I didn't recognise him."

Jonathan checks out my book display. "If I'm honest, your format needs changing or sharpening up. You've done it before so maybe you or the fans are getting a bit bored with it now? Why not do 'a day in the life of 35 speedway riders'? Why not follow different people that you like round? Riders, referees, promoters and that. Maybe write a book on Chris Holder or Darcy Ward? Not Lewis that would be boring and not Troy as he'd be throwing his dummy out all the time. Chris Holder is really laidback – he rides hard and lives hard off the track. He doesn't give a monkey's. What they get up to is unbelievable! You only have to look at his Facebook page to get some idea of how wild it is. Maybe you should go to Poland. When I went there the crowds were huge and they were mad. It was like watching *Tom & Jerry*, I thought I was in a cartoon when I saw some bloke get his arm blown off with a firework. No one's done a 'no holds barred' book on a speedway rider. Sure some of the retired ones have done autobiographies but no one's really interested in that. What they'd really like to know about is what speedway riders get up to now and not hear about it after they've retired. You would never want to follow a Dane – it would be the most boring book ever written! Thinking about it, you should definitely do a 'no holds barred' book on Chris Holder. He's gonna be world champion – he lives his life to the full on and off the track. Girls love him and Darcy – they love the glamour of speed. You won't have heard of him [I have] but we've had Arthur Sissis here for two weeks. We've known him since he was 13 – what a talent! Have you seen the Junior Moto GP? They get up to 160 mph and they're only 15! You should see the birds! Arthur went to Italy for a trial to become a Red Bull team rider. He just gets there and they provide the bikes, mechanics, gear and everything. He'd never been on a bike before yet he was chosen out of 500. He's doing that for two years but it's speedway he really loves!"

Speedway workers Bryn Williams and Paul Watson stop for a chat. Paul is part of the regular Thursday night Arlington press posse but King's Lynn are his first speedway love from their first season in 1965. Paul's work provides privileged behind the scenes access. Some riders make a positive impression ("Lukáš Dryml always calls me 'Sir!'") but he worries about the impact of other riders, "There's a really good team spirit in the pits when there's six riders or six riders and their guest but, if the other one is there – that's rarely, of course – a black cloud hangs over the place. I doubt he'll ride again for Eastbourne this season."
[Jeff] "It say's in Kevin's [Ling] press release that he is."
[Paul] "They'll probably use rider replacement or, like last week, when it said he would ride, they already had Edward Kennett lined up."

Bryn Williams doesn't let the grass grow beneath his feet. "Len [Silver] wants me to do the mic for a poxy parade – I thought it was 2 p.m. but it's 10 o'clock! It's a slack week for me. Ipswich was off, Friday Lakeside, Saturday Rye House, Sunday King's Lynn, Monday Rye House, Tuesday Isle of Wight, Wednesday King's Lynn, Thursday Isle of Wight, Friday Lakeside, Saturday Rye House, Sunday, Monday off, Tuesday Isle of Wight, Wednesday King's Lynn, Thursday Swindon."

Speedway clubs at the Elite League level divide into the "haves and the have not's" according to Paul, "Some clubs have all the money – teams like Coventry and Poole."

[Bryn] "Will you be going to the promotion relegation meetings? They could be really interesting."

[Jeff] "What, lots of 5-0s."

[Bryn] "No, 0-0s"

[Paul] "I think you'll find Edinburgh won't qualify and, if it's Birmingham, it'll be completely different!" Unable or unprepared to stop for a chat en route to the referee's box, second-half announcer/presenter Kevin "100% professional" Moore arrives frighteningly early but rushes past to bagsy a place in the referee's box. In answer to my question, "What's Kevin Moore doing here?" Bryn responds, "Nothing! He's hoping Edwin doesn't turn up!"

Out on the track, both sets of riders enjoy a trip on the parade truck with acquired taste presenter Mike Bennett who apparently labours under the impression that the crowd missed him during the fortnight's hiatus in shale action at the Norfolk Arena. "It's been a while – you've probably forgotten what to do! Phwow, smell those burgers. Let's wave on the home straight – that's you, come on! [sighs]. It's going to be a long night." Mike Moseley stops by my book display to point at them individually, "Haven't got it, haven't got it, don't want it, got it, got it. Every year my wife orders one of these for Christmas and I say I don't want it cos I can read it in the trackshop." A young lady lingers by my table to speak to Mike. He warns her, "Don't say anything otherwise he'll write it down."

[Jeff] "Who are you?"

[Mike] [points to her Simon Lambert Racing logo] "There's a clue."

[Jeff] "You don't look like a Simon."

[Lady] [laughs] "I'm his sister."

[Jeff] "I saw Simon race excitingly at Scunthorpe."

[Sister] "You were there? Oh, yeh, I saw your table."

[Mike] "I was there but I was taken ill before the meeting. It's a long way to go for that."

[Jeff] "Simon rode really well."

[Sister] "He did."

Talk of Simon Lambert inevitably brings up my suspicion that Kevin Moore owns some too-tight Simon Lambert Racing Y-fronts.

[Sister] "He sponsors Simon – he's really nice."

[Jeff] "I know, he's very sincere, keen on his speedway and he sponsors riders like your brother, Luke Bowen and Barrie Evans."

[Sister] "He is nice. Simon is here tonight if you want to chat to him? He's here with Jerran Hart."

[Jeff] "Running wild?"

[Sister] "Jerran's injured."

[Jeff] "Okay, hobbling wild!"

The dulcet tones of Edwin Overland cuts short our chat. Mystic Meg-like, Edwin looks into the future and pronounces it jolly interesting. "As we start a new month, it looks like an interesting month...really they don't come much tougher than a meeting against the champions elect!" With Edwin located in the eyrie of the referee's box and stealth diva Mike Bennett stood out on the centre green, the to-and-fro of their repartee adds to the atmosphere, bonhomie and joy of any speedway evening at the Norfolk Arena. With signature stream of semi-consciousness, Mike joshes with the Monarchs riders and fans, "You guys have done enough winning – we'd like to win tonight!"

188

Sight of Olly Allen going back from the tapes to make last-minute adjustments to his bike by the pits gate allows Mike Bennett to show he's speedway's equivalent of Andy "snakes on a plane, what's that about?" Townsend. Mike clutches desperately at some early verbal straws to 'entertain' us, "So drama straight away!" When the race does get underway it only lasts as far as the second bend until, after he fails to gate, Olly Allen lays down his bike in the hope of a disqualification for Ryan Fisher (or a rerun). Apparently communicating to us from a parallel psychic universe, Mike Bennett wonders, "Is this a case of *déjà vu*?" An irate King's Lynn fan is in no doubt that Ryan Fisher – rather than Olly's theatrical professionalism after a poor start – is the real culprit, "You dirty bastard! You're pathetic!" While the medical staff briefly hover around Olly, Mike Bennett tells us, "I've got to say one of the things ambulance staff do to check they haven't got concussion is to ask what day of the week it is. Asking a speedway rider that!? I ask you!" Barbara Horley orders a rerun with all four back. It's news that straightaway prompts Mike Bennett to visualise his record collection. No part of his life is too mundane to crowbar into his speedway presentational work, "Don't know if we have Status Quo's 'Rocking All Over the World' to play, the opening lines of that might be appropriate!" [1] Whether the crowd li-li-li-like Mike Bennett's musical tastes or wit remains unclear, but he definitely has the verbal dexterity and boldness that is usually solely the territory of narcissistic evening class performance poets from an obscure provincial town. Ryan Fisher wins the rerun comfortably but doesn't bother with a victory lap of celebration, possibly in anticipation of a muted or hostile reaction from the Norfolk Arena crowd. The front of the Official Raceday Magazine carries a prescient headline, "Lynn fans make me more determined to win". In the interview with the American reproduced as the magazine's front-page news, Ryan reveals that he would consider doubling up again if the opportunity arose and also the shock revelation that, "I always get booed by the fans at King's Lynn, even when I haven't done anything wrong, but I like it." Ryan fails to add, 'I li-li-li-like it, like it, yes I do!'

Fresh from his mangled pronunciation of Lasse Bjerre ("Lass-ARH BEE-AIR"), invariably fractionally out of sync with events – as he's phoning in his comments from the other side of the world – Mike wonders aloud if Ryan can "feel the love" of the home-straight fans long after he's back in the pits. The second race of the night gets to the second bend of the third lap until Adam Roynon locks up, sees his front wheel crumple underneath him to spit him from his bike for a painful looking tumble ("Aw, good looking tumble"). Barbara Horley awards the race while inside the trackshop Johnny Barber tells me "'little shit Adam Roynon'. He's a little shit cos I like him and he keeps getting injured, oh, and he's a Northerner!"

Nowadays a proud father, Nathan Hollands briefly pauses from his many raceday duties around the stadium. "I haven't been to Weymouth but I've only heard bad things but I can't comment as I haven't been. Stoke, I don't like the track – the people are nice but the track, well? The clubs with big crowds know how to promote and the ones with small ones don't! To be honest, for Keith and myself, running the National League team is to give them a ride – so long as they're improving that's the main thing. Someone has to finish bottom and this year that looks like it might be us!" After Adam Roynon's fall and Cal McDade's engine failure gifts the Monarchs a 5-0 heat advantage, they follow up with a comfortable but processional maximum heat advantage from Kalle Katajisto and Kevin Wölbert to take the scores to an already problematic 3-14. 'U Can't Touch This' plays over the speakers and Mike Bennett notes, "You can see why they are the League champions elect!" By the standards meeting so far, the drawn heat 4 represents something of an improvement in fortunes for the Stars. Prior to heat 5, a King's Lynn fan loudly advises Ryan Fisher, "Don't you turn left!" Unlikely to heed any advice from Norfolk-based fans, Ryan Fisher wins easily. Seeking any explanation (no matter how flimsy), Mike Bennett sympathises with Kozza Smith about his last place, "Clearly Kozza was underpowered in that one".

[1] "Oh here we are and here we are and here we go".

Johnny Barber is barely able to contain his excitement about a photograph planned for next week at the Norfolk Arena. "You know Phil Hilton – the speedway photographer? Next week he's lined up Lasse Bjerre, his dad and Kenneth is going to be here as well as Aaron Summers – you know, the blonde one from Birmingham – he's going to send the photo to the *Speedway Star* with the caption "Goldilocks and the Three Bjerres!" This is the sort of stuff Bennett would never dream with coming up with!"

[Mike Moseley] "You realise he's gonna write that down."

[Johnny] "Oh well, it could be any Bennett! At Mildenhall they once said 'and next week Eastbourne No. 1 and captain Gordon Bennett!'"

Photographs are suddenly all the rage. Johnny can't resist a photo of my Danny Bird Racing baseball cap ("it's for my book, I'm thinking of going round the tracks and writing a book"). Elsewhere in the stadium sight of Mike Bennett with his microphone is enough to instil reluctance in even the most chilled of speedway riders. "Kevin Doolan is down in the pits helping the boys out. We're going to have a word – he was here but he saw the mic. We'll get him later!" The chance to craft the ultimate speedway book isn't something to pass up lightly. "Jonathan Chapman thought my books were getting a bit stale. He suggested doing 'a day in the life of a speedway rider' (35 times)". Johnny's not so sure I understood him correctly. "What he really meant was – how about a year in the life of a speedway promoter and football manager!"

Out on the track without Goldilocks or the other two Bjerres, Lasse tries a speculative last-gasp run round the outside of bends three and four only to then find his route blocked by Matthew Wethers. With Lasse about to strike the bend-four safety fence, sensibly he decides to swiftly slacken off and coast to the line gesturing as he goes at referee Barbara Horley as if he's suddenly remembered to audition for *Vision On*! His virtuoso display of youthful Danish petulance gifts second place to William Lawson on the finish line. Unable to escape because of his injury and, probably, to get his punishment out of the way, Kevin Doolan finally succumbs to the penetrative questions that are the hallmark of all truly great Mike Bennett interviews. In response to Mike's rictus grin and casual question, "It must really hurt to see the boys struggling like this", Kevin gives good avuncular but really has no choice but to toe the party line, "Yeh, it really sucks! Everyone is giving 110%, they're just a little off the pace!"

Edwin Overland's interval announcement about my book discombobulates Mike Bennett, "I wonder if I could do something like that?" I'd certainly pay over the odds for any book written by Mike Bennett. Given his long involvement in the sport, let alone the way overconfidence hangs about him like a cheap aftershave, I'm sure it would make fascinating reading. The advent of the typewriter ensures that no joined-up handwriting is required. However, given the difficulty Mike clearly has – even after many decades practice – actually verbally marshalling his lava flow of thoughts into effective or illuminating descriptions of the real-time cut and thrust during any King's Lynn speedway meeting, serious doubts must still remain about whether Mr Bennett really can "write down what I see at speedway". Like myself, Edwin is desperate to get hold of a copy of this – as yet – unwritten book, "Can you put me down in Chapter 7?"

Obviously, the lightning repartee between Edwin and Mike is an oral joy after the solo stream of consciousness that precedes it. The effortless lunge and parry, wit and retort of their off-the-cuff conversation immediately marks Mike and Edwin out as the Norfolk Arena's equivalent of highly thought of stoners Cheech and Chong, albeit without the American accents and drugs. "Edwin, you've got me thinking, I really do think I should write a book on this season and we won't be changing the names to protect the guilty that's for sure!" Supposedly happier working with pictures (and animals), Mike Bennett's subsequent statement "I don't read many books but I can

190

tell you that Michael Lee's book is a great read. No holds barred! Whatever you think of his life, it's well worth getting!"

Speedway author and Monarchs fan Gary Lough is down from Scotland. Olly Allen's first-bend first-race tumble failed to impress him, "He dived like a B-LOUSE".
[Jeff] "Like a what?
[Gary] "Like a B-LOUSE, a big girl's blouse."
[Jeff] "I thought you were talking about a Scottish mouse."
[Gary] "I've got to go, I'm on updates duty".
[Jeff] "See you at Glasgow?"
[Gary] "I'm not a glory hunter but I'm not going because Sheffield Wednesday are playing Brentford on Sky. I could see both but [pause] nah!"

With the scores far from poised at 22-34, Kevin Wölbert falls on the pits turn and is disqualified. The rerun ends as a close contest when Kalle Katajisto edges inside Olly Allen on the first bend. Like a post-modern sound engineer endlessly practising the same trick, after three and a half laps of every race Mike Bennett clicks on his mic and, though we can already hear the roar of the bikes live anyway, over the loudspeakers we get the additional treat of the hypnotic thrum of speedway bikes racing interwoven with banal interjections. You'd pay good money to hear this kind of soundscape at Tate Modern but, accompanying every race, it soon verges on tiresome. On this occasion, Mike switches on his microphone in order to provide us with yet another oh-so-important but thrilling insight, "Yes, a well-deserved wheelie for Kalle Katajisto!" With his team patently out of sorts, Stars team manager Rob Lyon extracts maximum benefit from the tactical options available. They follow up their 8-1 in heat 6 (through Allen and Bjerre) with a 7-2 in heat 11 from Tomáš Topinka and Adam Roynon. Mike Bennett needs no second invitation to pucker up his lips to whisper sweet nothing towards the vicinity of Rob's nether regions, "Well, a bit of inspired team management by Rob Lyon as the black-and-white works its magic!"

Heat 13 pits Olly Allen and Tomáš Topinka against Ryan Fisher and Andrew Tully. It's a line-up that stirs Edwin Overland's fertile imagination, "Heat 13 looks a particularly interesting one to me – it really does!" An unsatisfactory start ensures that the initial attempt to run this "interesting" race fails to reach the first corner. News that Barbara Horley issues "a warning to the rider in white [Ryan Fisher] to remain stationary at the start" prompts the biggest cheer of the night (so far) from the home-straight grandstand. Olly Allen then nearly doesn't make the rerun. From the centre green, Mike Bennett tries to help resolve the situation by telegraphing Olly's emotional state to other potentially interested parties, "Message for Olly Allen's pit crew – not happy!" With the race still to get under orders, Nathan Hollands wanders by, "What's the score?"
[Jeff] "35-42."
[Nathan] "35-42!"
[Jeff] "You could still win."
[Nathan] "Could do [pause] theoretically."

Moments later Jonathan Chapman also passes by. He's changed into a rather smart Simon Templar-esque brown jacket with a dapper back flap styling feature and the somewhat obscure words (to someone of my generation) "Super Dry JPN" written on his garment. "It's a good crowd tonight – we threw it away in the first 12 heats!" Jonathan also admires my Danny Bird Racing baseball cap, "Funny enough, I was just thinking about Danny Bird the other day. What a waste of talent!" I understand all might not be lost, "He still can't come back? Can he?" Jonathan feels differently "He should have paid his fine, then he could have come back by now if he'd wanted!"

191

Given a second opportunity, Ryan Fisher ensures a drawn heat 13. The penultimate race is won comfortably by Monarchs No. 2 Kalle Katajisto to record a four race maximum 12 points. The only real drama in the race is a wild finish from Kozza Smith, "Wow! Bit of a scary finish to that one but, thankfully, Kozza managed to stay on!" Prior to the last race of the night we experience the treat of some centre-green interviews. Jonathan Chapman confides over the stadium speakers, "It's been a difficult night but it's not all doom and gloom…yeh, we started on the back foot but I'm positive! We're not going to come out of it too bad considering we're against the best team in the League…Rob [Lyon] is here now and I'm sure he'll give his opinion." Mike Bennett requires no second invitation to fawn over Robert, "Very quickly, it didn't start the way you wanted."

[Rob] "Clearly Edinburgh will be good champions and congratulations to them but we're building for next year!"

[Mike]"But, they, haven't won the treble!"

[Rob] "No [laugh] we have twice."

[Mike] "They'll certainly clinch the championship this weekend – congratulations – we know what it's like because we've been there and done that!" Mike also pressgangs Matty Wethers into service and cunningly, with one heat to go, has question that's both correct for tonight and also the season, "It's not over yet?"

[Matty] "Yeh, mathematically it could still go wrong but, yeh, we're not gonna let it go."

[Mike] "You could have eased off."

[Matty] "We didn't come out to be second best, we came out to win at whatever the cost."

[Mike] "You'll soon be champions but, hey, we know what that's like – it's nice but we like to share it around! I'm going to be on one of Mike Hunter's DVDs so I'm chuffed about that."

Edinburgh's No. 2 Kalle Katajisto extends his maximum with a win in heat 15 and, with Ryan Fisher second, the Monarchs give no impression of easing off as they win comfortably 42–53. With many exciting Premier League fixtures still ahead before the season closes, Mike Bennett has some good news and bad news for the fans, "I'll be off next week but back the following week." Edwin Overland abandons the referee's box (to do "media interviews" in the pits) so Kevin "100% professional" Moore gets to take over presentational duties for the second half. The combination of a lack of scorecard in the Official Raceday Magazine throws into yet sharper relief Kevin's trademark bereaved Speak Your Weight machine style of presentation. Though it's a Wednesday night, some Edinburgh fans still came to Norfolk. They conduct their post-meeting analyses in the bar but also by the urinals in the gents toilets, "Kevin Wölbert's mechanic thinks Barbara Horley doesn't like Germans." "She got two decisions wrong – I thought Olly Allen should have been excluded in heat 1." With four races of the second half already completed John Campbell is half way through a celebratory pint in the bar surrounded by fellow Monarchs aficionados. "We're having a drink to celebrate. Just one, mind! We'll be having another at Stoke on Saturday and at Glasgow on Sunday!"

1st September King's Lynn v. Edinburgh (Premier League) 42-53

CHAPTER 23

Glasgow

"It's difficult, there's so many other bits going on in the world – speedway is getting smaller!"

5th September

With quite a few hours before the tapes rise for this afternoon's Premier League local derby meeting between Glasgow and Edinburgh, there's already a considerable crowd of people gathered on the rough ground of the car park close by the pits gate. While there's a mix of vehicles from the swish to the much loved but slightly battered, the age profile is much more veteran than school. Hardly a surprise given speedway's national age profile but also expected here this afternoon since, prior to the meeting, the Scottish branch of the WRSA hold their annual lunch and AGM in the Ashfield Stadium bar. Despite the real intensity of the passion for their respective speedway clubs, Glasgow and Edinburgh supporters mingle amiably. Glasgow fan and STARS vice chair Alison Chalmers introduces me to Ronnie Anderson – one of the directors of Edinburgh speedway (whose modesty means that he omits to mention that he's sponsored many riders over the years including Les Collins and Robert Ksiezak). Alison originally met Ronnie on a golf course in Cyprus. Though only formally confirmed as 2010 Premier League champions last night at Stoke, Ronnie and his colleague Geoff Craythorne (SWRSA treasurer) both already wear T-shirts emblazoned with the phrase, "2010 Champions". Alison is here with her daughter Laura who rushes over with some injury news, "Have you heard our jinx has struck again? We were supposed to have Rempala but he crashed!" It's not news to me: "Yes, at Edinburgh when Rymel broke a bone in his neck.." Alison corrects my misapprehension. "No it was last night in heat 6 – he was run over and his crash helmet split in four. His chin hit the track and his helmet shattered into four. It did its job I s'pose! We were supposed to have Jade Mudgway too but we've Jake Anderson instead. I don't know why!" Alison certainly knows her speedway and also has quite a reputation for the accuracy of her pre-meeting results forecasts. "They say I'm the prediction queen – I'm going for 41-49."

Track prep

Pits scene

It's hard to get into the Speedway Office this afternoon because the area directly outside it forms the front of the stage for presentations to the Scottish branch of the WRSA. There's an impressive crowd of branch members – many of them smartly dressed, some proudly displaying their respective team colours. SWRSA President Jimmy Tannock sports an impressive chain of office. With hardness of hearing likely to afflict some of those present, they massively amplify each speaker's words but this doesn't distract from the convivial atmosphere. I dash past into the inner sanctum of the Glasgow Tigers Speedway Office seconds after the seated but attentive crowd are told, "I've got 12 copies of the accounts here. I'll put them on the tables and give you a two-minute thumbnail sketch of what goes on". Inside the office, co-promoter Alan Dick sits behind a desk piled with impressive quantities of paperwork. It's been a difficult season, though the wooden spoon will go to the Redcar Bears. "We've had a bad year jinxed with injuries again this season. You can't help these things but it isn't made any easier by our local rivals doing so well! They're champions every other year. We're pleased for them, of course, but it's added pressure!" [Jeff] "These things are roundabouts and swings."

[Alan] "I'm not so sure about that anymore! Like many people in speedway, we've had a struggle with crowds. We're averaging 700 when we need 800 – we've only had that twice this season, so far! Edinburgh will bring 100 or 150 today so we should do okay. Edinburgh are a powerhouse team – incredible! They've got 28 away points so far this season already. They've only lost away twice – at Berwick – by a big score and I forget where else. It's phenomenal! They've even won three times at King's Lynn! No one does that!" Talk of declining crowds prompts me to mention that some clubs have supplemented their income by successfully running stockcar meetings, "Rob Godfrey says they get big crowds, who drink the bar dry and eat all the food." Alan's already well aware of the various revenue raising initiatives of other promoters. "Buster Chapman tells me that they do that there too! Every week they get big crowds and they also drink the bar dry and sell out the food. People say they get a massive amount a week. Stockcars definitely pays for their speedway (they only break even, at best). I've never seen the appeal of stockcars myself. Ipswich wants to drop down – they only get 600 a week and you can't survive on that! Poole are the model on which all speedway clubs need to run, if they can. They're the only major sport in town, they get full coverage on the back page of the local papers in Poole and Bournemouth pretty well every night and they get a staggering amount insponsorship a season! Then they do have a commercial manager whose job it is to wine and dine someone – sponsors, local newspaper sports editors and that – throughout Dorset a couple of nights every week! It's very, very professional. Really the best! No one else is anything like it."

[Jeff] "They say Dudley have big crowds."

[Alan] "It's all the old Cradley Heath fans – have you been?"

[Jeff] "Not yet!"

[Alan] "I suspect they're mostly older fans and it's the young fans who are the life blood of any club. They're the ones any speedway club need to attract to have a future!" Quite what else the future holds or might require, I don't get to learn since the phone on Alan's desk rings endlessly (mostly with callers keen to establish if this afternoon's meeting will go ahead).

Glasgow Tigers official (and member of the BSPA results team) Michael Max strolls past in the mid-afternoon sunshine, "It's a lovely day but I'm exhausted. I was at Scunthorpe Friday and Newport last night so it's been a lot of driving!" SCB referee Dave Watters joins us clutching a laptop – the essential tool of the modern referee's trade – and a bottle of chocolate yoghurt. Michael Max embraces his inner housewife, "Dave Watters always has the whitest – and I mean the whitest – shirts in speedway."

[Dave] "I give them to the mother-in-law."

[Michael] "There was a football referee called Alan Ferguson who always tried to be a bit different and he once came out in an all-white strip and, afterwards, Jim McLean – the manager of Dundee United – said the ref was brilliant but bloody awful! Very funny! Hope you've got a pen cos there's lots of changes, the latest version of the team means we're now up to four fit riders and one who's not 100%, so five in total!" Dave Watters officiated at Berwick versus Redcar last night, "Because of the eight falls we had 47 minutes of delays but I managed to get the last eight races run in 45 minutes. At one point there was a chance the Berwick Bear was gonna ride [pause] he had the No. 8 on his back. Jade Mudgway impressed me as well – until he fell."

[Michael] "Last night at Newport, the track was magnificent! So magnificent, Masters took 0.3 seconds off the track record. The floodlights were okay. The track was the best it's ever been! Sadly Ronnie Allen did foul-up in heat 15 when Masters got his bike stuck under the airfence on the crown of the first and second bends. Ronnie didn't put the light [red] lights on until the first bend of the next lap. Masters was trying to get up but that was really dangerous – given he was the ref when Garry Stead was injured, he should be more careful! I said to him, 'That was downright dangerous,' and Ronnie replied, 'You don't know what I was thinking'. I said, 'I don't, but I know what I was thinking and it was downright dangerous!' but he wasn't having it: "There was no danger!'"

Though eventful nights were had at both Berwick and Newport, Dave Watters reports that wasn't the case at the Elite League Pairs meeting. "Chris Durno rang me after the Ipswich meeting and said that there was only one pass all night because the teams were so imbalanced by the time they got to stage it. Chris expected the semi-final to be better but it was Poole against Joe Jacobs." Michael Max's pre-meeting duties call him elsewhere. Before he dumps his laptop, papers and yoghurt drink in the referee's box prior to his track inspection, Dave Watters lingers for a few more words. He's heard on the grapevine that I'm not presently welcome at both Weymouth and Stoke, "Speedway is full of people with strong opinions. I don't mind what they say on the forums – in fact, I quite enjoy it because I have a thick skin. But I'd be worried if you wrote about me because you can be quite scathing."

[Jeff] "Can I? I just try to be honest."

[Dave] "It must be hard not to be brutal given all that goes on and how bad it can be at some places! [nods towards my *News of the World*] What's Wayne Rooney been up to now?"

[Jeff] "He's allegedly been sleeping with a £1,200 a night call girl and her friend. At least, he's heading in the correct age direction nowadays!"

[Dave] "Don't let bad reactions put you off what you're doing! Back in 2004, I had just attended the referee's seminar in York prior to my first meeting as a trainee. I arrived at my training track and they were unaware it was to be my training track which upset the promotion right from the off. The referee for that first meeting turned up and smoothed everything out, pointing out an e-mail that had been sent from the SCB. We began by doing the track walk and noticed many things that the promotion had done during the winter to improve the stadium. Also we noticed that the capping on top of the fence was not up to standard (something we had been told to look out for during the seminar) so after the track walk the referee and I set off to find the promoter. The clerk of the course advised us he was in the changing rooms. We went to the changing rooms and walked in. There, standing on the bench completely naked and drying himself off following a shower, was the promoter. The referee started to talk to him and as soon as he mentioned that the capping was not up to standard, he blew his top he was effing and blinding saying how much time and effort had been put into the stadium not to mention the amount of money that had been spent during the winter break. During all this I was stood directly behind the referee, looking at what was going on and thinking 'what have I let myself in for?' and getting more and more embarrassed by what was happening in front of me. I couldn't quite believe what was going on. I had never seen anything like the promoter was really going off on one, at some

195

point I must have just smiled a little bit with the embarrassment and that was when he gave me both barrels. All I can recall was his parting shot: 'And you smiler, you can fark off, if you think you are going to referee at my track!'. I couldn't believe it. I had been a trainee referee for about 15 minutes and had been told I would never referee at my training track. The poor referee calmed things down, however, and I was allowed to continue at the training track. He had had a difficult night and hadn't even started a race ..."

There's a party atmosphere among the Edinburgh fans inside Saracen Park. Mary Kelly wears yet another version of the Monarchs 2010 Premier League Champions T-shirt, "I got it for Karen. They were selling them last night at Stoke. There was a great atmosphere. I must away and get my spot next to my husband who's a Tigers fan!"
Gary Lough's dad Alan is as friendly as ever, "I'm surprised Gary's not coming today."
[Jeff] "Isn't he staying in to watch Sheffield Wednesday versus Brentford?"
[Alan] "They got humped 1-0."
[Friend] "I thought things were going to go badly after Berwick."
[Jeff] "Where else have you lost?"
[Alan] "At Workington, but we also lost at King's Lynn at the start of the season. Apart from that, it's been good!"

Though the turnstiles have hardly opened, it's announced that "If you've got your raffle tickets ready, we're going to have the raffle now". Unless they draw the raffle after the sale of only about ten tickets, I suspect this must be the raffle from the WRSA meeting in the bar. Two men arrive in rather showy fluorescent kilts while, on the centre green, Mystic Meg (a.k.a. Michael Max) forecasts a ferocious welcome from the Tigers, "I'm sure they'll be out to add a derby scalp to their record!" Michael conducts the rider introductions and parade with his usual bonhomie, "It's only fitting we give the Monarchs fans a chance to greet their riders". Without Derek Sneddon to boo, Ryan Fisher ("the next man needs no introduction and is one of the best riders in the Premier League") is the pantomime villain for the more boisterously partisan of the Tigers fans. Keen to set the narrative and, with a more than a hint of getting your excuses in early, Michael tells us, "Let's say hello to the Tigers – it's more of a select side with injuries dominating!" Apparently entertainment remains the ultimate goal of the afternoon, "No matter what, the idea is to have fun and I'm sure that the Monarchs fans will do that today no matter what happens…let's remember it's the country's number one family sport and let's keep it that way!" There are also visitors to welcome: "Hello to all at the Scottish Ducati Club in hospitality unit number two" and myself "bastion of authors".

Once again this season, the Glasgow track attracts critical comment including from its own supporters. So much so that Tigers co-promoter Stewart Dickson actually addresses these concerns in print (in the *Speedway Star*). "I can assure our supporters that we are looking at various options to improve the standard of racing for next season. We cannot do an awful lot this year but we will exhaust a whole load of avenues before we decide on what course of action to take. There has been a lot more shale added in recent weeks to try to give the track something extra and that is an ongoing process. We definitely got it wrong last close season when we took away some of the banking and that is something that will definitely be rectified during the winter. We do appreciate that our fans are not happy with what they are seeing and we are addressing the problems, but it will be next season before we will see the true results of our efforts." If these grumbles weren't enough, fellow Tigers co-promoter Alan Dick also identifies another peculiar (albeit less talked about) factor. "I have no idea why it is but throughout the league I have noticed that the away teams seem to be having the better of things off the starts. This is most strange and I can't recall it ever happening in this magnitude before. It has a huge effect at our place as the

196

chances of passing at the moment are somewhat limited so gating is paramount." The imperative to gate is clearly a lesson that Ryan Fisher needs no second invitation to learn or apply. Jake Anderson of the Tigers is in second place at the first bend but, then, almost stops stock-still to cause Jason Lyons (who guests in place of injured Glasgow captain Joe Screen) to shut off and allow Matthew Wethers past. Up front Fisher flies along at quite some pace. So much so that Michael Max observes, "I suspect that was pretty quick." Jokingly Alison Chalmers suggests she's already seen enough, "I'm gonna go home now and have a glass of wine. This is the third week of this!"

Alison's afternoon didn't start promisingly. "When I was sat at the WRSA lunch, Laura signalled through the window 'Lee Dicken' and I thought she was joking. Lee Dicken's form is pathetic!" Captain Lee Dicken's column in the programme says he'll sit out this weekend in order to try to recuperate from the cumulative impact of his recent injuries but, with replacements for Jade Mudgway thin on the ground, instead he steps back into the breach in the Tigers No. 6 race tabard. When the reserves race gets underway, we see a battle royal between William Lawson and Lee Dicken ("Two riders taking every single bit of shale"). Behind them both Ashley Morris and Jake Anderson add to the entertainment when they mount the white boards round bends three and four on successive laps. Judged purely on artistic merit, Morris's traverse has slightly greater style and also benefits from the surprise element. Like many others, Tigers fan Tom Bryce notices the track changes over recent years. "Les Collins could pass from anywhere. Shane Parker could ride the outside brilliantly – and the inside – I suppose we were spoilt but it's different now!" Kalle Katajisto touches the tapes before heat 3 gets underway and soon finds himself relegated to the equivalent of speedway Siberia after John Campbell reacts to his exclusion by having him start 15 metres back. If the meeting result was ever in doubt or if the Monarchs needed to massage their overall aggregates points difference, John Campbell would probably send out William Lawson instead. Predictably enough, barring mechanical difficulties, 15 metres proves an unbridgeable gulf and Kalle Katajisto finishes 25 metres adrift of third when he finally crosses the line.

Speedway fans and riders both know that severe physical injury can be only a split second away, irrespective of the severity of the crash. Michael Max suggests we all, "Take a moment to reflect on the very serious injuries sustained by Adrian Rymel – a very popular rider at Glasgow – hopefully the signs are good though small and, hopefully, they're positive." Andrew Tully's comfortable heat 4 victory wins faint praise from both Michael ("I s'pose his gating isn't the sharpest strength but he has this afternoon") and Alison Chalmers ("He usually only gets 3 [points] a meeting – he's got them all at once!"). The fifth race of the afternoon features the first genuine passing manoeuvre of the meeting – if you ignore those on the first corner or caused by mechanical difficulties – when Matthew Wethers passes Nick Morris on the last bend of the second lap to gain third place in a drawn heat. Alison Chalmers isn't exactly a big Monarchs fan. "I've never known champions hated like Edinburgh are this season! How can a 16-year old like Nick Morris find himself at No. 3 [for Glasgow] on an average of 4.76 when Kalle Katajisto spent most of it at reserve? Last season King's Lynn looked as strong as this Edinburgh side but, imagine, if they'd kept Ward at reserve most of the season? Bringing in these 7-point riders and then getting rid of them before they've ridden 12 meetings isn't speedway! They didn't sign a Brit – Ashley Morris – almost until they were champions."

Over in the pits, Michael Max corners the supremely affable Bert Harkins for a brief interview. Though nowadays resident in the Hemel Hempstead area, Bert retains a Glasgow accent, albeit one slightly softened by his years down south. Bert's jokes haven't improved with his time away, "As you say, it goes in cycles – usually motorcycles!" Ignoring the audible groans from the crowd,

197

Michael Max then serves up one of his trademark awkward 'Have you stopped beating your wife yet?' type questions that he just loves to doorstep unsuspecting interviewees with! "What do you see as the future of this great sport?" With the pin already out of this metaphorical political grenade, Bert answers with masterful but bizarrely elliptical diplomacy, "It's difficult, there's so many other bits going on in the world – speedway is getting smaller! The GPs are fantastic but these derby meetings are great!" These type of sensible sounding but ultimately fact-free nonsense answers are the bread and butter of political life. Clearly it's a world Bert would thrive in, if he hadn't spent his life on or around the shale.

After a scoreless first ride, Jason Lyons's disappointing afternoon continues with a 180 degree swivel at the crown of bends three and four (when in second place). This causes carnage amongst the Morrises. Nick Morris lays down with zeal while Edinburgh's Ashley Morris bumps into the bend-four safety fence. Lyons's exclusion is inevitable. At the time Michael Max blames Jason's unexpected manoeuvre on him "hitting a hole or a rut". Afterwards the *Speedway Star* would report Jason's clutch spring went and injured his hand in the process. Tom Bryce isn't surprised, "The Glasgow jinx hits Lyons! He's been going well everywhere and, I see, he won the Cumberland Classic [in Workington] last night." The rerun sees Andrew Tully provide the second proper passing manoeuvre of the afternoon with a swoop outside the Tigers young but impressive Australian Nick Morris on the fourth bend of the second lap. Alison Chalmers isn't Andrew Tully's greatest fan, "He's one of the most arrogant riders I've ever seen here!" Glasgow's first heat advantage of the afternoon arrives in heat 7 via a race win for Lee Complin [guesting in place of Josh Grajczonek] ahead of Kevin Wölbert. Third-placed Lee Dicken proves something of an immovable object for the hard-chasing Monarch Kalle Katajisto who explores the outside racing line on bend four for consecutive laps but is stymied by heavier shale. Though this narrows the scoreline to 18-24 Alison's much more enamoured with the novelty of the situation. "Did you know it's the first time Kevin Wölbert has graced us with his presence? He's always busy on a Sunday! Did you hear what time we finished last week? Twenty to seven! The red lights failed at heat 3 and took 20 minutes to fix. We had two bad crashes that had the ambulance on the track and then, just after six before heat 13, they said 'We're going to have a collection for the Riders' Benevolent Fund'. Why couldn't they do that when fixing the red lights?"

Michael Max catches up with Stewart Dickson for some thoughts on the afternoon so far and soon learns, "The boys are still battling away."
[Michael] "Obviously it's a disappointing run but so much is down to injuries – this is not a bad side but devastated through injuries!"
[Stewart] "You can run excuses all day but the bottom line in this game is results."
[Michael]"There's plenty of positives for the future – Screeny is going to be a big influence on and off the track, I believe."
[Stewart] "We're going to improve the track here – put some banking on and get some better racing for the fans!"

The possibility of a Glasgow revival briefly flickers into life for the duration of the first lap of heat 8 but, with the Tigers on a 5-1, Anderson falls on the second bend to gift the Monarchs a draw (rather than narrow their advantage to only 2 points). Glasgow actually also look likely to get a 5-1 in heat 9 until Andrew Tully falls when third and, slightly ostentatiously, stays down on the track until referee Dave Watters illuminates the red lights. Unlikely to be enraptured with Andrew Tully no matter what he does, Alison Chalmers isn't impressed, "He was so at it! Why – that's professional cheating!" With a more than hint of collective disgruntlement at the news that there will be a rerun, Michael Max puts his legendary familiarity with the rulebook to good use, "The referee doesn't have the authority to award it as all four riders haven't completed two laps!"

198

Reviewing her own version of Michael Max's job description (and ignoring the notional help he provides to Stewart with his managerial duties), Alison notes, "For a centre-green presenter, he spends an awful lot of his time nosing in the pits."

Bert Harkins is another who takes in the action from the pits. "I'm here for the Scottish Riders' reunion. 65 people tried to fit in with the derby meeting." Waving his arm expansively and slightly proprietorially at the panoramic scene in front of him Bert burbles with some pride, "It's a lovely compact stadium with lovely red shale and proper grass on the centre green! Lovely! It must be one of the oldest tracks – with Sheffield – it goes back to the '40s and '50s. It's a shame speedway doesn't get more publicity nationally!"

A short distance away Edinburgh co-promoter and team manager John Campbell stands in a central vantage point but close to the away section of the pits. It's a strategic position that enables him to see the action on the track in one direction and the activity amongst his riders in the other. "We're the team everyone wants to see and, of course, everyone wants to beat! That means you get a great atmosphere and good racing, wherever we go! I was saying to one of the media people earlier that Ryan Fishes rides everywhere very well whereas the rest vary. If we clicked as a team – which we haven't yet – we'd get 70!"

[Alex Harkess] "This is the ref that fined me 150 quid for swearing at him. I told him I never effin' swear at referees and I also told him – in the time when the sport is under real pressure – why can't you make it 50 quid?"
[Alan Dick] "He put it back to 150 quid after I spoke to him! When are you putting in Berwick?"
[John] "We don't know yet."
[Alan] "Why not?"
[John] "We might get knocked out of the play-offs yet."
[Alan] "We could do with a meeting as we're not going to be in the Young Shield."
[Alex] "We're very committed to the Scottish Cup as part of the calendar."
[Alan] "Good."
[Alex] "Is it second bottom for the third year running then, Alan?"
[Alan] "Yes, but not the wooden spoon!"
[Alex] "Sooo, it is second bottom three years running then!"
[Alan] "Yes."
[Alex] "I just couldn't resist asking."
[John] "We could have meetings right to the end of the season."
[Alan] "We won't – so can I schedule a meeting here, then?"
[Alex] "Of course."
[John] "Sure, no problem."

The meeting properly slips away from the Tigers during heats 10 and 11 with successive 5-1s for the Monarchs (though Jason Lyons does finally get on the score sheet with a solitary point). With a friend, Laura Chalmers now watches the race action from close to the apex of the first bend having also already stood this afternoon on the home and back straights. It doesn't make the spectacle any easier to take and, as a loyal Glasgow Tigers fan, she's definitely not consoled by my enjoyment of Saracen Park, "You're lucky to have a stadium and speedway club like this."
[Laura] "I know, I just wish we were better."
[Jeff] "That's speedway."
[Laura] "I'd still like better."

Tigers team manager Stewart Dickson tries to hit back using his tactical options. Nick Morris doubles his second place points in heat 12, while heat 13 sees Lee Complin go one better when he rides a brave outside line past Andrew Tully on the first corner as a prelude to a battle royal

199

with Ryan Fisher. He emerges victorious to earn praise from Michael Max, "A very, very fine race". Though these points massage the scoreline, the situation is still arithmetically hopeless (according to Michael Max's *ad hoc* calculations prior to heat 14), "The Monarchs just need one finisher in that race to guarantee the match, er, maybe two finishers." When the race gets underway, Travis McGowan battles on the first lap to gain and retain his lead from Kalle Katajisto, whose second place ensures a Monarchs victory. Tom Bryce praises the Australian, "He's not the most stylish rider McGowan but he gets the job done!" Alison Chalmers takes vague reassurance in the 41-48 scoreline, "I predicted accurately but just over 14 heats." Guest Jason Lyons's haul of one point from four rides this afternoon mystifies her. "He was my husband Robert's first favourite – when a raw 19-year old he was so exciting – we followed him everywhere! I've always followed Jason Lyons's career. He's one of my all-time favourite riders. I always look for his results but I've never seen him this poor! It must be an off day but it shows he's approaching the end of his career." As a counterpoint to the various Monarchs 2010 Premier League Champions clothes of allegiance proudly worn by Monarchs fans, there are a couple of ABE ("Anyone but Edinburgh") T-shirts adapted from the chip-on-the-shoulder football World Cup version ("Anyone but England") favoured by passionately patriotic Scotland soccer fans.

The last race of the meeting has all its action on the back straight. Travis McGowan leads until Wölbert gets in his way. This prompts him to knock off and, thereby, allows Complin to overtake. Fisher also accelerates past, so much so that with great velocity he smashes back first into the bend-three safety fence. Somewhat exultantly Tom Bryce exclaims, "He tastes a lot of shale!" Alison Chalmers admires the experience Travis McGowan brings to the team, "Some of the speeds he goes into that second bend you'd think – oh no! Probably that's his Elite League experience. He's had big boots to fill but everyone likes him. When Sky were at Somerset, he said how lovely Glasgow was as a club." Ryan Fisher's impact on the third-bend safety fence holds up proceedings, "Sorry for the slight delay for the repairs to a damaged kickboard – thankfully the only thing today!"

Quite a knot of Edinburgh fans stay after the meeting to celebrate as their riders go round on the parade truck (in the company of Michael Max). "Here they are if you want to love them or leave them! There's only six of them cos Ryan Fisher has disappeared to his van to negotiate his way out!" These Monarchs fans exult and some sporting Glasgow fans also clap politely. Referee Dave Watters enjoyed the meeting but now finds himself blocked into the car park so decides to sample some of the nearby amenities. "I can't get out so I'm going to go over the road to get a bottle of pop – from Honest Abdul's, supposedly." Alison Chalmers's dad, Danny Wilmoth, makes his way to the exit. "The biggest surprise is William Lawson. He's gone right down the tube – only last year he went Elite. We tried to sign him because he did so well here but, luckily, we didn't!" After her dad leaves, Alison tells me that though he sounds Irish, he's 100% Scottish. "He first came in 1946 – he followed the Ashfield Giants and then Glasgow White City. Riders of that era were people like Ken Le Breton and Tommy Miller. He used to walk here from Bishopbriggs. Their faces were covered in cinders. He says they used to be crushed with 40,000 here and now you can count the crowd!" There's still quite a knot of fans on the home straight when Jason Lyons exits the dressing rooms. He's almost unnoticed as he picks his way anonymously through the crowd holding a big holdall and a can of Carlsberg. Alison tells me, "You know what he was? [pause] A pastry chef until Sean Courtney discovered him. What a change of career!" Further reminiscences are cut short by sight of Josh Grajczonek dressed inappropriately (according to Alison), "Shorts – they're not for Glasgow!"

200 I return the small table they so kindly lent me to the Trophy Room in the undercroft of the home-straight grandstand. It immediately feels like a small but significant step back in time. Though white ceilinged, the room feels dark since it lacks windows but also because it's absolutely ram-packed with every conceivable type of trophy and memorabilia. Commemorative wooden boards decorate the walls. These outline triumphant moments in the Football Club's history while, close to the ceiling, there's an almost continuous line of pennants hung on display. Each trophy cabinet is packed with cups, plates, medals, photographs and sporting knickknacks. The gentleman there is proud to point me in the right direction of what exactly to admire or take in. "That's a picture of when they had the greyhound track here. We've been here since 1934. [1] We were in another stadium down the road. I can't see the photo of the record attendance here versus Clydebank. I think it was 32,000. In the '60s they had a concrete start gate but they got rid of them when so many people got hurt!" Filing cabinets, chairs and a large-size old-fashioned television obscure the commemorative panel that celebrates Ashfield Football Club's rich tradition. From what is visible of this list, it's clear that the club experienced their golden era sometime around the turn of the last century. At least, that is my surmise given that they were the Scottish Cup Winners in 1893-94, 1894-95, 1904-05 and 1909-10. They were also losing finalists in 1913-14 and 1920-21. Other honours include trophy success in the Scottish Intermediate Cup, Glasgow Cup, Glasgow Intermediate Cup, League Cup, North Eastern Cup, Maryhill Charity Cup, Glasgow Charity Cup and the Kirkwood Shield. It's a different world located only a few yards away from where the public stand every week in the home-straight grandstand to either watch the speedway or the football.

The relationship between the football club and speedway club is mutually beneficial but the exact nature of their partnership has undergone subtle change in recent years. There was a time when rental income from the speedway club apparently counted for much more than it did until the football club enjoyed greater fortune on the pitch and the promotion their success provided. Consequently, viewed from a neutral speedway perspective, the football pitch has assumed greater importance and, consequently, appears to encroach much more than previously. This is only visible and/or important on the bends where the laws of geometry dictate that the rectangular shape of the centre-green football pitch nowadays intrudes on the natural sweep of the speedway track bends. Nonetheless, judged by Stewart's comments over the tannoy and in the speedway trade press, significant changes are afoot for 2011. Alison Chalmers anticipates these changes will come to fruition, "They're going to widen the back straight six or eight feet!" Quite how they can do this, when brick walls ultimately form the perimeter that separates the field of play from the stands is a mystery to those, like myself, without building expertise.

Walking out of the stadium with Ian Maclean, his nearly seven decades of speedway give him a longer-term perspective, "We used to go to Blantyre. It was always a very happy experience. The facilities were awful though! "Saracen Park's changed over the years. I remember when the speedway track was put in and the terracing steeply banked. I passed it on the tram in the morning going to secondary school in the late '40s. The football team was at the top of the tree in those days and, I know, they got big crowds. I don't know when the greyhounds started? It was when they left Firhill (Partick Thistle), early '60s perhaps? The big bar outside was a very popular entertainment venue then – it was a club (The Ashfield Club) but I don't think it had anything to do with the football club. When the Tigers moved to Saracen Park – about 11 years ago – the football club was in the doldrums with very few attending. I know this to be true. Presumably the rent from Tigers – which must have been substantial versus gate receipts – put them on their feet, helped with promotion, something that now requires a bigger pitch! Owners of stadia often get

[1] A highly polished brown board – partly obscured by historic team photographs and a can of furniture polish – is headed "Ashfield Football and Athletic Club, Saracen Park." It then reads "This SCHEME was inaugurated by the OFFICIALS COMMITTEE and MEMBERS of the above CLUB on the 4TH OCTOBER 1934, and work commenced on the GROUND in FEBRUARY 1935. The SCHEME was officially opened on the 31ST OCTOBER 1937."

Glasgow: *"It's difficult, there's so many other bits going on in the world – speedway is getting smaller!"*

jealous of what appear to be big speedway attendances without knowing anything about the costs of running a team. Now the football team is doing well and, fortunately, all concerned realise that it's a symbiotic relationship!" A trip down memory lane doesn't alter feelings in the present, "No one seems happy at speedway, anymore – I'm not anyway!" A contributory factor to Ian's lack of sparkle is yet another home defeat and the disappointing performance of today's guest (for Joe Screen). "Jason Lyons got 1 – it's the second time he's guested badly for us – I doubt they'll ask him again! We only lost by 7 so a good performance might have made all the difference."

5th September Glasgow v. Edinburgh (Premier League) 44-51

Glasgow: *"It's difficult, there's so many other bits going on in the world – speedway is getting smaller!"*

CHAPTER 24

Somerset

"If he saw a lake on the way to speedway, he'd stop off and fish!"

15th September

When two speedway clubs with the same race-night clash, whoever has the shorter history in that league switches to their alternative race night. For their fixture with the Edinburgh Monarchs, Wednesday becomes the Somerset Rebels race night. The initial attempt to run the meeting on August 25th fell foul of the weather and, with dark clouds overhead and strong winds buffeting the Oak Tree Arena, another postponement remains theoretically possible though unlikely since some of the Monarchs riders are in the pits already almost ready to race. Oblivious to the gale-force winds that batter the clubhouse building, Rebels promoter Debbie Hancock works hard in the compact and slightly cluttered office that is the nerve centre of speedway operations. It's also the administration centre for all clubhouse bookings. The phone rings very regularly, "I just had Eric Boocock on the phone pretending to do a Scottish accent. It was awful and would fool no one!" The Hancock family certainly sweat their assets and, outside by the main road, a large sign attempts to excite the curiosity of passing motorists with talk of their facilities, catering skills and possible uses for the venue (from weddings to Bar Mitzvahs). According to Debbie demand is very high. "We've got loads of weddings here and we treat everyone as an individual and try to do exactly what they want! Nothing is too much trouble and the same applies to treating the riders and staff as people. When Jimmy Holder was injured I kept in touch, took him down to Poole to save Boycie doing it and stuff like that. You really get to know them! Doyley has just been injured and it doesn't take anything to ring and find out how he is. I know he appreciates that. I told him I did that with Jimmy and he said 'I know'. It's a shame that no one at Poole has thought to get in touch with him so far."

The arrival in the bar area of the clubhouse of two young men carrying ping-pong bats interrupts our conversation. Without a table, they expertly knock back and forth one of

Bath time preparations

Rider of the year ballot

203

those small sack-like balls used to hone your ball-control skills. Debbie asks the taller of the two – who turns out to be Christian Hefenbrock the Rebels No. 1 (after he dropped down to the Premier League from Elite League Wolverhampton) – in a concerned manner, "What's hurting?" Christian stretches, "My collar bone." Debbie goes to put her hands in the vicinity of the injury but then stops herself, "I would massage it but I'm not qualified!" Rebels press officer and programme editor, Ian Belcher, resists using his healing hands but needs no second invitation to immediately ride one of his hobbyhorses. "It's ridiculous that a rider's Elite League average is doubled when they come down to the Premier League! Someone did the research over the winter with all the riders and found that the ratio was really 1.5 or 0.75 if they go the other way. That would be much fairer!" Debbie has other more prosaic concerns, "I keep being worried whether we'll get into the Young Shield but I chat to the man who knows – Ian – and he tells me we're alright."

Debbie leaves Christian to his ping-pong bat-led recuperation to duck behind the impressive length of the clubhouse bar. "My hero and mentor Rosco is coming down tonight. He's been fantastic! He volunteered to help – he didn't have to! He's so passionate about speedway and knows so much. I've really enjoyed 95% of the season. In a funny way cos we've had such a difficult start, I've learnt more! I've got in touch with all the promoters and, because I was always needing riders, I've got to know tons of them too. In the end, I had to start a database of all the riders' names to make it easier for myself. When we had the 10th Anniversary meeting called off I had all the GP riders down here – Jason, Hans, Chris and that. Jason walked me round the track to explain exactly why they couldn't ride. Imagine your hero – standing out with him in the rain – while he goes through it all! I learnt so much but, then, I did at the AGM. I just listened for three days. Being the only woman in a man's world could have been funny but, ignoring I'm a farmer's daughter, they've all made me feel at home. Some more than others! I'm just myself so they can see who I am." Debbie's not just passionate about Somerset but her speedway generally, "I was surprised by how Peterborough fell off [on Monday] but you could see they might. Bjerre rode poorly while Chris Harris is flying and Krzysztof Kasprzak rode better as the meeting went on."

So far this season not a single Somerset meeting escapes the interest and attention of Ian Belcher. Travelling great distances with fans, other club officials and riders, Ian gets a unique insight into their outlook and personalities. "Steve Boxall was a natural on the bike but he couldn't do anything off it. If it wasn't going right, he couldn't tell you why. Bish said, 'I'll be his manager, if you like?' He needed a manager cos he was easily distracted. If he saw a lake on the way to speedway, he'd stop off and fish! He used to turn up the next week here with the bikes as dirty as when he left the week before. He had all week to clean them! When he didn't turn up at Newport, he didn't call or anything. I dunno what planet he's on?" Like Premier League speedway fans the country over, the arrival in town (in this instance, on the outskirts of Highbridge) of the Edinburgh Monarchs promises both entertainment and a severe test for the home team. "Tonight should be really good as we have two teams with nothing really to race for. Unless Stoke win by 50 against Newport – and you don't know with them, they could win or get thrashed – and we lose by 50, we'll be in the Young Shield! People complain but Edinburgh have done everything within the rules and, interestingly, they replaced Tabaka – after he'd ridden 12 meetings and before the new averages came out – so they can have him back at the start of next [2011] season on a 3-point something average. They did that with [Max] Dilger but he was still rubbish when he came back!"

Speedway merchandise manufacturer and trackshop entrepreneur Andy Griggs has relocated from Norfolk to Somerset. The grounds of the Oak Tree Arena house his new warehouse and his nerve centre of operations in a section of light industrial buildings close to the pits gate. Behind the substantial door of his new manufacturing facility, Andy's hard at work, "Rush jobs have come ill this afternoon for Matt Ford and Ritchie Hawkins who's just become a dad last week." [1] I wonder, "Is Matt getting some Elite League champion's gear done then?" but Andy bats off my suggestion, "Ha ha – not yet!"

Andy runs a high-tech operation if judged by the impressive number of industrial sewing machines in evidence. Each sewing machine has a computerised control panel. The largest has four workstations and the smallest only one. There is also an industrial heat press, transfer press and an impressive cutter plus, mounted neatly on the wall, there are numerous, varying sized metal templates. Jagged edged is their standard look. There's also a separate office – guarded benignly by a friendly older black dog lolling on a chair – where Andy tweaks the designs on various large-screened computer monitors. The workshop and office both have an array of pictures on display. Some of these pictures showcase the breadth and range of Andy's badge and logo manufacturing over recent years. The clubs represented include Rye House, Peterborough and Somerset (as you'd expect) but also shows off the wide variety of work undertaken for other clubs and societies. [2] Given, the military or martial arts leaning of his customers, I half expect Andy to salute or put me in a headlock. Even more excitingly, the inner sanctum that is Andy's partitioned office workspace is festooned with speedway related photographs. Pride of place (or, at least, the one that catches my eye) is a smiling and glamorous Suzi Perry apparently cuddling Andy (possibly because he's wearing a tie). Whenever possible, Andy travels overseas to watch his speedway. There's a large-sized team photo of Polish speedway team Czestochowa. It's of indeterminate but recent vintage with a line up of Edward Kennett, Antonio Lindbäck, Nicki Pedersen, Lewis Bridger, Seb Ułamek and a big Brown Bear Mascot (name unknown). With rush jobs to complete, Andy's preoccupied whizzing back and forth from the computer screen to fastidiously check the single-station industrial sewing machine as it embroiders a badge on some good quality collared casual shirts. Though distracted, Andy still has time to offer a morose forecast on the likely result of the Elite League play-off semi-final second leg between the Panthers and Bees, "Peterborough will win on Monday but not by 14!"

Despite the strength of the wind and the strong possibility of rain, I set up my book display table in the lea of the entrance gates adjacent to one section of the home-straight grass banking. Wearing a Magnus Zetterström sweatshirt, Roy ("battered husband of Diane") Phillips asks, "Who are you then?"
[Jeff] "I do books."
[Di] "I see you've met my husband."
[Jeff] "Have you been to watch Magnus in the GPs?"
[Di] "Nah, we've watched on the telly."
[Jeff] "Will he be back next year?"
[Di] "He's really enjoyed it but I don't think so because they've got too many Swedes – Lindgren, Jonsson and Lindback – so it's very unlikely! He's thoroughly enjoyed it though." As befits her status as Zorro's No. 1 fan, Di has an extensive range of Zorro-related memorabilia and clothing, "I've even got a key ring." Roy shrugs, "So long as he don't turn up in the spare room over the

[1] A baby boy called Bodi Alfie Hawkins.

[2] Cannon Professional, the Carp Society, Blondepoker.com, RAF Vulcan 1957-1984, Gorehounds Scooter Club, Sammy Wright Karate School, Battle of Britain Memorial Flight, Microsoft Professional, St Andrew's Cobra Martial Arts Association, Black Cats, Royal Navy Helicopter Display Team, Red Arrows, Teesside Academy, Shukokai Karate, United States Navy Top Gun Fighter Weapons School, Original Shukokai Karate, BAE Hawk, Milton Keynes Kitsune-Gari Judokwai and a Union Flag with a logo underneath that reads "These Colours Never Run!" There's also another display that lists various company logos that Andy has also produces including Honda, Ready Power, Minster Motors, AT Johnston, Silo Budo, TRM Racing, The Money Centre, Lawtronic, Butters Group, Freshtime, Manor Fresh Ltd, Bryan Thompson Windows Limited, Pegasus Freight Lines Ltd, Solanum (Growing Trust) Castle Cover, MBNG, DRW Howling Transport Ltd, Style Roses, Crisp Malling Group, Moulton Bulb Company Ltd and The Modernizer.com to name but a few.

Somersset: *"If he saw a lake on the way to speedway, he'd stop off and fish!"*

winter – that's what I'd worry about! I've known him since he was at Poole. He's a nice bloke. Always has time for everyone. He says speedway is an entertainment as well as a sport so there's no point waving your hand and dashing back to the pits. You have to entertain people too! And he certainly does that!"

Though always happy to chat about Magnus Zetterström, Di's distracted by the need to make last-minute arrangements ahead of tonight's fundraising venture for the Somerset Riders' Equipment Fund (SREF). "Tiny Tim is to commentate from the centre green in a bath of gravy to raise money for SREF. Debbie and Bill said it was fine but now the ref needs to approve it! I'm going to have to sort it out." Sat forlorn in the middle of the large-sized Oak Tree Arena centre green under darkening skies, an old-fashioned bath awaits its occupant and gravy. Di clutches a clipboard with a wad of sponsorship forms headed with an explanatory message from Tiny Tim. [3] Talk of the devil ensures Tim arrives, though there's no explanation about why gravy now substitutes for jelly. He's told the news that the referee Mick Posselwhite must approve his proposed altruism, "If they say I can't cos of health and safety that's ridiculous!". Demand isn't what it was for the Somerset Clean Cut Sports recordings, "No one has got any money! Most weeks Pete [Ballenger] only sells two DVDs. I must learn not to speak so fast and get so excited but I'm really enjoying it." Tim waves away my suggestion ("If you had rubbish racing, you'd stay calmer") with some passion: "We have brilliant racing here every week – it's fantastic! Unbelievable!"

Our conversation ends when under jet-black skies an early arrival despairs at the sight of the bowser hard at work on the OTA track, "Blimey! They're not gonna water it with all that up there, are they?" Another early bird is 9-year old Henry Atkins – the Somerset Rebels team mascot. Henry and Tim make an unlikely combination stood together. Tiny sings his praises, "He slides the bike like no one else I know!" Henry tells me he's ridden four years and, somewhat strangely, is nicknamed the Wasp. "I'm called the Wasp cos I go quick. I'm like lightning! Whaw!" Later on, after Henry's put in some fast exhibition laps prior to the meeting, his dad proudly highlights his skill on the bike as well as some of riding achievements. "Henry would have been British grasstrack champion but for a loose spark plug last year. On the trophy he has this year, previous winners include Joe Haines and Steve Boxall and, if you go back to 1976, Paul Bentley. Last time he binned it [fell off] over there [fourth bend] for the first time in four years but he was straight back out there tonight [where it looks extremely slippery] and loved it!"

Di returns in frustration since she's not so far found the referee, "He's not here yet!" Through bitter experience, hardworking but unassuming Newport and Somerset track photographer, Hywel Lloyd nowadays keep his own counsel. "People ask me what's going on [at Newport] but I say I don't know. I just take the photographs! I really don't know. They say one thing and do another! I dunno how much money that [club sponsor] dentist has but it must be quite a lot. If I was him and I had that much, I'd have bought the club! Say what you like about Tim [Stone] – he fell out with everyone and me more than most – but, perhaps, he needed me because the Argus don't ever send anyone down there but they keep putting my photos in. So I must be doing something right. He loved Newport speedway! Many more people realise that now." Able to access all areas of the stadium, Di asks if Hywel could kindly share his photograph of the magic moment when Tim actually lowers himself into the slop of a bathful of cold gravy on the centre green. "I'm not talking to him – he's got me in enough trouble in the past. If it's politics, I'm staying out of it!"

[3] My name is Tim Lang a.k.a. Tiny and in one meeting of the season I will be doing my DVD commentary of the whole Rebels match from the centre green in a bath of cold jelly to raise funds for SREF

Somersset: *"If he saw a lake on the way to speedway, he'd stop off and fish!"*

Judith 'Mighty Atom' Rourke strategically sets up her 50/50 raffle table so that everyone who enters the stadium passes close by. Sight of the first load of gravy going out to the bath prompts her to recall previous fundraising events organised by SREF, "We had a cut-out of Emil Kramer with his face missing and Tiny put his head through and everyone threw wet sponges at him." [Di] "He does one every year – he's great at helping us raise some money for SREF. It raised about £250 last year and this year we're hoping for £300 or something around that."

Filling the bath will take many journeys to and from the clubhouse out to the middle of the centre green. Tim already wanders past with his fifth empty bowl but shrugs, "Me and my big mouth, eh!" I'm not so sure about the liquid they use, "That looks like water to me." Di's adamant, "There's gravy mix out there!"

Minutes later when Tim passes with his sixth load of the afternoon, Roy Phillips comments, "What's that – the gravy train?"

Well-travelled trackshop man Bill Gimbeth is on the first day of yet another speedway track tour (albeit without his regular roommate Dave Rattenberry). "I'm here today, Eastbourne tomorrow and Plymouth Saturday, Buxton Sunday and Poole on Monday. I think Coventry are going to win it – they've come good at the right time." Speedway historian and co-author of the acclaimed *Homes of British Speedway*, John Jarvis, comes over all wistful when he recalls how many meetings and speedway tracks he used to visit each season. "I used to do 180 a year! This year I've only done 50 – most at Newport where I haven't missed one yet! That's 38 I think? I've been keeping notes to make sure [*Homes of British Speedway*] is up to date but nothing much has changed. I help Rob Bamford who does the updating nowadays. There's probably seven or eight new training tracks to add but nothing much really. It's too comprehensive really. Some bloke did some research and got in touch to say 'Luton didn't run in '36.' They did in 1934 and in '35 as a training track so, probably, that's wrong but, apart from that, it's probably too accurate really!" Coventry co-promoter Allen Trump bridles at my suggestion that Coventry are now favourites to win the Elite League play-offs. "I don't think we're favourites. Poole are a very good side but, if you come late and hit form – like we have – then, anything can happen! Not only did we come late during the season but even during Monday's meeting. They couldn't even use black and white! I'd like to say we planned it but we didn't!" Itinerant Monarchs fan Dick Jarvis wears in his trademark discoloured light blue anorak and is keen to see another strong performance from Edinburgh, "Oh no it's you!" My claim "I'm your lucky mascot!" is quickly rejected by Dick, "What! Except at Berwick you mean!"

Unusually Steve Miles comes along without his wife Sarah, "She's not here because she's had a big operation."
[Jeff] "What, had her tongue removed?"
[Steve] "Not that major an operation! I can't believe the other night! It sums up our season the way we [Peterborough] fell away!"
[Jeff] "You should beat Coventry at your place but probably not by 14."
[Steve] "I dunno. They beat Ipswich by 2 points recently and Chris Harris only got 6 [actually paid 9]. Krzysztof Kasprzak always went well at our place for Poole."

Like small children the world over, Tiny Tim is suddenly assailed with pre-bath nerves. The credit crunch has even impacted innovative but worthy fundraising schemes like tonight's, "I've only got £4 sponsorship money so far tonight and two of that was from you! Flippin' shocking, innit!"

The threat of rain means that they dispense with the usual pre-meeting pleasantries of the rider parade and lengthy introductions in favour of a prompt start. The main man with the microphone I suspect is Nigel Thomas (though, looking at the programme, it could equally be Jordan Satchell).

Somersset: *"If he saw a lake on the way to speedway, he'd stop off and fish!"*

Whoever it is, they're certainly not short of words or opinion. "There was a theory that the Edinburgh Monarchs would bow their heads outside the pits gate to take your applause on being champions but they're getting on with their bikes. Because of the weather, we're going to go without the parade. The Rebels have won the toss and will take gates one and three." To add to his pre-bath misery Tim, like the rest of the crowd, endures a 10 minute shower prior to heat 1. However, it's all in a day's fundraising and with some fanfare but little ceremony Tim steps into the bath and sits down, "It's big and it's not pretty; and that's just Tim!" With his promise kept, Tim then proceeds to commentate from the bath. Stood on any centre green swivelling round as you follow the riders circling the track at high speed requires sufficient knack to avoid dizziness. In his bath, Tim swivels even more ostentatiously to keep up with the action he commentates upon! Though damp under tyre tread, Matthew Wethers and Ryan Fisher immediately make light of conditions to relegate Ritchie Hawkins to third and Christian Hefenbrock to last to record an opening heat 1-5. "Hey, take it easy you Monarchs, it's not like the Premier League championship depends on it!"

Despite the dampness, both sets of riders appear to race flat out. Somerset hit back with successive 4-2s to level the score. Sam Masters's heat 3 win features lusty battles to stay ahead of Kalle Katajisto. Tim continues to cut a slightly forlorn figure sat in his bath, "I think Tim is slowly wishing it was a bath of jelly as originally intended. The night's wet, the camera's wet, it's slopping everywhere!" An incredibly fast-looking Andrew Tully ("well, considering the conditions, that's the fastest time tonight – 57.04") beats a determined Cory Gathercole in a drawn heat 4. Tim's predicament continues to delight the presentational team, "Well, Mike Atkins is going over there to torture Tim with a cup of tea. I reckon he'll ask for it to be poured on him." I stand with a small knot of fans on the terraces overlooks the fourth bend adjacent to the fourth bend. Bonhomie is in short supply. They're definitely not enamoured with Tim's work on behalf of SREF or, indeed, the attention given to it between races. "Pour it on his bollocks, we really don't care! Guffaw, guffaw, I bet you're glad you've come now so you could listen to this!" Notoriously not the greatest lover of wet shale under his tyres, Somerset captain Shane Parker is relegated to the rear of heat 5 field after only one lap and remains there. Up front, Ryan Fisher comfortably sees off the challenge of Sam Masters. Possibly invigorated by his earlier alfresco version of ping-pong, Christian Hefenbrock wins heat 6 so comfortably that he's able to stop almost a yard from the finish line! Second place goes to new dad Ritchie Hawkins to deliver a maximum heat advantage that converts a Rebels 2-point deficit into its opposite.

There's still fun to be had at bath time although the quality of the jokes start to diminish, "Tim said he had a blue one as well!" Heat 7 sees a lively rush from the start line to the first bend, only for Cory Gathercole and Kevin Wölbert to absolutely batter each other in their battle for second. Kevin retains his advantage until the third lap where he temporarily slows enough to let Cory past. Crossing the line behind Kalle Katajisto, Cory stares studiously straight ahead and goes back swiftly to the pits without so much as a nod or a wave to his rival. The 50/50 raffle is drawn with some ceremony (£100 first prize, £51 second). Though the winners quickly make themselves known, the whereabouts of the collection is altogether different kettle of fish. "I haven't got the ticket here any longer but I have the winner here. If someone can tell me where Di is that would be great!" With the track still tricky, the inspiration of recent fatherhood continues to drive Ritchie Hawkins to excel (and add a race win to his previous paid one). However, the real action is behind him as Rebels guest Simon Lambert and Matthew Wethers give no quarter in their determination to take third. Last at one point, Wethers showcases the form that's made him so consistently reliable this season. Using cunning and track craft in equal measure, he works his way back up into second place by the chequered flag. The announcer stops just short of issuing an All Points Bulletin at the stadium exits, "If Di is around – anywhere local to the ref's box – if she could come to the

---

Somersset: *"If he saw a lake on the way to speedway, he'd stop off and fish!"*

referee's box? Thank you!" After the first eight races fly by in 35 minutes, there's a slight delay for remedial track work. With time to fill, the search for Di expands to include the 50/50 draw winners, "Oh, they've disappeared, we had some winners here looking for Di." With a hint of irritation to go along with the irony, one of the Rebels fans in front of me exclaims, "Oh, there's Di on the top of Brent Knoll!" There's so few illuminating things left to say that the announcer consults the club mobile phone, "We've got some text messages!" One suggests Tim could warm the gravy by having a wee in the bath. "Urgh!" exclaims the disgruntled fan.

Luckily, before even worse text suggestions arrive, the strong gusty wind dries the track. Shane Parker double-underlines the changed conditions with a comfortable heat 9 win and, with Sam Masters third, the Rebels heat advantage gives them a narrow 2-point lead. Back in the pits Matthew Wethers bats off congratulations about the significance of his role in the bizarrely score-lined [44.5-44.5] draw in the first leg of the Elite League play-off semi-final between Wolverhampton and Poole. "Actually, it was one of my lesser performances at Wolverhampton. I wasn't that pleased! I'll be going down to Poole on Monday and I hope they want me back doubling up again next season." Given the high calibre of the competition and the importance of the occasion, 4 points from four rides is far from poor but, doubtless, Matty's perspective is coloured by his two point-less rides (one of them an exclusion). In the next race much more notable for the arrival of dust, Christian Hefenbrock easily sees off the challenge of Kalle Katajisto and Kevin Wölbert in the next race. The bane of innumerable speedway meetings over the decades, tonight's dust is a pleasure to behold since it means the forecast rain still isn't here. Completely unrelated to meteorological and track conditions, shortly afterwards, Tiny Tim abandons his bath on the centre green. In a meeting that sees the lead seesaw throughout, Matty Wethers and Ryan Fisher hammer home a maximum heat advantage only for the Rebels to return the favour immediately through Sam Masters and Simon Lambert. Sam Masters's great speed early doors means he can overcome a last-bend engine failure since he's already got sufficient distance to coast over the finish line to win.

In the trackshop Andy Griggs decides to test my powers of observation with a quiz about his own workshop office, "What photos did I have on the wall then?" Before I can list them extensively my admiration for Suzi Perry prompts Andy to interject, "That's the only one you noticed not the Hans Anderson one or the Edward Kennett – you just looked at the Suzi Perry!" With a 2-point lead to protect, the Oak Tree Arena curatorial team set about an extensive track grade. To pass the time there's the treat of an interview with Alun 'Rosco' Rossiter discussing his divided speedway loyalties. "I've got good memories of riding at Poole and Swindon is my home town and I love them but I have to do what's best for the team and my team is Coventry! Deep down, I didn't think we had a chance but it's pretty special!" Some ('ungrateful') fans grumble that the Sky Sports contract with the Elite League and the concomitant dictates of the television schedules ensure that the actual play-off teams get selected prior to the completion of all the fixtures! "We're short-cutting the supporters – the season don't end until October 30th so I can't see why the cut-off is so early? I've gotta watch what I say, in case I get fined, which I seem to a lot nowadays." As if the early cut-off weren't bad enough, in the last few days before the formal cut-off date, confusion reigned about who had or who hadn't exactly qualified. Indeed, at one point, it looked likely that (before they completed their late-season implosion) Lakeside would occupy fourth place ahead of Coventry, despite the fact that (at that point) they would have ridden one more meeting than the Bees! In the end, the results went against Lakeside and went for Coventry. Nonetheless, most unusually, Rosco is unprepared to offer his opinion, "I can't comment in case I get fined – suffice to say, we got through everything thrown at us!" Rosco is altogether happier to answer questions about mid-season team changes to the Bees line-up that – with the benefit of hindsight – enables them to gain momentum and, thereby, kick on into the play-offs as the

Somersset: *"If he saw a lake on the way to speedway, he'd stop off and fish!"*

form team of the Elite League. "With the three changes, there's Kasprzak and, er, I forget now – help me Nigel!" The sound of the two-minute warning and sight of the riders on their way out saves Rosco from any further floundering as he tries to recall the line-up of the team he manages!

It takes Ryan Fisher until the fourth bend to bump his way past Cory Gathercole in a drawn heat 13. The penultimate race of the night features a master-class in team riding from Shane Parker and Simon Lambert to hold William Lawson behind them. Bizarrely, it's something of a collector's item since it's Simon Lambert who has to slow to wait for Shane Parker before he then proceeds to team ride him home with great acumen and tactical awareness. Trackshop man Andy Griggs looks on approvingly, "Good old Lambert – he's been a good guest!" While we wait for news of the line-ups for heat 15, the text messages come in thick and fast. "This says 'come on Edinburgh!' I reckon they must be Edinburgh supporters". If the Rebels draw the last heat, they'll be another of the few teams to actually defeat Edinburgh in the Premier League this season. Unfortunately the presence of Ryan Fisher – who jets off faster than green grass through a goose – in the race thwarts their ambitions (as does his race partner Matty Wethers finishing ahead of Sam Masters). This last-gasp Monarchs heat advantage sees the meeting end in a 45-45 draw. Despite damp conditions, the Oak Tree Arena lives up to its oft-cited reputation as an exciting speedway venue. Somerset perform creditably as a team (with the exception of Kyle Howarth), while Edinburgh enjoy double figure contributions from Wethers and Katajisto to go along with a paid maximum from Ryan Fisher.

15th September Somerset v. Edinburgh (Premier League) 45-45

Somersset: *"If he saw a lake on the way to speedway, he'd stop off and fish!"*

CHAPTER 25

Plymouth

"My missus reckons it's because it's got Devils in the name!"

18th September

The sixth and final round of the GB Under-15 Championship is on at the shortest and most westerly speedway track in Britain – the St Boniface Arena in Plymouth. Luckily the summer holidays are over so routes down to the South West are no longer choked with holidaymakers and caravans. Nonetheless, it took the Freemantle family around four hours to get there from Steyning in Sussex. Similarly it's taken the Hazelden family nearer five hours to journey across from the Eastbourne area. Earlier in the week the speedway world was rocked to its foundations by news that club chairman Phil Bartlett sought buyers for Weymouth Speedway club. Given the importance of local derby fixtures for the Plymouth promotion and public alike, I ask Devils founder and promoter Mike Bowden if he would bid and, thereby, massively expand his speedway empire. "You're kidding! On a crowd of 120! We get more than that for a practice on a Saturday! He only paid £45,000 for it from Whitie. Perhaps Weymouth, like Newport, is a town where they don't want speedway? We were just at Newport and they only had 120. Steve Mallett's tearing his hair out – I dunno how they survive!" Changing the subject, when I look ahead to this U15 round, "This should be a good meeting this afternoon" Mike replies, "I dunno know about that but it's sunny!"

Since this afternoon Plymouth stage the Under-15 Championship and then this evening the National Trophy clash with Weymouth, Mike has numerous tasks to get on with but still kindly takes the time to suggest where to pitch my book display table. This attention to detail is one factor that enables Mike to buck the trend and run his club at a profit each season (despite declining crowd numbers) since the Devils National League reincarnation at the St Boniface Arena. After I quickly set out the entire Methanol Press back catalogue, my stall attracts little or no interest except for Mike Bowden's grandson, Adam. He immediately runs off to the nearby programme booth, "Mum, mum! I'm in a

Start girls

Under orders

speedway book!" I'm not privy to Angela's reaction but Adam is soon back to chat, "You always pick good meetings to come here. Last year, it was Bournemouth and this year Weymouth and the Under-15s!" Earlier, another of Mike Bowden's affable daughters (Ruth) is happy to chat amiably at the stadium entrance gate when not supervising or helping new U15 arrivals. "Dad's over here, like Blakey, panicking about things and people he hasn't told me who are coming. I got the worst job cos you really have to check every van carefully to see how many they're trying to bring in. Today, it's a nightmare getting all the vans parked! It's full already and I'm missing three. Some of them have ordinary vans but others are massive!" Fortunately, the smaller size of the Weymouth team means fewer vans later, so parking logistics should be less of a nightmare later. The admission charges for this afternoon's Under-15 meeting are extremely reasonable. It's £3 for adults, £2 for OAPs or the disabled, and £1 for a child. Programmes are free but, nevertheless, are more than fit for purpose. From inside the programme booth, Adam's mum Angela is happy to chitchat, "Where are you from?"

[Jeff] "Brighton."

[Angela] "I've heard of that."

[Val] "Everyone has heard of Brighton beach! Hasn't it lost its pier?"

When I arrive back at my book display table, Adam's desire to help and his natural salesmanship prompts him to try to sell my books. I overhear Adam say to the lady stood close by to the display, "£200 and you can have the lot!" Sadly, my books are apparently as presently unsalable as Weymouth speedway club. In common with speedway production companies the country over, Devils DVD man David Hawking's DL Actionsports survives in difficult trading conditions. "It's been a slow year. I used to do Somerset but, cos it was on a Friday, I'd a bloke to do it and he told them I wasn't doing it any more so Clean Cut got it. Steve from ReRun told me that Clean Cut pays Bill Hancock £xxx a season to film there! That's before he's got there from the Midlands. I don't see how that can work?"

Until dedicated fans ensured that their local club embraced the worldwide web, Plymouth speedway used to give Stoke a run for their money for the least impressive Internet presence. Thankfully this situation changed some time ago for both clubs. Previously, if you'd been keen, interested or foolish enough to bother to click on the Stoke link on the BSPA website, you found yourself directed off onto an apparently random sports page from the BBC Radio Staffordshire website. The Devils now wholeheartedly embrace this newfangled technology as a result of the work of George Skinner and Mike Simpson. Though generationally and by inclination, George is reluctant to describe himself as the Plymouth Devils speedway Webmaster that – to all intents and purposes – is what he is. "Since we started on April 3rd we've had over 650,000 visitors from 28 different countries! We're averaging 4,000 a day except for one strange day when it went up to 10,000. I did it cos I'm a speedway fan – the original website died. Through old George – who doesn't know much about websites – and my colleague Mike Simpson – who does – we got it together. We found that the dotcom address was available and things went from there. Mike Simpson has put hundreds of websites together and he's never known one take off so fast and carry on going, like the Plymouth speedway one has! My missus reckons it's because it's got Devils in the name!" Though now retired, George always had a fascination with figures. "I could remember the customers' phone numbers and account numbers when I used to sell glass fibre. Back in '74 when I took over our turnover in a year was £60,000 excluding tax and, when I left in 2002, we were doing £80,000 a week excluding tax. When we started there was no such thing as a glass fibre industry!" George's mission this afternoon is to take some attractive photos of the Plymouth Devils merchandise on sale in the trackshop to then solicit orders for these products on the website. "My plan today is to take photos of all the equipment we have for sale. Mike isn't an entrepreneur. We've already sold a scarf to a gentleman in Latvia. Our sales have been clothes mainly, so far. We've got a few ideas about how to increase visitors but I can't tell you about that." And what more uniquely passionate token of your speedway infatuation can there be than a Plymouth Devils thong? Already available in the track shop and, surely, an essential item of memorabilia for any online shop?

Some of the Sittingbourne speedway massive – a.k.a. Dick Jarvis and Les Drury – are on tour again this weekend. Dick Jarvis is pleasantly surprised at the reasonable level of prices charged by the Plymouth promotion in comparison to some of the tracks they visited. "When Weymouth staged the Under-15s they charged full-price adults (£10) and full-price programmes (£2)."

[Jeff] "It's for a good cause since I'm sure all the monies went to the BSPA."

[Dick] "I'm sure they did. When we got there last night for the Isle of Wight meeting, the car park bloke said, 'Have you come to buy the club? I hope so! Everyone hates that solo safe sex practitioner in there!'"

[Les Drury] "And when Phil Bartlett went on the mic to announce he was selling, half the people cheered and he said, 'That's why I'm selling!'"

Robert Peasley is here from Oxford to take in both meetings. He knows his speedway onions and wastes no time letting me know that riders in both the 250cc and 500cc Under-15 Championships can discard a 'poor' score from one of their meetings. "The riders drop their bottom scores. They're all young lads and it's in case they can't make one meeting or, because they rely on their parents, in case they can't take them. Even if he doesn't score, though, Robert Lambert will win!"

Given the close interest he professes in young speedway rider development, it's something of a contradiction that Derek Barclay isn't in Plymouth to see these championships conclude. His failure to travel widely or bother to see so many meetings nowadays – since the implosion of the CL version of Wimbledon – doesn't appear to crimp the volume or accuracy of Derek's opinions on the British Speedway Forum. As usual his Parsloes 1928 nearly Internet persona exemplifies the ongoing BSF trend toward vituperation (rather than genuine debate). Indeed, Parsloes 1928 nearly has recently been in fine rebarbative form. [1] Rob Peasley takes his usual generously benign view of people's characters, "I think Derek and Jayne's dispute might be about what he wrote in the programme."

[Jeff] "It didn't sound like that. He said something like 'apologies are fine IF reciprocated – and I did NOT appreciate being reported to the authorities last year for simply requesting the 1-7 of a team for the purposes of programme printing deadlines.'"

[Rob] "I remember when I was doing the Oxford programme and they didn't get on so well with Mildenhall and we didn't know what our line-up was or what we would have cos we had two riders injured. So when I rang up Graham [Drury] to discuss his team, I said, 'I can tell you five riders' and he said 'Well, I can tell you four'. It didn't help get the programme done. When I could tell him the complete line-up, he told me the other three riders. Fortunately, the programme printers (Presto Print) were great and turned it all around on the day of the meeting. I was

---

[1] Buxton promoter Jayne Moss's opinion that Jay Herne might have too high an average to be included in the Bournemouth Buccaneers team prompts the always level-headed Parsloes to fulminate, "Frankly I think that's one of the most disgraceful things I've ever heard written/said at this level of the sport". Gently chided to back down off his always handy high horse by other posters, Parsloes reiterates his sincerely held – often frighteningly late night – opinion ("I hold by my view") and insists, "surely anyone caring about the League would rather see a team go into the play-offs able to use their own rider at No. 1 rather than utilise guests". To outside observers, strongly held opinions about the speedway equivalent of the number of angels dancing on a pinhead probably isn't that exciting. Nonetheless, this post is definitely (either deliberately or accidentally) insulting to the time, thought and money put into British speedway – with especial emphasis upon rider development – by Jayne Moss and her family. Rather mildly she comments, "At the end of the day it doesn't really matter what you or I think it is down to the management committee to approve any team changes in line with the current regulations. As for implying I don't care about the NL you are way off target there. If that was the case, why run a team in a third division for the last 16 years, as we have, which takes a considerable amount of time and commitment on a limited budget?"

Plymouth: *"My missus reckons it's because it's got Devils in the name!"*

sometimes a bit too forthright in the programme! I used to write my match reports about what I'd seen but that got the club into trouble with BSPA sometimes because of what I'd written!"

Referee Christina Turnbull officiates at the first meeting of the afternoon: the Under-15 Championship. When off duty, Christina and her partner Mark are keen speedway fans, often seen at Arlington Stadium. Recently they've been notable by their absence. "Mark refuses to return after the abuse I got at Eastbourne during the Poole meeting. You expect that people will question your decisions during the meeting and, of course, that is their right. I don't mind that at all. But some of the things that were said went a long way past what is acceptable for a so-called family sport. No one should have to put up with comments like that no matter what people think they have done. To be fair, some fans did come up afterwards and apologise saying that they thought it was unacceptable too! So it's a shame that a small minority ruin it by saying such unacceptable things." Mike Bowden's comments on the loudspeaker system often enlivens race night at the St Boniface Arena. This afternoon is no different. "Would all the riders and parents pay attention? There'll be a riders' meeting in the pits at 12.45 when you will be able to take two laps of practice. The meeting will start promptly at 1.30." This is news to SCB official, Christina, "I don't know where that came from? I thought the meeting was supposed to start at 1.00?"

No Under-15 Championship meeting would be complete without the presence of organisational stalwart and young rider development enthusiast Graham Reeve. He flies about the place like a man possessed meeting, greeting, advising and mentoring. Graham knows everyone including myself, "Hey, John, how are you?" Graham's understandably very proud of the championships and positively delights in the enjoyment of the riders as well as their families. "We could do with a few more fans but we publicise it the best we can! Next year we're gonna call it the British Youth Championship rather than the Under-15s because some of the riders are in limbo after they finish in this, cos they're not old enough to get into the National League. Reece Naylor won last year but he was too young to get a team! Of this year's lot, Brandon [Freemantle] will get a team but lots of the others won't be old enough, so changing it to the Youth Championship should sort that out!" After an hour or so of complete disinterest from fans, riders, families and officials alike, a lady looks highly likely to purchase *Quantum of Shale* until Adam Bowden rushes over to sabotage the possible sale, "Don't buy that if you don't buy the *Speedway Star!*" Her contemplation interrupted, the lady decides to buy neither publication. After he studies the cumulative score chart to date, Robert Peasley returns with further advice on the complex scoring system in operation at these championships. "Both classes [250cc and 500cc] are already settled. Adam Portwood could score 18 today but he would have to drop a 16 and that would give him 84 points and Brandon Freemantle is already on 86!"

The meeting gets underway at about quarter past one and, from the very first race, dust eddies off the shale. The basic format of the event is to run a set of six races involving every engine class (125cc, 250cc and 500cc) before a brief break for demonstration rides and a track grade. There will be three such batches before the 125cc (heat 19), 250cc (heat 20) and 500cc (heat 21) finals. Shortly after the second race of the afternoon ends, Kidderminster-based businessman and Birmingham owner Tony Mole arrives – casually dressed as if he's just come back from sailing – to study these young riders in action. Race times vary between the different engine classes not least because the 125cc support races only race over three laps rather than the traditional four. Despite the difference in age, engine size and speeds, incredulity greets Graham Hambly's announcement that the wining time for heat 4 is 98.86 seconds! To ongoing widespread amazement, Graham repeats this exceptional statistic three times. This probably indicates that he doesn't have the time or inclination to question the information placed in front of him. For many more 'sensitive' speedway promoters, such an approach would be the ideal relationship with press and public

214

alike to their public announcements and analyses.

Plymouth Devils team manager, Gary Spiller, looks forward to tonight's meeting against local rivals Weymouth in the National Trophy with anticipation. He's been to Radipole Lane so many times he's lost count. So much so that even his wife has memories of the place. "My wife was stood outside the bar on the fourth bend – admittedly she'd had a few sherbets – and commented on the track, ('I've seen smoother McCoy's crisps') and that Sam Knight laid into her saying she was a guest so shouldn't comment because she's a guest of the club. She was told she'd have to pay next time!" The rider with the brightest kevlars (a distinctive purpley-pink colour) on display here, Nathan Stoneman, is also the busiest rider of the afternoon since he rides in both the 250cc and 500cc Championships. He falls back-first into the fence on the apex of the first bend on the second lap of heat 8. Though he immediately leaps to his feet and remounts, the race has been stopped and awarded by referee Christina Turnbull. The lure of the stadium microphone proves too great for Mike Bowden in light of his severe anxieties about speedway stowaways. Ignoring the St. Boniface Arena isn't on the US-Mexico border, quite where they'll hide within the stadium grounds is difficult to figure out. "We would ask you all to leave the arena in an orderly fashion after the meeting! We'll reopen the gates at 6 p.m. tonight. It's nice to see so many of the senior riders here to pick up a few tips from the youngsters! Let's hope for a nice safe afternoon's racing and let's hope we take our revenge against Weymouth tonight!" Stood leaning against the open-air wooden grandstand close to the start line, Devils Webmaster George Skinner studies the race action in absorbed fashion. "We didn't have speedway for 35 or 36 years. I couldn't see how they'd manage to stage it here! I came with my wife when they opened and she got covered in shale. We got back and opened the wine and the magic words came out, 'the next time we go'. Now when she goes away for a fortnight with her mum, she rings up for the results!"

Apart from the fact that they only race three laps, the 125cc races are made even more notable by the fact that – under the rules of the competition – the riders' dads are allowed to go to the start line to wish their sons luck and offer last-second words of instruction or encouragement, just prior to the rise of the tapes. Quite who is reassuring who isn't clear, particularly since their concentration, the noise of the bikes and muffling affect of the crash helmets is bound to lessen the impact of any last-minute words of advice. This afternoon's hardest working rider Nathan Stoneman temporarily leads heat 10 (in the 500cc class) until the fourth bend where he's aggressively brushed aside by Adam Kirby whose steely ruthlessness reveals why he currently lies second in the cumulative standings. Though still on his bike, Nathan only gets as far as the second bend of the next lap before he pulls off the track.

Proud grandfather John Hazelden crouches below the safety fence three yards down from the start line prior to the start of heat 11 that sees his grandson Jordan start off gate one. "I'm here watching how he starts!" Jordan rides with confidence but starts slower than the other two riders in the race. However, as they exit the second bend Jordan finds the inside line for a split-second opportunity to blast up the inside into second place. His granddad exclaims (unheard) words of encouragement, "Go on, Jordan! Go on! Oh, he's backed off! He could have had him but lacks the confidence. He likes the track." Indeed Jordan looks stylish and in control of his speedway bike, "It's a point and he's getting better and he's enjoying it!"

With the second set of races complete, we get to enjoy yet another incredibly extensive track grade. George Skinner is as mesmerised as the rest of us, "Usually they only do a couple of laps." High up on the far banking that overlooks the apex of the third and fourth bend in one direction and the railway track and dual carriageway flyover in the other, Dick Jarvis offers some words of praise, "It looks nicer here. They've definitely got rid of the bumps, which is probably why they've lost so much at home this season!" In addition to pride in their facilities, I suspect that the Devils look ambitiously to the future, "It's probably for their Premier League application." Dick grimaces, "Can you imagine what they would be like on the first bend? It would be carnage! They'd be rebuilding the fence all the time but it could be cheaper with all the heat 12 abandonments! I must say, I'm impressed with the track – it used to be like motocross. When you think we've had 14 races, some demos and all this grading in one hour – it's great!"

Though it's not widely known amongst the fan base (or even by the rider himself), Seemond Stephens recently became the all-time top points scorer for Plymouth. Pete Lansdale – who rode for the club between 1949 and 1954 – used to hold this record. To commemorate the occasion (and as a surprise for Seemond) George tells me, "I've had a trophy made up to celebrate the fact. At the bottom I've had written, engraved I should say, for 'Consistency and Loyalty'!" Like many speedway fans George enjoys a lifelong fascination with many different varieties of motorcycle. "I bought a BSA 650cc new in 1959 when I was 18 for £168 and a few pennies and, after years of twitching on about it, I bought another 1959 650cc. I got it for £915 but it's been valued at £1,500!"

Once the second session of track grading finally ends, it's back on with the action. Though we already knew the championship winners for both the 250cc and 500cc classes before a wheel turned, many of the riders still compete lustily. The third bend of the third lap of heat 15 (250cc class) illustrates this collective zeal and desire. Nathan Stoneman leads but that doesn't stop a sudden dramatic cut in front of him by namesake Nathan Greaves. Without contact, the element of surprise separates Stoneman from his equipment. Rob Peasley looks on approvingly, "You could see that they were really going for it!" It's lucky Rob is here otherwise I wouldn't properly understand the complex scoring system that applies to the participants in the various finals. If you qualify for the final, the points you score prior to your participation in that race get scrubbed from your score chart since the rules of the competition dictate that the first-placed rider receives 18 points, the second 16, the third 14 and the fourth 12. Should there be enough riders in any Championship, then the fifth-placed rider receives 11 points, the sixth 10 and so on. Even after 35 years watching the sport, such a scoring system boggles my mind and is so complex I immediately think it might well be suitable for the Speedway Grand Prix Series when they next decide to fiddle foolishly with its format. Heat 16 sees Tyler Govier get a lesson in the rough and tumble of speedway racing when Andrew Ross falls in front of him on the second bend. Though Tyler takes evasive action, it upsets his concentration and he soon rides onto the centre green to drop out of the race. Beset by the slings and arrows of other people's misfortune, Tyler doesn't react happily but looks forlorn and at something of a loss to know exactly how to seek justice or retribution.

Rob Peasley is a keen judge of speedway flesh. Though the white-helmeted Keiran Vaughan won the final of the 125cc class, the red-helmeted faller Anders Rowe catches Rob's eye. "The rider in white won but the rider in red looks like a speedway rider. We think we spotted an age differential but, maybe, he's just small rather than younger!" Not all fans feel happy with the logic of the points awarded to riders in the final. "The boy who won the meeting [Anders Rowe] falls off in the final so only gets 12 points whereas the rider who got no points during the meeting [Jack Collins] is in the final and is awarded third so finishes with 14 points! That can't be right?!" The final of the 250cc class sees a battle of the Nathans won by the Greaves version ahead of the Stoneman variety. That said, third-placed Robert Lambert – who has "ruthless" written on his bottom – is crowned 2010 Champion. Locally based Nathan Stoneman was 14 yesterday. Sadly, his excess rides of this afternoon possibly cost him in the 250cc Championship after Nathan Greaves's win in the final ensures – at the last moment – Stoneman slips from second to third in the overall standings. In the 500cc class, Brandon Freemantle swept all before him all season and, though he doesn't require the points or the victory, he fires imperiously to yet another win in the 500cc grand final.

The compact character of the St Boniface Arena circuit ensures during any race that no rider really gets away from the rest of the field. Both the reality and the perception of this closeness adds to the entertainment for regular fans. "We've had some breathtaking meetings here this season – the one that really stands out was against Team Viking. It was a draw, but they would have won if they'd had reserves. We haven't done so well but that's because we're a top heavy team with sacrificial reserves! People complain but that's Mike Bowden's prerogative. When we own a speedway club we can do what we want!" Unusually this season, Plymouth won't take part in the National League end-of-season play-offs. Rob Peasley has strong opinions, "I don't want Bournemouth to win the play-offs because they're a poor fourth, 20 or so points behind the top three. It wouldn't seem right!" It's a point of view that prompts philosophical questions, "So in a Coventry/Poole final, you'll be supporting Poole?" Rob won't consistently apply his own methodology, "Er, I dunno about that!"

In the car park afterwards I catch a few words with the rider in the number 25 race tabard – Joe Lawlor who (along with Saul Bulley) provided the demonstration rides on their 85cc machines. "Probably this is my favourite track of the season! I dunno why, it just turns easily!"

18th September GB Under-15 Championship Round 6 125cc Support Races Winner: Keiran Vaughan
250cc British Championship Winner: Nathan Greaves (Overall Robert Lambert)
500cc British Championship Winner: Brandon Freemantle (Overall Brandon Freemantle)

CHAPTER 26

Plymouth

"They're doing a job where they could end up in a wheelchair for whatever they're paid!"

18th September

Apart from the fewer vans parked up inside the stadium already, when I arrive back at the St Boniface Arena riders entrance gate there's a ground-hog day *déjà vu* all over again type feel. That said, the dress code is definitely much smarter. Mike Bowden's daughter Ruth looks ready for a smart upscale dinner party while her father eschews his casual clothes in favour of a more dashing dark jacket with prominent BSPA badge set off by a collared shirt and tie. Away from her speedway race-night duties, Ruth works in Social Services contracting. She's well used to negotiation, people management and a demanding work environment that requires working to tight deadlines. She handles the arriving riders, mechanics and officials with friendly but firm diplomacy. Her father is never too busy to pop back to check what happens and isn't reluctant to offer advice, "He's like Blakey – you gotta know how to handle him!" Ruth is an articulate conversationalist and takes a refreshingly matter-of-fact view of life, "We only know a fraction of what goes on. We kid ourselves about our place in the universe. We need seven hours sleep a night and should drink two litres of water a day but, beyond that, we're all mammals really!" Ruth knows her way round motorbikes but resists the inclination to parade her knowledge or to get caught up in the tittle-tattle or gossipy backbiting that's sometimes the *lingua franca* of the riders' van car park prior to (and after) a meeting. "I don't care what the speedway riders earn or don't earn. If it's £8 or £800, its their decision what they risk for that! They're doing a job where they could end up in a wheelchair for whatever they're paid! I wouldn't do it!" Ruth's sister Angela interjects, "She used to mechanic for Mike from the age of seven." Ruth makes light of her extensive experience, "I used to do everything for him." Angela adds, "She don't watch anymore, like me. Dad used to take us everywhere."

Though most riders are already here, a stream of vehicles draw up to the entrance gate. Man of many hats but questionable ability, Weymouth chairman, promoter and team manager, Phil Bartlett arrives in a sleek American styled black large-sized people carrier notable for its alloy wheels and personalised number plate. Effectively, it's the after version of a white van after an appearance on *Pimp My Ride*. Roomy enough for many large sized passengers, tonight Mr Bartlett arrives with Weymouth's presenter and webmaster Tim Helm and charming ex-Wimbledon but latter-day Wildcats speedway fan Allen Boon, Snr. (but, sadly, without Phil's glamorous partner and Wildcats Ace commercial head honcho, Samantha Knight). Allen is 73 next week but remains, even after many decades watching speedway, as engaged and enthusiastic about the sport as ever. "We had brilliant racing last night at Weymouth. Some races you could have thrown a blanket over all four riders! Adam McKinna fell off – bits flying off his bike and that – and got straight up. Whereas Dan Halsey fell off and he was on the track for 20 minutes and got carried off to hospital! It all depends on how you fall, doesn't it?"

My book display table is in a similar place as earlier for the GB Under-15 Championships. It's strategically located a short distance away from the entrance turnstiles and programme stall en route towards the toilet block, pits area, trackshop and, of course, the track. On the table adjacent to my left, they sell *Speedway Stars* and *Speedway Star* calendars, while next to that DVD man David Hawking sets out his stall prior to going off to film the meeting.

With his hair gelled into his distinctive ginger bed-head style, trademark sunglasses and an untucked white collared shirt (without tie) that would make him feel cold later if he were less hard, Phil Bartlett wanders from the vicinity of his expensively sleek parked vehicle with some pre-meeting fried food bought from one of the St Boniface Arena refreshment stalls (that earlier some Plymouth fans advised me against). While Phil strides purposefully off to the pits with a confidence that belies his lack of tactical speedway team management acumen, the bloke next to me remains sure that the Wildcats will put up a good performance. "They've got a good side with McKinna and Cockle! What do you think of René Bach then? I think it'll be a Newcastle versus Edinburgh final. It should be really exciting! Newcastle have Dakota North, Mark Lemon and Kenni Larsen too. Edinburgh have Ryan Fisher and he's awesome!" Judged by the way that the Plymouth Devils were late to embrace the worldwide web and, until they got their latest website, were then reluctant to update it – you could be forgiven for thinking that Internet usage wasn't a big priority for those who support the club. Apropos of nothing, the youth next to me says, "I've put on my Facebook page that I hope Matt Bates breaks his leg." Given that Matt rides at No. 3 for the Devils, my assumption is that this greeting must have some sort of theatrical background, "What to wish him good luck like they do before plays?" In fact, this message has no theatrical intention, "What's that?"

My explanation of theatrical superstition is cut short by ex-Exeter Falcons promoter, David Short who is here tonight having recently rediscovered his love of speedway. "I did some team management here and some other things but, not being involved, I drifted away but I've come back now! I go to Plymouth and Somerset. People are upset, like I am, about Exeter speedway but they don't believe me when I say Colin [Hill] didn't leave enough to reintroduce the sport! Nor are they happy when I blame English Nature!" No trip to Plymouth speedway would be complete for me without a chat to Paul 'Grizzly' Adams. However, tonight it's going to have to be since he's not here. Luckily, I'm able to catch up with his sister Julie Rickard and her daughter Laura. They're both fanatical Devils fans though Laura's speedway attendance has to fit round the demands of her Egyptology and Ancient History degree at the University of Swansea.

Smooth track

Poster

Plymouth: *"They're doing a job where they could end up in a wheelchair for whatever they're paid!"*

Nonetheless, she still packs in a lot of speedway over the summer, despite the intrusion of a successful re-sit. She enjoys university life but prefers the convenience and predictability of living on campus in Halls of Residence, ("I've moved from room number 13, to 15, to 5 and now I've moved to number 23"). Contrary to press reports and the attendance figures released by the organisers, Laura believes that the attendance at the Cardiff Speedway Grand Prix declined in 2010. "I thought the crowd was less this year – there were definitely no Poles! The racing was really good though!"

Though the result of tonight's meeting will make no real difference to the overall standing of either side in the final National Trophy table, the bragging rights any local derby between these two teams bestows ensures there's a buzz about the place. With racing not too far off, quite a queue of fans still have yet to come through the turnstiles. Once inside, some fans linger to consider whether to buy a book, calendar, or DVD but, mostly, they trundle off to their favourite spot within the stadium grounds. To the right of my table the back doors of Seemond Stephens's van remain open. Sat on its sill are a gentleman and Seemond Stephens's mum. She tightly holds the leads of two small dogs dressed in smart bright coats with Asian style patterns. It's news to Seemond's mum that her son is now Plymouth's all-time top points scorer. When I mention this fact to Laura Rickard, she already knows and can, with absolutely no hesitation, recite Pete Lansdale's vital statistics.

The calm of this pleasant September evening suddenly ends in a commotion at the table next to me after a man in a baseball cap worn the wrong way round draws attention when he raises his voice with the youth stood there. The gentleman is clearly angry and their age, size, height and weight difference is instantly noticeable. With his back to me, the man holds his face a fraction of an inch from the youth in the manner of prize boxers at a press launch. Some further passionate but indistinct discussions ensue where both parties give a full and frank exchange of opinion. People watch but don't intervene. Instead, like myself, they just stand and gawp – whether they're at the programme stall, stood close by, queuing to get in, sat on the back of their van, run over from other parts of the St Boniface Arena or are in the substantial sized gaggle of fans stood on the mound that, when they face in the other direction, overlooks bends one and two. Discussions soon predictably escalate into the violence the onlookers anticipate. The gentleman knocks the youth dramatically to the ground with a slap to the face. Unprepared to concede whatever points they discuss, the youth gets up, pushes his face close up and stares wilfully at his attacker only to then be knocked to the floor again with a loud slap. Though the youth is quick up onto his feet – to stand stock still with his face inches away in true Audley Harrison fashion – almost as rapidly, he's again knocked to the floor by the force of the next blow. The youth looks shaken but insolent while the gentleman remains extremely angry. This confrontation ends, when the gentleman is suddenly held back by a chap in a fluorescent sleeveless jacket and a traditionally worn Devils cap. Close by, Gary Spiller is also held back while, in almost cartoon caricature fashion, he smoulders like a tractor tyre on a farm bonfire.

The reaction of the majority of people is just to stand and watch the drama unfold but, almost as soon as the man in the fluorescent jacket calls a halt to this sudden confrontation, urgent conversations all around break the silence. Probably dazed, the youth runs off in the direction of the programme booth. Strangely, all of a sudden, everyone's got an opinion as well as expertise and insight. Without context, this confrontation is reported to the police who are now said to be on their way to the stadium. Contrary to detective dramas on the telly, all anyone can reasonably report is the events they saw (if they did see them or chose to say they saw them). The reportable event effectively started when both parties locked their heads close together by the display table of *Speedway Star* calendars. Ruth Bowden appears by my table to ask rhetorically, "What sort of

Plymouth: *"They're doing a job where they could end up in a wheelchair for whatever they're paid!"*

man hits a 17-year old? What sort of sport condones this sort of thing? Ruth turns to Seemond Stephens's mum who's still sat in the doorway of her son's van, "So you just sat there and watched a 17-year old get hit?" She replies, "I was looking after my dogs! I'm a 65-year old woman. What was I supposed to do?" A police car and police van arrives so Ruth departs. "What does she think I should do? He was lucky it was only three."

Rather than the aggressive style of policing style often seen on 70s television shows like *Starsky & Hutch* or *The Sweeney,* the Devon Constabulary appear to operate in the modern low-key friendly manner, possibly in order to diffuse any lingering tension but also to maximise the information they gather. They arrive comparatively mob-handed in a police car and a police van – possibly under the mistaken impression that there could be a need to take quite a few people down the station to help them with their enquiries. After members of the public identify me as a witness, a policeman and a blonde-haired policewoman soon arrive at my book display table to take down my basic particulars. They emphasise that they intend to continue to question all and sundry in order to establish/investigate exactly what just happened between the two protagonists inside the stadium. They promise to return in 15 minutes to take a statement. Moments after they leave in the direction of the pits, Graham Reeve passes walking quickly in the opposite direction en route for the car park. I call out to Graham for advice. "Like I've already told the police, I'm just a speedway fan close to the fracas. I'd prefer that any dispute could be amicably resolved without violence and or the involvement of the police." Many other potential witnesses quickly melt into the knowing anonymity of the crowd. Given the proximity of my table to the fracas, it's impossible to deny the claims of others that I was a well-placed witness to this incident. Graham's definite that the rule of law should be upheld, although he's not personally going to stay around to uphold it! "Say what you saw! Call me next week and I'll fill you in on what's really happening!"

Rob Peasley pops to my table enervated by the incident, "The police will definitely be wanting to take your statement!" Fifteen minutes later instead of the return of the original two officers, PC Harrip (Badge No. 6923) arrives to take my statement. Prior to doing so I inform him that I'd prefer not to be involved or make a statement as well as ask his advice. Rather than answer my questions, PC Harrip points to a small object on the breast of his jacket and says, "Just to let you know that everything you're saying has been filmed and recorded."
[Jeff] "Shouldn't you have told me that before we started?"
[PC Harrip] "I'm telling you now!"

PC Harrip effects surprise that I could believe that he had a legal obligation to inform me that he would film and record my conversation prior to doing so. Clearly I'm no expert but it seems highly likely that prior permission should be sought and warning given. While, I fully understand that the digital recording of evidence allows the police force to corroborate statements taken from witnesses in the likelihood of later dispute, this 'accidental' use of his equipment illustrates why some people don't automatically trust the integrity of the police. Contrary to my expectations and unlike television drama, PC Harrip laboriously writes out my comments longhand. Luckily for him, albeit in rapidly fading light, he has my book display table to rest on. Behind us the speedway meeting gets underway. Though I can hear the roar of the bikes, to all intents and purposes it might as well take place on the moon for all the attention I can give it. Hardly satisfactory after a long trip here from Brighton. The meeting is a stop-start affair with a substantial delay for a crash in heat 2. PC Harrip's future career as a dictation secretary might be hampered by both his lack of shorthand and his laborious handwriting. Inevitably, if regularly taking statements, an element of précis is involved. It's also a given that PC Harrip's familiarity with the language used and/or required by the courts dictates that he uses slightly stilted much more formal phrases than those of everyday conversation. Nonetheless, it's still a surprise that his word choice is a greater factor in 'my statement' – of events that I rather than he witnessed – than I'd expect. With hindsight and in the cold light of day, it's very easy for people to ignore the explicit and implicit pressure of this slightly fraught situation and say, 'well, don't sign it'.

PC Harrip sets to his task in dedicated fashion. He tends towards the noncommittal and aloof rather than the friendly. Probably an understandable reaction to a laborious but routine task in darkening unfamiliar surroundings. Either way, there's limited small talk except for his observation, "You're an Aries!" Fading light isn't the only extraneous element to impinge on PC Harrip's intense concentration as he writes out the statement since we're continually interrupted by other people keen to put over their tuppence worth (but not make a statement). While they can't influence this statement, they're certainly keen to provide additional context. An angry lady is one of the first to approach us and she tells PC Harrip, "He deserves locking up!" PC Harrip is polite but firm, "Could you go away – I'm trying to take a statement here!" Police officers escort Ken Bates out of the stadium to Mount Charles Police Station. [1] It's not long before another man comes up to tell PC Harrip, "He wanted hitting a long time ago." With a vague hint of exasperation, PC Harrip politely but firmly says, "Please go away!" Yet another man comes up to offer PC Harrip the use of his torch. "Nah, it's okay, thank you." Like everyone else who interrupts, this man also has a strong opinion, "He's had it coming for some time and totally deserved it." PC Harrip remains polite ("Thank you") but continues to write.

Keen to record my statement in the language of the court, PC Harrip insists on calling the incident "an assault" whereas I'm keen to stress that I identify it as "a fracas". Obviously, no consideration is given to possible provocation prior to or during this meeting. We take a considerable time over the statement and, while I can hear the meeting continue, frustratingly I can't watch it. In fact, by this time we can't see much at all until a second policeman comes along to shine a torch on the many pages of the statement. Again, I stress that I don't want to escalate or even intervene in the situation. After the statement is read back, slightly amended and signed, PC Harrip gives me an information leaflet produced for the Criminal Justice System entitled "You've reported a crime … so what happens next?" What happens next is I'm told I'll almost certainly hear nothing about this ever again. What then happens next is that the police leave the stadium to go and sit in their car outside for quite some time (to discuss matters unknown).

Spat out after my involuntary but tangential brief encounter with the early stage workings of the Devon arm of the judicial system, in darkness I pack up my table and books. By the time, I wander up onto the banked area that overlooks the first bend, unfortunately (for me) heat 8 is already over in this Plymouth versus Weymouth National Trophy meeting. Against all predictions, Weymouth flew into an early 10-2 lead but, according to most accounts, Phil Bartlett's tactical and strategic ineptitude marshalling the rider resources available to him effectively ruins any chance of a Wildcats victory. [2] Rather than linger on the cool terraces, I make my way to the pits in order to (hopefully) briefly chat to club officials about the events of the evening. I ask a morose-looking

---

[1] Next day I learn, "All charges were dropped – it was self-defence!"

[2] On the British Speedway Forum, Rob Peasley notes, "It was only just completed in time before the 9.30 p.m. curfew, after a number of reruns in the opening races, with Ben Reade getting well and truly entangled in the safety fence after picking up drive in heat 2 and ending up with a foot injury. Weymouth looked hot favourites to win early on taking a 10-2 lead but with Simmonds and Stephens both unbeaten, Plymouth had the match won with a heat to spare and could afford to keep their maximum men out of the final heat in which the Wildcats took a consolation 5-1. Some weird team management from Weymouth with trump card Gary Cottham, given reserve rides in all the wrong places; some good action with Nicki Glanz, Jamie Pickard (who's improved no end since I last saw him) and Tom Brown, all producing some good passes. The Plymouth track has improved a lot since my last visit in 2007." In his report for the *Speedway Star*, Graham Hambly comments, "Plymouth recovered well from a disastrous start". In the same issue, promoter Mike Bowden offers some praise. "The referee and officials did well to see that the remaining 12 races were completed in an hour [after Ben Reade's crash caused extensive damage to the safety fence]. It was a good win for us despite being down to a six-man team and proved to be a very entertaining and exciting meeting."

Plymouth: *"They're doing a job where they could end up in a wheelchair for whatever they're paid!"*

man with the words "Machine Examiner" written on his shirt, "How come the pits seems so deserted?"

[Man] "Everyone is pissed off in the pits. Well 95%! It's shit!

[Jeff] "Where is Mike Bowden?"

[Man] "On the centre green."

[Jeff] "Where is Gary Spiller then?"

[Man] "On the centre green."

[Jeff] "Everyone's on the centre green?"

[Man] "Some wish they weren't here at all!"

Standing on the centre green at the farthest point away from the pits area in the vicinity of the third bend, possibly isn't the ideal location from which to manage and or motive the Plymouth Devils riders. However, it is a tricky spot for curious policemen to reach easily. Moments later as I stomp away from the stadium Graham Hambly issues an appeal over the stadium loudspeaker, "Would Gary Spiller please come to the pits as soon as possible?" Without being on hand to witness it, it's impossible to know whether Gary's return is a request from his riders, officials or the police. If there's any lesson to learn from tonight then it's always best to bring a jumper if you expect it to be cool later. It's also a good idea not to comment on situations you don't witness or hear and, even if you do, it's not always easy to exactly recall these for a written statement, even shortly afterwards. Before I pick up my dew-dampened table to leave, a kindly Plymouth Devils fan stops me, keen to say, "I really must apologise. This sort of stuff doesn't go on here usually!"

18th September Plymouth v. Weymouth (National Trophy) 48-44

Plymouth: *"They're doing a job where they could end up in a wheelchair for whatever they're paid!"*

CHAPTER 27

Sittingbourne
"We'd had 50 races and finished within the curfew"

19th September

The usual hubbub of pre-meeting activity at the Old Gun Site is in full swing shortly before the "MTD Group Credit Crunch Team Event – Second Leg" gets underway. Today's meeting is programmed to have a comparatively meagre 54 heats! It's jointly organised by the Dragons Amateur Speedway Club and Sittingbourne Speedway but wouldn't go ahead without "the financial support of the MTD Group of Companies" (based in Romford) particularly "company representatives John Strong, Diane King and her daughters Lillie and Masie". It's the third year of operation and popularity for the Dragons Amateur Speedway Club. "We are a small bunch of friends who have joined forces to offer all amateur speedway riders the opportunity to develop their skills and enjoy the support we all love in a friendly and relaxed atmosphere." Though the DASC has "gone from strength to strength" they don't rest on their laurels and in the programme stress the ongoing need for feedback. "We welcome your comments in order to continually improve. A comment book is available in the riders' viewing area should you wish to leave comments for our team to address." Without regular National League fixtures, meetings like these have become the bread-and-butter competitive speedway at Sittingbourne.

In retrospect I should have come to last weekend's better attended 40th anniversary meeting to savour the atmosphere and to enjoy this milestone. That's certainly the opinion of Paul Heller, one of Sittingbourne speedway's friendly training instructors. "You should have been here last week for the fortieth anniversary meeting! We had everyone and everything! Some of the old riders and old bikes – Japs, Jawas, the Men in Black, quad bikes and everything. As the last quad bike crossed the finish line it was 4.59 and 20 seconds. We'd had 50 races and finished within the curfew. I expect someone was there waiting to ring the council!" To my untutored eye there have been stadium infrastructure improvements since my last visit, most notably what looks like to be a new hut. Yet to change into the distinctive trousers that have become his trademark when he start marshals speedway meetings, Ian Glover disabuses me of this notion, "No, it's not a new hut!" So much for my memory, "It's newly painted then, that's more or less the same thing!"

The terrapin hut that serves as the Sittingbourne Speedway clubhouse-cum-canteen looks the same as ever and inside, behind the service counter but in front of the kitchen area, there's a warm welcome from Alison. Prior to the racing, Iwade track supremo Graham Arnold pops in (dressed in his distinctive paramedic-style overalls) to check all is fine during his pre-meeting supervisory circuit. Graham is his usual understated but direct self. "You should have been here last week. It was nice and sunny but mad! We had 50 races – too many really! If there'd been an accident we'd never have got it finished." Away from the grassroots – like Ian Glover [Lakeside] and Terry English [Eastbourne] – Graham's also involved at the Elite League level of the sport. "Lakeside haven't run for three weeks and they didn't run in July. When Paul Hurry came back, how was he supposed to do well without any races?" Like many in the sport, Graham relies on speedway's bush telegraph for his news rather than the trade press. "I don't get the *Star* no more.

Mark Loram said 'Why do you get that – it's the *Farmers' Weekly*!' So I don't anymore. They don't put in anything about us – probably because of the Central Park thing. They didn't put anything about the 40th Anniversary meeting! We did chase them again in March to put something in but despite positive noises, sadly, it didn't happen." Demands elsewhere call Graham away, though throughout the stadium preparations continue in the pits, on the track and the canteen hut. A loud-voiced lady calls out to Alison behind the kitchen counter, "Do you want the door open? Only to learn, "Nah, Graham wants it shut cos of the dogs that are roaming around!"

Dressed in his well-worn eggshell blue anorak, Pits Marshal Dick Jarvis stands clipboard in hand watching the frenetic activity going on all around him. He believes Phil Bartlett's ineptitude as team manager cost Weymouth valuable points in the Premier Trophy last night at Plymouth. "If Weymouth had had a team manager they'd have won that – Bartlett's a tosser – if only he'd used his reserves properly! He kept giving Gary Cottham the rides he should have given Bob Charles rather than manage it properly." Dick Jarvis's travelling partner in crime Les Drury introduces me to one of this afternoon's riders – Alan Elliott. His fame still goes before him in the Canterbury area after he "stepped in" to score a point for the visitors when they were a man short on their trip to the principality on the 2nd September 1977. [1] Aberdare-based Alan laughs off his notoriety and contribution, "I'm 67 now but I got a point then. I used to stand in for lots of people for lots of different teams."
[Les] "No one used to like going to Newport."
[Alan] "I've actually been at Newport racing with world champions and others who were second, third and fourth in the world! Needless to say where I came."
[Les] "Malcolm Simmons didn't like riding there! He always broke down on the way to the world championship qualifier at Newport."
[Alan] "Some riders found it difficult. If you missed your line, the next thing was the fence!"
[Les] "It was diamond shaped."
[Alan] "It was very narrow. That was a long time ago and I didn't start riding again until about six meetings ago. I went back to do it because I simply didn't have anything to do. I'm a psychotherapist. My qualifications are in mechanical engineering but it was the way I managed that eventually led me to that. In mechanical engineering, it's all about getting the job done and, even now in psychotherapy, I

Sign in

Between races

---

[1] Dick Jarvis later tells me, "Alan made his comeback at King's Lynn and he was amazed anyone remembered him. We saw his name and you just say, 'Are you the same Alan Elliott?'"

225

look on it like that. Whatever it is, the aim is always getting results. There's all sorts of techniques you can use including CBT, psychodynamics, existentialism. I was senior therapist for Sanctuary helping people with things like stress, depression and relationship problems. I'm hoping to go and live in Spain at Torrevieja. There's lots of ex-pats so, with an ageing population, you'd expect to be counselling people with things like bereavement problems and the like. When I'm not here, I've got a GSX 1400 Suzuki that I ride round on and give it a bit of a hammering!"

Given Alan's youthful enthusiasm, age-defined participation in speedway and positive outlook on life, let alone his day job, I can't resist asking, "What is the secret to mental health and wellbeing?" Alan replies without hesitation, "It all depends. If you lead an active life, you should try and find something to do and be happy. Don't dwell on things. Definitely don't dwell in the past. It's looking in a rear-view mirror – you'll crash into what's in front of you going forward. You should face challenges one at a time. We've faced problems before and we'll face them again. Look on it as less of a problem and more of a challenge. Take it one step at a time and don't make demands on yourself. Always get flexibility in there – maybes, perhaps, and possibles. Don't take on anyone else's problems and get to see a professional, if you can. Always celebrate what you've achieved and what you've done rather than compare it to a target. For example, if I walk as far as I can and see how far I get and walk 96 miles, that's great. If you had a target of 100 miles you'd look at it differently and wouldn't see what you'd really done. Life is short and, as you get older, you shouldn't slow down. You should speed up as you have less time to cram it all in!" With life to live to the full, ahead of his races Alan bustles off to study the Old Gun Site track.

Also in the pits is well-travelled Ipswich speedway fan Mark Shrimpton. Though he lives in "Felixstowe near Ipswich (Walton to be precise)", like quite a few others, Mark went to Plymouth last night and now, this morning, is some distance away in Iwade. "Ninety odd races in a week can't be bad! Ipswich is me first team and I can safely say the second is Edinburgh. For 25 years or so. I've been following Edinburgh since 1989 for most of their away ones. When I first started going away it was a combination of Milton Keynes on a Tuesday, Wimbledon on a Wednesday, Ipswich on a Thursday, Hackney on a Friday, Sunday was either Rye House or Mildenhall. So, the question was who was on tour on a Saturday? I got chatting to a couple of people and one of the Ipswich fans is a Monarch fan so it went from there! What with Ipswich not being so good [this season] and Edinburgh being so good, I've seen both sides of the play-off." This year Ipswich's season closes with a promotion/relegation play-off against whichever team emerges victorious from the Premier League play-off series. "In the previous two years in the play-offs, the Elite League team have wanted to win but I'm not necessarily convinced that that is the case this season." Apart from following the Witches and Monarchs, Mark has other speedway goals. "I always set myself to go to every track, if I can. Two years out of every three isn't bad going. This year is a bit lower than normal. I average 90 meetings a season and I don't drive, so it's quite an achievement! I've been to 24 different countries following speedway, if you include Argentina where I'm going to in February 2011. I've been half way round the world and back to see speedway!"

Upstairs in the referee's box built on a section of the battlements that give the Old Gun Site its name, John Strong greets me by telling everyone else there, "He always criticises me in his books – says I'm incoherent and that!"
[Jeff] "I only say nice things about you in this book."

If speedway is a family sport on and off the track, this also applies to officials and volunteers, "I'm not announcing today, I'm the referee! My son is announcing instead – Chris – it's his first time so he'll probably be a bit bland." Back downstairs close to the pits and adjacent to the table where competitors sign in, some ladies gossip. "There's a bike for sale – whose is it?"
"Chris Neath's."

Sittingbourne: *"We'd had 50 races and finished within the curfew"*

"How much?"

"£300."

"£300! It's just the frame!"

Looking through the programme for this afternoon's meeting I exclaim, "It's 54 meetings!"

[Les Drury] "It's 54 heats not 54 meetings! Not one of these namby-pamby short meetings."

[Dick Jarvis] "I'm on the centre green today so it should be nice and peaceful."

The comparative serenity of a Sunday lunchtime in Kent is soon interrupted by bikes warming up but also John Strong's dulcet tones over the stadium loudspeaker system introducing my latest book, "No holds barred – he told me earlier that he doesn't lie – he just misrepresents facts! We're a bit short staffed up here in the box today cos Bryn [Williams] and Chris Golding are on duty at King's Lynn." Before John starts his refereeing duties, he introduces his son Chris to the crowd with a polite request, "Be gentle with him – he'll give you the announcements clearly and concisely." Heading back over to the canteen I bump into Stuart Lee-Amies – father of Chelsea, Chardonnay and Mercedes, "All the girls are here!" I tell Stuart, "It wouldn't be the same without them!" Shortly afterwards I spot all the Lee-Amies girls and their friends wheeling injured speedway rider Jerran Hart around at great speed on his wheelchair! Sat in the wheelchair Jerran looks cold despite his grey tracksuit trousers and a hooded top. Before the posse wheel him elsewhere, rather politely in response to my good wishes he tells me, "I'm good, mate – thank you!"

Over the speakers Chris Strong delivers the first phrases of what, hopefully, will be a long career in speedway presentation, "And a big thank you to our sponsors [breaks up]." Sadly, the quality of the amplification distorts the messages conveyed. Chris welcomes all and sundry in a calm manner including, "John Bryant who looks like something out of the Mafia. He's taking team management very seriously wearing an all-white suit and sunglasses." My book display creates no interest but fans do share their thoughts on the world of speedway. One fan tells me, "Since Eastbourne switched to Thursday, we go to Lakeside on a Friday – the music is better there too!"

The joy of speedway at Sittingbourne is that it caters for all ages (from 8 to 80) and genders. This 54-race meeting sponsored by the MTD Group showcases bikes of varying vintage, riders of vastly differing abilities and attitudes from the competitive to participatory. Irrespective of actual or perceived ability, once the tapes rise, some riders just can't resist giving it their all. Everyone races quicker than they plan on a speedway bike. They slide their machines but, most of all, the key factor is that they're out on the shale living their dream, albeit sometimes rather slowly. The very name of the sport – speedway – encourages some riders to go all out to maximise their velocity, perhaps not fully realising that haste (vividly described in Yiddish as "the beggar's on his third village already") is invariably at the opposite end of the continuum to reflection. Even in those races that the bikes tend to lean more to the vertical than the horizontal, you can still guarantee that there will be far greater concentration and acceleration from the last bend to the finish line. Irrespective of the ability of the rider, pretty well everyone opens the throttle wider on the straights.

If you're an experienced rider like Alan Elliott then you're able to blend savvy with zeal to burst into third place on the third bend of the last lap of heat 3. The racing doesn't lack drama. Comfortably ahead in heat 5 by some distance, Jim Wannell falls on the third bend of the second lap and, though there's tons of time to avoid this fallen rider, white-helmeted Lawrence Fielding is drawn inexorably towards Jim in the manner of a spaceship dragged into a black hole. With predictable inevitability Lawrence clatters into Wannell at a speed approaching something circa 5 mph. The crowd gasp "Oooh!" Shortly after, making it sound like there's been a bereavement, Chris Strong bursts onto the tannoy system to soberly inform us, "Our thoughts are with the riders at this time." Mad keen speedway (and Mildenhall) fan Michael Flattery attends with his family. "After the meeting I'm gonna go out to the centre green. See all that dirt that's building up on the fence, I'm gonna help clean it off!"

The seventh race of the afternoon only lasts as long as it takes the riders to get to the fourth bend where the blue-helmeted Jon Stevens vies with the yellow-helmeted Scott Day. Sadly Scott's afternoon soon takes a painful twist after he comes off his bike. This causes carnage ahead and behind him. Jon Stevens evades an immediate fall but continues without control until he smacks into the safety fence mid panel between the fourth bend and the start line. He's soon on his feet and fares much better than the closely following white-helmeted Ben Holloway who falls awkwardly onto the shale to injure his shoulder. Though apparently minor, this prompts an incredibly long delay for medical attention and fence repairs. Dick Jarvis looks on and can't help but admire the robust but practical design of the safety furniture at the Old Gun Site track. Comparisons with Plymouth immediately spring to his mind, "It takes so long to rebuild there. If the fence here is damaged, we can just add in another panel quickly and easily!" Resigned to the fate of others, during the long delay Graham Arnold shrugs as he watches the buzz of activity out on the fourth bend. "The problem is the riders are trying too hard! Jon Stevens has only been back riding three months and he goes out there and he wrecks his bike for no reason!" When the racing resumes, inaudible announcements because of the grunky speaker system manage to completely confuse me about the racers on show or even which heat is being run. In two short races my scorecard is reduced to an unintelligible mess so much so that, with appointments elsewhere, my frustration prompts an early departure from Sittingbourne.

19th September Dragons Speedway Club & Sittingbourne Speedway: The MTD Group Credit Crunch Team Event – Second Leg Winner: Speedway

CHAPTER 28

Peterborough
"I don't like to eat before the show as it gives me indigestion."

20th September

Already in his second season of ownership at the Peterborough Panthers, club owner and successful businessman Rick Frost (along with Julie Mahoney) has invested substantially to reconfigure the Panthers on and off the track. [1] With greater professionalism in all quarters, expectations heighten. Though likely to have been seen as a given at the start of the season, the Panthers qualification for the end-of-season Elite League play-offs does represent an achievement of some note in their fortieth anniversary season. Given the club were Elite League Champions in 1999 and 2006, their stuttering performances over the final weeks of the 2010 regular season didn't bode well for the first leg of the semi-final at Coventry. Despite leading by 4 points after six races and only trailing by 2 with three races to go, the Panthers then shipped three successive 5-1s to end with what many pundits feel is an insurmountable 14-point deficit.

Catering

In the new-look 2010 version of the Panthers programme ("The Bite"), Rick Frost nevertheless strikes a positive note in his column (Frost Bite) about both the League and the task ahead. "Without the play-offs the League Championship would have been decided back in June and we would have been robbed of the drama and tension that we've all personally experienced over the past few weeks … we do have an unbeaten record here this season, so our target of 15 points is not an impossible task by any means." At the entrance gate to the stadium, ex-Miss Fina Invader Wendy Jedrzejakski carefully scrutinises early arrivals to ensure that no one blags their way into the vast East of England Showground prior to the official opening of the turnstiles. Fortunately I'm here with the permission of co-promoter Peter Oakes so formalities get smoothly completed. Wendy also works at Birmingham speedway, "Graham Drury said to me the other day, 'You know you're in one of Jeff Scott's books'. I said, 'I know, I'm in quite a few of them.'" Many of those intimately involved with the sport

Tension mounts

[1] So much so, the club reported a loss of £140,000 at the end of the 2010 season.

ignore books, magazines and Internet forums in favour of a powerful speedway grapevine that works best face to face. Mobile phones and, increasingly nowadays, Facebook, also help fan these fast-moving flames of the speedway grapevine.

The significance of the Elite League play-off semi-final and finals, dictates Sky Sports Speedway arrive in full force to capture every delicious moment of the end-of-season circus they effectively invented (or, at least, suggested so strongly that this play-off system to select the champions became inevitable). Though there's over two and a half hours to go before the scheduled start of tonight's live broadcast, BSPA press officer and hardworking sports journalist Nigel Pearson lurks by the key Sky outside broadcast vehicle – the catering unit! A wide selection of cold food is already laid out, while a handwritten menu advertises the various hot dishes available to the Sky Sports outside broadcast staff. They serve "Sky Sports Crew Menu" between 5 and 6.30 p.m. Written by hand on a white board, it suggests that the Sky outside broadcast menu changes on a regular basis. [2] Smartly dressed in his relatively stylish collared Sky Sports team anorak, Nigel Pearson closely studies his dining options while authoritatively clutching his Sky Sports HD clipboard in his right hand. Over ten minutes early for feeding time, Nigel tells me, "Its 5 o'clock we eat."

[Jeff] "What for the talent?"

[Nigel] "No, for everyone! I don't like to eat before the show as it gives me indigestion. I just pick at the salad."

[Jeff] "Very healthy!"

[Nigel] "Not really, I have the scotch egg!"

[Jeff] "It should be a good meeting tonight."

[Nigel] [doubtfully] "Well, hopefully. The problem is the two meetings [broadcast simultaneously]. My dad was at Wolverhampton last week and he said the delays were quite long. The problem was that they'd had two heats at Coventry before we'd even had one because Ty Proctor went through the tapes. At least this week the programme has the Poole scorecard in it, so fans can fill that out while they wait."

Shortly after, still in more or less exactly the same location, Nigel stands deep in conversation with Colin Pratt and his co-presenter and partner in commentary crime, Kelvin Tatum. They chew the fat and although their conversation is inaudible, the sound of Nigel's voice rings out across the tarmac. They're oblivious to the arrival of Rick Frost only a short distance away in a sleek black Range Rover Autobiography with a personalised number plate. The i-player interview column written by co-promoter Peter Oakes's grandson Josh Gudgeon in tonight's programme reveals that Rick also has a Rolls Royce Phantom and a Mercedes CL55 AMG. Rick Frost also reveals that he admires Isambard Kingdom Brunel, Tiny Rowland and Sir Alan Sugar for achieving "so much in their lifetimes".

Another hardworking well-travelled man is Pete Ballinger founder of the Clean Cut Sports speedway DVD Empire. They film on a weekly basis at Coventry, Wolverhampton, Belle Vue, Somerset and Peterborough. "I'm in the [Elite League] final no matter what happens!"

[Jeff] "Are Peterborough going to be there?"

[Pete] "I doubt it, cos of tactical rides they effectively need 20 points and that ain't gonna happen! Coventry are a different team to what they were two months ago, let alone at the start of the season." Stood at the back of the home-straight grandstand we watch a pair of tractors circuit the

[2] For this particular speedway meeting the slightly bourgeois media-luvvie menu choices are Beef and Mushroom Pie; Pan Fried Fillet of Salmon with Dill and Shallots Beurre Blanc; or Pasta with Feta Cheese and Provencal Sauce. In addition staff members can have chips, new potatoes, carrots and fine beans – even if these don't particularly go that well with pasta! For dessert there's a choice of chocolate fudge brownies or bananas and custard as well as a strawberry and clotted cream torte. In addition, there are also fruit and yogurts as well as a comprehensive section of hot and cold drinks.

Peterborough: *"I don't like to eat before the show as it gives me indigestion."*

336 metres of the East of England Showground track. It's a virtuoso exhibition of formation tractor grading with a big newer blue tractor circling in close harmony with an older red one, both catching the eye with their whirling daisywheels. They've definitely got their work cut out since the addition of circa 100 tons of new shale earlier in the week wasn't turned and so failed to properly bind in with the old shale. Away from the cameras and public, allegations of track doctoring would prompt heated arguments amongst riders, officials and staff. At one point there was talk of pulling the meeting and, the next day, both the BSPA management committee and Sky Sports rebuke Rick Frost over track conditions.

[Pete] "They like to churn up the start every week – dunno what difference it makes!"

Also eye-catching, but not quite living up to its name in my opinion, the usual East of England Showgrounds stadium infrastructure is supplemented by a prominently displayed large screen above the third and fourth bend.

[Jeff] "The giant screen is a bit smaller than I imagined! Though, they say, size isn't everything."

[Pete] "It'll be irrelevant if they don't plug the audio feed in. Last week at Coventry they didn't, so after 6 heats everyone had stopped watching! They have Peter York to entertain there, of course!" Though Pete travels the length and breadth of the country, he rejects my suggestion that he must be part of the sport's in-crowd given his involvement in the warp and woof of speedway as well as with its cognoscenti. "I prefer not to post about speedway on Facebook now. I was politely advised by someone higher up in the sport that perhaps I shouldn't."

[Jeff] "Were you a keyboard commando then?"

[Pete] "No, I just had an opinion!"

Sat on a chair by my table outside the smartly dressed Peterborough Panthers trackshop, I have the ideal vantage point to watch the world walk by. The animated conversation between Nigel, Kelvin and Colin finally breaks up with Kelvin calling out to Colin as he departs, "See you later – watch out for that track!" Colin has a determined expression and, as he bustles away, he says, "I'm just going to have a look at that track now!" Later – possibly after his scotch egg – Nigel Pearson looms over my book display. "So this is the entire Jeff Scott catalogue!"

[Jeff] "I prefer *oeuvre*."

[Nigel] "Do you write about the Sky meetings much nowadays?"

[Jeff] "I haven't for a while, nor the GPs."

[Nigel] "Tell you what, they're much better this year. The racing has been really good. You wouldn't be able to complain about that."

[Jeff] "If Jonathan Green came back, I'd start writing about them again!"

Nigel confirms that the pressure of his work commitments ensures that he rarely has time to surf the net. "I can't remember the last time I read your blog."

[Jeff] "I said some nice things about the speedway World Cup in *Motorcycle News*."

[Nigel] "Jeff Scott nice about BSI/IMG shock!" Always approachable, Nigel is keen to put me right. "Paul Bellamy is actually a really nice chap! Thoughtful, approachable, really cares about the sport, really wants it to succeed! I get on well with him. He's sincere about speedway. I know you'd argue he gets well paid so should but that doesn't always go together! I think you'd be impressed if you met him." There's been wild talk on the Internet forums by those outside the sport's charmed circle that Sky might be more disenchanted with speedway than they used to be. Nigel pooh-poohs such outlandish suggestions, "Sky love speedway! Sports [audiences] are down across all their platforms so there's no denying that speedway is down too! But not only are they committed to speedway but we're holding up so much better than other sports! It's a product they love – lots and lots of programming – and have invested in substantially. You have to remember that we were against the Football World Cup and you only have to see the empty seats in football

Peterborough: *"I don't like to eat before the show as it gives me indigestion."*

grounds, like I do in my commentary work, to see the scale of the problem elsewhere!"

Attendance problems aren't solely restricted to this side of the pond if recent news about the substantial numbers of unsold seats at recent early-season NFL games is anything to go by. Even more problematically for American Football when attendances fall below a certain level, the clubs and broadcasters are contractually obliged to enforce live television blackouts within a 140 mile radius of the affected stadiums. It's a contractual obligation that's unlikely to ever apply to the shale. Nigel's incredulous, "If that happened here, speedway would never be on the telly! But seriously, we both know that we'll all be here again at this time next year! Speedway has many loyal fans that are really committed to the sport. Sky loves the excitement! Those BARB figures you quote [on your blog that I don't read] – what's their credibility?"

[Jeff] "They're the industry standard that advertisers use for *Strictly Come Dancing, X Factor* and the like."

[Nigel] "Oh, I see. Our figures are definitely down."

[Jeff] "Not that it's for me to say but Sky need to find a way to quantify the number of people who watch on different platforms other than the telly. If you're a Sky subscriber, others can watch on their PC or laptop. Plus there's all the people who watch online for free in other countries. If you add all that up, it would look a much better number!"

Bananas in hand, Mr. Potassium a.k.a. Craig Saul, is early for his announcing work from the referee's box. Craig used to rove the pits and gambol on the centre green at the East of England Showground. Nowadays the poshly titled "Head of Presentation" Darren Fletcher fulfils these duties on a race night for the Panthers, in addition to his regular football commentary work on Radio 5 Live (where, weirdly, he often sounds remarkably like Nigel Pearson). Craig is still the presenter at Rye House Speedway and enjoys a similar Master of Ceremonies function for Barnet Football Club. Sadly they haven't started the season well and most recently lost against Rotherham. "Actually we were the better of the two teams on Saturday until the last 20 minutes when they scored four!" Away from the track and the hallowed Underhill Stadium turf, Craig travels widely on behalf of one of the world's leading shed manufacturers. As a frequent flier he's well used to turbulence ("the Nantucket sleigh ride – it's where they used to harpoon a whale off Newfoundland and ride along behind it until it had exhausted itself"). He's also enough of a man of the world to be unshocked by male facial jewellery, "the no jewellery rule in football that was supposed to apply to speedway but, I think, no one told Shane Parker for a while!" By their own high standards, Rye House endured a poor season to finish only fifth in the Premier League! While fans' hopes remain high about facing King's Lynn in the Young Shield quarter finals, Craig isn't so optimistic, "No one can make any changes to their team after September 15th – so it's guests, rider replacement or 3-point National League riders for everyone from now on! We're pretty weak so I'd expect King's Lynn to beat us." Craig's stretched in his full-time paid work ("Shed sales are slightly down but holding up well") but also very busy at Rye House. "There's been mission creep! I started with Len just doing the announcing but now it's the presenting, stuff on the website, visitors' notes in the programme – but nothing else – and the press releases!" Though he's got firsthand access to characters on and off the track, Craig takes a sympathetic view of people's foibles and various idiosyncrasies as well as appreciating the cyclical nature of racing form. "I reckon Brendan Johnson is feeling the pressure of being British Under-18 Champion because his form has gone downhill since he won it! Everywhere he goes, people will say – I know I introduce him as 'the Under-18 Champion' – he's the Under-18 Champion! Three years ago it was Lewis Bridger." With information to check, people to greet and informal networks to reignite, Craig bustles off muttering about technical matters. "I hope they connect the [audio] feed to the big screens because last week no one could tell what was a white helmet colour and what was a

232

Peterborough: *"I don't like to eat before the show as it gives me indigestion."*

yellow!"

Ex-Peterborough Panthers programme co-editor Sarah Miles breaks her self-imposed vow of silence to outline the trials and tribulations of her recent post-operative care and recuperation. Panthers club Chaplain, the Reverend Michael Whawell, stands patiently listening a yard or so away. Michael wears his erudition lightly. "Dickens is such a humorist. I'm re-reading *Dombey and Son*. I take it to the crematorium. I get there very early and spend time knocking off a few chapters. It's the first [English] novel that ever dealt with the impact of railways on society and features the first ever railway fatality! Mr Carker is famous for having a mouthful of teeth." I'm not sure that this is so special, "We all have?" Michael adds, "Not glittering ones." Michael's understated but sincere pastoral care recently included the Oakes family after Peter's wife Pam fell seriously ill, due to complications after a major heart operation. Despite the initial grim prognosis, Pam's rallied, shown resilience and fortitude to make determined steps towards recovery. "Understandably Peter Oakes appears bewildered. His wife is very game! He really doesn't want to come here because he doesn't want everyone asking how she is all the time!" On my journey up from Brighton, on Radio 4 they discussed sound and memory. "They say perfect pitch is your memory of the sound of your mother's piano". The programme also discussed the rare neurological condition of synaesthesia that allows some people to see the colours associated with musical notes, "Many say D minor is yellow and A major is emerald green!" Completely unfazed, Michael effortlessly switches from great literature to classical music segueing from Charles Dickens to "Sir Arthur Edward Drummond Bliss, his colour symphony – that bit at the start of the Proms – is his red! He was a bit of an old goat, they say."

Dedicated Panthers diehards Graham and Hilary Rouse are keen to secure their favoured seats in the home-straight grandstand. Hilary remains rudely dismissive ("Are you still doing your scribbling?") in contrast to her always-affable husband Graham who retains a positive outlook on life. His quick glance to compare the Peterborough and Coventry team line-ups in the programme sees Graham immediately identify an unlikely Peterborough secret weapon – their French reserve Mathieu Tresarrieu! "He's a hard man to pass." In addition, Graham believes the really key rider for the home side wears the No. 2 race tabard. "I don't know what Buczkowski will do – he's usually spectacular! It was such a shame last week – three riders rode well, two excellently and two didn't turn up." Like many riders, officials and fans, Brian Oldham closely studies the type of track the Peterborough curatorial team prepare for tonight's season defining encounter at the East of England Showground. "Everyone is out there. It looks like a ploughed field. Trump comes along with hunks of bark, the two refs are out there – Jim Lawrence and Dan Holt – along with Colin Meredith. Bomber, Colin Pratt and Allen Trump are all stood looking together. It's clear that there's been lots of water put on it – they've tyre packed it and put some shale on the top of it. We looked at it and thought that's another ploughed field! If they try to doctor the track too much, it'll suit Bomber down to the ground!" Brian can see little way back for the Panthers, "A Poole versus Coventry Elite League final would be a very interesting meeting."

Over the stadium speaker system Panthers team manager Trevor Swales talks platitudinously about the night ahead then requests full support from the Panthers faithful, "The riders can hear them so it's important the fans get behind the team!" Though the stadium is extremely crowded, if I were the promotional team I'd nonetheless be disappointed at the turnout for this crucial meeting. My only real comparison is the Elite League play-off final second leg held here a few years ago against Reading. That night, the stadium was full to the point of absolutely rammed. In the pits, Nigel Pearson and Kelvin Tatum sit atop their commentary position. It's a structure that looks part Meccano experiment and part pagoda. Every rider, mechanic and official is ready for the off. Bikes gleam, kevlars look smartly shale-free and the brilliant blondness of Krzysztof

Kasprzak's recently dyed hair catches the eye. The bikes and riders for the first heat stand stationary in the area of the pits designated on race night as the pre-push-off holding area. There is a sense of anticipation though, presently, fans and competitors alike remain becalmed since in the live ping-pong match of alternate televised races, Poole versus Wolverhampton have the honour. However, when Freddie Lindgren falls on the first lap at Wimborne Road, the Peterborough pits immediately fire into life as their two-minute warning sounds. We're told, "If possible, televised races will alternate between Dorset and Central England."

Pre-meeting speculation that the Panthers need to immediately hit back against the Bees is sensible presupposition but proves wildly optimistic since Krzysztof Kasprzak wins the first race in a new track record of 58.4 seconds. Even more ominously, Kenneth Bjerre looks completely out of sorts as he finishes last. Coventry's highly regarded reserve Przemyslaw Pawlicki is so keen to get out there that he initially forgets his yellow helmet colour. When the correctly attired riders eventually get under the starter's orders of referee Jim Lawrence, the general tension plus itchy fingers on the clutch results in an unsatisfactory start. Returning confidently to the track where he suffered an ill-starred early season in the Panthers race tabard (before he moved to Coventry), Lewis Bridger leads the rerun easily until Mathieu Tresarrieu falls on the corner at the start of the second lap and is disqualified. While we wait for the third attempt to run the second race, head of presentation Darren Fletcher strikes a positive tone with the crowd about the first heat disadvantage, "Only a minor reverse in the first one but, of course, that did widen the Bees lead a little bit!" The re-rerun sees the riders occupy the same race order (white, blue, yellow) as the rerun until a mistake by Lewis Bridger – on the transition from the third to the fourth bend – gifts Norbert Kosciuch the lead. Stood in the crowd at the apex of the first bend, I'm showered in shale each time the riders pass. The shale is definitely damp so we're definitely more splattered than stoned. Indeed the shale has a peculiar mud porridge clay-like consistency – if judged by the piece that lodges in my ear – almost as if it had been rushed directly to the East of England Showground from a pottery evening class.

Between races, though there's no problem with the sound feed, indistinct pictures on the giant screen limits the entertainment value of racing beamed to us live from Poole. Nerves continue to plague the starts. Heat 3 features two unsatisfactory attempts. The Reverend Michael Whawell hopes that the additional time for reflection given to Barker and Kennett will impinge upon their performance, "I reckon the two Coventry lads will be well psyched-out by now!" Ben Barker wins the race so, with Rory Schlein out of sorts and Edward Kennett third, Coventry's second heat advantage in three races further extends their lead to 4 points on the night and to a possibly insurmountable 18 points overall. In the pits the Reverend Michael Whawell introduces me to Darren Fletcher whose work for Radio 5 Live has this weekend taken him to the Stadium of Light to watch the Sunderland versus Arsenal fixture. "Sunderland deserved the point. I was in Steve Bruce's office afterwards and he said so many big clubs are sniffing round Jordan Henderson. He's on a five-year contract so they'll get a load of money." Darren moves off to do his job that tonight basically gifts him the slightly unenviable task of trying to enthuse the understandably deflated Panthers faithful. Michael enjoys his own close connections with Darren, "Managing Director of Mansfield 103.2 Tony Delahunty gave us both our jobs in sports broadcasting! Tony used to do sports on Pennine Radio – I regularly used to do the God slot and was chatting one day and Tony said, 'Why don't you do the rugby?' We have another connection because Darren's got a mate who owns the nearest pub to Mansfield's ground!" Though it's Trevor Swales's job to motivate the Peterborough team, Darren believes that he might need additional help via Michael's upstairs connections, "We might need you!"

234

[Jeff] "Is that for an interview or to put pressure on the Lord?"

[Michael] "Hah! A bit of pressure. I'm not here to guarantee a win."

Peterborough: *"I don't like to eat before the show as it gives me indigestion."*

[Jeff] "It looks unlikely."

[Michael] "It does. The result's not in doubt but I suppose it's the tension. In terms of experience they [Schlein and Iverson] should have beaten those two [Barker and Kennett]. It's not our night!"

While we wait for the start of heat 4, Darren manages to corner one of the Swales family for a brief interview, "It's a lifting job, isn't it?" The pre-existing psychological barrier of Coventry's 14-point lead appears to weigh heavily and, apparently, is compounded by home rider anxiety about the race surface. Wayne's categorical about what's required from the Panthers riders, "Don't bother about the track, just get out there and show what you can do!" Talk of shale prompts Michael Whawell to break off from his study of the action from Wimborne Road to observe, "The Poole track looks very slick and dusty!" Michael senses heat 4 could be the turning point the Panthers require to kick-start their evening since it features the combative Australian Troy Batchelor, "Batch rode wonderfully here on Friday – he beat Leigh Adams three times!" This observation barely leaves Michael's mouth before Darren Fletcher echoes him about Troy over the stadium speaker system. ("I just said that – he's cribbing my best lines!") Also out in heat 4 is Panthers heat 2 race winner Norbert Kosciuch. Michael's been in conversation with his landlady, "Christina said – because Norbert lodges with her – he won that race because she gave him prawns and noodles for tea!" Until the last bend, it definitely looks like this innovative prawn and noodles diet should be a mandatory feature of contemporary speedway life in the ongoing search for the fractional advantages required to find the next British world champion. Unfortunately, though Norbert races with speed and confidence, Chris 'Bomber' Harris really relishes the track the Panthers curatorial team inadvertently created for tonight's meeting. Bomber picks his moment to power past Norbert and take the chequered flag. Up in the referee's box, Craig Saul prefaces his announcement of the official results with the words "the not-so-secret weapon …" Even worse for Peterborough, Troy Batchelor retires from the race and, thereby, gifts Coventry yet another heat advantage as the score balloons to 9-15.

Things look so shockingly desperate that Trevor Swales immediately calls an impromptu team meeting behind the closed doors of the Panthers dressing room. Though we're all excluded from this pep talk, we've all got a shrewd general idea of the content of the discussions. Darren Fletcher suspects blunt exchanges will "kick start this meeting" and spark a revival after "a tepid start". Veteran of many marathons, Michael still runs regularly but also subscribes to *Runner's World* magazine. "Did you see the motivational article by a middle-aged woman entitled 'I get to … go running?' It's a mantra she uses all the time to appreciate the things she gets to do that she used to take for granted. She didn't look at life like that until she went running but, now, she thinks: I get to make the tea, I get to help with the homework and, of course, I get to go out running! Did you see in the paper Brighton was described as the sort of town that gives the impression it's helping the police with their enquiries?"

If Panthers fans feel let down by the first four races of the night then – despite the impromptu motivational team talk – things take a distinct turn for the worse after Coventry's Richard Sweetman fires from the gate in heat 5 to win comfortably. Worse still, Rory Schlein concedes second place to Krzysztof Kasprzak on the last bend of the first lap. Even the Reverend Michael Whawell can no longer remain taciturn, "Oh come on! You'd think Coventry were the home team – that really is awful!" With the cushion of a comfortable lead, Coventry team manager Alun Rossiter is unlikely to require great oratorical flare to gee up his riders. However, as the Panthers team apparently implode, Rosco merely has to do what he does: sit back, smile, pat his riders on the back and offer token words of encouragement. After Krzysztof returns to the pits from heat 5, Rosco tells him, "Good stuff, Krzy, keep it up!" The Bees 1-5 takes the score to a ridiculously comfortable 10-20. Heat 6 features Panthers No. 1 Kenneth Bjerre. Michael hopes for significant

Peterborough: *"I don't like to eat before the show as it gives me indigestion."*

improvement this time out, "I don't know what happened to Kenneth in heat 1 – they'd not done anything dramatic to his bike! Umm, we're not going black-and-white yet! I'm surprised! [glances in programme] Ah, actually, probably a mistake to waste it against Chris Harris." Out on the East of England Showground track, formation track work by the tractors entertains during the mandatory lull to watch another televised race from Poole. Colin Pratt stands close to the fence. He intently watches these curatorial endeavours until Ben Barker comes up to him gesticulating, argumentative and with fingers wagging. Michael shrugs, "Ben has issues it seems!"

Away in the far distance, on the big screen at the opposite end of the stadium Chris Holder overtakes Adam Skornicki. It's a manoeuvre that prompts Kelvin to shatter the comparative calm of the pits area with a scream, "Whoa! Woo, who, what an overtake!" Engaging yourself in loud conversation would be frowned upon in many circles but, perhaps, this is how Kelvin keeps psyched-up to the ecstasy levels that typify his commentary work with Nigel Pearson? Desperate for a fight-back, Michael sets extremely tough targets for the Panthers commercial team, "We want the Lord God Almighty as a sponsor!" With the riders under orders, revving their bikes to the max as the tapes rise, Michael exclaims, "Go on – get out – somebody!" That certain somebody is Krzysztof Buczkowski. He leads until the third bend of the third lap until his bike stutters and temporarily judders to a halt. It's a sight that prompts Michael to come over all Victor Meldrew, "Oh, would you believe that!" Moments later, Krzysztof's bike fires throatily back into life but the damage is already done since Chris Harris now occupies the lead. By the standards of recent races, this drawn heat is a Panthers triumph of sorts though it fails to dent the deficit. Darren Fletcher prefaces his latest interrogation of a member of the Swales family with a lengthy observation, "Wayne, 10 points behind on the night – 24 on aggregate – it's not a lack of commitment, we just cannot get started!"
[Wayne] "Nah, we just seem to be on the back foot tonight ... we've discussed things, geed the boys up but it's not happening!"
[Darren] "It's not over till the fat lady sings but she's warming up at the back of the pits!"

The next race of the night sees Troy Batchelor start to show the form of three days previous that saw him thrice best Leigh Adams. Sadly, a fall from French secret weapon Mathieu Tresarrieu results in a drawn heat. Michael looks on disconsolately, "They can let us win races all night – it doesn't matter!" While we wait for further race action, talk turns to the beauty of the British motorway system, "In Birmingham in the '60s I was one of those that went to look at the M1 when it opened. It was two white concrete strips with a grass verge down the middle!" No sooner does Michael enquire plaintively about potential tactical options, ("How about giving one of the reserves a black and white?") than his wish comes true. Krzysztof Buczkowski is handed this responsibility in heat 8, "He's a nice lad – he speaks and shakes hands." Continuing his ongoing investigation into tonight's stuttering display, Darren Fletcher asks the Panthers No. 3 for an explanation, "Rory, what's wrong tonight?" Michael doesn't wait for his reply, "Rory's not been the lad he was when he first came here, he's gone off – before he was superb!" Coventry's Richard Sweetman makes no real attempt to line up at the tapes for heat 8 and is soon disqualified by referee Jim Lawrence in breech of the two-minute time allowance. He's then replaced by returning zero, Lewis Bridger. Michael's not optimistic, "Bridger will now put in the ride of the night, you'll see!" In fact it's Krzysztof Buczkowski who shines to gain a double-points victory while Lewis finishes last. With Norbert Kosciuch third, the Panthers gain their first heat advantage of the night to narrow the scores to 23-28. Breathtakingly optimistic, Darren Fletcher asks Peterborough team manager Trevor Swales, "Is that the turning point for the Panthers? For the first time tonight, there's something to cling on to!" Trevor plays along, "Yeh sure…I think we've too many people not firing!" Darren persists with his optimism, "Maybe we can fire in the 5-1s like Coventry did last week." Trevor has no choice but to publicly agree, "Yeh, sure."

Peterborough: *"I don't like to eat before the show as it gives me indigestion."*

While Edward Kennett warmly hugs Peter Oakes with a ferocity that betokens genuine affection, Craig Saul kindly promotes my books over the speaker system with his moniker "the sage of the age" only then to make me sound totally bigheaded with the (erroneous) claim it's my "self-proclaimed styling". Interview with Trevor over, Darren tells the assembled Panthers faithful, "You've got to remain optimistic at the Showground tonight. Maybe, just maybe, something could happen!" This optimistic statement over, Darren switches off his roving microphone and laughingly turns to Peter Oakes to say, "Did you see that pig fly by? If we get a 5-1 here we'll only be 15 behind on aggregate! You've got to be optimistic!"

If the Panthers best hopes hang by a thread, heat 9 sees the meeting fire into life when referee Jim Lawrence controversially excludes race leader Rory Schlein after he slightly locks up on the far bend and Chris Harris falls off behind him. Bellowing into his microphone, we can hear Kelvin's appraisal of the incident, "He looked out of control – both riders looked out of control [pause] that's an exclusion for the rider in red!" Though hard to believe it possible, Peter Oakes exclaims even louder than Kelvin, "What?!" Sensibly avoiding a possible fine by the sensible legal tactic of repeating the opinions of others, Darren takes to the speaker system, "Nigel Pearson and Kelvin just said Rory isn't going to be too pleased with that [watches replay] it looks like not the best decision by the referee ever!" Indeed, it's the kind of peculiar decision that makes you want to phone a friend. Predictably enough, there's real clamour to use the pits phone. With their opinions sharpened by a sense of righteous indignation, Trevor Swales and Rory Schlein both give their tuppence-worth to Jim Lawrence before they then reiterate a politer version of their opinions under the roving arc light in front of the Sky Sports cameras. Keen to review the incident dispassionately and/or have their prejudices confirmed, people crowd round the pits television monitor or squint at the replay loops on the giant screen. The bare bones of the incident is that Schlein and Harris definitely made no contact. Varying schools of thought place different stresses on the response to Rory's slight lock-up. I have some sympathy with the strand of opinion that expresses incredulity at the idea that the race leader can earn a disqualification when the rider behind him falls. Jodie Lowry expresses the Coventry school of thought cogently, "What would you do then? Bomber had to put it down cos Rory got out of shape. The alternative is to run into him!" Darren explains the pit scene to the crowd, "I think you've all seen the replays so you'll understand why tempers are running high here in the pits." Rarely needing a second invitation to grumble, Rory's adamant that he has been discriminated against, "I got a little bit out of shape on turns three and four – no more than anyone else!" Prior to the rerun there's a slight element of a kafuffle around Chris Harris after he ignores heartfelt suggestions he intervene with the referee to try to make him rescind his decision. Understandably, and sensibly, Chris deems that the referee Jim Lawrence's decision is final. Peter Oakes's grandson Josh Gudgeon remains nonplussed, "Why can't referees look at the replays and say, 'I was wrong?' Everyone would respect them for it – even the Coventry fans." Darren Fletcher doesn't have to search very far to find an ex-World Champion to comment, "You've seen some bad decisions in your time, what did you think of that?" Michael Lee comments, "Yeh, very disappointed about it. The rider in front can go where he wants and the rider behind has to avoid him! I don't want to say anything that'll get me into trouble but, yeh, well …"

While this storm of indignation or indifference reigns in the East of England Showground pits, the audio feed from Poole supplies a surreal counterpoint when Tony Millard gurgles, "That's the icing on the cake – marzipan and all! … wheelies in unison and all!" With the earlier poor performance on the track almost forgotten, Darren just can't get enough perspective on the incident, so gleefully snatches yet more words with Trevor Swales, "You were extremely vociferous on the phone to ref." Unable to deny his understandable anger, Trevor confesses, "Yeh, you know, it's one of those things. [Pause] I'm not going to say what I actually think, am I? [Pause] I regret my swear words!"

Krzysztof Buczkowski wins heat 10 but sadly it's an out-of-sorts Kenneth Bjerre who catches the attention with his last place. It's a performance that perplexes management, fans and Michael Whawell alike, "There we go, I dunno what's wrong with him? Maybe he's not feeling well or something? Buczkowski's got twice as many points as anyone else riding at No. 2, which is a pig of a position! I just don't know what's up with Kenneth Bjerre – this is the man who's lowered the track record three times this season!" Darren manages to catch an always reticent Chris Harris for a few (brief) words on the talking point of the night, "He got a bit of grip – the ref made the decision not me!" Michael listens to Bomber's explanation intently, "You can imagine it would be a candidate for the shortest book in the world – *The Thoughts of Chris Harris*. Taciturn is a word that springs to mind." Michael Lee pops over for a few words with the club chaplain, "We played into Coventry's hand by how we prepared the track. It wasn't what we expected! Don't get me wrong – they all have to ride it – but it's given us no chance!" Krzysztof Kasprzak enlivens heat 11 on the second lap when he hits the airfence as he exits the second bend. Indeed, Krzysztof smacks into the inflatable safety furniture with such velocity that the safety fence boards behind the aircushion bend and rattle noisily. Rick Frost exclaims, "Bad one!" There's huge but barely controlled panic as paramedics, officials, riders and mechanics from both teams rush over to inspect and console Krzysztof. The impact punctures the airbags and decimates the fence around. Darren relays updates to the crowd and almost glories in the "deep wet and murky outside line" Krzysztof rode before he personally crash-tested the equipment. Built of stern stuff, bottle-blond Kasprzak quickly reassures concerned teammates and competitors that he's alright ("He's even found the time to exchange a smile with Ben Barker"). To fill the time, Darren grabs Wayne Swales for yet another probing interview that he prefaces with the most ludicrously optimistic rhetorical question of the night so far, "If the Readypower Panthers get 5-1s for the last five heats, you go through by a point." Wayne isn't so easily convinced, "What can you say? We've left it too late. I can only apologise to our fans."

Richard Sweetman storms to his second win of the night in the rerun of heat 11 to, thereby, guarantee Coventry progress to the Elite League play-off final against Poole. With Peterborough's Elite League silverware ambitions at an end for the 2010 season, over by the trackshop many fans stream away early towards the car park. These early departures include Graham Rouse, "That was embarrassing. A lot of people have gone home early!" Though the teams share the points over the final four heats, it hardly massages the final scoreline of 44-49. In the trackshop Andy Griggs isn't likely to be overwhelmed with demand for the astonishing array of clothing and merchandise he stocks in the distinctive black-and-red livery of the Panthers. Krzysztof Buczkowski is the only Panthers rider to excel (paid 15) and, even if you could fit all the letters of his name onto the back of an anorak, it's unlikely that Andy would even be able to shift these on a night like this. Andy isn't keen on excuses, "I can't stand how people complain about track conditions! Funny how, out of 14 riders, it's always the team that's losing that moans!" That said, with the milk of human kindness in short supply, equally Andy doesn't want to bathe too deeply in the warm glow of Alun Rossiter's post-meeting comments, "I wish Rosco would shut the flip up! He talks like a professional tit." Coventry fans are out in force tonight at the East of England Showground – particularly on the back straight – to celebrate their triumph with gusto.

20th September Peterborough v. Coventry Elite League semi-final second leg: 44-49

Peterborough: *"I don't like to eat before the show as it gives me indigestion."*

CHAPTER 29

Dudley

"He doesn't turn it until – as they used to say – he can read the labels on the beer bottles!"

5th October

The success of the 2010 season is the Dudley Heathens club emergence on the National League speedway scene. Shrewdly built upon the pent-up nascent demand of Cradley Heath fans for a speedway club closely linked to their presently defunct club, the promotional triumvirate of Nigel Pearson (Chairman), Chris Van Straaten (Club Partner) and Gary Patchett (Club Partner) along with Will Pottinger (team manager) in combination with the dedicated Cradley Heathen Supporters' Club has, retrospectively, been hailed as an obvious low-risk investment. With speedway fans already well served in the Midlands area at Birmingham, Coventry, Stoke and Wolverhampton, the assumption that attendance levels would be significant and sustained for the duration of the season was far from certain. Especially since Dudley's organisational structure is premised upon a split of their race-night activities between the stadiums at Monmore Green and Perry Barr. On the lower cost base of the National League, consistently impressive attendances deliver significant weekly financial benefits to this risk-taking and visionary triumvirate. Though in some quarters, some speedway fans resent the windfall nature of their sustained profitability, such a financial outcome is a rarity in contemporary British speedway (let alone in the National League). Setting aside the 'drinks all round' robust financial performance, results on the track have also been significant. Many of the Heathens NL riders quickly established themselves as fans' favourites and, in any other season, their ongoing improvement would usually result in significant silverware for the Dudley trophy cabinet (exact location unknown). However, this season there is intense competition at the top end of the National League.

My initial attempt to witness the Dudley dream first hand was sabotaged by poor weather prior to the original staging of the Golden Hammer individual event on July 12th. In fact the rain was so heavy that if the trophy had

Programme stall

239

been left outside it would soon rust, if made of the 'special' gold usually used for speedway commemorative prizes. Sadly I missed the restaging of the Golden Hammer (won by Simon Lambert) so it's good to finally make it along to see the Heathens autumnal National League play-off semi-final first leg versus the Buxton Hitmen. When I pull up inside the Monmore Green Stadium entrance gates, Chris Van Straaten and his son Karl stand deep in conversation next to a small knot of three mad-keen Wolverhampton fans. In the few moments it takes for me to grab my stuff and make my way to the gates, Chris Van Straaten has shot off back to the seclusion of the speedway office doing his best Major Major impression. Luckily, earlier in the season, I spoke with Chris Van Straaten at Arlington about the successful reintroduction of Dudley: "The crowds have taken us by surprise at Dudley. Really taken us by surprise and they're not my [Wolverhampton] fans. Well, 10%, but 90% are Cradley fans. You can tell they haven't been for a while because we sold out of programmes on the first night out – people want those, of course, the first night. Programmes are dead nowadays. Since I've been in the sport it's, at least, 35% less than it was. Understandable because there's no news in them and, with technology nowadays, you can get your news elsewhere and print your programme sheet. Because we sold out we did a reprint – we had to because so many wanted them – and we only have 20 left of those. When I was a kid Dudley used to have so many sports in the borough – cricket and football – and now there's nothing! Whereas in Wolverhampton they have everything – the athletics stadium, Molyneux, us, horse racing and the dogs. When we wanted extra car parking for the final last year, nothing was too much trouble for them. We could have everything. Of course, the local politicians said some very positive things about us [Dudley] but that was at election time so we really have to get them on our side. We've had them all down to see for themselves! Of course, we can only do it for two years, otherwise it's not fair on the public. We need the carrot of the sport returning to the borough. It has to! You can't run this indefinitely without some action!"

Back at the entrance gates, Karl Van Straaten guards cum supervises arrivals tightly clutching a clipboard. Karl's engaged in deep in conversation about the West Midlands topic du jour – the exact team line-up of the Coventry Bees. "If Pawlicki had ridden one more meeting he'd have been in the team and Ginge would have been at reserve!"
[Jeff] "I'm Jeff."
[Karl] "I know who you are. I'm not speaking to you. You put me in your book."
[Jeff] "Ah. I thought your joke was good."
[Karl] "Not many people got it. I'm not saying anything to you."

Dave "the Hat" Haddon is happy to talk, "I'm only 19 short of 9,000!" It's an astonishing headgear collection, even in a sport that attracts multiple obsessives. Dave proudly wears the latest addition to his wardrobe – a Vargarna cap with a centrally placed weird wolf's head logo (apparently swimming). Karl politely enquires, "Is that the old-fashioned one?"
[Dave] "What?"
[Karl] "Is that the retro one?"
[Dave] "I dunno about that – it's the old one."
[Karl] "So, it is the retro one!"
[Dave] "It's the old one!"
[Karl] "THAT is the retro one!" [Sighs]

Ignoring the size of his cap collection, Dave's any promoters' ideal speedway fan since – even though the season isn't yet complete – he has with him the completed application form (concession version) for his 2011 Wolverhampton speedway season ticket. Wolverhampton pits marshal Kevin Davies arrives and immediately asks Bill Gimbeth, resplendent in a Redcar Bears shirt, "Can I borrow your shirt to clean the car with?" Talk soon turns to further analysis of this

Dudley: *"He doesn't turn it until – as they used to say – he can read the labels on the beer bottles!"*

season's Elite League champions – Coventry – who triumphed at Poole last night. Despite just winning this coveted silverware, Kevin is quick to highlight weaknesses in their line-up, "Barker and Bridger did nothing!"

Over by the left-hand set of stairs that lead up into the swishly impressive Monmore Green Stadium home-straight grandstand, programme seller Keith Fletcher patiently sets out boxes that contain tonight's programme on the table he's just taken from the boot of his car. Keith's cup also doesn't exactly overflow with joy at Coventry's triumph. "They deserved it but I can't say I'm pleased." Fellow programme vendor, Sarah Jones, ponders 'what if?' scenarios, "If Bomber had been injured in that race [heat 6] who knows how it would have turned out? It was Lewis who ran over him so who knows how he would have reacted?" No sooner do the turnstiles open than a loud alarm sounds within the main grandstand. Ten minutes later three policemen in reflective yellow fluorescent tops arrive to investigate. During the factional lull after an initial rush of programme sales, I quiz Keith and Sarah about their allegiances. Keith is a "dyed in the wool" Wolves fan, "I support Dudley as well to be honest with you in the National League. Sarah's just started helping me this season. I can't get anyone else to come on a Tuesday night."

Sarah is keen to underline where her allegiances lie, "Wolves is my team not Cradley – if I like a National League team, it's got to be the Isle of Wight!" Sarah pointedly asks the next fan to request a programme, "Are you gutted?"
[Keith Stellard] "I am, especially when I've had a bet on Coventry for the last two seasons but this year I didn't! Yes, I'm gutted!"

Programme seller Keith Fletcher's been going to the speedway since 1961. "I've been working down here 30-odd years. I used to work with Dave [Rattenberry] and John Millard doing lots of things until I started doing the programmes." Sarah's reluctant to tell me how long she's been coming ("37 years – my age – that's why I don't like to say!") but is much happier talking about her all-time favourite Wolverhampton riders. "The present one now is Tai Woffinden, then Ronnie Correy and Sam Ermolenko. Back in the '70s it was Hans Nielsen." It looks like there's endless demand for the Dudley programmes. Two staple topics of conversation intersperse purchases – Coventry's triumph and the price of the programme. If Sarah isn't repeatedly sharing her perspective with fans ("the turning point was when Bridger ran over Harris – if he'd been injured that would've been it!"), she responds to the question, "How much are they?" To my mind, this is a surprise most frequently asked question given that you'd expect – this late in the season – Dudley fans would by now know the cost of their own programme? Sarah soon corrects my misapprehension, "No, no, no! Last week [for the Golden Hammer] it was £3 that's why!" Keith admires the fans here. "The crowd is surprising, isn't it? There's some Brummies and Wolves fans and the odd Coventry fan plus a few from Stoke but 90% are Cradley fans!" Poole supporter Sally Knight is the first person to sound genuine in her congratulation of Coventry. "I'm disappointed, but the best team won! Not over the season but the play-offs! When Bridger ran over Chris Harris, I think it surprised everyone that he sprinted back to the pits. The only really bad thing was seeing Rosco's smug face at the end. I wish I hadn't seen that!"

Buxton co-promoter Jayne Moss stops to collect a wodge of programmes and I ask her about a team line-ups spat that Derek Barclay recently alluded to on the British Speedway Forum. "He's just a programme editor. I wasn't going to be spoken to like that just because I wasn't at my computer at that minute! It's good that he gives his time but, then, so do many people. That's speedway – everyone puts in a lot of time! Fair enough, he wanted some information. The rule is that the home promotion has to declare their team first. I wasn't going to have anyone telling me they'd make up my team for me! He sent me these long personal messages. I think he thinks he's more important than he is! He's just a programme editor. When we went there [to

Dudley: *"He doesn't turn it until – as they used to say – he can read the labels on the beer bottles!"*

Bournemouth] I didn't see him. I don't think I'd know him. If he stood next to me, I'd not recognise him." Buxton and Belle Vue fan Charles McKay cuts short our conversation, "I've just been to Czecho. There wasn't a very big crowd at the Marketa. I must say I smiled when I heard Rye House [National League Pairs and NRLC] had been called off [due to the weather]. Jane's similarly philosophical about the need for restaging, "I did too cos it means we'll have Cookie riding there now!" Craig Cook rides for the Buxton Hitmen tonight but so does the most exciting speedway rider I've seen this season – Jason Garrity. When I sing his praises to Jayne, she smiles, "You're not the first person to say that. He always gives 100%! Sometimes you shut your eyes but he really tries! Lots of speedway fans really take to him. He's got quite a following!" Jayne's football-mad Manchester City and Buxton supporting son Josh is keyed-up for tonight's meeting. He modestly bats off my congratulations that he's already top scorer for his football team with five goals in two games. When I ask, "Are you going to win?" Josh fires back with some assurance, "Yeh, easy-peasy." Jayne counsels against his overconfidence, "Woof! I wouldn't say that!" Josh isn't open to his maternal advice, "I would – we will!"

Reading Racers club historian, Arnie Gibbons arrives in plenty of time before tapes up, "I was at Wimborne Road last night chatting about child benefit with Derek [Barclay]. He's a bit of a leftie." [Jeff] "What Derek Barclay at an Elite League meeting? Is that allowed?"
[Arnie] "Oh absolutely! He claims to be a Poole supporter nowadays! It's a shame that Coventry got a 5-1 in heat 10 because, as a neutral, I'd have liked it if it'd gone down to the wire." I resist quizzing Arnie about the coalition government as ill advised, given his close connections to the upper echelons of the Liberal Democrats. Arnie does lead me to think that there may be some budgets that could be constructively reviewed, "I live in a constituency with the National Military Band School. So, obviously, trombones are vital to the defence of the country!" I'm not so sure this would be a sensible 'cut', "They say some music can be intimidating and strike fear into the heart of the enemy!"

Programme sales still continue apace. Keith tells me, "We'll sell about 575 tonight – sometimes it's 600 – about the same as we sell at a Wolves meeting!" When I quiz Keith and Sarah about what could be done to improve British speedway, Keith replies, "More English riders!" Sarah believes training could be the key, "Get the Government to put up schools so we can get more English riders!" If they were in charge of the BSPA, changes to the organisation and structure of the sport in this country would result, "Get rid of the play-offs! Poole finished top of the league so they're the winners!" On the subject of winners – although she was here at the time – Sarah knows what they broadcast earlier on the telly, "Chris Harris was on *Midlands Today* at 6.30 p.m. tonight with the trophy – his back was bruised!"

In front of a substantial crowd on the upper and lower home-straight terraces, Heat 1 sees Lee Smart and Micky Dyer of the Heathens surge into a lead. So much so that when Craig Cook falls on the third bend of the second lap, he lingers long enough on the shale to ensure the race stops. Understandably SCB referee Mick Bates disqualifies him but, with Dudley on an almost certain 5-1, theatrical boos greet Cook on his long trudge back to the pits. Presenter Ian 'Porky' Jones issues a timely reminder to the more robustly opinionated members of the Dudley faithful, "You can say what you want about me but do remember that there are kids at the front!" There are also kids on the track according to Wolverhampton club historian Mark Sawbridge. "I'll tell you two to watch out for. Ashley Morris (16) can turn a bike on a sixpence – which is a rare skill for a youngster – just watch him in the next race! Whereas Tom Perry, he doesn't turn it until – as they used to say – he can read the labels on the beer bottles! You can tell Tom Perry is a typical grass-tracker, he can't gate to save his life! Mark Loram, Chris Morton, Peter Collins and Chris Harris all started out on grasstrack and – because you've got such a long run into the first bend – you never develop the habit. It helps that Ashley and Tom are both Wolverhampton lads! I hate to say that the crowds have been bigger than for Wolves. Every meeting here has been brilliant! We've missed a couple down here. It's like joining some sort of religious sect if you say you go to see Dudley, they look at me as if I've been brain washed! It's been great. If you think about it, it's been 15 years since Dudley Wood closed. I reckon we should forget all of that old Wolves/Cradley rivalry as it's well and truly in the past!"

With the riders up at the tapes for heat 2, I point out that Jason Garrity is one to watch. Mark's yet to see him in action, "I don't think he rode the last time they were here." As usual, Jason Garrity fails to gate but soon leans on Ashley Morris in the first bend. They then traverse the corner inches away from each other before Garrity thrusts his way into the lead as they exit the second bend. Jason wins easily though his speed and frequent slight lock-ups do create the impression that, at any moment, he could still unexpectedly tumble from his bike. Sportingly, 'Porky' admires what he's seen, "It has to be said he was absolutely flying!" Earlier Dudley announcer Stuart Sargeant kindly complemented my work ("I've enjoyed your books") and, before heat 3 starts, he bigs up *Shale Trek* with a dig at his presentational partner in crime, "that's about 240,000 more words than you, Porky!" With words the *lingua franca* of his business, Porky isn't ever short of an immediate retort, "Next year – your autobiography is out – 40 words!"

The third race of the night sees Adam Allott gate and lead from flag to flag. Behind him, between bends two and three, Tom Perry excitingly blasts from fourth to second to give good chase throughout. Mark Sawbridge looks on admiringly, "See what I mean about Perry? It's like a magnet drawing him to the fence!" Untroubled team riding from Buxton's Nick Morris and Jason Garrity then delivers a maximum heat advantage in heat 4 that gives the Hitmen into a lead they hold on to. When, for reasons unknown, Nick Morris slows on the last bend he's waved forward by his teammate Jason Garrity. Arnie Gibbons luxuriates in seventh heaven, "My two favourite teams this year are Dudley and Buxton, Wolves is my favourite track and this is a meeting that means something!" If this meeting is something to savour, then the food Arnie had on the way up still causes some anxiety, "I had an American chicken sandwich at the Services on the way here. It could have been worse. I asked the woman what was American about it and she said it was the batter. Sounded more Scottish to me!"

The return of Craig Cook back out onto the track prompts Porky to goad the Dudley faithful, "Show your appreciation for Cookie!" Theatrical boos ring out as well as a solitary shout of bravado, "Come over the fence and do it!" It's a topsy-turvy race. Jake Andersen gates with Tom Perry second as they exit bend two. Garrity surges past Perry round the third and fourth bends before Cook comfortably passes both Garrity and Anderson. On the third bend of the second lap, Garrity drops to fourth before he battles his way back into third and then – with a blast up the inside on the run-in from the last bend to the finish line – he snatches second by the proverbial tyre knobble. It's the kind of closely fought overtaking galore-type heat that deservedly gives the National League its reputation for excitement. Heat 6 is a much more meat-and-potatoes affair after an engine failure on the third bend robs Nick Morris of the lead to gift Micky Dyer and Lee Smart a maximum heat advantage. The fourth maximum heat advantage in four races arrives via Adam Allott and Robert Branford who combine to stretch the Buxton lead to 6 points. The bare fact of their victory on the racecard disguises the fact that though he finishes third, Ashley Morris pressured, probed and harried both Hitmen for the entire duration of the race. *Express and Star* speedway reporter, Tim Hamblin, enquires of the knowledgeable fans around him on the terraces, "Who is the oldest in this then?"

They say that many hands make light work and this certainly appears to be the race-night

---

Dudley: *"He doesn't turn it until – as they used to say – he can read the labels on the beer bottles!"*

approach to start-line supervision for the Dudley Heathens. Prior to the start of every race, Dudley start marshal Keith Kershaw supervises the riders on gates three and four; while another (mystery) man in overalls supervises the riders in gates one and two. Once the riders line up to the satisfaction of both men, the overalled man steps aside onto the centre green to allow the registered official in the black-and-white striped top [Keith Kershaw] to formally supervise the actual start under the control of the referee. I can't say that prior to a race that I've ever noticed two start marshals in operation at any other track in the country but, come to think of it, I've never really looked! At Dudley, each man holds up the tape (between gates one and two or between gates three and four) in contrast to tracks where there's the traditional solitary start marshal. The fine line between helpfulness and pedantic harassment is often difficult to judge – though, usually, it's only focused upon away riders. Here at Dudley, prior to heat 8, it's difficult to understand on what basis a non-licensed man in overalls can take it upon himself to exercise the regulatory duties of a licensed start marshal stood only a yard or so away from him? The man in overalls obviously relishes his work, judged by the zeal with which he insists Jason Garrity adjust his position on gate two. It's a nitpicking display that prompts me to ask the man next to me, "Who's he?"

[Max Cartwright] "The start marshal."

[Jeff] "No, he's not – the start marshal is on gates three and four."

[Max] "Garrity's lined up too close to gate one."

Whether or not such intervention distracts or irks Jason Garrity, we'll never know. However, we can all see with our own eyes that Garrity arrives into the first bend in last place. Super keen to get back on terms, Garrity powers away from the exit of bend two, zooms along the back straight and really launches himself into the third bend where – though he doesn't touch him – the blue-helmeted Ashley Morris reacts with surprise at such close attention and falls. With Jason Garrity amongst them like a bowling ball through skittles, Robert Branford and Micky Dyer also both do well to stay on their bikes. With carnage threatened on bend three but not quite fully wrought, Garrity finds himself disqualified. Most of the crowd greet this decision with insouciance though, personally, I can only imagine the referee Mick Bates makes this decision based on perceived intent or lack of control, since there was no actual contact with the fallen rider. Tim Hamblin notes, "Jeff Scott predicted that at 3.30 p.m. over a cup of tea. " Half-admiringly Max Cartwright comments, "He saw the gap and just went for it!" In an attempt to solve the mystery of the wannabe extra start line 'official' in the overalls, I pop over to consult Arnie Gibbons, "Who is that?"

[Arnie] "I think he's the assistant start marshal."

[Jeff] "Is there such a position? He hasn't hassled any Dudley riders yet!"

[Arnie] "That's not unusual. He's probably an enforcer for the older start marshal."

[Jeff] "Am I the only one in the stadium who thought Garrity was unfairly excluded?"

[Duncan Gusterson] "I thought he'd passed blue and then pulled a locker to avoid Dyer."

[Arnie] "I thought he was going to knock off Dyer and Branford so got disqualified for that."

[Duncan] "I thought Morris fell off when he pulled the locker."

[Jeff] "Are you a Buxton fan then?"

[Duncan] "I am but I'm impartial! I thought he went for it and got through the gap and blue fell off two seconds later."

It's all moot anyway since the rerun gets underway with only three riders plus a start marshal and a wannabe "assistant start marshal" who exhibits an arriviste's zeal in his supervision. Sadly for Dudley fans, Ashley Morris gets out of shape and drifts across the track. So much so that he creates a giant gap for Robert Branford to seize a lead he fully capitalises upon. After the race, Porky is either blessed with incredible eyesight or a fertile imagination, when he claims that (despite his helmet), "You can see the disappointment on Ashley's face!"

Dudley: *"He doesn't turn it until – as they used to say – he can read the labels on the beer bottles!"*

After a slew of 5-1s, we witness a run of drawn heats. The exclusion of Adam Allott for a tapes offence at the start of heat 10 brings crowd favourite Jason Garrity back out onto the track and prompts Porky to observe, "Oh, it's like having a curry with lots of spice in it!" Sadly bike trouble prevents Garrity from executing any of his trademark inside blasts. Nonetheless we still enjoy an engaging duel for second place between Micky Dyer and Robert Branford. They exchange position throughout until Dyer's ambition trumps calculation or circumspection to result in his fall on the apex of the final bend during a last-gasp dash for glory (to, thereby, gift Garrity an undeserved consolation point). While we wait for the next race, Mark Sawbridge inadvertently reveals the frightening depth of his speedway memorabilia obsession. "I was watching eBay on Sunday like a hawk and there was a Cradley race jacket from 1982 signed by Phil Collins. Guess how much it went for? It was up to £492 when I let it go!" Max Cartwright takes a brief jaunt down memory lane, "I went to my first speedway meeting in 1947 – I was 12 – and if I'd had a programme (I couldn't afford one, if you know what I mean) it would be worth £200 now! There was 30,000 when I went on a Sunday afternoon. I've been going ever since. I was interviewed on the telly last week for a programme called *Inside Out*. It'll be shown next month on BBC1." Craig Cook races to his second victory of the night in heat 11, despite a last-gasp blast up the inside that fails by a yard from Barrie Evans (who casts off his earlier lacklustre form).

During the interval I make my way to the Dudley Heathens Supporters' Club trackshop. There's a good selection of merchandise and, when I snatch a few words with Simon Priest, he tells me, "All the money comes back into the club." Simon also lets me know that he's "On the Supporters' Club committee along with Andy, Paul and Will P. The four of us helped start it two years ago! Everyone has worked really hard and it would be nice to think that we'd helped speedway in some way! We've enjoyed it and I just hope something comes of it!" Though the Heathens trail by only 6 points at the interval, Buxton look strong opposition. "It's exactly the repeat of last time they were here. Evans and Anderson have struggled. That Garrity reminds me of Tomasz Gollob with that move. If he'd waited a lap, he'd have got past! Actually he reminds me of a young Kenny Carter!"

When the racing resumes, Buxton make a reserve switch to bring Jason Garrity in for Lewis Dallaway. Once more he starts slowly (this time off gate one). The race is still only a few yards old when Garrity slides underneath Tom Perry as they enter the bend and, as a result, he slews across the track to fall. Tim Hamblin is adamant that Garrity took Perry's leg away and, shortly after, news that referee Mick Bates orders all four back, is roundly booed. Max Cartwright is adamant the referee's made a howler, "I think he's a Buxton fan him!" My slightly tongue-in-cheek observation that Perry should be excluded is given short shrift. We then enjoy a long break. Mark Sawbridge has a plausible explanation for the delay, "They say Perry's bike was clogged up with shale. Arnie was saying that he's seen Garrity fall off on the way to the start line – you instinctively like a rider like that!" Continuing in problem identification mode, Max Cartwright has little optimism ahead of the rerun of heat 12, "Perry can't gate, that's his problem – he's a grass tracker." When said rerun finally gets underway, Tom Perry sensibly adopts an 'after you Claude' approach to let Garrity into the second bend first. It's a wise move as the Hitman gets totally out of shape on the second bend and, as a result, interferes with the smooth progress of his teammate Robert Branford by driving him sharply towards the airfence. It's a wayward manoeuvre that allows both Franklin and Perry to get away. There's a loud cheer from the Dudley fans at Branford's clear annoyance with his teammate. Garrity quickly stifles their delight with overtakes past Tom Perry on lap two and Franklin on lap three before a win in some style. It's yet another lovely NL race that showcases multiple overtakes as well as a determined zeal to race for fresh air ahead of your rivals. Though it's academic, Mark Sawbridge wonders, "Should the ref have called that back, do you think?"

245

Dudley: *"He doesn't turn it until – as they used to say – he can read the labels on the beer bottles!"*

Retirement for Craig Cook and a win for Lee Smart with Barrie Evans third, give Dudley their first heat advantage in seven races and tantalise us with thought of a fight-back with the scores at 37-41. It's a prospect that only lasts as long as it takes Adam Allott to gate swiftly in the penultimate race. With Allott already up front, Garrity jostles Jake Anderson in the first bend without success. After, by his standards, biding his time, Jason Garrity then subjects his rival to one of his signature blasts up the inside just as both riders' race into the third bend of the second lap. Astutely realising that Garrity is part speedway rider and part bowling ball, Anderson sensibly backs off and decides there's always another day to duel with this particular tearaway 16-year-old. Though this race puts the meeting beyond reach, National League play-off semi-finals take place over two legs so it remains vital that Dudley perform well in heat 15. While we wait to learn who's nominated to ride, Mark Sawbridge asks, "Do you get *Backtrack*? I was reading one issue where Michael Lee said lots of nice things about Reg Fearman and, in the next issue, they had a really strangely worded apology!" Since Garrity's ineligible having already had his seven rides (for paid 17), Buxton send out Adam Allott and Robert Branford who, although they're split by Lee Smart, deliver yet another race advantage to take the final scoreline to 40-50.

Stood by the Supporters' Club trackshop, I listen as departing Heathens fans share their thoughts on tonight's encounter with the staff. "Bit of a waste of time signing Barrie Evans. The only time he did something is when we got 60 odd. He rode for Stoke for about six years so he's not going to get any better is he?" Another man tells the trackshop lady, "We need a bit of passion" only for her to retort, "They're the better team, what can you do?" Simon Priest wants to discover my impressions after my first ever visit to see this National League incarnation of the Dudley Heathens. I compliment the crowd size and atmosphere ("It's a return to the '70s"). Smiling proudly, Simon nods, "It's all we've ever lived for since the '70s and the '80s!"

Buxton fan Charles McKay questions the legitimacy of Jason Garrity's disqualification in heat 8 but then concedes, "Okay, he went in hard but what was that assistant start marshal about? He hassled Garrity and, once the red mist comes down, that's it! I've never seen two start marshals! If anything goes wrong, you see the head man not the assistant!" A short time later Arnie Gibbons wonders. "Would there be any mileage in the *I-Spy Book of Speedway Anoraks*? I didn't see Charles until the end – the two start marshals is an amazing talking point amongst the anoraks. Buxton were robbed, it should have been 20 points. These are my two favourite teams!" Stuart Sergeant interjects, "Did you enjoy that? A great meeting and an enthusiastic crowd!" And Arnie replies: "Dudley underperformed. There was passion on both sides and a great atmosphere! If you go to Belle Vue, you're behind glass, the remaining fans are scattered round the stadium and there's no noise! The Buxton fan you spoke to said, 'Have you been reading any of his books?' I said, 'Not only have I read them but I'm in them too – like you will be!' I think that's worried him."

The always conscientious speedway reporter Tim Hamblin returns from his usual in-depth post-meeting interviews in the pits. Dudley Heathens captain Lee Smart is always available for a few words: whether with his teammates or the media. A keen student of human nature, Tim's very impressed with the serious attitude Lee takes toward his responsibilities as captain. Tim also praises his leadership skills. Since Lee needs no second excuse to deliver genuine words of encouragement or praise, "It's amazing how he mentors a young team from the lofty height of 22!" One post-meeting talking point in the pits is, of course, Jason Garrity. "People say he's going to get to the top or kill himself or kill someone else. I spoke to Lee Smart about him and he said some nice things. 'You can't take anything away from Buxton. They're good, they're solid. They've got young Jason at reserve and he's just something different. He rides with his heart on his sleeve. He's all out! Give the boy some due – he's got the courage to do it, so fair play to him. He makes riders look for him. And as soon as you've got that mental edge over them, your game's up.'" Tim

Dudley: *"He doesn't turn it until – as they used to say – he can read the labels on the beer bottles!"*

reflects for a few moments on his own judgement of Jason Garrity "He just has to make sure his shirt is all numbers and not letters!"

5th October Dudley v. Buxton (National League) 40-50

Dudley: *"He doesn't turn it until – as they used to say – he can read the labels on the beer bottles!"*

CHAPTER 30

Kidlington

"I still send in the occasional piece to the Mail. We haven't been running for three years so, obviously, it gets more and more difficult!"

9th October

Though Cowley Stadium continues to stage greyhounds, sadly the roar of speedway bikes isn't heard there any longer.[1] The club name is kept alive with invitation meetings at other tracks but, with no real regular race action of speak of, it has fallen to Oxford supporters to represent their club. Though a good number of speedway clubs have active supporters' clubs, Oxford fans are known for the BBQ and bingo evenings they host to coincide with every televised round of the Speedway Grand Prix. These gatherings continue to be held at the Kidlington Green Social Club based in a town cum village on the outskirts of the city. Kidlington Green Social Club remains pretty well exactly the same as it did on my previous visit two years ago. Modelled on trade union clubs that used to be everywhere, it's a large functional building surrounded by a big car park that's part tarmac and part rough-hewn ground. A members-only establishment with a choice of bars, snooker room, dance floor, a sea of tables and a substantial number of different seat types. Regular patrons occupy most of the building but, at the rear of the building, there's a bar that's still large by most pub standards. There's also a patio-style garden area with wooden benches where tonight's BBQ will be cooked and hardier smokers regularly congregate. The bar serves keenly priced alcohol to supplement tonight's BBQ food.

When I arrive, the compact kitchen area is a bustle of activity, while outside the BBQs have been sparked into life to start to slowly cook the burgers, sausages and chicken legs you'd expect to enjoy at such an event. At the opposite end of the room from the kitchen area, there's a giant screen, speakers and an impressively large scoreboard to help us enjoy and understand the final Bydgoszcz round of the 2010 Speedway Grand Prix Series. Outside in the car park, close to the cage where they store the soft drink crates in higgledy-piggledy fashion, I bump into Cliff Peasley who's shocked and delighted by what he's seen in today's *Oxford Mail*. "They have a double-page spread in the *Oxford Mail* on Wiggy! I was amazed [mimes double take] to see two whole pages because we don't see that anymore!"[2]

---

[1] Since the end of the 2007 speedway season. Interestingly the stadium did stage a grasstrack meeting there in late 2010. At least this indicates it could still quickly be readied for action and also that the owners aren't completely ideologically opposed to bikes in action there. Whether speedway bikes will ever return is, of course, another matter way above my pay grade.

[2] One of speedway's most colourful and charismatic riders, Simon Wigg passed away on the 15th November 2000 at the age of 40. At the pinnacle of his speedway career, Simon finished runner up in the 1989 World Speedway Championship held in Munich (behind Oxford rider Hans Nielsen). Wiggy was also five-times World Longtrack champion and six-times British Grasstrack champion. The *Oxford Mail* article publicises a reunion of the Oxford Cheetahs held at the Plough Pub in Wheatley on 24th October – the day Wiggy would have been 50, if he hadn't died of a brain tumour. The article features some fantastic photographs including a brilliant slightly old-fashioned photo of a speedway race in full throttle along with an interview with ex-Oxford rider George Major (who rode for the Cheetahs in 1961, 1963-64 and 1969-70) and also features his memories of Oxford Speedway in poetic form. Speedway reporter John Gaisford also knew Wiggy, "He was not only a great rider – he was a reporter's dream. He was upbeat, open and a real showman – and he is sorely missed on the speedway scene." Simon Wigg had two spells for the Cheetahs from 1984 to 1986 and from 1988 to 1990.

The closure of Sandy Lane after 58 years of activity leaves a massive hole in the lives of many Oxford speedway fans. Like his son Robert, Cliff Peasley has (where his health allows) thrown himself into fundraising collections at speedway tracks everywhere on behalf of the Speedway Riders' Benevolent Fund. Though he's too diplomatic to name names, not all speedway clubs are created equal, let alone as honestly responsible as you'd like to hope. "When we started to do the SRBF collections, Bernard [Crapper] warned us that at a certain club – I won't name them – all the collections when they came in used to be exactly the minimum required. Bernard said if it was a few pounds more or a few pounds less, you'd understand. They weren't that generous there but to always be the exact money was strange!"

Grilled food

With a couple of hours to go before the doors open to the public, outside on the patio the bustle of preparation ramps up further. Three BBQs specialise in different cooked items. In charge of the burgers is Paul Guest, the chicken legs Ashby Hope while Rob Peasley looks after some large (suspiciously pink-hued) sausages. Rob industriously separates strings of sausages from a giant plastic bag as he absentmindedly heats the first batch. "It's fallen off the last few GPs. We always get 40 and quite a few people might come along tonight as it's the last one of the season. Nowadays the Speedway Grand Prix BBQs are run by the OSSC (Oxford Speedway Supporters' Club). Basically it's exactly the same BBQ but a different group running it. [3] SOS (Support Oxford Speedway) had actually done it for ten years and raised a lot of money. They did 84 BBQs or something like that. We're using their equipment actually – we borrowed it from them, it's what they built up. You couldn't do it without the screen, scoreboard and amplifier. With it looking like Oxford wouldn't come back, they questioned whether to carry on? There's still no return in sight! Paul Guest who's cooking the burgers is the actual organiser, secretary and that. Ash – Ashby Hope – is doing the chicken legs and Mike Coombs is the treasurer. Gav is the chair but he's got a very young baby. Mandy Dougan buys all the food and that. Neil who's in the kitchen used to be in the SOS too, actually he's not in either group but he's carried on – he's very important because he helps Mandy prepare all the food. Neil does all the salads and that. He's our head chef, having picked up his skills during his army

---

[3] The programme for tonight's event provides news of the Oxford Speedway Supporters' Club end-of-season party to be held on Saturday 20th November. It also lists the OSSC club committee members: Gavin Beckley, Paul Guest, Michael Coombs and Ashby Hope. The regular OSSC volunteers are also listed: Neil Smith, Chloe Smith, Robbie Lucas, Rob Peasley, Colin Perkins, Mandy and Jack Dougan.

Kidlington: *"I still send in the occasional piece to the Mail. We haven't been running for three years so, obviously, it gets more and more difficult!"*

days. He was in a road accident the day before one of the GPs but he still turned up all smashed up!" 15-year-old Chloe Smith interjects, "I am part of this team with my best friend Tash Bartlett [also 15]. We live in Wiltshire – Amesbury and Tash is from Salisbury – cos every other weekend I come to see my dad – Neil Smith – and he's the cook so we help out. I'm the 'Find a Cheetah' game girl!"

[Rob] "You can't say no to Chloe."

[Chloe] "I have persuasive skills."

[Gavin] "I'm the bingo caller. I was here last Sunday and the barman said, 'You're really good at that bingo. Do you memorise them all or do you make them up?' I said, 'Nah, I read them off a board!' This is the tenth BBQ this year except for Cardiff because everyone tends to be there!"

As he distractedly turns the chicken legs, Ash winds Chloe up with some slurs. "No, Tom Daley [diver] isn't gay! He's Tash's favourite that's all. Saying he's gay that's just your insecurity! Any man who feels threatened always claims attractive men must be gay. Tom isn't and neither are JLS!" Shortly after, Chloe tells me, "I've read your book but I'm not in it! I don't think I was there. It's my third or fourth year helping."

Like his dad, Rob Peasley's delighted with the coverage in the paper about Simon Wigg but wishes that developments at the stadium also made the club newsworthy. "I still send in the occasional piece to the *Mail*. We haven't been running for three years so, obviously, it gets more and more difficult! Today's article on Wiggy is in the news section not the sport. The last double-page spread was 2008 and was on Hans Nielsen. As soon as I said 'Hans Nielsen' they said 'Wow! We'll definitely give you a double page' but, since then, it's been harder and harder!" Rob travels widely to watch his speedway. He recently went to Pardubice to watch the Czech Golden Helmet. "We watched the Elite League Play-Off final second leg without sound and tried to predict what would be said. When we got back, 13 races were "crucial" until it was over! What I want to know is what has happened to Moley? He only appears once a meeting nowadays!"

I quiz chairman Gavin Beckley about the profitability of the BBQ nights, "Sadly the treasurer isn't here so I can't tell you! The third, fourth and fifth ones did well but, overall, we've more than broken even. So long as we haven't made a horrendous loss, we'll be happy. All have broken even. Obviously, we've got nothing to raise money for so we'll see what happens in the future. We're happy to keep it ticking over and it helps keep the name alive. Which is what we should be doing as a Supporters' Club and why we are here!" With Gavin on hand, Rob deputises him as a food taster but doesn't make the sausages sound that appetising, "They look purple inside but that's because they're pink sausages!" Nevertheless savouring his taster mouthful, Gavin reports, "It's not hot right in the middle. I reckon it needs a bit longer. If we can make it to the end of the season without food poisoning, we've done well!" Returning to his earlier theme about the purpose of the OSSC, Gavin continues, "It's nice to think that if something happens at the stadium and, things change, that we're keeping a small fan base ready for them! We try to keep the name involved in speedway. We sponsor the Ben Fund – either a heat or a rider – depending on who's riding. We sponsor ex-Oxford riders' testimonials – riders like Johno, Dean Barker and Billy Hamill. Was it this year we sponsored Crumpie, Paul? Obviously the Oxford side has been in second halves at Coventry so we've tried to help Pete Seaton with the lads. We take a couple of coaches to Cardiff and that's a laugh. That's all we can do – we can only try! The problem is you've come to the least entertaining one tonight. The first one was the fight between Rob and the screen!"

[Rob] "It was a steep learning curve! It was all a bit pink that night and, of course, because Jason Crump's got orange kevlars, he looked quite camp!"

[Gav] "Croatia was an absolute nightmare because it was called off! We lost the Sky signal and, obviously, because there's no live speedway people get a bit antsy. But, luckily, we'd Sky +'d the

Kidlington: *"I still send in the occasional piece to the Mail. We haven't been running for three years so, obviously, it gets more and more difficult!"*

Swedish GP and people got a couple of quid off future events."
[Chloe] "Note down that Ashby said he didn't want me to come next time."
[Neil – Chloe's dad] "Who said that?"
[Chloe] [Points to Ashby] "He did!"
[Gav] "It's okay. You can keep coming. We need someone to wash-up! The biggest draw this season has been my baby daughter Elizabeth. She was born on May 18th and came to her first meeting at four days old! If she's not here, the crowd definitely want to know where she is!"
[Chloe] "You can't take any photographs – only from behind!"
[Jeff] "Is that your best side?"

When the doors open, there's quite a rush of people keen to bagsy seats with the best vantage point for the big screen. During a lull in the rush at her entrance desk, Mandy tells me, "It's £8 to get in – £7 if they're SOS members. For that they can eat all they want including puddings, they get a scorecard, raffle ticket and a bingo card – where it's £5 for a line and £10 for a full house – so it's very good value!" In addition to this, there's also a sweepstake that costs £1 per rider and, included with the entrance fee, is a scorecard provided by the OSSC. Fortunately this is professionally produced and accurate unlike the organisers' official Speedway Grand Prix page. Posted in slapdash fashion, this informs us that Hans Andersen is in for a busy night since BSI/IMG website list him twice in each heat that he's programmed to race in!

Attempting to double my luck, I randomly draw Andreas Jonsson and Chris Harris. They're selections that ensure I watch their races attentively throughout the night. Dedicated Sandy Lane trackman Nobby Hall continues to visit the stadium very regularly. "I've been going down to the track every day or every other day but it's getting worse and worse!" Liam Mills interjects, "My grandson says it's a grasstrack now, you can't see the difference between the go-kart track and the speedway track. I went down there and asked permission for the keys and Maureen – the manageress – wouldn't let me have them. I went down with Pete Seaton to pick up the Oxford speedway grader but they said it's the property of the stadium! Relations are at an all-time low!"

The size of crowd an Oxford speedway BBQ attracts bodes well for the future, should the speedway ever return to the city. Gavin welcomes us all with a few words, "There's lots of people here tonight – many more than we expected so thank you for that! There's food outside – it has to go tonight – it won't last until next year! Jeff Scott is here with his books tonight – *Quantum of Shale* and others he can tell you about. He's got lots of special deals, I forget what, but he can tell you." Sales are unlikely to be robust if gauged by the reaction of a woman who learns the *Track Directory* costs £4.99. "I'd like to get that but I ain't got the money!"

Once the action gets underway there's an attentive atmosphere but, in between races, people go to the bar, eat, or chat with their friends. Rob Peasley briefly breaks off from his duties. "I haven't finished. We have to serve desserts and then clear up, wash up and that. We usually finish at half-nine to ten. It's nice to see Nobby. There's a letter from two Aussies, three pages from the back of the *Oxford Mail*, in response to the Greyhounds not wanting £80,000 a season from the Speedway. They're staying with Nobby. We probably won't see Tai in the GP next year, he ain't ready. Give him a few years. Nicki [Pedersen] always flies round Bydgoszcz and although he's 11th, he's only 12 points behind Holder so he could qualify!" Also drawn to my table for a chat is long-time Oxford speedway fan Ralph Gilbey. "I started in '49 when I was eight – taken by my uncle from Kidlington – and I carried on until the last day. I'd a tear in my eye when it closed. I used to live in the same village as Dickie Worth. I remember the first great Dane – Arne Pander. He was great until Les Owen decided to nail him half way down the straight at Coventry and he was never the same. I never saw trouble or fighting in the crowd only a bit of banter. I was fortunate enough when [Nigel] Wagstaff was there I asked if I could go to the pits. Todd Wilshire was there and, of all people, my hero Hans Nielsen. He was really nice and not the man you saw on the track. He even apologised for leaving Oxford [in 1993] but they weren't paying him enough. Living where I did, Enstone – where Dickie Worth lived who ran Oxford Speedway for four years and also ran his own bus company – is nearer to Swindon. Oxford was always my team. The third time I went to Wembley – there was Nigel Boocock, Ove Fundin and what have you – we came out and couldn't find a bloody bus to go home! Black as the ace of spades. Speedway has been my life!" Ralph believes Poole fans are quite fickle, "I lived in Bournemouth in my early teens and, if they started to lose a meeting, they got up and walk out. They did that then, they do that now. In about 1950-something, I saw the American novice Ernie Roccio killed at West Ham in the last race. Everyone denies [name redacted] did him but he did! Ernie flipped over the wrong way and went through the bottom board. He broke the bottom board fence, slipped under it and out over the greyhound track. From articles I read, he was dead when they got to him. The promoter at the time – a big blustery fellow, I can't think of his name – didn't cancel the meeting but ran the second half!"

On the screen, crowd celebrations at Bydgoszcz are slightly muted by Tomasz Gollob's foot injury (sustained away from the track in a Motocross accident). Luckily, he's been so dominant in the 2010 Speedway Grand Prix Series that he's already champion. The expected battle for the final eighth qualifying place for 2011 also fails to ignite. Nonetheless, the Oxford fans in Kidlington enjoy the evening to the full. Rob Peasley gives his own expert opinion on the likely wildcard selections for 2011. "Janusz Kolodziej has been in two GPs and reached the final twice. Tai has been in eleven and not made the final once. I think Kolodziej has to get a wildcard! To me, the wildcards are almost picking themselves. It should be Nicki Pedersen, Emil Sayfutdinov, Andreas Jonsson and Janusz Kolodziej but stupidly they'll probably put in Tai instead of Kolodziej. If you look at it, Tai has 49 points from eleven GPs whereas Emil has 33 from five and two of those he was injured! Emil should definitely be in there before any of them because he's brilliant! One problem with the Speedway Grand Prix that they've got to look at is how just qualifying for the semi-final and final in each round means riders pull ahead. This year's Under-21s were over three rounds and it was a three man run-off after the three rounds. The key difference was they don't have the semi-final and finals, so there's less opportunity for any rider to pull ahead!"

After the Grand Prix ends (at 8.32 p.m.), we watch the podium presentations in Bydgoszcz and enjoy the post-meeting rider interviews. Our prize draws are made and there's quite a queue of winners who drew Andreas Jonsson in the sweepstake (indeed, someone had his name twice). We all get £8 as a result of our good fortune. After the "Find the Cheetah" competition finally gets a winner (£116), Colin Pollard from Save Our Speedway takes to the microphone for a few words about the equipment previous fundraising efforts purchased. "It's your grader but you can't put it in your back garden! We took the decision to loan the grader – after we get permission from the Stadium – to Peterborough [low boos] – it's only Trevor Swales we have any problem with – but also we'll use it at Leicester and, if we can benefit a new club, that has to be good!" Rob Peasley refuses to be drawn on the specifics behind the antipathy the fans here tonight clearly have towards Trevor Swales. Rob explains elliptically, "Cos of things that happened!" Moments later, he clarifies his gnomic statement further, "Because he was involved with Colin Horton". With the bingo about to get underway, Gavin reviews a season of successful Speedway Grand Prix OSSC events, "We've had a good time, good laughs and a couple of hairy moments. Would you support us if we ran again next season?" The assembled crowd are in no doubt, "Yes!" Gavin smiles sheepishly, "Thank you. That makes it clear and all worthwhile!"

9th October OSSC Speedway Grand Prix BBQs 2010 Winner: Oxford Speedway

Kidlington: *"I still send in the occasional piece to the Mail. We haven't been running for three years so, obviously, it gets more and more difficult!"*

CHAPTER 31

Poole

"He used to ride with both wheels on the safety fence, like it was the wall of death."

27th October

Poole need a win by more than 8 points to ensure the Pirates 21st home speedway meeting of the season finally delivers some silverware for their trophy cabinet from their 2010 team of all talents. Comfortable at the top of the table throughout the Elite League season, the Pirates surprised many when they succumbed to the in-form Coventry Bees in the final of the play-offs introduced to big-up the end-of-season drama for the satellite television broadcaster Sky Sports. Back in May, the Pirates beat Eastbourne 63-29 while, in August, they nearly repeated the medicine 61-31. However, Eastbourne's season of two halves saw them perform creditably in all their home Elite League 'B' fixtures as well as go on a KO Cup run that eliminated both Lakeside and Wolverhampton. Even the Eagles No. 1 Matej Žagar has greater zest over the closing weeks of the season. So much so that it's now a possibility that he could race at Arlington again next season. The Eagles team manager Trevor Geer told the press, "Matej is talking about coming back and he is not just doing that to keep his options open. I know he would love to stay. He's enjoying it here now. He's got it set up and he likes the track now. Six weeks ago I would not have thought it but I know now he definitely wants to stay at Eastbourne next year." The Slovenian still has to build bridges with some sections of the Arlington fan base who question his commitment or highlight his ongoing inability to win heat 1. Perhaps indicative of a corner not quite yet turned, Sunday's first leg ended with the Eagles only 8 points ahead after Chris Holder snuck past Žagar. Afterwards, Chris Holder was quick to praise the Slovenian, "Matej was on the outside but gave me enough room to race. Fair play to him, he could have been a lot harder. We bumped together but it was better than tangling and both of us going into the fence." With every point vital, a lead of 10 would be preferable to the 8 the Eagles actually bring into this contest. Matej's lack of steel in the final analysis could prove very costly unless he suddenly rediscovers it this evening.

Long queue

Close contest

Eastbourne trackshop manager with the perpetually put-upon expression, Martin Dadswell, parks up in the Wimborne Road stadium car park massively early. Though reluctant to be drawn on his forecast, Martin notes morosely, "We needed to win by 20 [pause] or 30 – don't ask me what we're gonna do!" The stadium buildings Poole speedway rent on race night from the Greyhound owners look unchanged. However, at the perimeter of the stadium grounds there's noticeable change including the demolition of the Conservative Club – now just a bare patch of rough ground guarded by a thin security fence – while a substantial new building has been built inside an impressively high wall topped with razor wire. "What is it?"

[Martin] "Climb over the fence and find out."

[Jeff] "What is it?"

[Martin] "Well, the giant sign outside says it's a police station."

[Jeff] "Strange they should demolish the Conservative Club then! Maybe they need bigger premises in Poole?"

With at least 60 minutes to go before the turnstiles open, a substantial number of anxious fans queue at both the available turnstiles handily positioned on opposite sides of the stadium. Eastbourne fan as well as an avid *Planet of the Apes*, speedway and *Star Trek* memorabilia collector, Alan Boniface bounds up with important news, "I see that Mroczka isn't riding." Alan's arrival prompts Martin to wonder, "I can't remember the last time I was here; probably the Cup Final [in 2008]." Alan's slightly more certain about the situation, "I dunno when I was last here – you came for the Cup Final when it was lashing it down but I didn't. We've been here all day. We left at half-ten – walked on the seafront and went to three pubs. No one really spoke in the car, which was embarrassing. Well, the bloke from Norwich's wife was interested in *Planet of the Apes* and *Star Trek* so that was good. I saw Bob Dugard with his dog. Bob always comes to Cup Finals."

[Martin] "Bob only comes to wind them up."

[Alan] "I said that's a new one and he said 'its Bonnie the Fifth'. I don't like that name I told him. My dad used to answer to that but I won't."

[Jeff] "What, Bonnie the Fifth? We need Matej Žagar to win heat 1."

[Alan] "He should win at least three out of five races then Joonas and Simon should get seven or eight. They all should. Kling will get one or seven, probably."

In the ever-lengthening queue that runs parallel to the Poole railway line fence and up the steps up to the posh entranceway of the deluxe back-straight grandstand, we join John Ling (father of Eastbourne's press officer, Kevin). In between deep draws on his cigarette, John contemplates the night ahead, "Matej summed it up well on Sunday when he said 'if we all get 6 we'll win!' They haven't got Mroczka so Doyle and that will all get extra rides. We just have to split them. It would be nice to sign off with something! But they're desperate to win, they'll be up to their tricks especially Holder. He's not really the nice boy they say he is. He's not averse to taking people off but it's a hard sport and there you go!"

With two payment points at the reception desk, the big queue moves smoothly through with surprisingly swiftness. Stood behind a small round table with a clipboard close to hand, tanned Poole co-promoter Giles Hartwell surveys the queue in his smart, rather fashionable Poole Pirates anorak. He also checks pre-admissions off from the guest list on his clipboard in the manner of a tour party manager at airport passport control, albeit without a metal detector or any form of pat down. Verifying credentials are often required as regular Eastbourne centre-green photographer Mick Hinves found, even though festooned in long lens cameras. His good rummage soon finds his BSPA press photographer pass. After another season of tight finances across the sport, any well-run business will seek to minimise the number of possible freeloaders. The previous week Giles was only too happy to explain his firm approach to me. "I'm sick of

Poole: *"He used to ride with both wheels on the safety fence, like it was the wall of death."*

people calling trying to get in for free. It's our Cup Final and we've got to try and earn some money! For the [Elite League Play-off] final we had to turn 400 paying customers away and I had a guest list of 200 people I'd let in for free! How come no one comes along to the Buccaneers meetings? Last Sunday we lost £4,000 and only had 200 people." It must take a substantial attendance to fill Wimborne Road Stadium (or, at least, meet the maximum number dictated by Health and Safety requirements). By my calculation, the loss of 200 adult admissions translates to around £3,200 gross revenues for the club.

Just inside the double door entrance to the downstairs bar cum viewing area of the back-straight grandstand, the always-friendly Poole programme lady isn't willing to make predictions, "I'm not sure we're going to win tonight." I'm pretty confident on the Pirates behalf but she's not, "We expect to make it but you can't take nothing for granted this season!" There's a homemade ballot box on the table so fans can vote for their "Poole Speedway Rider of the Year 2010". The stability of the Pirates team this season is such that there's only eight riders in the list and, to my untutored eye, Gary Havelock looks the least likely winner so I vote for him. Any ballot paper with two votes or more is deemed spoilt. My observation about the voting form ("there doesn't appear to be a box you can tick for Chris Harris") elicits the *sotto voce* response from the programme lady, "I think you'll find he's not a Poole rider!" The winner will be announced at the Pirates annual dinner dance that, this season will be held at the Premier Inn on Westover Road in Bournemouth. When fans discuss the cost of tickets for the dinner dance (£38.50), the consensus is that, in times of recession, they might prove prohibitively expensive ("I reckon they're struggling") particularly with the taxi fare, if you live any distance away from the venue.

Members of the extended speedway family are out in force tonight at Wimborne Road. One of them is the Under-18 British Champion Brendan Johnson. I'm surprised at his lack of a plaster cast, "Haven't you hurt your wrist?" Brendan fiddles with a large-sized slightly bling metallic watch, "I have."
[Jeff] "I expected to see you in a cast – are you making light of it?"
[Brendan] "It's a bang but I'm okay."
[Jeff] "Are you spending the winter here or the summer in Oz?"
[Brendan] "I'm off on Monday until January 20th. It's time to go as I've just had to put on a woolly jumper the other day. I can't wait!"
[Jeff] "Has your dad organised a chaperone?"
[Brendan] "[laughs] He doesn't know any!"
[Jeff] "Who's going?"
[Brendan] "Quite a crowd of us: Kyle Newman, Josh Auty, Kyle Howarth, Cal McDade and Adam Wrathall. It should be a laugh!" [1]

Robins pits crew organiser Darcia Gingell is here with her partner ("I won't tell you who I'm supporting but it's not Poole"). After another season of disappointment for them and the retirement of Leigh Adams, talk soon turns to the likely makeup of the Swindon Robins 2011 line-up. Darcia tells me, "We'd like Matej back but it's not going to happen!" Darcia implies she already knows the identity of next season's Robins No. 1 but hints this information is so confidential she'll have to kill me if I know. Maybe the confident talk on the grapevine that it's either Hans Andersen or Scott Nicholls is wayward? Either way, Darcia continues, "They're going to confirm all the riders shortly. Simon [Stead] is definitely back cos there was a ceremonial handing over of the captain's armband to him by Leigh Adams."

Speedway reporter (with close Poole connections) Paul Burbidge, strides through the bar area en route to his vantage point in the press box at the back of the home-straight grandstand. A

[1] Cal McDade withdrew two days beforehand after a crash when riding for the King's Lynn Young Stars in the National League.

Poole: *"He used to ride with both wheels on the safety fence, like it was the wall of death."*

hard-working speedway journalist who writes regularly for the *Speedway Star*, nowadays Paul also enjoys sufficient respect and status to have his own column on the BSI Speedway Grand Prix website. Though he moves in the rarefied circles of the speedway in-crowd and travels extensively internationally (albeit without a credit card), Paul approaches his work with the wide-eyed enthusiasm of a speedway fan. Without taking his privileged access for granted, Paul clearly delights in his proximity to the race action and, of course, speedway's inner sanctum. All this ensures his copy remains current, interesting and breathlessly insightful. Paul wears his knowledge lightly. "I'm doing all the tracks next year for the GP! I'm doing the blog, which is fun! I tell you what, all the [GP] tracks have been brilliant this season! The racing has been exceptional but, I tell you, the field they have for 2011 is amazing! Getting Kolodziej was a masterstroke. I do feel sorry for Hans Andersen but you can only have 15 riders. I'd bet my own money that Hans will win the Copenhagen GP. He's a great bloke and always has time and always has a story. I might be doing some more [SGP] reports for the *Speedway Star* next year." Some reporters have been on that particular speedway beat for a few years. "More like 20 years! I expect in 20 years I'll be saying what they are! There's only so many times you can go to all the same old places again and again! What BSI are doing with the wildcards makes sense too. You might as well give some of the young and upcoming riders a go to see what they can do. Perhaps we'll see the likes of Darcy Ward, Maks Bogdanovs (from Latvia) and Martin Vaculik (from Slovakia) in the Grand Prix next year? But I don't make these decisions, so I can only speculate like everyone else. I must get a credit card cos it can be a bit tricky without one. When you travel with BSI it's okay because they sort out everything – entrance to the tracks and the hotels – but, when you're not, it's a different matter. On Ryanair, you always ask for priority boarding and then leg it to the gate, rush on and get the seats with the leg room – job done!"

Paul expects Poole to win comfortably tonight, "Not having Mroczka should be a big advantage. He was flying early season but his form has fallen off a cliff ever since about June when he got injured." Poole isn't Paul's only speedway responsibility within Dorset, since he also reports on the beleaguered National League Weymouth Wildcats. "I think it's run its course with Phil [Bartlett]. If Garry May takes over there'll be a big difference but now that Phil's put it up for sale at £1 it could mean someone will be tempted to come in and buy it. It's not only £1, of course, cos there's the liabilities! I reckon the National League needs to bring in someone to really run it. I haven't met Peter Morrish but he seems to make some funny decisions." I tell Paul it's still strange to visit Poole and realise that Gordie Day is no longer the press officer. Paul visits Poole regularly, "I haven't seen him much this season. He's kept himself to himself. I saw him at the Final but that's it!" [2]

Upstairs in the swish glass-fronted back-straight grandstand are tables with panoramic views that the club reserve for guests, sponsors and diners. A good number of people wait patiently in line for self-service hot food. Midway along there's an impressive collection of trophies but, when I question their provenance, the lady sat by them tells me, "They're from the greyhounds not the speedway!" Sat next to his wife Barbara – who has her Ruth Rendell novel close to hand – Gordie Day positions his seat so that he can chat with his wife but also overlook the first and second bends as well as enjoy an almost completely uninterrupted view down the length of the back straight. Making light of the ongoing after-effects of chemo, Gordie looks the same as ever and is his usual friendly, wholehearted but modestly understated self. He's anxious that late season race conditions aren't exactly optimal, "The presentation isn't great and the track is crap. It rained all day yesterday and overnight until half-nine this morning. It's rideable but not raceable. It'll be

[2] Gordie's visits to Wimborne Road were somewhat curtailed in 2010 by his successful course of chemotherapy treatments for bowel cancer. Since an operation before Christmas that saw him spend 9 days in hospital, scans have revealed that Gordie is – thankfully – now in remission.

Poole: *"He used to ride with both wheels on the safety fence, like it was the wall of death."*

gate and go."

After the rider parade and introductions, in the first race I'm astonished to see the Eastbourne pair of Matej Žagar and Lewis Bridger comfortably lead a processional race. These are the kind of positive thoughts you keep to yourself in the deluxe surroundings of the Poole hospitality area. Well luckily I do, since, in fact, it's Poole who wear the red-and-blue helmet colours. My own stupidity explains how comfortable "Žagar and Bridger" look since they're really the young dynamic Australian partnership of Chris Holder and Darcy Ward. Tonight's commemorative programme is an impressively glossy full-colour affair with a certain heft. There are an astonishing 19 pages of adverts in a publication that only has a total extent of 40 pages. According to the front cover of this impressive document, tonight's clash takes place on the "27th Ocrtober". Success won't automatically attract significant sponsorship without considerable effort. With bicep tattoo partially displayed, in his column co-promoter Matt Ford proudly alludes to the off-track commercial success that complements the Poole Pirates vim and vigour on the track. "I'm just about to complete my 12th season of racing here at Poole Speedway and in that time I hope that each year we have improved. But look around. The place is crammed with advertising and sponsors names everywhere. Everybody wants to share in the Poole Speedway experience. All the businesses and respected entrepreneurs who link with this club know they're getting value for money and a personal one-to-one service like no other sporting enterprise. It sounds crass, but all of them are friends. Genuine friends. They help make Poole Speedway what it is today. To everybody that's helped put this show on the road for the past eight months a sincere thanks. Your TLC and help towards promoting Poole Speedway has not gone unnoticed and I am sincerely grateful." Stirred up by Matt's Summer of Love style message, if I could find – or, at least, confidently identify – a close at hand sponsor I'd give them a big, fat, wet, sloppy kiss! Away from the metaphorical snog in, the programme details some "stats amazing" about the "Holder/Ward team partnership" who – after you include tonight's races – rode together 86 times for the Castle Cover Pirates this season. They enjoy a close relationship on and off the track since they live together in Poole, ride together for Poole and Torun (at least they did until Darcy got dropped late season in favour of Jepsen Jensen) while Darcy mechanics for Chris at the various Speedway Grand Prix rounds. In a sport that loves statistics, they've been consistently 100% young Australian ("no worries"), while the bare statistic that 37% of their races result in a Poole 5-1 requires no further comment. Arguably even more important, they've only conceded maximum heat advantages on four occasions. Repetition doesn't dull the Poole fans' enthusiasm for the sight of a Holder/Ward maximum heat advantage. Indeed the Pirates fans are collectively "stoked" so greet their Aussie heroes rapturously as they cross the line to win Heat 1.

Since he relinquished his press officer duties, race night's taken on a different complexion for Gordie (when he's not been absent convalescing). "It's great, I can sit up here and watch the racing and chat to all my friends. I might pop briefly to the pits but it's somebody else's show nowadays. So it's nice just to be able to be up here to watch and chat with people. I never used to be cold but, stood in the pits tonight, I was freezing. Matt told me to go upstairs because he wanted me better for next season!" After many years service at the club, both as a fan and also working behind the scenes, it's no surprise Gordie knows so many people so well (or for so long) – whether they are riders, officials, staff, fans, sponsors, media or visitors. Gordie wears his encyclopaedic knowledge and insight lightly, though it's clearly founded upon his love of meeting and talking with people. He wistfully recalls the late Sid Hazard. "He rode in the first ever race at Poole – he was an absolute star and a lovely gentleman! I didn't meet him until '96 when he was fairly late on in life. [Turns to Barbara] 'Was it about ten years ago that Sid died?' We'd just talk about the club or his life or anything. It was fascinating. He was a lovely gentleman. With a club like Poole, you get to hear the history or what people say is the history but Sid used to say, 'You don't wanna

Poole: *"He used to ride with both wheels on the safety fence, like it was the wall of death."*

believe this or believe that – this is what happened!' And he'd tell me based on what he actually saw or knew at the time. Pat Smith – Pete Smith's wife – she was a Crutcher, she often says, 'How did you know that?' and I'd say 'Sid told me!' It was always a pleasure talking to him. It's funny they used to say to me, 'You gave him another five years of his life', I dunno, he was a true gentleman and added something to mine. Sid used to have a monthly blood transfusion – he used to go in 85 and come out 75. We'd play snooker together and he'd be knocking in these big breaks. He was so competitive! When he used to ask the score, I'd say he was about 30 odd ahead and he'd say, 'The trouble with you is that you're not competitive.' He was – over everything! He was a lovely man. He'd beat me at snooker and then he'd ask if I'd like to play shove ha'penny. Sid drove like a 20-year-old. He had great reactions! I took him to the Isle of Wight one night and he rode around on a 1952 Jap. He said afterwards, 'If they'd given me another lap I could have got into a broadside!' Although he was 85, he was still acting as though he was 25! Sid would say, 'you should have been at Poole Speedway since you were 12'. Sid was a huge star at Exeter Speedway too. He used to ride with both wheels on the safety fence, like it was the wall of death. They used to pay him an extra £5 if he could get both wheels on the fence to entertain the crowd. Of course, he could! Sid used to say, 'It was the easiest £5 I ever earned!'"

Gordie interrupts his own trip down memory lane recalling the energetic and incomparable Sid Hazard when he catches sight of Jason Doyle coming out for the second heat, "What is Doyle wearing?" With a keen eye for detail, Gordie immediately spots Jason isn't in his regulation Poole Pirates team suit but, instead, tonight prefers to wear a completely different set of garishly patterned kevlars. Leon Madsen wins and, with the strangely dressed Jason Doyle third behind Lewis Bridger, the heat advantage sees the Pirates move into a 6-point lead. Passing is definitely at a premium tonight. This is double-underlined in heat 3 when the vastly experienced Bjarne Pedersen is unable to get past the fast-starting Simon Gustafsson. Though the glass of the grandstand deadens the noise of the bikes, our elevated position and panoramic view makes it much easier to appreciate the racing lines taken. In addition, Gordie's expert guidance identifies the incredibly specific overtaking spots there are on tonight's version of the Wimborne track. In the drier summer version of the track, it's usually possible to get drive coming off bend four but, with the shale solidly packed and damp underneath tyre treads, riders who try this option find their success almost nonexistent. Nonetheless, despite the sodden shale, it still remains possible to overtake with a dash round the inside line of the second bend. The Poole Pirates riders exploit this manoeuvre with some regularity throughout the night. Strangely the Eastbourne Eagles riders either remain inattentive or nonplussed since they repeatedly fail to block this manoeuvre but, more significantly, refuse to indulge in it themselves! The temporary setback of the Eagles third race heat advantage is soon forgotten after a maximum heat advantage from Davey Watt and Jason Doyle in heat 4. This moves the score to 16-8 and levels the tie on aggregate.

While they grade the track Gordie asks, "What would you say the crowd was tonight?" It's a hard question to answer though it's easy to see that tonight's attendance isn't up to the level of other key meetings I've seen at Wimborne Road. For example, it's only three or four deep in places on the first and second bend. Geordie studies the situation, "There's probably about 500 on the first and second bend, around 1,100 in the grandstand as there's spaces and it holds 1,200. There's probably 200 or so in front of that grandstand so I reckon there's around 2,200 which was a fair to middling crowd for 2008." The mystery of Jason Doyle's peculiar race suit continues to vex Gordie during heat 5, "Wait till I get down to the pits." Barbara Day takes a practical perspective, "Maybe he ripped them?" After a pointless first ride, Matej Žagar pressures Bjarne Pedersen for all four laps. Though he has the ideal tableside vantage point upstairs in the back-straight grandstand, throughout each race Gordie fidgets on his seat, stands up or dashes the short distance to the edge of this particular balcony to drink in the race action. Absorbed in the

Poole: *"He used to ride with both wheels on the safety fence, like it was the wall of death."*

moment, the intensity of Gordie's concentration belies his stated insouciance about the outcome, "Sorry, I was too busy watching Bjarne ride a nowhere line – not defending the inside and not defending the outside!" Earlier Bjarne gave Gordie one of his baseball caps festooned in the logos of prestigious teams and sponsors. The Dane's home-track expertise allows him to best the Slovenian because, according to Gordie, he "just pinched that little bit of dirt". Heat 6 sees the Holder/Ward combination back in action. Darcy's inside overtaking manoeuvre on the transition from the first to the second bend meets with Gordie's approval, "Here's the place to do it! Round the line – vintage Havelock!" Unusually stuck back in third place, Chris Holder struggles to get the traction he requires to overtake Joonas Kylmäkorpi, "It 'ain't gonna happen there [bend four]. Let it run! Let it run!" While we wait between races, Gordie wonders if I've noticed that the advent of faster, easier-to-ride speedway bikes stifles the ballet-like jockey skills frequently shown by the stars of yesteryear. "When you watched the Moran brothers, Dave Jessup or Michael Lee you saw how busy they were on the bike – they were always up and down the bike. Riders don't do that now since the bikes are so easy to ride! Lots of people don't know what they're seeing or what to look for. When riders are up at the start, I say to people: 'What are you looking at?' You can learn so much if you see whether they are up the bike or leaning back." Gordie's surprised to learn that one of the most exciting meetings I've seen this season was at Lakeside (versus Poole). "Have I ever seen a good meeting at Lakeside? I went when it was a smaller track in '93-94 when it was the London Lions. When Mick Barnes was the ref. He would have a cup of tea and I'd check everything off for him from the tapes to the safety fence." Gordie's got more stories to tell than most people have hot dinners. "We were walking in Salisbury and someone said, *'Big Issue?'* I said, 'No thanks' and half a minute later they said, *'Big Issue?'* I was just about to turn round and say something when I realised it was Martin Yeates. An hour later, we were still chatting. I asked him if he had old videos of himself riding and he said he had nothing so I did him a DVD of three meetings for when he came along to Poole that Wednesday. When I saw him next he said, 'I didn't realise I was that good! In that meeting against Milton Keynes I made five starts.' He couldn't believe his reactions!"

10 points to the good, the Pirates start heat 7 brightly but Woodward and Gustafsson of the Eagles soon pin Leon Madsen back in last position. Gordie implores the young reserve to get a yard or so closer to them, "Come on, Leon! Give him something to think about! Show him a wheel!" Though the drawn heat leaves Poole 10 points ahead on the night (and two on aggregate), Gordie looks disappointed, "I thought we were going to get 5-1." Davey Watt's race win misses its usual musical accompaniment too, "There's a single by the Kinks: Davey Watt!" Since relinquishing his press officer role, Gordie's consciously kept to the background to leave his replacement, Stephen Allen, free reign to stamp his authority on the Pirates media and PR function. The significance of Poole speedway within the town, the county and the sport generally inevitably means that this particular media and PR role is a demanding one. "They say no one is irreplaceable! Steve does a good job. If you see someone with a microphone, I'd want to know who they were and what they wanted? When they'd got what they thought they'd needed, I'd always say, 'Did you know there's another story?'" The characters that make up the rich tapestry that is the sport of speedway, inevitably, have also been a part of Gordie's life. "What about old Floppy? I remember seeing him on a sunny day here when he was pushing his toolbox to the pits in a wheelbarrow. When I asked him, 'Are you a builder's labourer?' He propped it up at an angle and said, 'It makes a bloody good chair!' I've seen all the frightening sights in this sport – including Bob Dugard's fists! I love Bob – he's one of the few people in the sport with the sport's best interest at heart!"

Though it's only heat 8, with Joonas Kylmäkorpi on a rider-replacement ride for the injured Tomasz Jędrzejak in a black-and-white helmet colour (and with Lewis Bridger a reserve switch for

Poole: *"He used to ride with both wheels on the safety fence, like it was the wall of death."*

Ricky Kling), this race could still be the decisive one in the 2010 quest by the Eagles for silverware. Lewis gates with alacrity from gate one closely followed by Joonas. Unfortunately for the blood pressure of the Eagles team management and fans, Lewis spends the rest of the four laps completely focused on making it to the chequered flag in the lead. Unfortunately, this means he completely ignores his race partner, apparently forgetful about the tactical opportunity of double points from the black-and-white helmet colour. Joonas remains on his tail throughout – repeatedly positioning himself so that a casual glance backwards will immediately reveal his friendly intentions. On the run-in from the final bend to the finish line, Joonas throws all caution to the wind and races wholeheartedly for the victory. From our slightly diagonal position opposite, to the naked eye it looks like this last-ditch effort for the flag proves unsuccessful. Joonas thinks so too given his indignant reaction with Lewis. Gordie's in his element, "Oh, oh, Jeff – Kylmäkorpi has just looked at Bridger and pulled the black-and-white helmet off! He's not happy! If Paul Carrington gives that, I'll go up and complain myself." Rather unbelievably referee Paul Carrington then does give the race win to Joonas Kylmäkorpi to widespread disbelief on the terraces and in the grandstands! It doesn't take much imagination to form a mental picture of the Pirates team manager Neil Middleditch questioning this decision on the pits telephone. Gordie decides not to storm over to see Mr Carrington, "Why would Kylmäkorpi be angry with Lewis? They know when they've won!" The 1-8 heat result narrows the scores to 27-24 and leaves Eastbourne ahead by 5 points on aggregate. I'm pretty surprised that Darcy Ward only manages third while Jason Doyle brings up the rear.

If the Poole Pirates last chance of 2010 silverware isn't to slip disastrously away, in heat 9 they need an immediate reply through Bjarne Pedersen and Leon Madsen (against the powerful but uncommunicative race partnership of Joonas Kylmäkorpi and Lewis Bridger). Vanquishing their rivals and the steepling anxiety within the crowd, the Poole pair race to a comfortable heat maximum, though this doesn't stop Gordie dashing up and down to the edge of the balcony. Generally the crowd reaction is muted, "Have you noticed how quiet the Poole crowd is? In the old days they'd be wild about that!" Nowadays, they certainly take Leon Madsen race wins in their stride. While we wait for Heat 10, Gordie bamboozles me with a difficult question, "What's gonna happen to speedway then?" I've absolutely no idea. Gordie believes a rebrand can't come quick enough. "It's not a bleeding family sport, it's an extreme sport on the edge! What can be more extreme than riders racing fractions of an inch apart on bikes without brakes for glory? While the present promoters remain, the sport isn't going to change or rebrand itself! It's an extreme sport on the edge but, to acknowledge that, would be dangerous for some people. They'll worry, 'but where's my money gonna come from?' I remember going to Oxford and Bernard Crapper saying 'We've lost £50,000' and I said, 'So you won't be back next season?' He smiled. If I lost £50,000, the bank would close me down – not tell me to try again next season!" Immediately prior to the start of every race the back-straight grandstand lights go out, so we can properly see the on-track action. Like sex with a stranger in a foreign hotel, the lights remain on throughout heat 10 as another maximum from Holder and Ward further subdues the fire of the Eastbourne fight-back (and give the Pirates an aggregate 3-point lead). Gordie's got a keen ear for speedway bike engine noise, even from behind glass. He turns to his wife Barbara, "Someone has a bike whose engine is very tight – I've a feeling it's the man in second [Darcy Ward]." Throughout heat 11, Matej Žagar probes for a way past race leader Leon Madsen. Gordie suspects that Zagar's going through the motions rather than genuinely attempting to find a way through, "There's no drive coming off four – he's made his mind up!" The Pirates gain another heat advantage since Davey Watt finishes third. During the interval International Financial Advisor, Poole programme contributor and speedway rider, Leah Elliott stops by for a few words with Gordie. Unlike most fans within the stadium she's sanguine about Paul Carrington's adjudication

Poole: *"He used to ride with both wheels on the safety fence, like it was the wall of death."*

in heat 8, "I think it was a wonderful decision because otherwise they could have put Žagar in!" Gordie's keen to explain who Leah is, "She's a good speedway rider, she rides in Sweden. She also contributes to the programme – how long is it now?" Leah furrows her brow, "I think this is my sixth year. I think I'm due a testimonial."

After the interval, Gordie's astonished to see Eagles team manager Trevor Geer decide to use his remaining tactical option in heat 12, "Have they gone mad – Lewis out in black and white?" Bjarne Pedersen's race win is no surprise, "Bjarne has been brilliant this season!" Trailing 5 points in arrears on aggregate with three races to go, the Eagles suddenly spark into life when Joonas and Matej race to an unlikely 5-1 against Chris Holder and Davey Watt. The penultimate race of the night sees Leon Madsen and Lewis Bridger battle for position at the start of the second lap. Unfortunately for Eastbourne's hopes, Lewis falls on the second bend. Though it would be better for his team if Lewis stays on the shale, instead he sportingly tries to clear the track but – a split second before he gets his bike onto the centre green – referee Paul Carrington puts safety rather than spectacle first and illuminates the red stop lights. Gordie exclaims, "What's Carrington playing at tonight? Oh well, 5-1 in the rerun." If bets were taken, few would wager their money on a race win for Cameron Woodward if up against Darcy Ward and Leon Madsen on their home track. However, the Eastbourne captain continues his season long run of powerful performances to lead throughout. Under great pressure from his rivals, Cameron also copes capably with the bike-decimating motocross-esque deep rut on the second bend that repeatedly threatens to throw the riders from their machines. With one race to go, the Pirates hold a slender aggregate lead of a solitary point. Though unlikely, a heat advantage from Žagar and Kylmäkorpi would take silverware back to East Sussex. The Poole fan next to me says, "We just wanna winner!" Throughout the 2010 season, Poole have been a team of winners except, of course, for their unfortunate collective blip in the most vital meeting of the season against Coventry. So it proves again as Chris Holder and Bjarne Pedersen combine to fire in a final race heat maximum. Gordie Day has the final word, "I think the word is stoked!"

27th October Poole v. Eastbourne Knockout Cup Final 2nd Leg 54-41

Poole: *"He used to ride with both wheels on the safety fence, like it was the wall of death."*

CHAPTER 32

Ipswich
"It was John's first season and he dressed up as a witch and rode on a bike!"

27th October

Ipswich guaranteed their participation in the end-of-season promotion relegation play-off in virtuoso fashion by securing bottom spot in the Elite League table with considerable time to spare. Witches fans, promotion and riders alike then had to wait for the end-of-season Premier League play-offs to run to their conclusion in order to find out who they'd face in an exciting clash on the last Thursday of the season before the official speedway cut-off date. Irrespective of whichever teams participate, past results indicate that these 'contests' between Elite League and Premier League clubs notoriously aren't close affairs. Wilder Internet forum posters with florid imaginations sketch a scenario that envisions Ipswich deliberately engineering their own relegation to the second tier of British speedway. It's widely held that their opponents Newcastle probably don't wish promotion to the Elite League. Equally there have been numerous press reports of low crowd numbers at Foxhall Heath. The first leg at Byker saw Kenni Larsen beat Scott Nicholls from the back to break the track record. Ahead by 8 points with five races to go, the Diamonds eventually went down to a narrow 44-46 defeat after a Witches last-heat maximum. If the Diamonds came to Foxhall Heath at full strength then, perhaps, the second leg of the promotion/relegation race-off would retain an element of mystery about it. Unfortunately, tonight Newcastle will be without Jason King (covered by rider replacement), Mark Lemon (Stuart Robson will guest), Derek Sneddon (re-injured his knee in the first leg, so Chris Mills guests) and Dakota North (heel injury, Simon Lambert guests). When I bump into Newcastle team manager and co-promoter George English outside the Ipswich speedway office my enthusiastic greeting ("This is what it's all about!") isn't met with a confident response. "Yes, it's just a shame we didn't win the other night. We were 8 up at one point but after we lost Dak that was it, really. He's a scoring reserve plus he takes two of the rider-replacement rides so, being without him, was like losing a rider and a half. We're pleased it's dry here tonight because we're at Edinburgh tomorrow and we would have had to come back here on Saturday, if it had rained, and then race at home on Sunday!"

[Jeff] "Are you going to the big match before your meeting?"

[George] "I can't. It's race day. I think it could be your year anyway."

[Jeff] "Isn't Andy Carroll gonna get a hat trick?" [1]

With Halloween a few nights away, enterprisingly the Witches announced a fancy dress competition in the hope that the chance to dress up and be judged by Danny King for the chance to win a prize will attract youngsters along from their half-term holiday. If accompanied by an adult, they'll also gain admission for a token price. In preparation for a spooky night ahead, the turnstile area of the Foxhall Heath stadium is decorated with Halloween masks, tape and fake cobwebs (or perhaps not given rumours of declining crowd numbers). To add further atmosphere, they have also hired a smoke machine for the night ("Don't be alarmed Johnny if you

[1] Newcastle United annihilate Sunderland 5-1 with a hat trick from Kevin Nolan and two goals from Shola Ameobi. Missing this derby match is just one of the many sacrifices George English makes to ensure that the Newcastle Diamonds speedway club runs successfully.

see smoke coming out of the turnstiles!"). Later on rather than billows of Hollywood-style smoke, we get to see an almost imperceptible light misting, roughly equivalent to the smoke created if you lit a box of Swan Vestas all at once.

Like race day the country over, prior to the arrival of the fans: tracks are prepped, trackshops dressed, kettles boiled, refreshments made (or reheated), turnstiles dusted down and programme stalls stocked. Johnny Barber unloads an impressive amount of Ipswich speedway merchandise and memorabilia. With rain not forecast until later, I ask Johnny, "Is it going to be a bumper crowd tonight?"

Cobwebs and spiders

[Johnny] "I certainly hope so but quite what a bumper crowd is round here anymore, I don't know!"
[Jeff] "Isn't it whatever Elvin King says it is in his *Speedway Star* reports?"
[Johnny] "We had 850 for a National League meeting at King's Lynn last night."
[Jeff] "It was Buxton in a double-header wasn't it?"
[Johnny] "Yeh!"
[Jeff] "What did you think of Jason Garrity then?"
[Johnny] "To be honest he's an accident waiting to happen! I know it's the first time he's been there and he's only 15 years old ... but! He got 3 or 4 in the first meeting and, in his last race of the night, he had an engine failure and crossed the line fourth and then ran alongside his bike before dropping it. It made me laugh anyway."
[Jeff] "Sounds unorthodox."
[Johnny] "That's one word!"
[Jeff] "Was Mike Bennett there?"

Trackshop bustle

[Johnny] "Mike Bennett doesn't do the Stars as it's not important enough for him. We had Kevin Moore instead."
[Jeff] "Don't you mean Kevin "100% professional" Moore?"
[Johnny] "Possibly!"
[Jeff] "Was he announcing like he'd learnt the job from a correspondence course? Or making comments like he was reading from a prepared statement that he simultaneously had to translate from a foreign language?"
[Johnny] "I dunno. Whenever Mike Bennett comes round to ask what we'd like promoting we tell him what there is and I always like to say 'and, of course, there's Jeff Scott's sensational new book'. When Mike runs through what he's got he'll say something like 'and there's books in the trackshop plus one particularly bad one!'"

A man interrupts to ask rhetorically, "I think this is the latest we've ever run here! Is there a sale on?"
[Johnny] "Every day is a sale. We've had four at Eastbourne so far cos they keep getting through in the KO Cup. We had

Ipswich: *"It was John's first season and he dressed up as a witch and rode on a bike!"*

a sale; a final sale; a final, final sale and then we had a final, final, final sale!"

Close by to the trackshop, Chris Ellis opens up and tidies the programme stall. She slits open all the boxes of programmes and then unpacks one ready for action. She's not a big fan of the promotion relegation race-offs, "I don't see the point of it personally! If no one goes up and no one goes down, what's the point? I hate the last meeting, it always seems so long before it starts again! Tonight the kids get in free if they come in fancy dress – three of them can win prizes! We've done up the turnstiles and brought in a smoke machine to add to the atmosphere but, once they're through, that's it. At some point all the kids will go down to the centre green as will Danny King. There'll be three prizes – the main one is a season ticket. They can't get in free without an adult so hopefully they'll bring a few. It's half term too!

[Jeff] "This is the first time I've seen the new shape track."

[Chris] "It's bigger and there's more room but we haven't had a home advantage. The Poles keep complaining they can't get used to it but I tell them, 'The old track is still out there so ride that!' But they don't! They go where they want and wonder why everyone goes past on the inside and the outside. You should see Scott Nicholls ride it, he's perfect!" Chris nods towards the dark brown damp-looking Foxhall Heath track. "It rained overnight but, after a little drizzle first thing, there's been nothing. It's damp in the air but they watered the track and it looks really nice, don't it?"

[Jeff] "Do you expect many people in fancy dress?"

[Chris] "Maybe, John [Louis] is going to dress up later!"

[Jeff] "What as?"

[Chris] "I dunno?"

ReRun Productions supremo Steve Girdwood reacts to news of the fancy dress competition with a trip down memory lane. "The first season I ever did here – 1989 – 21 years ago! It was John's first season and he dressed up as a witch and rode on a bike!" That would certainly be a sight to look forward but it's unclear if we're going to have that treat.

Sat in pride of place in the centre of the kitchen-cum-rest area inside the Ipswich's Witches Speedway Office building is another succulently moist fruitcake baked by Chris Ellis. Before he disappears back off to the inner sanctum of his office with a copy of *Shale Trek*, ("I hope there's no foul language in it this year – that was awful!"), John Louis suggests that I help myself to a piece. When she's not on the phone with callers keen to find out the latest weather at the track, Chris Ellis hovers in the doorway to chat with Pat and Sue about the goings on at last Saturday's end-of-season dinner dance.

[Sue] "How did you feel on Sunday morning?"

[Pat] "I was stiff from all that dancing."

[Sue] "I didn't feel too bad but I stuck to the vodka all night."

[Pat] "We left about one – what time did you leave?"

[Sue] "1.30."

[Pat] "It was really good but I think that's because all the riders were there. The Poles went early because they were taking the Newcastle meeting seriously but Ritchie and Joe both stayed until late."

[Sue] "They'd pulled though, hadn't they?"

[Pat] "Yeh, I think they were sisters."

[Chris] "Kozza must have fallen ill with appendicitis the next day I reckon."

[Sue] "There were loads of photos on Facebook the next day of girls posing with the riders. They sat in a group and didn't dance much."

[Pat] "What about the one in the white dress? This year's [music] man was much better. I thought he worked the crowd and knew what we wanted. He played the older ones' music – the younger ones can dance to ours but the older ones can't dance to theirs."

The dinner dance compere apparently used new technology to enhance the evening's enjoyment, primarily by flashing photos from the event (almost as they happened) onto a large screen. Witches team manager Pete Simmons arrives to grab a quick cup of tea to take out on duty with him to the pits. Looking even taller than usual in the tight confines of the kitchen, he strikes a triumphant note, "We've won away!"

[Chris] "It took until heat 15."

[Pete] "An away win is an away win I say, so it's worth celebrating!"

Altogether a different height, shortly after Danny King arrives for a cuppa.

[Pat] "When's the wedding?"

[Danny] "Saturday week."

[Pat] "Have you had your stag night yet?"

[Danny] "Saturday."

While the kettle boils, Danny sits on the portable gas heater.

[Pat] "Are you going anywhere nice?"

[Danny] Nah, not really."

[Pat] "I meant on honeymoon."

[Danny] "Oh, my missus is a teacher so we're going on a Caribbean cruise at Christmas. You know there's a strong smell of gas in here?" [2]

[Pat] "It's you sitting on it!"

Danny gets up and studies the gas dial of the portable gas heater suspiciously. "Are we expecting a lot of kids tonight [on the centre green]?"

[Pat] "You'll be busy."

[Danny] "You know there really is a strong smell of gas!"

[Pat] "It's you! It's lucky no one's allowed to smoke or we'd have all been blown up by now!" Still possibly emulating Trigger from *Only Fools and Horses*, Danny 'gasman' King leaves and, with a definite click, Pat ensures that the dial is safely in the OFF position, "It was him – the plonker!" John Louis's friend Sue solves the mystery of why I've recently got emails from John (someone I'd always previously assumed was slightly technophobic). "It's me that writes the emails – while John dictates them – he reads some carefully but not yours! This winter the project will be to try to teach him to use the computer. I know he'll like it. He gets me to look things up and I made a big saving on his car insurance and that impressed him."

ReRun's Steve Girdwood is in buoyant mood after last night's Poole and Eastbourne clash in the KO Cup Final Second Leg at Wimbourne Road. "What a brilliant meeting! Fantastic racing, great atmosphere and a good crowd; Sky would have loved it! It was the cream – the icing on the cake. From a professional point of view, to have two teams in a cup final it didn't matter to me which team won because they'd both buy them. If Eastbourne had won, I'd been up all night getting them done for the dinner dance. It's a shame Poole weren't Elite League champions but it's okay for Clean Cut. They have four tracks and I have five so I'd expect to do better than them, but you don't know?"

Ipswich fan and ex-presenter (still much missed after his premature retirement) Kevin Long lingers at the programme booth. Chris Ellis greets him excitedly, "Isn't it wonderful about Scott and Sophie! Sophie's due date is the 17th May." Kevin's out of the baby loop, "I dunno what has changed." But Chris isn't, "They never said she couldn't ever, just she might not!" After they catch up on gossip and news, Kevin glances at my book-laden display table and comments sardonically,

[2] Snow would strand the newlyweds on their honeymoon at Heathrow Airport. After two days they gave up and were offered an alternative break a few weeks later.

Ipswich: *"It was John's first season and he dressed up as a witch and rode on a bike!"*

"Someone said earlier these make very good coffee table books [pause] not on the table but as the table!" Kevin doesn't have much time for the thin-skinned hypersensitivity of some of his erstwhile speedway presentational colleagues. "Anyone who puts themselves in the arena – riders, officials and announcers – it's fair game for you to write about their idiosyncrasies and foibles. Either you're part of the show or you're not! Your work stands for itself. There's no point going on Facebook, like Mike Bennett after the World Cup, thanking everyone you can think of in the hope that people will reply and say something nice about him! Chris Simpson at Birmingham is another. He did something thanking everyone on another fantastic season at Birmingham. If people want to praise you, they will without you having to ask them. I've done all the Super7evens for ReRun this season and, when they had the meeting at Peterborough, Mike [Bennett] wore the yellow suit he wears when it's cold. It was amazing Craig Saul wasn't doing it as he's part of the presentation team there. Mike came over to us and said, 'I'll be giving lots of plugs don't worry and if you need me to be in the shot I'll be the one in yellow!' Kevin Moore and Simon Lambert will be here tonight." I interject, "Kevin "100% professional" Moore you mean – that's how Mike Bennett sometimes describes him." Kevin shrugs, "That implies he makes his living at speedway presentations!"

After Kevin goes off, a familiar-looking lady whose name I can't quite place attempts to dissuade someone from buying any of my books. "Don't buy his book, he just makes things up. I'm in one of them but I didn't say that. Luckily no one will know it's me except for Chris Schramm." Talk soon turns to an Ipswich campaign that fell short of her expectations, "At the start of the season they said what a brilliant team they'd put together but I immediately thought we'd finish bottom. I was disillusioned by May. It's lucky they banned the public from press and practice for the last two years, otherwise we'd know all about the team before the season had even started! That said, there's a gap in the fence so you can watch it anyway!"

With an end-of-season sale in the trackshop, I'd expect that Johnny will let the presentational team know of this opportunity, "Will Stephen Foster drop by?" Johnny's doubtful, "It's highly unlikely – he's only been here twice and that was probably by accident!" Widely travelled speedway historian, Arnie Gibbons exits the trackshop with a pertinent possible line of enquiry. "The question you should ask Mr Barber is why has he got a "We Love Premier League Speedway" stickers and no "We love Elite League Speedway" stickers in an Elite League's speedway team's trackshop?" My explanation fails to convince, "Maybe it's his stealth campaign to encourage the promotion to consider dropping down to the Premier League?"

With only days left of the speedway season, Arnie's end-of-season itinerary isn't yet fixed since he likes to leave his speedway viewing options open. "I might go to Rye House but it depends on the weather. If I don't, I don't. I didn't go to Poole last night because I had to meet representatives of Lidl about a supermarket they want to open in my area. They have planning permission – it's been vacant for 30 years because the Co-op forgot they owned it for 20 years!" Not much escapes Arnie's attention, "Did you notice the quiet return of James Clement last Friday at Weymouth? And did you see that the obscure Russian you hadn't heard of last year – Artem Laguta – will be riding in the speedway Grand Prix next year?"

After a home defeat on Sunday night, the consensus amongst the contingent of Diamonds fans who've come down from the North East isn't that bullish. "As long as they do better than the last time they were here – in 1984 – when they lost 60-19 or something like that!" According to local rumours, Ipswich Town Football Club manager Roy Keane could be at Foxhall Heath stadium tonight. While we wait to sight him, or his dog, keen Ipswich Witches fan and security man Lee has got some pertinent questions about the future of the club, "Would people really be happy if we went Premier League?" Kevin Long is adamant, "Of course they wouldn't! There was a good

Ipswich: *"It was John's first season and he dressed up as a witch and rode on a bike!"*

analysis on the British Speedway Forum the other week that showed that the cost difference between the Premier League and the Elite League isn't that much! When it was lighter, I stood on the top of the grandstand because you get a good view and I counted 275 people. When you think we have 200 season ticket holders, it's not easy to survive on that."

[Lee] "Do you know anyone who might buy it?"

[Jeff] "You need someone's who's very optimistic to buy any speedway club."

[Lee] "In a recession, who is really gonna buy it? It's been a hard season. At the trackshop, they're moaning every week but who is going to buy memorabilia for a poor side? It's great to see a good crowd and, if Newcastle lose by 15, they'll have done well!"

Witches presenter Stephen Foster welcomes the Newcastle fans to Foxhall Heath prior to the traditional Witches two-by-two Noah's Ark rider parade. While the various riders wave to the crowd from the stockcar circuit, an Ipswich fan tells me, "it might be close if we fall off in the first five or six heats like we did at Newcastle!" Scott Nicholls sets the tone for the night with a comprehensive win ahead of the Diamonds star rider Kenni Larsen. With a maximum heat advantage in the next from Ritchie Hawkins and Dawid Stachyra, security man Lee doubts the wisdom of his possible close-contest prediction, "I think I got that a bit wrong!" In contrast to many other fixtures this season at Foxhall Heath, the Witches riders proceed to hammer home a slew of maximum heat advantages. With race wins from Danny King and Robert Miśkowiak, after only four heats Ipswich lead 19-5. Despite their comfortable victories, Lee remains to be convinced about these two particular riders. "Miśkowiak and Danny aren't really heat leaders! Would Miśkowiak even be a second string at Poole? Danny's of the age where he really needs to be knocking on the door." If, in heat leader terms, these riders don't quite do what it says on the tin, then the same can't be said about the *Evening Star* local newspaper since it gives welcome comprehensive coverage to all things speedway. "They said in yesterday's *Star* that there would be an exclusive interview with Scott Nicholls tonight. You'd have thought it might be news that they'd brought his contract from Coventry or that he was definitely here next season but it was about his personal life! Not being funny, if you bought that you'd be disappointed. He was very careful not to reveal where he'd be next season – it didn't sound like he'd be here anyway!"

Though a force at Premier League level, Kenni Larsen's Elite League speedway education continues with a heat 5 lesson from Danny King. It's a drawn heat since Aleš Dryml falls on the second bend of the third lap to gift Adam McKinna a lucky point. At the moment his erstwhile rival fell, Adam's some distance away at the back apparently about to win his own slow-riding competition. In the context of the meeting so far, a drawn heat counts as a mini fight-back. The gulf in class between Scott Nicholls and every other rider on display at Foxhall Heath gets further illustration when he rears massively at the start of heat 6 but, despite his terrible gate, by the time the riders exit the second bend, he's taken the lead! At least, there's a close race for second place after Chris Slabon makes a last-gasp dash for the chequered flag and, according to referee Graham Reeve, bests Stuart Robson on the line to give the Ipswich Witches yet another maximum heat advantage. The seventh race only lasts as far as the apex of bends three and four where the Diamonds guest No. 3 Chris Mills flamboyantly challenges Dawid Stachyra only to get massively out of shape and then unceremoniously clattered from behind by René Bach. With nowhere to go, Bach really couldn't avoid his teammate. To a low grumble of disapproval from the terraces, Bach's initially disqualified by the referee. However, Stephen Foster is soon back on the microphone to let us know commonsense prevails, "After discussions with the rider, the referee Graham Reeve has agreed that Chris Mills was the rider at fault for that crash." With Mills out of the three-rider rerun, the shaken and stirred René Bach fails to challenge the Witches pair of Stachyra and Miśkowiak as they saunter to the Witches fifth 5-1 in seven races. With the scores less than poised at 32-10, Stephen Foster takes a few moments to try to quiz Ipswich promoter John Louis, "The Elite League

---

Ipswich: *"It was John's first season and he dressed up as a witch and rode on a bike!"*

next season surely, John?" John chooses his words carefully, "Let's hope so." Stephen presses with a rhetorical question, "Now, surely, every fan wants to see the best riders and Elite League racing?" John parries with a slight digression, "The Elite League does need sorting out! Well, one or two people do want to see it a little bit bigger but I don't know if any Premier League clubs want to come up!"

Given the gulf in firepower on display tonight, it would be understandable if all but the most frighteningly ambitious second-tier clubs refuse to contemplate such a move up on commercial grounds alone. Well-matched riders in team competition on a well-prepared track are essential ingredients if you wish to stage entertaining absorbing speedway meetings, irrespective of the notional level of the competition. On the subject of competitions, Stephen Foster suddenly adopts a serious tone as if he's about to announce something momentous like the winner of *Strictly Come Dancing* two weeks early. In fact, he's keen to let us know, "Danny King will be doing the judging of the Halloween fancy dress contest." In an attempt to massage the scoreline rather than initiate a real fight-back, Newcastle Diamonds manager George English sends Stuart Robson out on a tactical for the heat 8 rider-replacement ride in place of Jason King. Ritchie Hawkins then gets caught out trying to predict the rise of the tapes to the extent that he gets his helmet caught on them! Strangely Hawkins isn't disqualified by the referee and manages second behind Stuart Robson. Steve Girdwood can't quite believe the evidence of his eyes, "Is that a Newcastle rider out in front? Oh no, it's a Lakeside Hammer!" Sunderland-born Robson also wins the next heat to leave the scores looking ungainly at 38-19. Heat 10 sees Scott Nicholls and Chris Slabon combine for their second maximum heat advantage of the night prior to an interval that will hopefully enable the Diamonds to regroup and act upon George English's words of encouragement.

Arnie Gibbons has feedback from the terraces albeit with the saltier words removed, "The view from the Newcastle fans that, if they wanted a crap ref, they'd have brought Jim McGregor!" With lawyerly discretion, Arnie gives his own reaction to the contentious decisions of the meeting so far. "I'm loath to criticise photo finishes without a camera but allegedly Slabon overtook Robson. It's all pretty academic! I think we can safely say Ipswich are going to win. Newcastle need an 8-1 and four 5-1s to draw but Ipswich would still win by 2 points on aggregate!" It remains a daunting task, even after a black-and-white helmeted Kenni Larsen becomes tonight's second Newcastle Diamond race winner. Nonetheless, this 3-6 heat score ensures Ipswich win on the night (and also on aggregate). With only pride left to race for, Simon Lambert separates Danny King from Ritchie Hawkins in heat 12 while Kenni Larsen rides combatively for four laps in heat 13 to hold Scott Nicholls at bay for the majority of the race until a last-gasp outside blast allows Scott to snatch second place on the line. Ipswich hammer home another maximum heat advantage in the penultimate race to take their total to eight 5-1s in 14 races. The bare bones of this heat score fail to tell the whole story since René Bach would have been a comfortable second but for his last-bend engine failure.

Friendly Ipswich speedway fanatic Rob Scrutton wanders round for a few words. He's a proud father who – for once – is out without his daughters, Mel and Kelly. His 18-year-old Mel isn't sure which university to go to ("It's probably going to be Warwick to do a maths or physics degree"), while his 16-year-old Kelly has just been awarded "Suffolk Young Volunteer of the Year" as part of their 125th anniversary celebrations. Every Saturday she's at her local pitch at 9 a.m. to train 40 10-year-olds. She took her dad as her guest when she got invited to a presentation dinner at the Bobby Robson Suite inside Portman Road. "The presentation was by Sheepshanks and I also got to meet some old Ipswich players – Mick Mills and Roger Osborne!" The opening section of Mike Oldfield's 'Tubular Bells' plays prior to heat 15 to give the night a proper retro feel. Stuart

Ipswich: *"It was John's first season and he dressed up as a witch and rode on a bike!"*

Robson follows up his heat 13 last place with an engine failure on the second bend of the last lap when placed third behind the impressive Kenni Larsen. With a comfortable 64-32 win to savour, many of the Ipswich faithful linger on the terraces, in the bar or by the trackshop to eke out the last few hours of their 2010 season. Gerry from Hastings stops by my table with a few words of praise, "When you read your books you feel like you're really there! Thank you." Nigel 'Noddy' Fordham reveals that tonight is his 108th meeting of the season. This takes him to a grand total to 4,963 meetings. "I've now travelled over a million miles. I achieved that at the beginning of October when I went to the Czech Golden Helmet. They promoted the meeting, for once, with posters and that so we got a big crowd there!"

After the crowd mostly ebb away, the Newcastle Diamonds management massive – George English, Joan English, Andrew Dalby and Ray leave the home-straight bar with their long drive back to the North East ahead of them. Characteristically gateman Ray strikes an optimistic note, "We've done a lot better than the last time we came here! It was 60-17 or something like that when we were all in one big league!"

28th October Ipswich v. Newcastle (Promotion Relegation Play-Off Second Leg) 64-32

Ipswich: *"It was John's first season and he dressed up as a witch and rode on a bike!"*

Afterword

I hope that you enjoyed the journey.

Phew! What a fantastic year I had and what another brilliant experience. I was genuinely overwhelmed with the kindness of strangers and amazed how people went out of their way to help me. There are, of course, exceptions to every rule.

Obviously all mistakes remain my own. If you have any comments, of either persuasion, please get in touch via my website on www.methanolpress.com

Every effort has been made to get in touch with all copyright holders but, again, I would be delighted to hear from you to make the appropriate credits or acknowledgements.

I mentioned earlier that I have been overwhelmed with help and kindness. I hesitate to name everyone as, inevitably, I will make a mistake and miss someone I'm extremely grateful to, so, with sincere apologies to those who I do manage to miss out I would like to thank the following people: Paul Adams, Peter Adams, Rachael Adams, Mike Amos, Graham Arnold, Ian Attwood, Mike Bacon, Pete Ballinger, Robert Bamford, Nick, Johnny, Bev, Molly and Colin Barber, George and Linda Barclay, Dick Barrie, Ian Belcher, Joyce and Malcolm Blythe, Tim Booler, Mick Bratley, Bob Brimson, Jim and Steven Brykajlo, Paul Burbidge, Brian Burford, Peter Butcher, John Campbell, Alison Chalmers, Jonathan, Keith and Cheryl Chapman, Steve Chilton, Jon Cook, Graham Cooke, Dougie Copland, Mick Corby, Dave Cox, ICA Crook, Lucy Cross, Dave Croucher, Dave Curtis, Martin Dadswell, Gordie Day, Alan Dick, Jem Dicken, Steve and Debbie Dixon, Ann and Jeff Dooley, Chris Durno, Graham and Denise Drury, Steve and Debbie Dixon, Neil Dyson, George and Joan English, Dave Fairbrother, Jim Fleming, Ben Findon, Richard Frost, Chris Gay, Arnie Gibbons, Bill Gimbeth, Rob Godfrey, David Gordon, Andy Griggs, Bert Harkins, Patricia and Tim Hamblin, Graham Hambly, Debbie Hancock, Steve and Jan Harland, Darren Hartley, Brian Havelock, Steve Hilliard, Steve Hone, John Hyam, John, Jordan, Karen, Mark and Judy Hazelden, Richard Hollingsworth, Dave Hoggart, Allison Hunter, Mike Hunter, Gary Inman, Tony Jackson, Sue Jackson-Scott, Billy Jenkins, Dani Johnson, Howard Jones, Sally Knight, Emma and Mark Lemon, Sheila Le-Sage, Kevin Ling, Kevin Long, Gary Lough, John Louis, Michael Max, Ian and Jean Maclean, Neil Machin, Julie Martin, Dennis McCleary, Keith McGhie, Charles McKay, Allan Melville, Steve and Sarah Miles, Laura Morgan, Chris Morton, Mike Moseley, Chris Moss, Jayne Moss, Hazal Naylor, Martin Neal, Bill Norris, Peter Oakes, Paul Oughton, Brian Owen, Gordon Pairman, Les Palmer, Dave Pavitt, Nigel Pearson, Rob Peasley, Di Phillips, Gary Pinchin, Mark Poulton, Andy Povey, Colin Pratt, Guy Proctor, Dave Rattenberry, Dave and Margaret Rice, John Rich, Giles Richards, Gareth Rogers, Laurence Rogers, David Rowe, Wayne Russell, Craig Saul, Mark Sawbridge, Rob Scrutton, Chris Seaward, Shiggs, Len Silver, Andrew Skeels, George Skinner, Derek Smithson, Claudia and Jan Staechmann, Tony Steele, Barry Stephenson, Trevor Swales, Bob Tasker, Peter Toogood, Stuart Towner, Ian Thomas, Christina Turnbull, Chris Van Stratten, Nick Ward, Vicky Warren, Dave Watters, The Reverend Michael Whawell, Bryn Williams, Steve Winter, Dave Wood, and Malcolm Wright.

To pick out anyone in particular would be invidious. However, I owe so many 'thank yous'. The book wouldn't look as lovely as it does without Vicky Holtham's artistic skills. The look and feel of the covers, website and book layout were all originally conceived by Rachael Adams. There would be many more errors than there are without the help of Vy Shepherd. Graham Russel has shown tremendous pedantry and knowledge to wrangle with my words to convert them into some sort of sense. Robert Bamford also kindly copyedited the Swindon chapter. Michael Payne was, like many others, there at the start and Billy Jenkins continues to offer encouragement, advice and

270

support. My true friend Sue Young encourages me often in so many things and really saved me when I needed that most – for which she has my eternal gratitude. Of course, without the love and guidance of my parents – Mary and Alan – none of this book or so many other things would ever have been possible. Finally, you can never have too many teachers and I was lucky enough to have been inspired to write my speedway books by a truly great teacher, poet, musician and wit – Michael Donaghy. He remains greatly missed.

Before I go, we only get one chance to make a first impression – this holds for speedway clubs as much as people. If you've read to here, it's safe to say that you've probably been bitten by the speedway bug (for which, apparently, there is no permanent antidote). We can all no longer go to speedway for the first time. However, we can take new people and relive this experience vicariously once more, albeit second hand. I always enjoy taking newcomers.

It just remains to say: if you go to speedway already why not make a point of taking even more friends and/or first timers this year? And, if you haven't been for a while or have never been, now is as good a time as any to start!

Yours in speedway!

Thank you for coming this far on my latest journey round the tracks.

Brighton

8 April 2011

INFORMATION

Jazz Musicians

www.billyjenkins.com
The one and only Billy J – the incomparable speedway/bowls loving Bard of Bromley and progenitor of a distinctively British kitchen-sink jazz sound

ACCOMMODATION

All the following warmly welcome speedway fans and have special rates for us:

Waverley Hotel, Workington
01900 603246
www.waverley-hotel.com

Beeches Guest House, King's Lynn
01553 766577
www.beechesguesthouse.co.uk

Lower Farm
Harpley, King's Lynn
01485 520240

Jurys Inn Glasgow Hotel
0141 314 4800

www.glasgowhotels.juryinns.com
Brent Knoll Lodge Hotel, Somerset
01278 760008
www.brentknolllodge.com

Aston Hotel, Sheffield
0114 261 5609
www.astonhotels.co.uk

Garrison Hotel, Sheffield
0114 249 9555
www.garrisonhotel.co.uk

FOR ALL THE LATEST NEWS AND FIXTURES GO TO:

www.speedwaygb.co

Other useful speedway websites:
www.speedwayplus.com
www.speedway-forum.co.uk
www.speedwayupdates.proboards103.com:8080/index.cgi
www.tattingermarsh.co.uk/blog
www.worldspeedway.com
www.subedei.proboards.com/index.cgi
www.keep-turning-left.blogspot.com
www.sideburnmag.blogspot.com
www.all4back.com
www.allspeedway.tv